Canada in the North Atlantic Triangle

CANADA
in the
north atlantic
triangle

Two Centuries of
Social Change

by

John L. Finlay

Toronto
OXFORD UNIVERSITY PRESS
1975

© Oxford University Press
(Canadian Branch) 1975

Cover design by
FRED HUFFMAN

ISBN-0-19-540237-5

Printed in Canada by
THE BRYANT PRESS LIMITED

Acknowledgements

Many people have helped in producing this introductory survey. It was Bill Smith, that kindest of colleagues, who first suggested that I undertake the task and who encouraged me to persist with it. Mark Gabbert and Tom Vadney have helped enormously, more perhaps than they realize, by their discussions of various topics and of writing in general. Doug. Sprague has been especially helpful and has greatly stimulated my thinking; it is to be hoped that one day he will publish his account of the founding of new societies. Above all, there is Lovell Clark. Professor Clark read and criticized much of the text in draft form; but he has also given generously of that interest and concern that all who know him recognize so well, and it is true to say that without him this book would never have been written. To him I am particularly grateful.

The task of reducing my handwritten copy to typescript was very ably performed by Mrs Jean Birch, Miss M. Kawata, Mrs J. Pritchard, and especially by Miss Blanche Miller. I have also been extremely fortunate in the editorial help I have received; Ms Tilly Crawley must be the perfect editor, and it has been a joy to work with her.

To all these people I extend my sincere thanks. I am also happy to record my debt to Norbert Montcalm. But finally I acknowledge with deep gratitude the comfort and support given me so unstintingly by my wife, Rosemarie.

To My Parents

Contents

1

The Presuppositions
of
European Society

What follows is a study of Britain, Canada, and the United States of America, three societies that, emerging from a common background and holding certain things in common, yet came to exemplify differing ways of life. The study begins, therefore, at that point in time when the colonial societies had developed sufficient identities to be considered separately from their parents, with lives and dynamics of their own. The second half of the eighteenth century, then, would be the place to begin. About 1750 began that chain of events that a generation later was to culminate in thirteen of the British colonies in North America gaining their independence and forming a new political entity. And if the remaining British North American possessions, the nucleus of what later would become Canada, were still colonial and very dependent, the fact that there existed on the border a similar but quite different alternative meant that already fundamental questions would be raised about the eventual identity of these colonies. A further reason exists for taking the mid-eighteenth century as the starting point. About this time the entire western civilization, of which the North Atlantic was the most advanced portion, was experiencing a revolution that was destined to usher in the modern world. In this case the parent society, too, was passing through a crisis, and so it is true to say that in all three instances new societies were being born.

Yet any attempt to jump directly into the account halfway through the eighteenth century would be impossible. The background to these diverging societies must be sketched, the common presuppositions and their variants must be noted, and from time to time the triangle must become a quadrilateral with the inclusion of France, the parent of Quebec and Louisiana. This introductory account, however, will not be chronological, but will be a thematic treatment of the major social determinants. It will begin with the religious dimension.

❈ ❈ ❈

The second half of the eighteenth century was the climax of a period historians call the *ancien régime*, in which the change from medieval to modern was in the main accomplished, and that is usually dated from 1648 to 1789. The latter date, that of the French Revolution, is readily recognized, but not the former. It was in fact the year in which the Treaty of Westphalia was signed, which brought to an end a savage Thirty Years' War that had begun over a religious dispute and that continued to be fought over religious issues. But it was the last of the wars of religion and marked the end of an era; future wars were to be fought increasingly over the more modern issues of trade and nationalism.

This does not mean that religion immediately ceased to rule people's lives, or that it immediately ceased to determine the development of societies. As late as the Treaty of Utrecht in 1713 Europe continued to refer to itself as Christendom, and as late as the Congress of Vienna in 1815 European statesmen could play with the idea of a Holy Alliance. But Westphalia did end wars of religion and it did settle the religious map from that day to the present. Minor changes in religious allegiance have taken place, of course, but essentially the distribution of the Christian denominations was frozen in 1648.

It is a map of bewildering variety and detail, but a drastic simplification will be in order. For the interest is not in the theological distinctions as such, but rather in the sociological implications of different religious beliefs and practices; that is, the manner in which a religion can spill over into the wider life of society and affect the way that its members view and value the world. For the purposes of this chapter then, the multitude of Christian denominations may be reduced to three basic types, the Catholic, the Reformed, and the Radical, each of which must now be defined and discussed.

But first it may be necessary to answer the protests that may have arisen. Why, it will be asked, is there no mention of the Lutherans, the first successfully to challenge the unity of Roman Catholicism? Why no mention of the Anglican Church? After all that Church was the established or official Church in England and in several of the North American colonies, and so should surely merit some discussion. But Lutherans have had little impact; their churches do exist in considerable numbers in North America and count adherents in the millions, but it still remains true that this Church has left little impress on society as a whole. The truth is that the Lutheran Church has been ambiguous in its break with Catholicism; in many ways it is very Catholic; and where it has struck out on new lines it has done so half-heartedly, leaving it to the Reformed Churches to push these beginnings to their logical conclusion. And Anglicanism is like Lutheranism in being very close to Catholicism; sociologically speaking, it is but a local variant of Catholicism. This fact was brought home very forcibly to the author when, a teenager, he was host to a French boy over in England to learn the language. The French guest, a (Reformed) Protestant, expressed a wish to attend divine service in the village, and so he was taken to *the* Protestant church, that is, the Anglican church; afterwards, however, it was almost impossible to convince him that he had not attended a Catholic service.

It is reasonable to begin with the Catholic grouping, for not only was it the first in the field, but it also counted, at the time of Westphalia, the greatest number of adherents. Catholics were to be found in almost all areas of Europe, but were particularly strong in the Latin countries—Spain, Portugal, Italy—and were also in a commanding position in southern Germany, the Austrian empire, and Poland; in view of the later heavy immigration into North America from these areas, the Catholic background needs to be understood. But of more direct concern for this study is the position of Catholicism in the two parent societies, France and Britain.

France had been deeply scarred by the growth there of the Reformed religion in the sixteenth century and by the subsequent religious wars between the Huguenots, as the Reformed believers were called in France, and the Catholic majority of the population. No accommodation between them was possible until after some forty years of fighting and such savageries as the St Bartholomew's Day massacre in 1572, when several thousand Huguenots were assassinated. Eventually in 1598 the Edict of Nantes granted the Huguenots a tolerated though second-class citizenship. The Edict recognized, however, that the majority of Frenchmen were Catholic with a Catholic monarchy. The year 1598 was, in fact, the high point of Huguenot fortunes under the *ancien régime*, for increasingly in the seventeenth century the Huguenot position was eroded by the Catholic Counter-Reformation and by the emerging absolutist state until finally Louis XIV revoked the Edict of Nantes in 1685. Large numbers of Huguenots emigrated, and France remained solidly Catholic.

In Britain the position of Roman Catholicism was very different. Until the nineteenth century it was a proscribed religion; indeed, ever since the reign of Bloody Mary (1553–8) and ever since the victory over the Armada of Catholic Spain (1588), Catholicism had been viewed with suspicion and even hatred. As late as 1780 anti-Catholic sentiment could paralyze London in the Gordon Riots. In England Catholicism, a secret and furtive religion, was to be found mainly in the West Country and in Lancashire. Scotland had its pockets of Catholicism, notably in the Highlands and Western Isles; from here Catholicism was carried to North America and traces may be found today in the Maritimes, for instance around Antigonish. Ireland was overwhelmingly Catholic, for ever since the days of the Elizabethan wars against them the Irish had made their Catholicism a badge of their nationalism and yearning for independence. In addition to these examples of Roman Catholicism there was, of course, the basically similar Anglicanism. It was the official, established Church in England and in Wales (that is, it was supported by tithes that were paid by Anglicans and non-Anglicans alike), and the separately named but identically conceived Church of Ireland was imposed in that country; in Scotland Anglicanism was weak and did not significantly affect that country's development.

Given such a widespread base, Catholicism was able to play a commanding role in the evolution of the North Atlantic community. To understand in just what ways it affected society it is now necessary to note the main characteristics of Catholicism.

A most significant element is the way in which the Catholic mind handles the problem of salvation. In common with all Christian groups the Catholics begin by acknowledging the immensity that separates man from God, the crossing of which gulf constitutes the work of salvation. But having once acknowledged the gulf that yawns before man, the Catholics immediately proceed to fill it in by the construction of 'bridges' by which man may be helped to cross the abyss. Prominent among the bridges that lie to hand are the sacraments (seven in number for the Catholics), and it is their prominence that causes this whole Catholic approach to be labelled the 'sacramental'. Implicit in this doctrine is the notion that any Catholic who, spiritually speaking, feels out-of-sorts can ease himself by resorting to the sacraments, and by doing so up to the point when he feels adjusted once more (say by practising more frequent Communion). But the system is wider than this; the whole doctrine of 'works' takes this concept further. Any action performed for the glory of God is a work, and a work performs in the Catholic scheme of things the same function as a sacrament. Fasting and pilgrimage are examples of works; so too would be the endowment of a chapel. The nature of this sacramental cast of mind is seen more clearly perhaps when contrasted with the alternative view put forward by Luther. For Luther the secret was 'Faith, not works', and by that slogan he meant not to deny works but to suggest that the inner reality was infinitely more important than the outward sign, and that once a person had faith then works would be the natural result. The Catholic direction is the reverse; the performance of an act in itself conduces to salvation, and even helps to faith.

It is easy to see how the Catholic doctrine of works and more especially of sacraments may appear as magic. The Church itself will repudiate such a term, but is prepared to speak of mysteries. Thus the Act of Consecration is a mystery, by which the bread and wine actually become the Body and Blood of Christ. For a different and more social illustration of the sacramental attitude, attention may be drawn to a recent eruption of Mount Aetna. The Catholic communities endangered by the lava flow organized a series of processions and services at which the intercession of the saints was invoked. A Protestant community would have used this time and energy to dig a ditch.

If Protestants are affronted by what they see as the magical elements in Catholicism, they are also pained by what they see as a tendency towards the fragmentation of the totality of the God-man relationship, to compartmentalize spirituality. What is meant here may be illustrated by the following examples. If all the faithful are sons of God it does not follow that all are equal brothers. Some are set apart, set totally apart by the sacrament of Holy Orders; as priests they are seen as superior, as nearer to God, and the laity is expected to approach God through the priesthood. Yet this does not imply that all should aspire to the priesthood. Indeed the Church takes the realistic but in one sense inconsistent view that very few are called to the priesthood, and seminary directors are eagle-eyed to weed out those who lack a true vocation. Perhaps an even clearer way of indicating this Catholic mentality is to consider the institution of monasticism. It is admitted that the monk's calling is a superior one, but once again it is recognized that not all are suited for such a life. But more than this; there is not one monasticism, but many different kinds, each catering to a different kind of spirituality. Thus for many the Benedictine rule with its balanced régime of physical work, study, and prayer will be satisfying. But for others a more austere rule will be required, say the Cistercian, which is reformed Benedictine and which stresses manual toil, while a few may be prepared to join the Trappists, an order committed to almost total silence. Such thinking characterizes the Catholic view of society, which is seen not so much as a grouping of individuals but as a congeries of groups each with its own distinct function and contribution to the whole. Finally this fragmentation may be observed in what is scathingly referred to by some Protestants as the 'Continental Sunday', that is, mass in the morning and recreation in the afternoon. When the high-Anglican Charles I (reigned 1625–49) published his *Book of Sports*, allowing games on a Sunday afternoon, he mortally offended the extreme Protestant or Puritan party in the land.

In addition to Catholic presuppositions in the field of socio-theology, Catholic concepts of church government and structure, often referred to as church polity, must also be distinguished. A leading hint here is the point already made that the priest is a man set apart; so crucial is the idea of priesthood that the Latin term for priest, *sacerdos*, is used to form the concept sacerdotalism to sum up Catholic thinking in this area. The principle of hierarchy that sacerdotalism implies comes out starkly in the gradations that prevail within the ranks of the priesthood itself. The priest, important though he is, is merely the lowest rung in a ladder that descends from the pope at the head down through the cardinals, the archbishops, and the bishops. The notion of authority flowing downwards is everywhere stressed; the priest receives ordination from a bishop, who himself has been consecrated by a bishop. The office of bishop is so important that such churches as the Roman Catholic and Anglican are known as episcopalian (from the Greek, *episcopos*, a bishop) and the Anglican Church of colonial America, having to give up such an embarrassing name at independence, took the term Episcopalian as its official name, certain that it was descriptive of its essential structure.

But the stress on authority imposed from above is communicated to the faithful in much more effective ways than these. A glance at the architecture of a typical Catholic church reveals the long nave leading the line of sight up to the most important element, the altar; reveals the fact that the altar, a 'table' set apart and rendered 'magical', is raised above the level of the congregation; reveals the fact that it is a 'holier' place than the rest of the church since it is railed off and used only by the priest; reveals above all the fact that no real provision is made for preaching: preaching, by stressing that preacher and congregation have something in common—reason—tends to put them on the same level. The gorgeous vestments of the priest drive home the distinction between priest and congregation during the actual service. Above all, there are the terms that are constantly on the lips of the faithful; pope is derived from the Italian *papa*, father, and this term is used in the vernacular in addressing priests. The paternalism, or sometimes the maternalism, of the Church is constantly insisted upon. And it goes without saying that such a paternal-authoritarian structure will tend to be traditional and conservative.

So far what has been described may be termed eternal Catholicism, the underlying style that may vary somewhat from time to time and from place to place, but to which the Church tends to return. It is also important, however, to say something of the particular style of Catholicism that was dominant in the period of the *ancien régime*.

It must be admitted that in this period Catholicism was not vital. In many areas and in many ways the Church had sunk into a deplorable lethargy. What life there was tended to come from the Counter-Reformation impulse that had begun in the sixteenth century and that was still strong in the seventeenth. This spirit was epitomized by the Jesuit Order. Founded in the mid-sixteenth century by Ignatius Loyola, a Spanish ex-professional soldier, it reflected its originator's conviction that firm discipline was essential to success. Such loyalty to the hierarchical principle was doubly precious to the papacy about this time, for there was the danger that the Church would split along national lines. This possibility was most pronounced in Louis XIV's France, and for this reason the terms used of such disputes reflect the French origin. Those, like Louis himself, who believed that the papacy could be played down and the national French Church stressed were known as Gallicans; their opponents, who argued that the Church was indivisible and centred on the pope, were referred to as Ultramontanes since the focus of their attention was beyond the mountains in Rome. Jesuits, true soldiers, looked to the centre—they were ultramontane.

And yet the strength of the Jesuits was that along with a military discipline they managed to be most flexible in matters of dogma and propaganda. It was this flexibility that helped account for their great success as educators, for besides a firm insistence upon hard work, high standards, and a classical curriculum, they were prepared to be innovative in method. Equally impressive was their success in the missionary field, where they flexibly incorporated native values into their own Catholic world-view. Their activities in the North American mission field bear witness to their readiness and ability to meet Indian civilization on its own terms, though the best example of Jesuit flexibility comes from China. There at the end of the seventeenth century they came close to converting large sections of Chinese society, largely because of their willingness to use rather than to deny traditional Chinese values. (In this particular instance the approach was condemned by the Church as being too flexible and they were ordered to change their line.)

The second major type of religion was that of the Reformed tradition. This brand of Christianity, which so looked to Calvin for inspiration that it is often referred to simply as Calvinism, had achieved a wide diffusion by 1648. Calvin, who had been born in France, moved in 1536 to Geneva, which became the 'headquarters' of Calvinism. A good deal of neighbouring Switzerland was loyal to Calvin's teaching, Holland was dominated by Calvinists, and, as has been noted, France had a significant Calvinist minority until 1685. Scotland had embraced a version of the Reformed religion as transmitted by John Knox, and the Presbyterian Church was the dominant religious force in Scottish life, as it was too in the transplanted Scottish communities in Ireland, especially in Ulster. Calvinist tendencies had appeared in England in Elizabeth's reign (1558–1603), but had never been countenanced and the so-called Puritans had been mildly persecuted. With the accession of the Stuarts this persecution increased, James I (1603–25) making the celebrated pronouncement that the Puritans should conform to the established Anglicanism or be 'harried out of the land'. A significant number did choose to emigrate and New England was the settlement of those who wished to build the Calvinist New Jerusalem in the New World. This English-derived Calvinism was reinforced by other Calvinists from the continent, so that by the eve of the War of Independence almost fifty per cent of the North American population had some kind of Calvinist background.

This successful spread, which quite dwarfed anything accomplished by the Lutherans, was a tribute to the compelling logic of the creed, a creed that was in most ways the complete antithesis of the Catholic. Calvin began with the fact of the gulf between God and man. But whereas the Catholics were eager to build sacramental 'bridges', whereas the Lutherans were eager to insist that faith could help one across, Calvin was prepared to insist on the terrible width and depth of the abyss. He felt that both Catholic and Lutheran solutions were wrong, for both in their different ways sought to limit God's power, both sought to 'bargain' with Him. Calvin would allow man no means of helping his own salvation, which depended solely on the grace that was in God's gift to bestow or withhold. Those to whom grace had been given were the elect; those to whom it had been denied were the damned. And it further followed from this stress on God's omnipotence that only God could know to whom grace had been given, and that this was known even before a person was born. Man was *predestined* to heaven or to hell.

Equally opposed to Catholic thinking was the polity of the Reformed Church. Calvinism held to the priesthood of all believers; there was no warrant for the idea of a priest as a man set apart. Rather it was open for all men to find their way to God, especially if helped by a knowledge of the Bible. The study of God's word was emphasized. Education was vital in Calvinist societies, literacy being a minimum requirement of the true religion. Church services became less sacramental, less 'magical', and more a spiritual identification with Christ's ministry; they became, above all, an occasion for preaching. Calvinist architecture bears this out. Their churches tend to be plain so as not to distract; to be square, which is a good form for listening though not for having processions; to give pride of place not to the altar (which in the sixteenth century would aggressively have been called a table) but to the pulpit. But if there was a belief in the priesthood of all believers there was also a realistic awareness that in the absence of any formalized structure there would be anarchy. Certain individuals were recognized, then, as officials, but not in the Catholic way of setting a man entirely apart. Rather there was a division of labour, so to speak. One was recognized to have the gift of ministering and was accepted as the pastor; another was theologically knowledgeable and so was to be charged with teaching; the overall direction of the Church was to be placed in the hands of suitable elders. And here, in the repudiation of episcopacy and its replacement by presbyterianism (from the Greek, *presbyteros*, an elder) was the origin of the name given to the Scottish and Scottish-derived Calvinist Churches. It is further to be noted that, in contrast with Catholicism, the flow of authority was not downward but upward; for instance the Moderator of the United Church of Canada, which incorporates the Presbyterian tradition along with those of other denominations, is elected to a limited tenure by delegates of the Church at large.

The social implications of the Reformed tradition are crucial. If order is valued, it is order on a very different basis from the episcopal. It is not so hierarchical nor paternal, and provided that the necessary qualifications are kept in mind, it may be said that Calvinism is more 'democratic'. Certainly James I spotted this implication in Puritanism when he summed up and dismissed their case in the lapidary phrase 'No bishop, no king'.

At the heart of this 'democratic' tendency lies a new concept of individualism. Calvinism brought man face to face with God and the problem of salvation. It provided no sacramental aids. For the Calvinist who could face the challenge and believe that he was of the elect, the result was an amazing belief in himself, an inner certainty that gave his every action a force and confidence seldom otherwise experienced. There was indeed the very real danger of coming to believe that the elect could not sin; this is known as the antinomian position, for this Greek-derived term indicates that its adherents are against or beyond the law. And it helps to account for the fact that in the hands of its believers predestination, which seems to mean fatalism, led not to resignation but to an active, severe morality that was to be forced upon the damned by those in authority (presumably the elect). Many find the logic of this position deficient, asking why one of the damned should be made to worship the God who has already condemned him to everlasting torment. Calvin simply declared that 'Man, being taught that he has nothing good left in his possession, and being surrounded on every side with the most miserable necessity, should nevertheless be instructed to aspire to the good of which he is destitute'. The result was that Calvinism was not so very different from the existing Catholicism when it came to enforcing conformity, and if Calvinism did not burn so many people as the Inquisition did it was not yet free from the attempt to force its views upon people. In fact the argument has been advanced by the liberal Catholic historian, Lord Acton, that the Calvinist theory of persecution was even more frightening than the Catholic, for the Catholics were working from an actually existing unity, the questioning of which could be presented as a threat to the very fabric of society. The Calvinist, who himself had shattered that unity by claiming the right to question, had to counter his critics by denying the validity of any other belief but his own; if a Calvinist persecuted it was because the belief in question was *false*, not because it was socially *disruptive*. The reader will wish to examine this argument, of course. But he may be convinced, and perhaps may go on to agree with those who have interpreted the McCarthy witchhunts of the America of the fifties as a modern, secular version of the Puritan self-righteousness that cannot permit deviance. In using the Salem Witch Trials of

1692 in *The Crucible* as a means of attacking McCarthy, playwright Arthur Miller was contributing to this interpretation.

But what of those who, to the key question 'Am I of the elect?', could not answer with a firm 'Yes'? Many Puritans, if not most, could not give a confident 'Yes' and so felt insecure. In the seventeenth century this became evident as the Puritans, lacking the sacramental aid of confession to the priest, took obsessively to keeping diaries in which they could wrestle with their doubts; Cynthia Wolff's article on 'Literary Reflections of Puritanism' in *Journal of the History of Ideas*, 1968, provides a fascinating glimpse into this activity. In a different way this greater insecurity of Protestants as compared with Catholics has been noted by the late nineteenth-century French sociologist, Emile Durkheim, who found that the former are more likely than the latter to commit suicide. A more amateur sociologist like this author would draw attention on the one hand to Lady Macbeth and on the other to the preoccupation of North Americans, latter-day Puritans, with personal cleanliness, such that today's houses are coming to have more bathrooms than bedrooms.

For those Puritans who felt insecure the problem became, then, to dissipate their sense of sin and uncertainty. By the seventeenth century two major revisions of Calvinist orthodoxy had gone some way to doing this. The first was the doctrine known as Arminianism, named for the Dutch theologian, Arminius, who about 1600 formulated a challenge to thorough-going predestination. He argued that God offered each man a choice between salvation and damnation, and that man, to whom free will was now restored, accepted or rejected that offer of grace. Such a view had to be rejected by the orthodox, and as dogma Arminianism never made much headway; but as a more liberal tendency it was always strong within the Reformed tradition, for its lack of fatalism was much more congenial to the western tradition. The second modification was worked out in England and above all in New England. This federal, or Covenant, theology similarly modified predestination by having God freely enter into a contract or covenant with man such that a person, having stuck by the terms of the bargain, could confidently expect the reward of salvation. In this way man's helplessness could be subtly changed into a sense of mastery over the world where, as Ralph Perry, a leading historian of American Puritanism, puts it, 'God helps those who help themselves'. Such doctrinal shifts may be viewed in part as responses to the psychological need to escape the terrifying implications of original Calvinism. There was a third way of accommodating Calvinism to western man's nature, and this was much more nakedly psychological, having dispensed with any doctrinal mediation. But this third way out will be treated a little later.

On many points, then, Catholicism and Calvinism differ profoundly. Yet on one particular they are agreed. Both are churches. Some will feel that this is a pointless identity, since the whole discussion is about different churches. But this is because the term 'church' is ambiguous. Frequently it is used to mean any organized religious group, but it should be kept for a certain type of religion; the implied contrast is with the sects. The nature of this distinction and its implications for society will become clearer after looking at the Radical wing of the Reformation.

The crisis of the sixteenth century was not only religious, it was social and economic as well. Protest movements were numerous; the best example would be the German Peasants' War of 1524–5. But if the source of discontent was social or economic, the language of the day was religious, and so it was inevitable that such movements should seek for a religious solution. But which religious group to appeal to? The Catholics were clearly identified with the establishment—there was little hope there. What of the Lutherans? After all, Luther was in his way a revolutionary. The peasants did appeal to him, but his reply was brutally disappointing, revealing that in social matters he was more Catholic than the Catholics. When informed of the outbreak of peasant violence he wrote, 'Therefore let everyone who can, smite, slay, and stab, secretly or openly, remembering that nothing can be more poisonous, hurtful or devilish than a rebel. It is just as when we must kill a mad dog; if you do not strike him, he will strike you and a whole land with you.' Then what, a little later, of Calvin? But Calvin had an aristocratic streak in him, and his polity was deliberately designed to avoid the excesses of too radical a break with order. The small bands of discontented were thrown back on their own resources, and in the early days of the Reformation were drifting aimlessly and ineffectually.

But by 1534 several such groups had converged in the North German city of Münster and had begun to organize their own system with which to cope with crisis. They founded what today would be called a commune. An earnest attempt was made to break down the false individualism that was poisoning relationships, and in an initial burst of fervour they decreed the abolition of doors. (This was quickly rescinded, for in medieval Münster this was to give the pigs and chickens that roamed the streets entry to the houses; even so only a grill was permitted.) Yet at the very moment that Christian communism was being spread, there was a countervailing development, that of the charismatic leader. John of Leyden emerged in Münster as the messianic organizer, putting his own image on the coinage and demanding that his subjects prostrate themselves before him. When polygamy began to be practised, John obtained more wives than anyone else—nine. This juxtaposition of egalitarianism and elitism may be paradoxical, but it is by no means an unusual combination; it may even be the norm. The United States was later to know many experiments along these lines and frequently the same combination was detected. The example that springs to mind is that of the Mormons.

Münster presented a fundamental challenge to established ways. Catholic and Lutheran, busily fighting one another, immediately joined forces and marched against the common enemy. Fanatically the Münsterites prepared for Armageddon, convinced that they would triumph. Like so many other millenarians they were wrong. Münster was taken, John of Leyden executed, and the communards scattered over Germany. Münster became the scare-story for years to come; at the end of the Civil War and the Restoration of Charles II in England (1660) the city's name could be used to indicate extreme anarchy, and the same usage was to be found in America on the eve of Independence, over one hundred years later.

It was at the time of the fall of Münster that Menno Simons entered the scene. In 1524 he had been ordained a Roman Catholic priest and since then had spent the time quietly in a remote part of Friesland, leading an average and not particularly edifying life. But in 1536 he experienced conversion, feeling that it was his special mission in life to help the persecuted Münsterites. In 1537 he was re-ordained for his new life's work by an earlier adherent of the commune movement, and in 1540 he brought out *The Foundation Book*, the basis for the denomination that is today called Mennonite in his honour. This new formulation of the communal impulse was characterized by a complete rejection of direct physical confrontation; in its place was a radical insistence upon pacifism.

This continental development was not an isolated example. Rather later in England much the same style developed. About 1580 Robert Browne began to organize a little group that would eventually develop into the Congregational Church. Similar groupings proliferated in the years that followed, reaching a high point in the 1630s and 1640s. A sampling of their names will say much about their nature: the Ranters, the Seekers, the Fifth Monarchy Men, the Diggers, the last two of which were the closest English approximations to the Münsterites. And the English equivalent to Simons was George Fox, who acted as the reorganizing focus about which these impulses could be fused. His Society of Friends, or Quakers, also repudiated violence in favour of pacifism.

Enough has now been said to make clear the earlier distinction of church and sect. The sects are formed from the more obviously disinherited, those who are or feel themselves to be rejected by the greater society. Churches operate on the assumption that there is a broad identity between the society and the religion. It is this identity that makes possible the practice of infant baptism—the child does not have to decide to enter the faith; merely by being born to members of the faith he is already a member. But the mentality of the sectarian is one of dissociation from society. He views the majority as tainted, to be avoided. Psychologically he demands separation and then a compensatory huddling together of the righteous few. Consequently he demands adult baptism, a sign that the initiate has deliberately decided to break with the main body and join the sect. Because in the Reformation period adult baptism meant rebaptism, this whole tradition is known (using the Greek prefix meaning again) as the Anabaptist; today's Baptist is merely a shortened form.

A new baptism, however, is not the only example of rebirth that the sectarian experiences. Attentive readers may have noticed that Simons had himself re-ordained. Luther and Calvin, who wished to *reform* the Church, had no notion of repudiating their original Catholic ordination. But for Simons the past itself was tainted, a completely new start was called for. Some sectarians even felt that a marriage performed according to the Catholic rite automatically lost its validity once they had been converted to a sectarian outlook. Many remarried their spouses according to the new law; but many, it must be confessed, seized the chance to change partners. The idea of rebirth was so pervasive that the key term reformation was not used by these groups; rather, they spoke of renewal. There was in sectarian thinking a crucially greater willingness to break with the past, with tradition, and to consider a future orientation. For instance the English Dissenters (as the sectarians were frequently referred to) were prominent in progressive movements, and in the nineteenth century formed the backbone of what was known as the Nonconformist Conscience, a tradition of enlightened social concern that will be dealt with more fully later in the book.

Rejection by and of the larger society pushes the sectarian into a compensating emphasis on brotherhood and equality, and the tendency towards 'democracy' is even more strongly marked among sectarians than among Calvinists. For instance there is a more thorough-going repudiation of structure, whether of bishops or elders; thus the Quakers have no priests or ministers of any kind. The significance of Browne's movement becomes plain, for the term Congregational draws attention to the fact that in this system the congregation, autonomous and self-sufficient, is the focus of attention, and that if any structure is to be built on this base, it is to be in the nature of a federation. To look ahead, the way in which such thinking may rub off onto more secular attitudes may be seen in the fact that in the United States the Baptists tended to be in favour of 'states' rights', and in the fact that in the Canadian rebellions of 1837 the sectarians were generally for the movement and for a program that favoured the backwoods areas over the centre.

The distinction between sectarianism and Calvinism is a blurred one. Partly this is because under certain conditions a sect could take on the characteristic of a church. New England Congregationalism had originally been sectarian, but in the absence of an entrenched church it quickly became the orthodoxy and lost its 'outsider' qualities. Indeed it was established, that is supported, by the colonial authorities, and became in many ways conservative. Although the underlying sectarianism was never lost, and was later to be re-emphasized, this new-world experience represented a significant shift of style in sectarianism. Partly it was because Calvinist churches could move in a sectarian direction. Presbyterians may have been 'insiders' in Scotland but in North America, lacking the firm support that, say, the centralized Catholic institutions could provide, they reverted to being 'outsiders'. And partly the blurring was due to the fact that to sectarians the main problem was a social-psychological pressure that was to be resolved by new kinds of organizations. Sectarian theology tended, therefore, to be underdeveloped, and many sects were content to take over a basic Calvinism. There were affinities, then, between the two impulses, and that this was so was borne out when Congregationalists and Presbyterians joined to form the United Church of Canada.

A trinity of religious styles has now been outlined, a long-established Catholicism and two challenges stemming from the Reformation, Calvinism and the sectarian impulse. But a fourth, which dates from the eighteenth rather than the sixteenth century, must now be added. It has something from each of the traditions, but combines them in such a way, and adds such distinctive touches of its own, that a separate treatment becomes necessary. This addition, which had immense impact on both sides of the Atlantic, and which was the third element in the United Church fusion, is Methodism.

By the late seventeenth century the fortunes of Protestantism were at a low ebb. Lutheranism, for example, had lost its early vitality and had become a dry, narrow orthodoxy. As a reaction against such desiccation there arose a movement in Germany, led by Jacob Spener, known as Pietism, that stressed a personal, brotherly religion, that emphasized an emotional and intuitive sense of Christ, and that was so suspicious of reason as to be in some ways anti-intellectual; the evangelical aspect was also emphasized and Pietists were active missionaries. A little later and somewhat to one side of this impulse was that of another German, Count von Zinzendorf, who gave a lead to a reconstituted group known as the Moravian Brethren. Here the emotional aspects were even more pronounced, though missionary activity was also important; Zinzendorf himself visited North America and it was because of his suggestion that the Moravian settlement of Bethlehem, Pennsylvania, was so named. Even so, Pietist-Moravian impact on the North Atlantic community was relatively slight, and completely overshadowed by that of their English counterparts, the Methodists.

In England the mass of the population was in a worse condition than in Germany. The Industrial Revolution was not yet in full swing, but the urbanization of England was beginning. The new towns lacked the amenities for a growing population, in particular the parishes to serve their spiritual needs. On the land the traditional, still in many ways feudal, relationships and communal structures were breaking down and social dislocation was rife. The Church of England was moribund, the clergy scarcely engaged with religion; in his six years as Bishop of Bangor, Hoadly never set foot in his diocese. A good many societies similar to the German Pietists were emerging in the hope of injecting some sense of purpose into the main body of Anglicanism. That group at Oxford University dominated by John and Charles Wesley and George Whitefield, and known as the 'Holy club', was but one among many.

Of these three leaders the greatest was John Wesley. He was ordained an Anglican priest and determined to work as a missionary in the newly founded colony of Georgia. This mission was a failure, and it caused Wesley to rethink his approach. But the venture was redeemed from total failure in that en route to the New World Wesley travelled with a party of Moravian Brethren. He was impressed by their outlook and incorporated much of their spirit into his own rapidly evolving religious thinking. This evolution was in fact taking him further and further away from his Anglican heritage. Wesley fought against the logic of this development and managed to die (in 1791) still a member of the Church of England. But by 1795 his followers had to take the plunge and constitute themselves an independent church. What was the character of this new denomination that forced it into separation?

Evidently the basic impulse was sectarian. Wesley made his greatest appeal to the uprooted; he was especially successful, for instance, among the coalminers of the Newcastle and Bristol areas. The sectarian impress may be noted in the way in which doctrine was played down. There was very little theology in the movement, and the only salient element was Wesley's determination to avoid predestination, a position summed up under the loose term Arminianism; here he parted company with Whitefield who was the founder of the small sub-sect of Calvinistic Methodists. Sectarian, too, was the prominence given to revivalist technique—the unashamed use of raw emotion to bring the sinner to Christ. Sectarianism may be seen also in the use of lay preachers, a development over which the priest Wesley long anguished. And it may be seen in the use of itinerant preachers.

But if Methodism was sectarian, and so qualified for inclusion in the United Church along with Congregationalism, it was sectarian with a difference. From the first there was a determination to hold the system tightly together in an efficiently structured framework. The local organizations of classes were grouped into circuits, which in turn were organized into districts, the whole held together by the connection, which was the name for the entire Methodist organization. Then, too, officials at various levels were fascinated by the possibility of quantifying the amount of holiness in an individual or group, and reports on such matters were constantly flowing from the lower to the higher levels. Superiors were ever on the lookout for those falling away from the standard, the most notorious of whom were accused of that particularly Methodist sin of 'backsliding' and were 'winnowed' from the church. Superimposed, then, on sectarian spontaneity was a most bureaucratic control system. It was not surprising perhaps that Wesley had a high regard for Loyola, or that in the absence of a strong theology the bureaucratic means should seem to become the end.

Commentators have seen this concern for orderliness as one reason why England made such a relatively smooth transition from a premodern to a modern, factory-disciplined society. It comes as something of a shock to the clock-conscious, precision-minded twentieth century to realize that there was a time when such values were not recognized. That Wesley's group could have been singled out as *Methodists* because they prayed at set times and generally ordered their lives in a methodical manner, is a reminder of how rare such ways were at that time. Contemporaries were certainly aware of the connection between emerging factory discipline and Methodism, noting for example their coincidence among the workers in the new pottery industry of Stoke-on-Trent.

A concern for social order was reinforced by a concern for political order. Like other sects, Methodism appealed to the outsider. But Wesley himself was of a marked Tory cast of mind; for instance he wrote a pamphlet against American independence. His followers, perhaps to convince the authorities that there was nothing to fear, were happy to continue to emphasize law and order. When in the 1790s the French Revolution was terrifying England, Methodism was hostile to it, and members who sympathized with it were expelled from the classes for being too 'democratic'. Somewhat later Wesley's successor, Jabez Bunting, would proclaim, 'Methodism is opposed to democracy as it is opposed to sin.' So powerful a combination was this concern for social and political order that the conclusion was early reached that it was Methodism that saved Britain from the recurrent revolutionary disturbances that scarred so much of the continent, and if recently this thesis has been questioned, it still illuminates many modern accounts of British society.

Yet another aberration from sectarianism was the Methodist stress upon an individual approach. Sects, for reasons already given, commonly stress the group, the social feeling, but such an emphasis was played down in the Methodist outlook. Similarly ignored was the sectarian preference for an apocalyptic solution, for the immediate ushering-in of the millennium. Instead Methodists put their faith in philanthropy, working for improvement over the long haul. Thus they were active in founding money-lending societies, schools, even dispensaries for the provision of cheap drugs. This practicality, together with the stress on the individual, was responsible in large part for the 'self-help' doctrine that was to be so rich a theme in the emerging industrial society of the nineteenth century.

So far this outline has dealt with conditions and developments in the land of origin, England. What of Methodism's spread across the Atlantic? It came to the future United States in the 1760s, but its growth was retarded by the revolutionary situation and the War of Independence, and something as British and Tory as Methodism was viewed with suspicion. But the war over, the Church spread rapidly, especially thanks to Francis Asbury, a British lieutenant of Wesley, who at the Revolution threw in his lot with the Americans and became leader of the Methodists in the United States. One oddity was that in the United States the superintendents were known as bishops. It was from the

United States that Methodism first penetrated into British North America—(if one ignores Newfoundland, at this time not officially a colony; in Newfoundland Methodism dated from 1765)—to the Maritimes and to Upper Canada. Somewhat later a more British tradition began to arrive with the early nineteenth-century surge of migration, and the Wesleyans (as they were known to distinguish them from their American cousins, the Episcopalian Methodists) eventually dominated.

In both North American societies the success of Methodism was immense. Although these were rural and not urban societies, the situation was still one for which Methodism was suited. The combination of local and itinerant preachers was ideal in societies where newly settled communities were rapidly becoming mature and throwing off still newer and rawer ones. The absence of a sophisticated theology and the use of lay preachers were boons to an impoverished backwoods suspicious of learning, yet hungry for emotional release. 'Self-help' philosophies were also in tune with the ethos of the land. It must also be remembered, however, that the Tory element acted as a counterweight to an otherwise radical outlook. In the United States Methodists tended to be against states' rights doctrines, while in Canada the Methodists drew back from the reformers of the 1830s when they sensed the revolutionary implications.

The foregoing discussion has occasionally spelt out the ways in which religion affected development in the North Atlantic communities and has rather more often hinted at other impacts. Before closing this section it remains to outline one particular theory of the interaction of religion and society. This theory deals with the third way, alluded to above, in which the more Calvinist-inclined sought to minimize their sense of insecurity.

At the beginning of this century the German polymath Max Weber brought out his study known to an English readership as *The Protestant Ethic and the Spirit of Capitalism*. In sketching the Weber thesis one begins by explaining the spirit of capitalism. By the spirit of capitalism Weber did not mean to refer to actual capitalists, or to the capitalist technique of breeding money; he knew that most cultures and most periods have provided examples of these. What was unique about the western tradition in the modern period was the emergence of a generalized climate of opinion where capitalist technique was widely diffused, and where there was a feeling pervading significant sections of society that the use of such techniques was a duty imposed on man. To illustrate his point, Weber drew attention to the contrasting pair, Jacob Fugger and Benjamin Franklin. The former was an early sixteenth-century German banker who by capitalist technique had become a multi-millionaire. But, argued Weber, he was an isolated capitalist not imbued with the spirit of capitalism, for when pressed by a friend to retire he replied that he was happy making money and would quit only when he ceased to enjoy it. For the eighteenth-century Franklin on the other hand such an attitude, making continuation depend on pleasure, would have been a dereliction of duty. For him the mobilization of resources and their reinvestment was looked upon as a sacred imperative; as Weber sums it up 'What in [Fugger's] case was an expression of commercial daring morally neutral, in [Franklin's] takes on the character of an ethically coloured maxim for the conduct of life. . . . Truly, what is here preached [in Franklin's case] is not simply a means of making one's way in the world, but a peculiar ethic. The infraction of its rules is treated not as foolishness but as forgetfulness of duty. That is the essence of the matter. It is not mere business astuteness, that sort of thing is common enough, it is an ethos.'

Now it is central to Weber's thesis that those who have the spirit of capitalism are overwhelmingly Protestant, not Catholic. He noted that in his own day the majority of industrialists in Germany were Protestant. He knew that the sectarians had been prominent in England's Industrial Revolution and that seventeenth-century observers had noted an economic climate suitable for capitalist growth in Huguenot France and Reformed Holland. It now became necessary to explain why Protestantism should have permitted the evolution of a spirit of capitalism, whereas Catholicism permitted but isolated capitalists. The key lies in two conflicting attitudes to work; they may be identified as the traditional (followed by most cultures throughout most periods) and nontraditional. The traditional attitude assumes that work is an evil, a necessary evil it must be admitted, to be avoided whenever possible. The classic illustration today would be the story told of the introduction of improved rice to the Indian subcontinent; when informed that the new rice would yield more than the traditional amount, the peasants reduced the acreage cultivated by the same proportion. Weber knew of different examples from his own day. On the German-owned farms of East Prussia the heavy work of mowing was performed by migrant Polish labour. When in the interests of quick harvesting piece-work rates were raised, the amount mowed fell! The traditionally minded Poles were satisfied with earning the traditional amount and preferred to take their increment in the form of increased leisure and not, as in modern western society, in the form of increased purchasing power.

It still has to be explained why a traditional attitude to work and

Catholicism should go together. Here one remembers the sacramental quality of Catholicism, what Weber openly calls the 'magical'. If the Catholic wishes for change he will tend to appeal beyond the world, to call for a miracle, and the Aetna example springs to mind. The Protestant, forbidden to rely on such devices, will be obliged to manipulate the world, to act within it. Work must take the place of magic. Then, too, the Protestant, especially the Calvinist, feels insecure. Work is frequently a way to tangible success, and success is presumably an indication that one is of the elect. Bear in mind that New England Covenant theology openly used the language of business to make its points; note, for example, the parallel drawn between 'a Covenant that is made between two parties, and the Law, which is the Covenant which is given us of the Lord: in a Covenant, first there must be conditions and Articles of agreement between the parties offered and consented unto: and secondly, a binding one another to the performance thereof by Bond, perhaps a pair of indentures are drawn between them. . . . It is just so [with] the agreement between us and the Lord.' Work is also a means of avoiding temptation and of drugging oneself so as not to have to face doubt. The Kipling poem in praise of digging ('How the Camel got his Hump' from *Just So Stories*) is a nice illustration of this Wasp attitude; another would be the fetish made of games in English public (North American private) schools, for if the sons of gentry cannot be put to manual labour a fit substitute can be found in games. Work is necessary to the Protestant because his religious simplicity minimizes the chance of praising God by, say, donating a stained-glass window, or by actually producing the window; moreover the Protestant rejection of the other-worldly means the impossibility of monasticism and related life-styles. The Protestant, therefore, has nothing but his work, his worldly success, to dedicate to God, and Weber has a fascinating observation on the fact that Catholic vocabularies lack a term for 'calling' and that the German word for profession (*Beruf*, from *rufen*, to call) was an introduction of Luther. And finally, at a more down-to-earth level, the Catholic year contained many holy days of obligation in which no work should be performed—in some areas of Christendom they came to more than one hundred a year, and this in addition to Sundays. It is often overlooked that there were two sides to the early seventeenth-century Puritan demand for Sabbatarianism. Evident is the call for a purer observance of the Lord's Day; not so evident is the fact that there was a call for an end to the excessive number of saint's days.

The Protestant needed a different conception of work from that of the traditional. But to hold the new work ethic looked dangerously like jumping out of the frying pan into the fire. As Wesley himself was aware, 'wherever riches have increased, the essence of religion has decreased in the same proportion. . . . For religion [by which he meant Methodism] must necessarily produce both industry and frugality, and these cannot but produce riches. But as riches increase, so will pride, anger and love of the world. . . . We ought not to prevent people from being diligent and frugal; we must exhort all Christians to gain all they can, and to save all they can; that is, in effect, to grow rich.' However, a means of short-circuiting the passage from frugality to wealth to temptation to sin did exist. It was to make money, but not to spend it; to accumulate wealth but not to enjoy it. Instead it was to be re-invested. The capitalist technique was now fully formed, the mechanism complete and self-sustaining.

Naturally the Weber thesis has come in for much criticism. Two of the many deserve to be mentioned here. The first would see the spread of the spirit of capitalism not as a function of religious belief, but of a group's status. That is, a sectarian group in England, say, frozen out of public life, will tend to enter the only real avenue open to it, the world of business. Support for such a view may easily be found; for instance, the Russian 'Reformation', which took place in the mid-seventeenth century, modernized the main body of the Orthodox Church but left a section of the more 'magically' inclined behind as the Old Believers; yet it was the Old Believers rather than the more modern Church that provided the impulse to the spread of capitalism. The second line of criticism would urge that Weber had the cart before the horse. Perhaps a changing economic world calls into existence a religion better able to validate the new norms.

But if the broad insight of Weber is accepted, what further applications might it have for the North Atlantic community? It will suggest a partial explanation of why the United States has forged ahead in capitalist technique and why New England was at the forefront of this process at the formative period. It will suggest that Quebec's problems are not solely due to exploitation by the Wasps, nor to the lack of resources in that province during the industrial take-off period. Rather, it will stress the Catholic mentality of the Québecois. Support for such a view is convincingly presented in N. W. Taylor's article 'The French-Canadian Industrial Entrepreneur and his Social Environment' in M. Rioux and Y. Martin (eds), *French Canadian Society*. A typical Quebec outlook recorded by Taylor would be this from a forty-seven-year-old shoe-manufacturer, the employer of 160 workers: 'I don't want to get too big. I'm happy so long as I get a comfortable living for myself and my family. The business has done well—better than I expected—and if I were rich I would have more work and worry. It's no use being a millionaire and in the cemetery.' The Weber thesis will also suggest why missionary work among the Indians has always been more successfully carried out by Catholics than by Protestants—for Catholics and Indians share a traditional scheme of values. It may also suggest that the Indian problem will be much more difficult of solution than may be supposed. It may suggest such a clash between Indian and Wasp values that the adoption of one must mean the giving up of the other, that any full integration of Indian into white society will destroy the Indians as a culture. Perhaps the extremist statements of Miss Kahn-Tineta Horn, a self-styled spokesman for Canada's Indians, who calls for segregation, are a recognition of this truth.

The question is evidently an immense one, and it will be for the reader to decide how big an interpretive role to allow the Weber thesis. Even American/Canadian football has been tackled on this basis (see the article 'Homo Ludens (Americanus)' in *Queen's Quarterly*, 1971). In what follows, there will be ample opportunity for considering further possible applications.

※ ※ ※

From time to time the foregoing discussion of religious development touched upon ideas that were to have radical implications for the evolution of England and the two colonial societies of North America. Yet despite the presence of these radical elements, it is clear that religion represented the forces of tradition and conservatism. After all, each religion was conscious of belonging to the more than a thousand-year-old tradition of Christendom; each looked back to Christ. During the *ancien régime*, however, there developed an alternative outlook that at many points was opposed to this religious tradition and its associated philosophies. By the latter part of the eighteenth century this challenge had emerged in many parts of Europe as the dominant intellectual current. But its roots lay in the seventeenth century and, if the compelling account provided by Paul Hazard is accepted, the beginnings of that movement known as the Enlightenment may be dated in the 1680s.

This is not to say that the change was a total one; total revolutions do not happen in history, and periodizing is a dangerous if necessary game. Indeed those who are over-inclined to mark a clear-cut break at about this point would do well to ponder Carl Becker's provocative

Heavenly City of the Eighteenth Century Philosophers, in which he stresses the similarities between the eighteenth and the thirteenth centuries. Probably in the end the reader will decide against this most extreme championing of continuity, but even if he does so his return to a late seventeenth-century *Crise de la conscience européenne* (the title of Hazard's book) will mean a richer and more balanced understanding of the Enlightenment.

This change of outlook was one that affected the entire western world. From Beccaria in Italy to Linnaeus in Sweden, from Franklin in the British colonies of North America to Kant in Königsberg and even to Radishchev in Russia, there stretched a network of shared ideas that encompassed almost all the significant thinking of the time. The greater part of Enlightenment activity and some of its most impressive achievements were centred in France, however, and the great names of the movement are overwhelmingly those who were French or who chose to write in French; Montesquieu, Maupertuis, Buffon, La Mettrie, Rousseau, Diderot, Helvétius, Condillac, d'Holbach, Condorcet, and finally Voltaire, the greatest of them all, are eleven out of twenty-five 'more important writers of the Enlightenment' listed by Norman Hampson in his study *The Enlightenment*. And if one work sums up this tradition it is the *Encyclopédie* that Diderot brought out between 1751 and 1772 and whose contributors were mainly French. So great, in fact, was the impress of French thought and style upon the Enlightenment that increasingly the French word *philosophe* is being used to refer to those within the tradition; provided that it is understood that *philosophe* does not mean philosopher, but implies rather 'member of the intelligentsia' or even 'man of letters', the use of the term is a fitting tribute to French dominance.

And yet there is a sense in which the movement was more English than French (and perhaps more British than English, since the Scottish school was a most important element in the Enlightenment). The reason for claiming this is not so much the fact that, to turn again to Hampson's list, six out of the twenty-five were from Britain (the next highest national total, incidentally), as the fact that it was an impulse from England that 'began' the Enlightenment. French *philosophes* recognized this as readily as anyone else. Thus when in 1751 D'Alembert, who for a while assisted Diderot as editor of the *Encyclopédie*, brought out the *Preliminary Discourse* as an advertisement both of the forthcoming *Encyclopédie* and of the *philosophes'* views, he wrote at length of the four 'principal geniuses that the human mind ought to regard as its masters'; they were Francis Bacon, René Descartes, John Locke, and Isaac

Newton, and of these the only non-Englishman was regarded as seriously flawed. And even when the initial impulses from England were taken into the French setting and developed there, it was to England that they eventually returned for their final formulation, for the thinking of Helvétius formed the starting point for the system of Jeremy Bentham whose Utilitarianism may be seen as the culmination of one strand of the Enlightenment.

This stress upon the British salience in the tradition means that it is justifiable to concentrate upon Locke and Newton and to see in their contributions the major characteristics of the new outlook. (Bacon may be played down, since it was his method rather than the content of what he said that linked him with the Enlightenment.) Since this is a study of the North Atlantic community, which is overwhelmingly British-derived, such an emphasis may be doubly justified. But there may be a second meaning to British prominence. Does Britain's key role as originator, as a major contributor, and perhaps most significantly as Utilitarian culminator, point to a sociological explanation of the Enlightenment? For this was the period when the bourgeoisie was beginning to displace the aristocracy and when values were increasingly being derived from a bourgeois way of life. And in this evolution Britain was the leader, as most of the indicators bear out. Thus by about 1700 England had the most developed newspapers and periodicals (which implies a mass, middle-class readership capable of supporting such novel ventures), had all but parted from individual, aristocratic patronage in favour of mass bourgeois support of the artist (so calling into existence in 1710 the first copyright law, the vital protection for the bourgeois artist selling in the open market), and had, through Defoe, produced the quintessential bourgeois figure of Robinson Crusoe, the isolated economic man whose individual efforts had imposed order on chaos. And more precise links between the new outlook and the bourgeoisie may be noted. It has been stated that in the mid-seventeenth-century English Civil War the Baconians were Parliamentarians hostile to King Charles I. By the 1680s, the decade of the Glorious Revolution, the links are becoming convincing indeed—as will be pointed out. While of the culmination, Utilitarianism, which also will be dealt with later in this book, it is enough at this stage to allude to Bentham's reduction of social philosophy to the pleasure-pain calculus, to the bookkeeper's double-entry drawing of a balance.

Both Newton and Locke had an immediate and extensive impact that is rather rare in the case of really influential thinkers. In the former's case the rapid diffusion of his ideas was even more noteworthy in that his system had to compete with the very satisfying one already in the field, Cartesianism; yet despite such obstruction Newtonian ideas had so penetrated the universities of Cambridge, Edinburgh, and St Andrews within a few years of their definitive formulation in the *Principia Mathematica* of 1687 that they were actually being taught there by some of the faculty—though the official philosophy, it must be admitted, was still Cartesian. The continent took relatively quickly to Newtonianism, as the bibliography of translations of and books on Newton amply testify; one of the most popular was Algarotti's *Newtonianismo per le Dame*, though the greatest Newtonian in terms of ability to convince a wide, influential readership was Voltaire. Locke also was quickly transmitted to a European audience. Before his ideas were fully worked out he himself had published hints of them in French in the journal run by Jean Le Clerc, a Huguenot refugee in Holland; and it was another Huguenot, the London-exiled Pierre Coste, who translated Locke's *Thoughts concerning Education* within two years of its first appearance in 1693. Incidentally, it was Coste who was Newton's first French translator.

That their views were so quickly absorbed into the thinking of Europe indicates how Newton and Locke were great, not only in their originality but also in their ability to sum up and convincingly present a completed picture of the intellectual trends of the seventeenth century. And so even though they interested themselves in different questions, there was a good deal of shared ground that, as will be noted, was more striking than the differences.

Newton's primary place in the intellectual pantheon is as a mathematical astronomer, though he did concern himself with other fields and produced such important works as his *Opticks*. Ever since the medieval astronomy based on Aristotle and Ptolemy had been impugned by Copernicus in the mid-sixteenth century, the tendency had been towards a theory that would explain the universe on the basis of mathematics and mechanistic models. This had been particularly true of the early seventeenth-century giant, Galileo, who had gone a long way towards working out a satisfactory theory of the heavens. But an overview that would account for all the observed facts was still lacking, and it was this deficiency that Newton was able to remedy. His theory of universal gravitation, the formula that every particle attracts every other particle in the universe with a force proportional to its mass and inversely proportional to the square of the distance involved, couched in a compelling mathematical explanation, set the seal on a century and more of progress in astronomy. Its most convincing attraction was that it handled all the scientific problems of the day; it worked in a way that even the Cartesian system did not.

Locke was more the philosopher in the traditional sense of that word, with a particular interest in two of its applications, political philosophy and epistemology, with the latter leading on to a fascination with educational theory. These two fields, though interrelated, deserve separate and extended treatment.

In the late 1670s when Locke was first beginning to attract attention, England was ruled by the Stuart King Charles II whose increasingly absolutist reign was drawing towards its close. Since Charles lacked a legitimate heir, the new king would be his brother, James II. What made the prospect of such a succession odious to many of the ruling class, and to many of the people too, was the fact that James was an open Catholic and gave every indication of being more absolutist than his brother. A movement to exclude James from the throne began to grow. It failed to prevent James from becoming king in 1685, but three years later the birth of a Catholic son and the prospect of a Catholic dynasty encouraged leading men to invite the Calvinist William of Holland (who was married to a Protestant daughter of James, and had a claim to the throne) to assume the English crown. Locke's early writings were in the service of this anti-James faction, and when James fell in 1688 in the Glorious Revolution, Locke became the philosopher of the new régime. His *Two Treatises of Government* defended the exile of one monarch and the calling in of another; but more importantly they contained ideas revolutionary in their implications for society.

Two key ideas dominated Locke's political writings. The first was an insistence upon the individuality of each man. Most readers will find this point so self-evident that they will be unable to grasp the originality such a position represented in the late seventeenth century. But until Locke finally demolished it, the accepted view had been that exemplified by Sir Robert Filmer (published in 1680 but written c.1640), which was the medieval and Catholic notion that all men were the descendants of Adam, that everything men possessed was by virtue of an inheritance or gift from previous generations, and that man, far from being an individual, was but one element in the primordial family. Hierarchy, a sense of one's place amid the various stations of life, was taken as given. The political corollary of this belief system was the theory known as the Divine Right of Kings; God, the supreme father, had appointed kings to be earthly fathers to their peoples. It followed that resistance to God's anointed representative was not merely a political crime, it was also blasphemy, an infraction of the command-ment 'Honour thy father'.

Against this view of society Locke postulated an original state of nature. There men enjoyed 'perfect freedom' and a 'state also of equality'. It was a state that had 'a law of nature to govern it, which obliges every man: and reason, which is that law, teaches all man-kind . . . that being all equal and independent, no one ought to harm another in his life, health, liberty or possessions'. Here was a most important concept, one that was to dominate thinking through the eighteenth century and beyond. Man had a *right* to life, health, liberty and possessions; these were not privileges granted to him by any earthly power but inhered in him simply by virtue of his human *nature*. Locke was championing, then, natural rights.

The second originality, and again one that will probably require an act of imagination to appreciate, was the closely allied notion that society was the result of individuals' choosing to come together. The fact that men possessed natural rights to life, health, liberty and pos-sessions did not in itself guarantee social harmony; indeed it would provide grounds for dispute, say when one individual pitted his natural right to a particular piece of property against that of another. To guard against this kind of anarchy, each individual agreed to accept curbs on the exercise of his natural rights, and so replaced the state of nature by society, which could arbitrate between rival claims. The relationship between ruler and ruled, then, was one governed by the terms of the contract that established the society. The people agreed to support the king if he in return agreed to use the powers entrusted to him to rule in the interests of society. It was, argued Locke, because King James II had broken the contract between himself and his people, by which he had agreed to rule wisely and in agreement with the fundamental laws, that it became justifiable to withdraw allegiance from him and form a new contract with William and Mary. Here, too, the older notion had been that taken by Filmer, who denied that society was a voluntary compact but held rather that it simply *was*. He insisted on that obedi-ence that all children owe to their father—was not the title of Filmer's book *Patriarcha*?

Locke's contributions to epistemology are to be found mainly in the lengthy *Essay Concerning Human Understanding*. Until this time the accepted view was that ideas were innate, that is, they were impressed on a person's mind at birth by virtue of the fact that man was God's special creation and made in His likeness. It followed that ideas were looked upon as fixed and established for all time. The following illustration may make this outlook a little clearer; at the same time it says something about a particular aspect of society that will be referred to later in the text. Pre-modern man had a very different conception of law from modern man. To put it dramatically we may say that medieval man never ever made a law. Such a statement will no doubt provoke the reader. What, he will ask, of Magna Carta? In 1214 England had no such law, in 1215 it did; therefore it must have been made to come into existence. But this is how modern man sees it, not how medieval man saw it. He, rather, believed that Magna Carta had always existed, and that the only significant thing about 1215 was the fact that in that year it first became necessary to make explicit what the law always had been. Law *declaring* was the key to pre-modern legislation, not law *making*; the first was the work of man, the second of God alone.

Locke rejected innate ideas. For him, a child's mind at birth was quite empty, a blank sheet of paper 'void of all characters, without any ideas'—or as he put it in the scholastic Latin of the day, a *'tabula rasa'*. If one went on to ask 'How comes [the mind] to be furnished? Whence comes it by that vast store which the busy and boundless fancy of man has painted on it with an almost endless variety? Whence has it all the materials of reason and knowledge?' Locke answered 'in one word, from EXPERIENCE'. In other words, the mind was to be seen as a box in which were sorted out and combined the various facts of the outside world. These facts came to the mind as impulses transmitted by one or more of the five senses, and through them, and only through them, was knowledge built up, step by step. Pride of place, then, was given to sense impressions, and because of this the Lockean philosophy is often referred to as 'sensationalist'.

Two points should be noted. Such thinking opened the way for a more relativistic method of viewing truth. Rather than truth being given once and for all, it was now seen as something towards which individuals and societies could evolve. As an example of this novel relativism may be cited Locke's own delight in showing that contemporary American Indian practices corresponded to other, earlier ones in the European and Mediterranean pasts. In other words, Indian ways could not be simply written off as pagan and irredeemably wrong; just as European peoples had progressed towards the truth, so too might Indians. Secondly, this kind of thinking demanded an emphasis on education. If the child's mind is blank to begin with and has to be filled, and if the way to fill a mind is via sense impressions and these alone, then a careful selection of sense impressions and a careful inculcation of these sensations should guarantee a mind well stocked with the right ideas. Suitable programming (to use the up-to-date term) would enable the child to become an adult with socially acceptable views; in brief, education seemed to promise a short cut to utopia.

So outlined, the systems of Newton and Locke seem to have little in common. Yet a little probing will reveal much basic agreement. One of the first points to grasp is the way in which the *philosophe* now goes about his enquiries. The older tradition of thinking had been that known as deductive; one began with a given truth and from that starting point deduced the consequences, any facts being of significance in so far as they conformed to and illustrated the expected consequences. The newer tradition was that known as inductive; here supreme importance was given to the facts, and from that starting point one at last induced some general conclusion, some truth. Closely allied with the inductive method was the experimental. The investigator was not to wait on the facts, observing them as they normally presented themselves to his gaze. Rather he was to go to them aggressively, and by performing experiments he was to force a conclusion from the facts. As Bacon, the great protagonist of the experimental method and for this reason so lauded by D'Alembert, put it, one should torture nature in order to make her yield up her secrets. And a generalization having been induced, experiment should be repeated to show that from any given set of phenomena the identical results would always flow, for only in this way would true mastery over nature be possible. A more convenient term for inductive-experimental is empirical.

Locke and Newton were clearly empirical in their methodology. As has been seen, the former insisted upon going to the facts, to the unambiguous sense impressions, and building up from them. And when he named the great informing principle 'Experience' he might as well have called it 'Experiment'. Newton made his methodological position clear when, doubts about it having arisen, he inserted the following caution into the second edition of the *Principia*: 'hitherto I have not been able to discover the cause of those properties of gravity from phenomena, and I feign no hypotheses'. In other words, his examination and analysis of the facts had not enabled him as yet to induce a law of the cause of gravity, and in the meantime he would refuse to make a guess.

This quotation brings out clearly another example of the new method, a willingness to acknowledge that the study was provisional, but that so long as it seemed to account for the observed facts and to do so in a better fashion than any alternative explanation, it would be pursued. Locke put this modest attitude clearly when he wrote of his own contribution to learning, 'it is ambition enough to be employed as an under-labourer in clearing the ground a little, and removing some of the rubbish that lies in the way to knowledge', and he went on, 'It is of great use to the sailor to know the length of his line, though he cannot with it fathom all the depths of the ocean. It is well that he knows that it is long enough to reach the bottom, at such places as are necessary to direct his voyage, and caution him against running upon shoals that may ruin him. Our business here is not to know all things, but those which concern our conduct.' There was, however, a less satisfactory side to this so-modern attitude. Both the Lockean and Newtonian cast of mind encouraged the belief that the 'how' questions were much more important than the 'why' questions. Especially in the hands of later and lesser followers there was the danger that too great a preoccupation with technique would lead to the ignoring of ultimate goals; the ecology boom of the late sixties and seventies is a belated recognition that 'why' questions cannot be ducked for ever.

Accompanying the use of an empirical-inductive approach was that of the quantifying method. This is what is meant by saying that the new science was mathematical. It was not merely that new and advanced mathematical technique was needed to communicate the Newtonian picture. That was certainly true, but mathematical technique had a deeper meaning. The medieval system had been qualitative, it used in its analysis the notion of 'qualities' or 'natures'. Thus it was the nature of 'earthy' things, say stones, to seek to be reunited with their own kind and so to fall towards the centre of the earth. It was also held that they became 'happier' the closer they came to their appointed place in the eternal scheme of things, and so fell more 'joyously' or faster as they neared the earth—such was the qualitative explanation of acceleration. Chemical questions were tackled on a similar basis. All substances, it was thought, were built out of four elements, earth, water, air, and fire, which combined to produce mixtures characterized by the proportions of the qualities they contained— thus a heavy stone differed from a light one in that the former had more earth in it, the quality of which was to have gravity and so to fall, while the latter had more air, the quality of which was to have levity and so to rise. Such a view was rapidly becoming old-fashioned even before Newton's day, for it had been cruelly satirized by Molière in *Le Malade Imaginaire*, where the candidate for admission to the medical profession, asked why opium caused people to sleep, answered 'Because there is in it a dormative virtue, the nature of which is to lull the senses'. Such a response indicated the failure of a qualitative explanation—it too immediately became circular. Newton's work, on the other hand, showed the superiority of a quantitative approach by which things were measured and their relationships established mathematically; that way a greater mastery over the world could be gained. It was an outlook generally shared in this period, which saw in England the beginnings of demography, the keeping of trade statistics (the very word a seventeenth-century invention), and the introduction of the expression 'Political Arithmetic', by which term was meant a nation's vital statistics.

Changes in method marked the first crucial shift of the new outlook. A second major shift was connected with man's understanding of motion, a shift that may be summarized as that from a static to a dynamic conception. The contrast between the Newtonian and the medieval will be instructive here, and it can be done in a way that will indicate whether the reader has the modern view of motion or whether he still holds to one that was exploded some three hundred and fifty years ago. It takes the form of a 'thought-experiment' in which such troublesome details as air-resistance can be thought away. Imagine a driver in a convertible driving along the highway at sixty miles an hour; the day is hot, the roof is down, and he is drinking a soft drink from a can. Being a litter-lout he thinks to dispose of the empty can by throwing it vertically upwards with all his might. The question now is, will the can land a little way behind the car (it having moved along the highway in the time taken for the can to go up and come down), a medium way behind, or a long way behind? In fact, choosing any of the alternatives given indicates an impossibly medieval mind—though classroom experience reveals that the majority will plump for one of these choices. To begin with it is medieval because of a willingness to go along with such qualitative phrases as 'with all his might', a 'little . . . medium . . . long way', and not to demand that they be replaced by quantitative measures akin to the 60 m.p.h. of the car. Even then, the choice of any of these alternatives is medieval since the true answer is that the can will fall back exactly into the hand that threw it. The Aristotelian-Ptolemaic universe was based on a theory of motion that held that the natural state of anything was at rest in its proper position; it was this theory that made the stone fall towards the centre of the earth—in some way it had become displaced from its true position and was hurrying to get back. The selection of one of the choices offered indicates that this view is still operating, for it is felt that when the can ceased to be held in the hand it ceased to have horizontal motion and had but vertical motion. For a modern, however, the view is that all things are moving unless they are stopped. The can had a horizontal motion before being thrown upwards, nothing stopped that forward motion, and so a vertical component was added to a horizontal one; the combination of the two produced a parabola that returned the can to the hand. A clinching question may be asked to check if the lesson has been learned. What happens if a bottle is let fall from a train travelling at speed? Many people actually do dispose of their litter in this way, fondly imagining that the bottle drops lightly to the track. A Newtonian will realize, however, that the bottle moves initially with the speed of the train, and all too often such objects become lethal missiles.

Now that something of the content of the Lockean-Newtonian scheme has been outlined, two previous points merely hinted at may be amplified. Earlier it was stated that Locke and Newton were great in part because of their ability to sum up the trends of the time; force may now be given to this observation by showing how the Newtonian belief that motion is the natural state and the Lockean notion that man can build up to some end fitted in with developments in seemingly unconnected fields. One draws attention to the literary quarrel that raged in the last years of the seventeenth century. Until this so-called 'Battle of the Ancients and Moderns' it had been the instinctive belief that no poem, say, could be composed that would better those of Homer and Virgil. The Golden Age lay in the past; the classics were the unchanging standard against which anything modern would, by definition, be inferior. Then suddenly, and mainly through the French critic Charles Perrault, this assumption was challenged. The moderns dared to assert that they could equal, perhaps even surpass, the ancients. The Golden Age, it might be, lay in the future. A little later these French moderns were joined by their English counterparts who fought their separately named 'Battle of the Books'.

It has also been asserted that the new thinking might have been connected with changes in the composition and nature of society. That hint was made on the basis of circumstantial evidence, the fact that so many of the changes took place in Britain, which was the leading bourgeois society at that time. Now the content of the Enlightenment may be set against the values of a middle-class world and their correlation judged by the reader. Those inclined to such an interpretation will seize upon the reverence for facts that can be observed and measured, and that can be used to change the world. They will note the studious avoidance of awkward ultimate questions and the concentration upon the more proximate ends. They will observe how Locke repudiated the medieval views about society that held that it was composed of sub-societies each with its own function, and replaced it by one that took the atomized, independent individual as the basic building block. They will snap up the fact that Locke insisted upon a contractual state, and based it upon the sanctity of property. They may also be interested to learn from Herbert Butterfield's *Origins of Modern Science* that even in France this same scientific movement was largely staffed by those of bourgeois antecedents.

This account of Lockean-Newtonian thinking has dealt with the changes that were explicit in their writings. But there were in addition implicit changes, changes that did not become apparent at once but emerged only with time. Indeed in some instances the later corollaries would have been repudiated by the originators themselves—but then this, after all, is a normal pattern. A good example of this kind of development was in the field of religion.

Both Locke and Newton were devout Christians, the former a Puritan who died to the reading of the Psalms, the latter one who devoted more time and words to the problem of the Apocalypse than he ever did to science. Moreover an inaccuracy in Newton's data led him to believe that the mechanism of the universe was ever-so-slightly faulty and doomed to progressive deterioration; that this did not happen was proof, he thought, of the constant beneficent intervention of the Almighty. Many Newtonians believed that their system revealed the order and majesty of God—Voltaire himself was a prime example—and studies were written using the new truths to support religion, for example John Craig's *The Mathematical Principles of Christian Theology*. What made it possible, however, for later writers to minimize religion and especially Christianity, was the fact that for both Locke and Newton religion was private; that is, their systems *allowed* religion but were not *based upon* it. Locke's state was not only contractual, it was secular as well. Newton refused to allow religion to infiltrate his science. It was as if, at this period, thinkers developed the habit of owning several different hats; when wearing a certain hat one was being scientific, when donning another one was moving to literature, and so on.

This chink having been opened, new ideas passed through and widened it to enormous dimensions. There were those who seized upon the fact that under the new rules God was to be minimized now that motion was the norm. In the past the action of God and of angels had been constantly required to keep the colossal fabric of the heavens turning. Now, however, it was possible to think of God who had indeed created the world, who had in fact given an initial flick to set it in motion, but who had then ceased to intervene in His creation. If God as clockmaker was a favourite Enlightenment image, it was often as an absentee clockmaker that He was portrayed.

But what more than anything else was responsible for altering the status of traditional Christianity was the way in which the age took Newton's and Locke's work as proving the superb power of the human mind. Having so long been prisoners of a world and universe they did not understand, the men of the early eighteenth century responded to these breakthroughs with disproportionate delight. At last the full potential of reason had been revealed. Two quotations from Pope, who in so many ways summed up the Enlightenment mind, deserve to be given at this point; his epitaph for Newton,

> Nature and Nature's laws lay hid in night
> God said, Let Newton be! and all was light

indicates the awe felt for the scientist and reason; his caution,

> Know then thyself, presume not God to scan
> The proper study of mankind is man

the way in which the approach was changing.

The two quotations make a further useful point. It was not that religion was being denied so much as being re-evaluated and defined. Few were prepared to deny God. What they did deny was revealed religion, above all any religion based on miracles, since for such beliefs no warrant could be found in reason. To make the point still clearer, and there is much in a slight difference, such beliefs were not reasonable. If, then, God was not to be found in any sacred book, in any arcane tradition, where was He to be found? Pope's first couplet provided the answer. Nature was the source of all knowledge, and from it one found one's way to God. But care must be taken to understand nature in the sense used by Pope and the greater part of the Enlightenment. Here nature meant the totality of God's creation, the universe and the world, the inanimate and the animate, the animals and man. It did not mean the emotional appeal of mountains, lakes, and sunsets that it did for Rousseau and the Romantics. Rather, what impressed was the order of the creation, the incredible neatness of God's arrangements. Enlightenment nature was the naked facts, which revealed a God of Reason. God was acknowledged, but reduced to the minimal status of Prime Mover or First Cause. For the religion of such an impersonal god the term deism is used, from the bare Latin *deus*, a god.

Deism was overwhelmingly critical, and this combative aspect drove it onward to a thorough-going skepticism. Anything that was not reasonable was to be attacked. More radical, perhaps, than an attack upon revealed religion was that mounted upon the institutional Church. The *cause célèbre* of the Enlightenment, the Calas affair, was basically one of anti-clericalism. This was the case in which a Huguenot father had been executed for the alleged murder of his son, who, it was said, was about to convert to Catholicism; in fact the son had committed suicide. Voltaire, who knew nothing of the family until he read of the case, was suspicious, ferreted out the facts, and mounted a campaign using the slogan '*Écrasez l'infame*' until he secured a reversal of the verdict and the rehabilitation of Calas. It should be noted in passing that the more savage attacks on institutional religion were to be found in those countries where it was all-powerful. Thus France, where the Church was a dominating institution and where it played a leading role in the censorship, was always marked by this hostile brand of deism, while England, where the established Church had to compete against a bevy of dissenting groups, was over such deism by the 1730s. The North Americas hardly knew conscious deism—the French colonies because they were effectively screened from it and the English because their churches were even more equal and competing than in the mother country.

Reason was also brought to bear to show up the stupidities of the legal and administrative codes of France, and for two years the Enlightenment even had a representative as Controller General or Finance Minister of the kingdom—Turgot, who strenuously sought to bring a rational approach to a chaotic situation. Many hated kingship as a non-rational form of authority. One of the best-known epitomes of a strain of *philosophe* thinking was that of Jean Messelier, communicated to the world by Voltaire; he looked with longing to the day that would see 'the last king strangled with the guts of the last priest'. Yet another way in which reason was applied was to subject the entire medieval period to scorn and derision; the best example here was Gibbon's *Decline and Fall of the Roman Empire*, according to which account the rational structure of the empire was brought down by 'barbarism and religion'. The compensatory praise given to things classical may incidentally be noted; it was to be an important characteristic of United States style in the first year of the Republic, as can be seen from the terms Congress and Senate and the architecture of the period.

Another reason why the medieval was repudiated was that its priest-ridden life was dominated by the concept of original sin. Until late in the seventeenth century the dominant view was that man was born with a propensity to evil and that society was necessary not so much to allow man to realize his potential as to act as a check upon his anarchical tendencies. This view was not entirely conquered in the Enlightenment, but increasingly voices were raised to insist that man was basically good, that benevolence was more characteristic of man than malevolence. It was a plea that shone forth most splendidly in the works of Rousseau. This was radical, indeed. But equally radical was the new idea produced when the belief in the naturally good man combined with the dynamic outlook already mentioned. The old idea of society had been that degeneration was inevitable and that history was accordingly cyclical. As the eighteenth century went on this was replaced by a belief in perfectibility and the linear progression of the human species. The most complete Enlightenment expression of this outlook was by Condorcet. Writing in the shadow of the Terror, he refused to give up his faith in progress, and in the final chapter of his *Outlines of an Historical Sketch of the Progress of the Human Mind* defiantly included the claim that 'we may conclude that the perfectibility of man is indefinite'.

Summary accounts inevitably distort the reality of historical development, and are particularly liable to mislead when it comes to broad periodizing. Yet when all allowances have been made it remains clear that the Enlightenment marked a radical shift in the consciousness of the western world. Indeed we may venture the judgement that in any society the degree of vigour of the Enlightenment was a measure of the society's modernity.

※　※　※

New religious styles, new philosophies of man and society—two ways in which adjustment was attempted following the break-up of the medieval world. But a third way was also needed, a more practical way that would enable societies to withstand the disruptive forces that threatened to destroy them as formed institutions. In the face of this chaos, epitomized in the Thirty Years' War, there emerged a new entity in which mankind could shelter. This was the state.

Modern man, especially twentieth-century man, takes the state for granted; it is everywhere and increasingly all-powerful. It requires an effort, then, to grasp that medieval man had but a rudimentary notion of the state. The focus of his loyalties was very different. On the one hand his loyalties were local and personal, to the lord of the manor, perhaps, or to his feudal superior who would not necessarily be the king, and on the other hand they were broad and even universal, say to the Pope as leader of the whole of Christendom. Such patterns began to break down by the close of the Middle Ages and increasingly in the sixteenth century and after. In England Henry VIII (1509–47), in breaking with the Roman Catholic Church, elaborated the theory that England was a truly independent entity whose ecclesiastical affairs did not need to be, could not be, appealed to Rome, a foreign jurisdiction. On the continent the truce of Augsburg in 1555 settled the religious fighting for a while on the basis of *cuius regio, eius religio* (loosely translated, 'He who rules chooses the religion'), which in a slightly different way made the same point as Henry VIII had done. In France there arose a school of political thinkers, the *Politiques*, who saw a way out of the civil war between Catholic and Huguenot that was tearing the country apart by transferring loyalties from religion, which divided, to the state, which could unify. And it was during this period that the sinister phrase 'reason of state' was added to the political vocabulary; so crucial was the state felt to be for the defence of civilization that the state came to have a rationale of its own, apart from and superior to that of the individuals who composed it.

These beginnings were taken further in the seventeenth century. Reference has already been made to the introduction of the science of statistics (originally directed to making the state strong by giving the rulers a better idea of their resources), and to Louis XIV's championing of Gallicanism. But any number of illustrations could be used to make the same point. In almost all fields the new centralizing power was at work, and the keynote of all its activities was efficiency. A particularly good example of the transition in outlook is warfare. In medieval times the basis of an army was the personal loyalty to their prince of the greater barons, and these in turn were supported by the same loyalty of their dependents. Increasingly, personal and individual links gave way to the mercenary band, loyal to its organizer, who in turn was loyal to the paymaster; while free to change allegiance (and during the Thirty Years' War there were some amazing changes that today could only be called treason), the semi-permanent identity of the band yet did permit a greater professionalism to develop. But more and more after 1648 it became clear that the mercenary had outlived his usefulness—he was too independent and so too untrustworthy. He was replaced by the modern professional soldier, not so much 'hired' by the state as 'owned' by it, with all his equipment and provisions supplied. It was at this time that the permanent army organizations and hierarchies came into being, and uniforms date from this period; in short, standardization became the basis for the new efficiency. The novelty of all this may be judged from the fact that the first inspector of the French army, the late-seventeenth-century General Martinet, has given his name, even in English, to any especially severe and demanding official.

But if military science provides the most convenient example of growing state energies, the most significant area of growth was economics. If the state was to be strong and to withstand the other states that were likewise growing, then the all-important field of economic activity could not be left to chance. The state had the right and the duty to intervene in all economic matters so that eventually economic growth should safeguard the state's power and, hopefully, ruin that of its potential rivals. The thinking by which this end was pursued was known as Mercantilism.

It is easy to caricature Mercantilism by presenting it as a theory that confused money with wealth. It is certainly true that a cursory glance at mercantilist writing will reveal a preoccupation with the flow of specie. But it must be remembered that during this period Europe was short of coinage. In particular a large trade was carried on with India and the Far East in luxury goods that could be paid for in cash only, since at this time Europe produced almost nothing that these people wanted. There was a danger that if this cash flow continued too long some countries would experience liquidity problems, for without fully understanding the theory, mercantilists were at least aware that too little cash within a system meant a downward spiralling of the economy. And it must always be remembered that this was a time before the extension of credit facilities began to take the pressure off the supply of coinage. Mercantilists may be pardoned for thinking as they did.

In the earlier days there had been an obsession with keeping coinage at home to the point of prohibiting its export. When this broke down as unworkable in practice it was replaced by a concern for the balance of trade. Laws prevented the importation of certain items, while exports were fostered at all costs, even to the point of paying bounties. In this way little money would be leaving the country but much would be flowing in as foreigners had to pay cash to buy their rivals' products. The state also intervened in the economy by actively participating in the trading patterns of the period. Both France and England had their various Indies companies, for instance. Other well-known mercantilist ventures were the French Company of New France, chartered by

Richelieu in 1627, and the English Hudson's Bay Company, which received a royal charter in 1670. The state made such ventures monopolies, for it was thought that in this way the promise of great profits would encourage merchants to enter risky fields where the initial returns might prove discouraging.

Above all, this mercantilist interest in the balance of trade as a long-term means of keeping coin at home was seen in the Navigation Acts. In England their effective origin was in 1651 when Cromwell had an Act passed to foster the English carrying trade; in the years following, other acts built on his base. These acts decreed essentially that goods coming into England had to come either in ships of the country of origin or in English ships. The thinking behind such legislation may be illustrated by the following hypothetical example. Suppose England to have a bad crop year and that grain is insufficient. The authorities would prefer not to import grain at all, since in paying for it money leaves the country. But too great a shortage may mean starvation and rioting, and so importing will have to be allowed. But then comes the question of shipping the grain. If competitive bids were asked, there would be a good chance that the lowest tender would be Dutch, for especially in the seventeenth century their ships were better, they carried fewer crew, and their insurance business, superior to any other's, kept premiums low. But to give the freight to a Dutch firm would mean increasing the amount of money leaving the country. By insisting on an English ship, even should the freight costs be twice those of the Dutch, the money would remain in England.

The importance of colonies will now be apparent. To a mercantilist, colonies were an essential adjunct to any powerful state. Not all goods could be produced in the mother country, and if they had to be imported it was infinitely preferable that they come from one's own monetary sphere and not from a foreign competitor's. Moreover the colonies could provide a market for the mother country's exports, and furthermore a market that could be denied to a rival power; indeed the colonies themselves were not to develop manufactures of their own but were to depend on the mother country for such supplies. Thus for the purposes of the Navigation Acts the entire British empire was treated as one trading area, and other great powers, notably the French, operated in the same fashion within their empire. The links that bound the system together and especially those that entrenched the primacy of the mother country were strengthened by the practice of declaring certain goods 'enumerated' commodities; these items, those of a more strategic nature, were not to be traded with any country but the mother country, which was in this way protected against any short-fall of essential supplies.

Mercantilism never worked with the precision demanded by the theory, and smuggling was perhaps the most successful industry that it fostered. But the important point to grasp is that the heroic efforts to make the system work, at a time when bureaucratic technique was rudimentary, were a tremendous testimony to the aspirations of state power and control.

What has been described was a tendency. Within that broad framework there was room enough for different societies to pursue different methods of governing themselves and of increasing their efficiency. On the continent the dominant pattern was that provided by France, the largest, most populous, most powerful unit of the day and culturally the arbiter of the rest. And since France was the parent of New France, that pattern must be outlined. Across the Channel, and again radiating out to the North American colonies, was the very different English pattern, and so this, too, will have to be sketched.

The decay of France that had marked the sixteenth century had been brought to a halt by the end of the century with the accession of the first Bourbon king, Henri IV (1589–1610); it was he who issued the Edict of Nantes. A line of strong kings, helped by a series of highly gifted ministers, of whom the greatest was Cardinal Richelieu (1624–42), began the recovery and brought the country successfully through the Thirty Years' War, which for France was much more a struggle for survival against the Austrian and Spanish Hapsburgs than a pro-Catholic crusade. The situation was a perilous one in which the logic of earlier French development was taken further. France had been through similar danger much earlier and had survived it by putting all efforts behind the leadership of the monarchy; as early as the fifteenth century France had allowed her kings a standing army, a radical departure justifiable only because the victorious English were on the point of dismembering the country. Now, in a similar crisis, it was natural for the Bourbons to reassert monarchical leadership.

So effective in fact was the impulse to royal centralized control that at the end of the Thirty Years' War it produced a reaction. In 1648 and intermittently for the next few years the old feudal ruling class rose up in revolt in the confused episode known as the Fronde. Despite certain successes (notably when the Parisian *frondeurs* broke into the royal palace and forced the queen mother to parade before them the boy-king, Louis XIV, an insult he never forgot) the movement was a dismal failure, for in truth the *frondeurs* had no program, nothing beyond an instinctive wish to halt the erosion of their dominant position. The Fronde, in fact, indicated the bankruptcy of all ideas apart from those of royal centralism, and in that sense contributed to Bourbon success. And Bourbon success was the establishment of a system of government known as Absolutism, which was enthroned in the reign of Louis XIV from 1661 onwards when, after the death of his minister Mazarin, he personally took charge of the affairs of France.

Absolutism, especially in France, was based on the cult of the monarch. Under Louis XIV this tendency was carried to its zenith. The theory of government was that known as Divine Right, a theory that claims that the king is set on the throne by God Himself, and accordingly that disobedience to this lieutenant is blasphemy. To heighten the aura of sacred majesty the Bourbons kept alive the practice of touching for the King's Evil; this illness (scrofula) was thought to be curable by the touch of an anointed monarch, and it is interesting to note that while in bourgeois England it died out at the beginning of the eighteenth century in the reign of Queen Anne, the last of the Stuarts, the Bourbons continued the ceremony into the nineteenth, the last to touch for it being Charles X in 1824. Louis was known as 'le roi soleil', the sun-king, and the device of a stylized sun was incorporated into much of the royal furnishings as a constant subliminal reminder of the king's splendour. At every turn the courtier was confronted by evidence of Louis' extraordinary pre-eminence.

Nor was this exaltation an empty show; Louis had the power to match it. He and he alone chose his ministers and he could over-rule them at will. He had the power to consign anyone to prison without cause shown or trial held, by the use of *lettres de cachet*. Thanks to his marvellous presence and to his tremendous application to detail and hard work (it is reported that never once did he miss a day's work and consultation with his ministers until the very end of his long, long reign in 1715), Louis was rarely obliged to make his power explicit— his total command was such that questioning never arose. But its reality was made plain by his much weaker successor, Louis XV, who, sensing opposition, made an open declaration of absolutist principle in the tongue-lashing he gave to the leading figures of the day: 'Sovereignty lies in me alone. The legislative power is mine unconditionally and indivisibly. The public order emanates from me, and I am its supreme guardian. My people is one with me.'

If the king was to be supreme, care had to be taken to crush any alternative power centre. Already there had been a hint of this in Louis XIV's Gallicanism. His predecessors had dispensed with the

French parliamentary system, the Estates General, which had last met in 1614. But Louis carried the assault further. France had long been divided into a dozen or so high judicial/administrative courts known (misleadingly for English readers) as the *Parlements*. These courts had the traditional right of remonstrating with the king over proposed legislation and even of refusing to register royal edicts in their journals, in which case the edict failed to have the force of law. Early in his reign the *Parlements* had shown signs of using these powers, but Louis had ridden roughshod over their protests. The *Parlement* of Brittany, a province with a long history of separatism, was made an example of, offending passages in its journal being ripped out by royal officials and its members exiled from Rennes, the main city of Brittany, to a lesser town for fifteen years. Those provinces that had their local estates were similarly humiliated, the provincial estates remaining as but empty relics.

The nobility was broken in yet other ways. To limit their control of the localities the governors of the provinces, who were drawn from the nobility, were outflanked by the creation of new officials, the *intendants*; these, who effectively date from Louis's reign, were creatures of the king and reported directly to him if necessary. Even more successful in diminishing potential Fronde reaction was the building of Versailles. This monstrous palace, deliberately built away from Paris and its mob memories, was designed to be so attractive that all important figures would want to be there. At Versailles, under the direct gaze of the king, they would be in no position to challenge his authority. At the same time, by bringing them to the centre, Louis was cutting the aristocrats off from their local roots and local support; they were being transformed from nobles into courtiers. What completed the transformation was the elaborate ceremonial that pervaded Versailles; it has been well captured by W. H. Lewis, a passage from whose *The Splendid Century* deserves to be given:

> Court etiquette was a life study. Who for instance could guess that at Versailles it was the height of bad manners to knock at a door? You must scratch it with the little finger of the left hand, growing the finger nail long for that purpose. Or could know that you must not *tutoyer* an intimate friend in any place where the King was present? That if the lackey of a social superior brought you a message, you had to receive him standing, and bareheaded? You have mastered the fact that you must not knock on a door, so when you go to make your first round of calls in the great houses in the town, you scratch: wrong again, you should have knocked. Next time you rattle the knocker, and a passing exquisite asks you contemptuously if you are

so ignorant as not to know that you give one blow of the knocker on the door of a lady of quality? Who could guess that if you encounter the royal dinner on its way from the kitchens to the table, you must bow as to the King himself, sweep the ground with the plume of your hat, and say in a low, reverent, but distinct voice, *La viande du Roi*?

The point was that such a mysterious world of ceremony effectively froze out the transient, holding the courtier at Versailles forever.

Finally, in noting the crushing of any alternative power centre, the censorship should be mentioned. Free expression of opinion could weaken such a monolithic structure, and so the *ancien régime* always retained the censor. It was fear of the censorship, in fact, that caused D'Alembert to pull out of the editorship of the *Encyclopédie* and leave its completion to Diderot.

Absolutism was characterized, then, by a monarchy that brooked no rival and no criticism. But in addition it was characterized by a certain climate of opinion that may be summed up as a longing for uniformity; there was a socio-psychological striving for unity and control. For example an absolute king, accustomed to perfect obedience, naturally found the existence of deviant groups within his kingdom disturbing. Thus it was that in 1685 Louis allowed the Edict of Nantes to be revoked, despite the fact that Huguenots were among the most loyal of Frenchmen, and despite the fact that those interested in economic matters, anticipating Weber, prophesied a loss of French entrepreneurial skill if these Calvinists were driven into exile. This same urge may be seen in the arts. Under royal patronage the various branches of the arts were organized and disciplined. The painters met at regular intervals and debated the manner of depicting different expressions, of portraying various emotions. Then the sense of the meeting having been summarized, it became the official manner and binding on the artists; and thanks to the vast financial resources of the crown available for purchases, prizes, and so on, the artists could be encouraged to conform by economic necessity. And it was fitting that the superb seventeenth-century French classical theatre dominated by Corneille and Racine should have produced passionate plays that yet conformed to very restrictive rules; the entire play was written in verse—undeviating Alexandrine lines each of twelve syllables, each pair of lines rhyming—and obeyed the classical unities of action (the main plot was not to be confused by sub-plots), of time (what was represented should be set in a time span no longer than twenty-four hours), and of place (the scene to move no more than would be feasible within twenty-four hours). Little wonder that the classical Voltaire, for all his love of England, condemned Shakespeare for his plays, at best piles of dung with the occasional jewel sparkling in them!

By now the alert reader will have begun to sense the contradiction that lay at the bottom of Absolutism. Louis was eager to make his country more efficient. He employed people selected on the basis of merit. The greatest example here was his minister, Colbert, who was of bourgeois origin, but there were many other examples of men promoted in the church, in the army, in the ranks of the *intendants* and the civil service, who owed nothing to aristocratic privilege. A determined effort was made to break through into a new ordering of society, and Louis's reign was in many ways the golden age of the bourgeoisie. But either the effort was not enough, or the aristocratic sense was too deeply engrained, for the middle class did not come into its own. By the end of the *ancien régime* the establishment was once again solidly aristocratic; the nobility was still almost wholly exempt from taxation and in control of the army, the church, and the civil service; the church was still a too dominant and too privileged element in society, not contributing its fair share to the state; the base of society was still a feudal one, for if serfdom had virtually disappeared, the manorial system with its compulsory dues and monopolies of mill and oven still prevailed. The town crafts were organized in guilds to which a worker had to belong and in which the theoretical graduation from apprentice to journeyman to master had long ceased to operate so that a small co-optive body monopolized power and perpetuated traditional methods and organizations; and despite Colbert's efforts there were still too many *internal* customs duties (as late as 1785 a new customs' wall was built around Paris, so that goods from the countryside could be taxed), anomalies in the law, and other obstacles to the full development of trade. That French society in the eighteenth century, in spite of some modernization, was still profoundly medieval may be illustrated by the following two examples. Participation in commerce was enough, in itself, to cause a noble to lose caste, to derogate from his aristocratic status, and such *dérogeance* was sufficient to taint the blood through all succeeding generations. It is indicative of the contradiction in French society that Louis XIV would make exceptions from this rule in favour of certain trades vital to the state but he would never abolish *dérogeance* as such. The functioning of the robe nobility is the second example. This was a type of nobility that paralleled the old, feudal, fighting nobility, the nobility of the sword, and that staffed the higher civil service, the ranks of the *Parlements*; by the eighteenth century the two kinds of nobility were beginning to coalesce and intermarry. A distinguishing feature of these higher civil service offices was that they were venal, that is to say, they were considered as a form of private property capable of being bought and sold. One could, if sufficiently wealthy, buy a judgeship, and thereby acquire noble status, if not for one's self then at least for one's children. What happened was that the successful bourgeois sold out, bought into the aristocracy, and left behind the middle-class world in which he had amassed his capital. This constant haemorrhaging of bourgeois talent into the ranks of the nobles speaks volumes about the tone of society under the *ancien régime*.

Having said something about the institutions of France it is now possible to look across the Atlantic to examine the daughter societies there. By the time that French authority in North America came to an end in 1763, a French presence had existed there for more than two hundred years and had spread over half a continent. The task of summarizing this experience, however, may be simplified by applying limitations of space and time. Much of French North America received but a faint French impress. Acadia, the maritime region of present-day Canada, was never important in the eyes of the administrators in France, and that part of the French empire was lost to the British at the Treaty of Utrecht in 1713. The same may be said of French influence over Hudson's Bay and Newfoundland. Louisiana and the Midwest were areas exploited by France only in the last years of French rule in America, and they too may be passed over in this survey. Far and away the main centre of activity and concern was the St Lawrence, essentially today's Quebec, and this will be the focus of the following section. And the enquiry may be limited in time, too. Accounts of Canadian history frequently begin in 1534, the year of the first visit of Cartier to the St Lawrence; with more justification they could begin in 1604/1608, the start of French settlement in North America. Both dates, however, are unsatisfactory. Early attempts at colonization were disrupted by English attack and by French distraction in the Thirty Years' War and Fronde, and it was only in 1663, when Louis XIV began the royal government of New France, that any real progress was made. Thus this society was effectively but one hundred years old when it passed forever out of French control.

When Louis and Colbert turned their attention to New France, there were fewer than 2,000 inhabitants. This tiny society was as yet unformed, and the French administrators may be viewed as operating in a laboratory setting with an almost completely free hand to create there the kind of society they wished to have in France itself but which tradition prevented them from achieving. Thus a tight control from above was only to be expected. The political institutions show this well. Effective power resided in the *intendant*, who had wide powers to direct the growth of the settlement. What could happen when the *intendant* was a man of ability and was backed by the authorities in France was shown by the striking advances made under Talon (1665–72). He was aided by a Sovereign Council, which was the equivalent of a *Parlement*, but with this crucial difference—venality was never permitted in New France, the king always retaining his right to nominate to the Council. And this fact of nomination should be stressed. Before royal government became the fact in 1663 there had been some limited election of higher officials, but under the new régime this practice was discontinued. Indeed throughout the remaining period of French rule there was only one instance of quasi-elective office. In the parishes the *capitain de milice* was chosen by the parishioners, since amid perpetual danger of war it was essential that the leader have the full confidence of his followers. But this was the one exception. Under this system of administration, then, the French Canadian lived out a life of minute regulation—prices, building codes, upkeep of the streets, entertainments, all bore the mark of central direction.

Other controls over the development of society went much further than this, however. The population was to be screened to ensure that it was capable of measuring up to the high standards set for it. As early as 1627, the date when Richelieu reorganized the affairs of the colony, intending immigrants were examined and the undesirables prevented from embarking for North America. And should any undesirables yet be discovered in the community, they were promptly shipped back to France. As part of this control Richelieu also began the practice of excluding Huguenots, an ironic decision since the pioneer of settlement, De Monts, had himself been a Huguenot. The Colbertian régime naturally continued these beginnings, though by 1760 some French Protestants were to be found in the colony. Not surprisingly, the population growth was not outstanding. The natural increase might have been spectacular (but then it was in all colonial societies of North America), but the growth from immigration was tiny, and by 1763 the population was not much more than 60,000. Another control was the attempt, almost completely successful, to turn the church into a Gallican institution. Yet another control was the complete absence of any printing press, which made the work of censorship much easier.

Even so the experiment was not free of certain characteristics that belonged more to the medieval world than to the emerging modern one. Alongside the *intendant*, and relating to him in an ambiguous way that dramatized the clash of old and new, was the governor. Given charge of the military affairs of the colony and of the conduct of external relations (subject to ultimate control from France, of course) and given precedence on ceremonial occasions, the governor was always a member of the nobility. The often vain and petty preoccupation with protocol is epitomized in the rule of Frontenac, whose courtly conduct was so disruptive that he had to be recalled from the colony. Then, too, the landholding system, the seigneurial system, was outdated. Large blocks of land were granted to seigneurs who thereupon assumed heavy responsibilities: they were to see to the bringing out of settlers; they were to make sure that the land was cleared; a manor house, the focus of the community, was to be built, and often a church endowed too; a mill was to be provided for the settlers. The returns for such outgoings are instructive. Economically they were insignificant; the seigneur did receive certain feudal dues from the *habitants*, as his dependents were called, and he did receive certain customary payments such as a set amount of fish—but all told these amounted to little; nor could he look forward to an eventual capital gain from the sale of the seigneury, for any transfer of the land, other than to the next heir, attracted the *quinte*, a tax of 20 per cent on the price received. (But then French Canadians did not see their land in speculative terms. For them it was a family trust, which explained the existence of the *retrait lignager*, which permitted any relative of a vendor to repurchase property at the selling price at any time up to a year and a day of the sale.) In fact, what the seigneur got out of the arrangement was prestige and precedence, the counterpart on a smaller scale of what the courtiers at Versailles were after and an indication of an old-fashioned viewpoint.

With modernity offset by such medieval survivals, was any genuine bourgeoisie possible? Recently certain historians have sought to claim that one did exist. And certainly by the mid-eighteenth century the population was big enough and the society mature enough to support an economy of some complexity. But it seems preferable to accept Eccles' judgement that while there may have been individual bourgeois they chose to live nobly. There was just too much that prevented society as a whole from accepting a middle-class outlook. New France, it seems, did not even have Colbert's imperfect attempt at a commercial law, the *code marchand*. Louis XIV may have given 10,000 livres for preliminary work on iron deposits, but he also gave 10,500 livres for a set of bells for a Quebec church. In a society where a yoke of oxen, vital to such an agricultural life, was worth perhaps 110 livres, and an indentured servant could be hired for as little as 60 livres a year, people would pay 8 livres for a private mass, and in their wills would tie up large amounts of much-needed capital for further masses for their souls; in one will almost 200 livres were so set aside. There were over eighty holy days of obligation in the year, which cut down the amount of work that could be done and which help to account for the attitude to enterprise held in modern-day Quebec, as reported in Taylor's article above.

This reference to the very Catholic quality of New France is a point that requires a brief elaboration, for here was one of the characteristics of the colony. Earlier, the pre-1663 developments were dismissed as relatively unimportant, but in the religious context these years were vital. From the start the impulse to convert the Indians had been very strong and so religion had bulked large in the life of the early settlement. Then too this was a time when the parent society was experiencing a wave of religiosity marked by great fervour and a somewhat narrow devotion, a good deal of which was channeled into New France; that Huguenots were to be excluded only intensified this fervent, crusading Catholicism. And the fact that the French state neglected the colony in these years allowed the church a disproportionate influence in which the Jesuit impact was especially noticeable. Such an impress was never lost. If Gallicanism was imposed, it did not wholly destroy a lingering ultramontane tinge; this tendency surfaced, for example, in 1868 when the pope was threatened by the loss of the Papal States and a French-Canadian contingent rushed to his aid. Even more persistent was the puritan quality of this Catholicism. These small illustrations make important points; of 674 births in New France before 1660 only one was illegitimate, and there was by 1690 only one more such birth; even under royal government Sunday ploughing could mean a heavy ten-livre fine. The links between *curé* and *habitant* that were early forged were tight indeed.

Before leaving New France perhaps one point should be made quite clear. This society was no tyranny. Some may be tempted to see the strict regimentation imposed by the civil and religious authorities as something alien to the real aspirations of the society, as something that was borne with resentment by exploited *habitants*. Such an interpretation of the situation would be false. To begin with, the *habitant* could not be said to be economically exploited. Consider one of the main sources of complaint in *ancien régime* French society, the tithe, the compulsory payment to the Church. The usual rate in France was one-thirteenth of a peasant's produce, but in New France the rate was less than half of this, one-twenty-sixth of the grain crop alone. Official direction was welcomed when there were so many dangers and difficulties to be faced. Indeed, had not the state stepped in with aid and supervision, the infant colony would doubtless have foundered. Rather what has to be grasped is the ethos of French society, whose eagerness to accept paternalism was intensified by the problems of a new-world setting. Perhaps the most illuminating evidence for this is the fate of colonial representative institutions. During the period of royal government some seventeen ad hoc assemblies were held. Such meetings were not truly democratic since free elections were not a feature and they had no genuine decision-making powers. But they did permit some dialogue and could have been the basis for meaningful representation. What happened? The last was called in 1702, but did not meet. Not enough leading citizens had the interest to take part. New France was quite content to be administered by those who knew.

To turn to the English tradition is to discover a very different path to modernity. This is not to say that seventeenth-century England was without its tendencies to Absolutism on the French model. In fact, in James I Christendom had one of the most logical and outspoken theorists of Divine Right; his four-word summary of the essence of monarchical Absolutism has been given above. In the reign of James's successor, Charles I, the high Anglican Laud was made Archbishop of Canterbury, and the 'thorough' persecution of Puritans that he mounted caused a great wave of emigration to New England. And it was in that same reign, in 1629, that Parliament was dismissed in the same manner as had been the Estates General in 1614. In its absence the king would rule by use of the prerogative. The royal prerogative was that vast but ill-defined reservoir of ultimate powers that, it was acknowledged, the king had to possess. (Today a vestige of the royal prerogative can be seen in the prerogative of mercy by which the sovereign may commute a judicial sentence, usually a death sentence; now it is exercised through the government of the day.) It was the Stuarts' aim, as it was the Bourbons', to meet the challenge of chaotic times by extending this uncertain principle until it supported the entire and not just the extraordinary business of the state.

The Bourbons were challenged by the Fronde, and came through with power enhanced. The Stuarts were challenged by quite different forces and were defeated. In 1640 Charles was obliged to acknowledge that the experiment of prerogative rule had failed and that a parliament would be necessary. There the pent-up fury of the opposition wrung concession after concession from Charles until finally the royalists were driven to take a stand. The more extreme critics, including a great many Puritans and representatives of the new bourgeois order, stuck by Parliament and the gulf between its supporters and royalists widened to the point of civil war. Charles was defeated, and defeated again soon afterwards in a second civil war. In 1649 Charles was condemned as an enemy of the state and executed. The way was opened for the emergence of the rule of the Puritans, the army, and Cromwell. The attempt to find an alternative to monarchy was a failure, however, and after Cromwell's death it quickly became evident that the only way out of increasingly grave difficulties would be to call back Charles's heir, Charles II. This took place in 1660, amid scenes of general rejoicing.

Charles II was wily enough to retain his throne for twenty-five years. But his brother James II who succeeded him marked a reversion to more normal Stuart ways. Within three years his tendency to Absolutism had alienated too much support and he was driven into exile, the crown passing to William and Mary. The Glorious Revolution of 1688, the Act of Settlement of 1700, which became necessary when it became clear that Queen Anne would have no heir and that the Protestant succession would have to be provided for, and the associated legislation of the time, completed the transition from monarchical Absolutism to a new style of government. It has been called parliamentary absolutism.

There can be no quibble about the qualification 'parliamentary'. It was not simply that the Triennial Act of 1694 made the summoning of Parliament at least every three years mandatory. Royal powers had been broken in deeper ways than this. Until about mid-century the English monarch had enjoyed that magical aura that set kings apart from ordinary men. This attitude is clearly revealed when men's responses to the Civil War are examined, as they have been by Christopher Hill in his beautiful study of the Stuart century. Even Parliamentarians could not fully break with medieval concepts, and they fought under the fiction that somehow the king was a prisoner of the opposition who, when taken by the Parliamentarians, would repudiate his royalist supporters. Oliver Cromwell, the modern man, horrified his questioners when, on being asked what he would do if in the press of battle he found himself confronting the king, replied that he would kill him like any other man. Against such widespread acceptance of the king's divinity the execution of Charles must be seen as one of the most crucial acts of the century; the absence of divine retribution proved to many that the king was after all a man. Divine Right did make something of a comeback after the Restoration—remember the date of

Patriarcha—but the exile of James and the succession of Dutch William, the ineffective and female Anne, and finally Hanoverian George helped to kill an idea that had no place in the new order of society. That Anne should have been the last both to touch for the King's Evil and to veto a parliamentary bill was fitting. Monarchical prerogative was ending, and the conduct of the nation's affairs was passing increasingly to Parliament.

The latter part of the term 'parliamentary absolutism' may also be justified—but only if one concentrates upon the working rather than the theory of the constitution. According to the prevailing theory, which Locke had done so much to establish, Parliament was but one element of the constitution obliged to share power with other institutions. This theory was variously formulated; it could stress a triple institutional framework, the legislature (Parliament, essentially the Commons, which decided what laws were to be and how taxes were to be raised), the executive (the king's government, which applied the law, spent the money, and carried on the public business of society), and the judiciary (the judges who adjudicated when any dispute arose); or it could draw attention to the different principles represented in the constitution, the king representing the monarchical virtues, the House of Lords the aristocratic, and the House of Commons the democratic, all of which had to combine in the legislative process since the veto of one element prevented the passage of any bill. The first formulation stressed the legal, the second the social distinctions within the constitution, but both agreed in insisting upon the negative virtues of checks and balances. For a generation that remembered Stuart prerogative did not wish to see a concentration of authority at any one spot. But this was merely a particular application of the theory. The general theory was the pervasive, still pre-modern notion associated with original sin, that the natural tendency of any institution, whether a unitary style of government such as an absolute monarchy, or a single branch of a government, was to arrogate power unto itself and become a despotism unless checked by the counter-tensions of other institutions. But as indicated, this was the theory; the practice was quite otherwise.

The social balance of monarchy, aristocracy, and democracy was a sham. The monarch, as has been noted, was ceasing to play a meaningful role. For instance the Hanoverians felt it beneath their dignity to attend meetings of their ministers, nominally their servants, and there were in addition the language problems that obliged George I and his minister Walpole to converse in Latin. So long as the first two Georges were given their annual Civil List grant by Parliament so that they could maintain the royal estate and pay the executive officers, they were largely content. The Lords was a small body, at this period some two hundred strong, and homogeneous in composition. Most members were exceedingly rich landowners who, having become aware of more bourgeois ways of making money and unhindered by any law of *dérogeance*, had diversified into property speculation and trade and commerce. They represented the wealth and enterprise of the nation, and on all fundamental matters were in agreement. The Commons was but an extension of the Lords. In part this was so because many heirs to peerage chose to gain parliamentary experience by having a seat in the lower house; in the 1761 election twenty-three such heirs were returned. Then, too, in England, as opposed to France, only the eldest sons of peers were noble, and the young sons being commoners could sit for life in the Commons; in that same 1761 Parliament over half the M.P.s had titled relatives.

But what made possible the entrance of so many noble relatives, and made sure that almost all the remainder of the 558 Members of Parliament were dependent on the Lords, was the nature of eighteenth-century political relationships. Crucial to the representative process was the franchise and how it was used. Approximately one-fifth of the members represented the shires, the agricultural areas. Here only those had the vote who had purchased land (i.e., they owned the land outright and did not lease it from another) worth forty shillings a year. Such electorates were small, averaging some 4,000, and amenable to the pressure of the greater magnates of the district, the peers. The other four-fifths of the members sat for the boroughs, though they overwhelmingly came from the same landowning class as the shire representatives. Which boroughs sent representatives had been decided at a more medieval period of Parliament's history and had been frozen before the eighteenth century. Thus by this time there was no necessary relation between a town's importance and the fact that it had representation. (This was not felt to be a flaw, necessarily. The basis of representation was not individuals, but interests. This principle is best illustrated by reference to the university seats. The city of Oxford and the borough of Cambridge were both represented in Parliament. But the two universities were also separately represented. For it was recognized that the interest of a university was different from the interest of the townsmen among whom it happened to be situated, and that no man should represent two dissimilar interests. This basis in interests gave rise to a corresponding but paradoxically opposed theory of virtual representation; a seaport like Bristol could be said to represent all the other ports that were not represented at Westminster.) Many boroughs had in fact decayed to the point of losing almost all their population, but they still returned Members of Parliament; the most notorious of these 'rotten boroughs' was Old Sarum, the original site of today's Salisbury, which in fact had no inhabitants at all. In addition there was no standard qualification for voting in the boroughs. In some the franchise was very wide and several thousands might vote, while in others a mere handful could decide the election. Only fifty-five constituencies had more than 500 electors; Portsmouth with 20,000 inhabitants had some 80 electors. Above all, it should be kept in mind that eighteenth-century elections lasted several days and that voting was open not secret, two factors that encouraged interference in the polls. The ease with which the outcome could be influenced may be imagined, though it is worth noting that English society, if not so status-conscious as the French, was yet sufficiently deferential for prestige to play as great a role in swinging elections as money. In the election of 1761, for instance, only 48 constituencies actually went to the polls, since in all the rest it was quite clear who, as the natural leader of the locality, ought to be returned.

The theory of checks and balances, of separation, had broken down at the social level; both monarchical and democratic elements had been swallowed up by the aristocratic. It had also broken down at the legal level. True separation demanded that the king choose his ministers from outside the legislature. But from a very early period the practice had been for the king's ministers to have seats in the Parliament, especially in the Commons, which had the right to control the supply of money. Kings seeking to be strong had recognized that to have their spokesmen in the legislature where they could control the business and especially the granting of money was a source of strength indeed. The post-1688 régime, in which the aristocracy had almost captured the monarchy as it had captured Parliament, saw no reason to change this very convenient arrangement, and so they took care to repeal by the Regency Act of 1707 the clause in the Act of Settlement that would have forced members of the executive to resign from the legislature. (But the compromise was retained that an M.P. could become a minister of the Crown only after he had offered himself for re-election so that his constituents could pass judgement on the fusion of legislative and executive functions. This requirement was abolished in 1926.) But the meshing of executive and legislature went further than this. Members of Parliament who were not important enough to be given high executive office and so become ministers were yet free to hold other offices under the Crown that brought them income of one kind or another. The Crown having become a rubber-stamp for the aristocracy meant that the aristocratic clique in power had available to it tremendous sources of patronage. So powerful was the patronage available to the king's ministers, in fact, that in any Parliament they could build themselves a majority by the careful distribution of offices—'places' they were called, and there was a large body of M.P.s known as 'placemen' who would obediently and mindlessly vote for the government so long as they continued to be rewarded with 'places'. It is not surprising that from the Glorious Revolution on, not one government was ever brought down by a hostile parliamentary vote until 1782. Finally to round out the meshing rather than the separation of powers note that by the Act of Settlement the judges, who were appointed by the Crown, were removable by Parliament; note, too, that the head of the legal profession, the Lord Chancellor, was a member of the government and sat in the Lords, of which House he was Speaker. Such interlocking helped make the aristocracy absolute.

Where one can quibble with the term 'parliamentary absolutism', however, is over the connotation of absolutism. Very definitely it was not an absolutism of the French kind. To begin with, French absolutism was a busy, ever-interfering activity; in practice the pre-modern attitudes of its servants might cause inefficiency but in intention it was a ceaseless, positive force. Parliament, on the other hand, was an absolutism of last resort so to speak, a power to be used if all else failed, but under normal circumstances unnecessary. The medieval attitude still prevailed that things would simply get done on their own and that sessions should be short and devoted essentially to the voting of supplies and to the negative work of redressing grievances. Only slowly was a more positive attitude to parliamentary work emerging. Then, too, France was centralized, England was decentralized. The patterns of local government indicate this. French towns and the provinces were under the watchful eye of the Crown, and run by the *intendants* and a host of officials. English towns were in most respects little islands unto themselves, while over most of England local justice was turned over to the natural ruling class, the lower reaches of the aristocracy, who were made into justices of the peace on the say-so of the local magnate and who in that official capacity controlled much of the lives of the bulk of the population. These J.P.s had no legal training necessarily and were not inspected from the centre, a lack of bureaucratic expertise that was an odd medieval hangover in an otherwise increasingly modern society. Nor did the English seek the same kind of uniformity as the

French. In the 1690s censorship was allowed to lapse. Four years after the Revocation of the Edict of Nantes England had a Toleration Act. It did not give equality to all religions, and Catholics and Jews were still strictly discriminated against; as late as 1780 London was paralyzed by the anti-Catholic Gordon Riots. Dissenters were in the second-class position of having religious rights but not full civil rights. The Test and Corporation Acts, first passed in the Restoration period, were retained to make positions in government, entry to Oxford and Cambridge, and so on, Anglican monopolies; in addition Anglicanism remained the established, tithe-supported church. But even so England was moving away from French practice and towards justifying Voltaire's quip that where France had one religion and three hundred sauces, England had one sauce and three hundred religions.

Above all, the difference between the two absolutisms lay in the fact that England had a constitution. In France everything depended on the king, and if Louis XIV ever did claim *L'état, c'est moi* ('I am the state'), he spoke truly. In England everything might be controlled by the aristocracy, but it did not depend on it. England might not have had a written constitution, indeed the experiment with one during the Interregnum between Charles I and Charles II had prejudiced Englishmen against one, but it did have a long tradition of documents produced in the clash of interests, and these regulated the positions of the protagonists. Magna Carta of 1215 was by no means the first of these and not the last either. In the Stuart period significant additions were made, in particular the Bill of Rights of 1689, which listed the iniquities of James II and condemned such practices. There were, too, such important developments as the entrenchment of jury trials and the improvement of the machinery of habeas corpus, the legal safeguard whereby the authorities had to show cause for detention and provide speedy trial or else release the suspect; the contrast with the *lettres de cachet* is striking. It does not matter that these documents represented selfish class advantage, or that for most ordinary people the administration of justice in France was superior to that in England. The important thing is that these documents and procedures existed, could be appealed to, and could be pushed to novel lengths by future generations. The result was that while in eighteenth-century France the tensions of society were such that they could be resolved only by revolution, in England the tensions were of a kind that could be settled by evolution.

It can be said that, in eighteenth-century England, dialogue, no matter how perverted or restricted, was possible, something that French society never experienced in that period. This difference may be highlighted by noting the 'invention' in England, and the complete absence in France, of the party system. Party politics is a development that comes only at a certain stage in social evolution. It demands a relatively large body of politically conscious individuals (which is in effect to say individuals who have a vested interest in the state and direction of the economy) who, while agreeing on the basic framework of political life, can yet disagree about the methods of working towards accepted goals. Choice is the keynote, and so a climate of change and in particular an acceptance of expansion are called for. Such prerequisites were satisfied in England about 1680; and the Exclusion Crisis, the same that had brought Locke to the fore, occasioned the first faint organizations that may be called political parties. Those who inclined to exclude James were called Whigs by their opponents, those who tended to Divine Right were dubbed Tories. From then until the close of the reign of Anne these divisions, while not equivalent to modern parties, were yet meaningful. And if they lost meaning under the Hanoverians, when the Whig dominance became total, the idea lived on to be resurrected towards the end of the century as part of developments to be dealt with later.

The comparisons so far made have always been simple ones—France with New France, France with England. But now that the examination turns to the English possessions in North America the comparison must become twofold, on the one hand the English offshoots with the French, and on the other the colonial society with the parent. In the first case the result will be stark contrasts, in the second a mixture of similarities and differences.

What would have astonished a Colbert about the English colonies was their heterogeneity. New France was homogeneous; it mattered little which part of the colony was being examined, the same pattern prevailed, its uniformity ensured by an ever-watchful parent society. How different it was in the English areas. At the time of the Declaration of Independence there were eighteen British colonies in North America, of which thirteen eventually joined together to constitute the United States of America. No two of these thirteen were alike. Each owed its inception, growth, and character to unique combinations of factors. For instance Virginia, founded first in 1607, had been from the beginning a colony dominated by large economic interests and the tobacco boom, while Massachusetts, founded 1620–30, was peopled by earnest Puritans whose impulse was not so much economic as religious. Since other colonies were founded from existing ones, over-spill from Virginia was responsible for the establishment of North Carolina,

Massachusetts threw off Rhode Island, New Hampshire and, much later, Maine. The best that can be done to reduce these thirteen to manageable categories is rough and ready indeed. It is possible to make a crude sorting constitutionally. By the time of Independence two colonies (Rhode Island and Connecticut) were charter colonies, enjoying a virtually independent and republican-like existence under the shelter of the British monarchy; three (Pennsylvania, Delaware, and Maryland) were proprietary, where power was vested in the owners of the colony subject to a good deal of interference from Westminster; and the rest were royal colonies run more completely as departments under the Crown. Or it is possible to sort them by region. In the south was a block of colonies (Georgia, South Carolina, North Carolina, Virginia, and Maryland) that in the main depended on the bulk export crops of tobacco, rice, and indigo, an economic basis that encouraged large estates frequently worked by African slave labour and an establishment given to aping the ways of aristocratic England. New England (Massachusetts, New Hampshire, Rhode Island, and Connecticut) was characterized by subsistence farming and the trade and commerce facilitated by the region's good harbours, strategic location, teeming fisheries, and by the people's enterprise. The middle colonies (New York, Pennsylvania, New Jersey, and Delaware) partook of something of both northern and southern characteristics.

More bewildering yet to the Colbertian observer would have been the diversity that complicated even these distinctions and split apart individual colonies. English settlers may have predominated, but there were plenty of other nationalities. The Welsh, Scots, and Irish were all represented in colonial America, though from among the British strains pride of place must be given to the Scots-Irish from Ulster. The Dutch had been established since the early seventeenth century in New Amsterdam and remained when that town was taken by the English and renamed New York. Sweden had briefly held portions of the Delaware valley. Germans were particularly strong in Pennsylvania. Huguenot immigration became especially heavy after 1685. The consequences of this open-door policy were that the population grew rapidly from both natural increase and from immigration, so that on the eve of Independence it numbered some 2.5 million, and that in time the society was leavened by non-English elements and ideas—to take one example the Declaration of Independence was signed by 56 people, of whom eight had not been born in the colonies and an additional eighteen were of non-English stock. And if the population map was variegated, so was the religious. The Anglican Church had been established in some colonies, notably in Virginia, but its strength was not otherwise marked. New England was Puritan, but then Puritan covered a great variety of groupings. German Pietists of various shades, Quakers in Pennsylvania in particular, all manner of offshoots of the Radical Reformation, Jews who had first entered North America via New Amsterdam, Catholics who had originally founded Maryland, all contributed to the richness of the American scene. Not that these denominations were equal— Protestantism and especially Calvinism predominated, and there was a continuing distrust of things Catholic; in 1745 the attack on the French fortress of Louisbourg was turned into an anti-Catholic crusade by the colonial troops, who ceremonially took along an axe with which to destroy the idolatrous altar and furnishings that the church would be sure to contain.

In every way the heterogeneity of colonial America was striking, and it is illuminating that the one Colbertian venture, Georgia, where emigration was controlled, land *holding* practised, and liquor prohibited, abandoned these ideals within twenty years of its foundation and reverted to the normal pattern. Yet to stress diversity is not to deny any common traits. After all these were English possessions, founded by essentially English enterprise. Instinctively they adopted English patterns. Despite the pressure of other stocks, the language was predominantly English. The books read, and eventually the books and newspapers printed in the colonies, were overwhelmingly English. Law was based upon English common law, and so jury trials and habeas corpus were taken for granted. The land system was for all intents and purposes that of English freehold, that is, land *owning*. Disregarding minor exceptions, each colony had some variety of the English constitution, with king, Lords, and Commons represented by governor, upper nominated house, and lower 'democratically' elected house. And the practice of local autonomy, so that local government remained the abdication of central responsibility and direction, was a very marked English trait; but with this difference, especially in New England, that formally democratic selection of officials was practised in the township meetings.

In the new-world setting, however, certain aspects of the English tradition were taken further, to the point that the English character began to seem faint and it became apparent that a proto-Americanness was emerging. The English myth of resistance to tyranny has been noted; the popular song *Rule Britannia*, with its refrain 'Britons never, never shall be slaves', dates from the first half of the eighteenth century. Americans were to elaborate this myth. In part it was a consequence of the way in which America was settled. The Puritan represented one extreme, the high-principled departure for the wilderness rather than compromise one's conscience; at the other extreme was the criminal, shipped or encouraged to ship himself to the New World to rid settled society of a pest. In between were to be found all shades of motivation. But whatever the precise reason, it is clear that the great majority who came to the New World did so because for one reason or another they were at odds with the prevailing situation at home. Whereas the New French population was selected for docility and did remain quiet, the Americans were very often the reverse of docile, and the history of colonial America was studded with instances of opposition movements, civil commotion, and even outright rebellion. There was in them a kernel of principle, a tinge of ideology, that distinguished them from the instinctive rioting endemic among the lower orders in England. The deference that existed in England was not so evident across the Atlantic.

This was immigration playing a role at the social level, forming a mix of people in which a critical attitude at least would be disproportionately strong. But immigration played a more intellectual role too. It had been a key belief of many immigrant groups, and one to be found especially among the Puritan sects, that they were the righteous remnant fleeing a corrupt society to build the New Jerusalem. By the eighteenth century this view had been reinforced by the Enlightenment belief that 'natural' America was more free of the corruption of kings and priests than was the Old World, and accordingly was the home of virtue. These two outlooks fused in the widespread assumption that America represented the quintessence of English liberty. That fragile flower might be in danger in the home country, but in the colonies it could be preserved. Watchful and valiant care, though, would be needed, and all society's critical awareness.

A second difference of degree lay in the class structure of colonial society. Britain was a mature society rooted in a traditional past, and one moreover where the population was pressing upon the means of support. Against such a background a well-differentiated socio-economic structure had developed. Thus while the basis of the English social system was land, only a tiny minority possessed such land. Many times that number were tenants of the great landlords, or slipping down the ladder were landless labourers working for their betters with no hope of ever changing their status. To a lesser extent in the towns, comparable distinctions were to be found. The master class was in control and the majority of workers could not expect to work their way up to join them; in certain trades the guild system hung on as it did to an even greater extent in France. In America the huge spaces and booming population made nonsense of such restrictions, and turned the colonies into middle-class societies in a way that surpassed Britain. Land was so plentiful, speculation so cut-throat, that the price of land was low and those who wanted land could reasonably expect to possess it, and outright. The impossibility of guild control of crafts and long years of apprenticeship quickly became plain in a society where there was a lack of tradition, high mobility, and a chronic labour shortage. Here, too, the ambitious could reasonably expect to acquire a business and to prosper. Of course extremes of wealth and poverty were to be found. But the extremes were not pronounced. More importantly, middle-class style was so pervasive that both small extremes of upper and lower classes subscribed to the bourgeois ethic. To make the contrast with New France is to say that whereas there the bourgeois hoped to live as aristocrats, in America the aristocrats were content to live as bourgeois.

This last consideration points to the third difference of degree. Americans believed in progress like no other people in the eighteenth century. No doubt the initial foundation of so many settlements as money-making ventures had something to do with this orientation towards future prospects. No doubt the Puritan heritage had much to contribute in this direction. And no doubt the selective operations of immigration and wilderness living had their part to play. But as Daniel Boorstin compellingly argues in *The Americans: The Colonial Experience*, the nature of the American environment operating on English presuppositions must have been sufficient to produce a belief in progress. And in such a climate the Enlightenment was fully at home. There were *philosophes* in colonial America, notably Franklin and Jefferson. But to refer to the American Enlightenment is to do much more than point to certain intellectuals. The very fabric of American society was in harmony with the notions of Locke. Long before Locke wrote *Two Treatises of Government*, the *Mayflower* Puritans had elaborated a theory of social contract, vowing 'to covenant and combine ourselves together into a civil body politic for our better ordering and preservation'. Long before Locke wrote his *Letter of Toleration* Americans were being forced by the very multiplicity of competing sects to a more pragmatic acceptance of religious diversity. As Boorstin puts it, what were in Europe intellectual constructs were in America self-evident truths.

2

The Establishment
of
New Societies

At the opening of this account the birth of the three separate societies—the British, the Canadian, and the American—from the womb of the previous imperial unity was dated about the middle of the eighteenth century. In that opening the statement was also made somewhat cavalierly that the entire western world was passing through a crisis, so that even the parent society Britain itself was profoundly affected. Now when the account focuses in on the crucial half century that ended about 1815, the formative period during which were laid down the main lineaments of the mature societies, an explanation of that claim must be given.

One of the most useful syntheses of this period has been that provided by the American scholar, R. R. Palmer. Taking as his province the entirety of the western world, from Russia to Pennsylvania, from Scandinavia to the Mediterranean, he traces out what he calls *The Age of the Democratic Revolution*. It is an age dominated by the American War of Independence and by the French Revolution, but Palmer drives home the fact that these are by no means the only revolutions that took place at this time. In fact, when Palmer has done listing the revolutions and near-revolutions that occurred in this period, it is difficult to find countries that were not touched by them. Revolution becomes the characteristic of the age, so much so that by way of shorthand the term 'the Atlantic Revolution' is frequently applied to the entire phenomenon.

These revolutions differed, of course, from country to country. But a thread runs through them all, claims Palmer. Everywhere there was a tendency for society to polarize. On the one hand were forces making for increased oligarchic control, the ever-tighter hold over society and government by the establishment. This account has noted, for instance, how in France the old sword nobility and the new robe nobility were uniting, and how under the weaker successors of Louis XIV the bourgeois advance was being checked and thwarted. On the other hand, and related to the oligarchic tendency both as cause and as effect, was what Palmer calls the 'democratic revolution'. He acknowledges that this term is a loose one, and indeed that the very word 'democrat' was barely used in Europe before the nineteenth century, but he insists, and rightly, that the term can be a meaningful one; it draws attention to a 'discomfort with older forms of social stratification and formal rank' and epitomizes an attitude that 'politically was against the possession of government . . . by any established privileged, closed, or self-recruiting groups of men'. Something has already been said of such 'self-recruiting groups of men'; the French *Parlement*, where the sale of office was openly part of the system, was one example. But it is on the British Parliament, where sham elections and bribery were the rule, that interest must be concentrated. Indeed the whole British experience in the second half of the eighteenth century well illustrates the polarization of oligarchic and democratic tendencies.

In 1760 George II, the second Hanoverian king, died and was succeeded by his grandson, George III. The new king was strikingly different from his predecessor. He was young, only twenty-two, and had much of the crusader in him, which is proper in those of that age. He had been appalled by the corruption prevalent in his grandfather's court, both political and moral, and was determined to end it. To give his determination an added edge was the fact that he was the first king since the Glorious Revolution who was not a foreigner and whose first language was English. 'I glory in the name of Briton' was his boast and confirmed him in his decision to be a true father of his country.

George III intended to provide leadership by being at the head of a team of ministers chosen by him on the basis of loyalty and ability. And immediately this resolve highlighted one of the most salient characterics of the British constitution, that it is always evolving, never fixed. In one sense what George III proposed was perfectly legal and constitutional. British government was (and still is, it is worth remembering) the king's government; to give one small but significant illustration, it was necessary to hold an election in 1761 because, George II having died, his parliament died with him and a new king required a new parliament. James II had picked his ministers, William III had done likewise, and there was nothing in the Glorious Revolution and Settlement to deny this practice. George III was quite within his rights in selecting whomever he wanted to carry on his business. At the same time, however, it has been noted how since 1688, and especially since 1714, the monarchs had slackened their grasp of the direction of affairs, and how the Whig oligarchs had increasingly taken over the control of the state. There were those, then, who would argue that the king, in seeking to take up the direction of the executive again, was subverting the constitution by reverting to practices over fifty years out of date. There was merit in both positions (though legality was with the king), and only the give and take of political and social developments would decide which was 'right'.

George III wasted little time and by 1763 had managed to install his long-time friend and mentor, Lord Bute, as his leading minister. The great Whig magnates, who had learnt over two reigns to look upon high office as their god-given right, were appalled and furious. In their rage they cast about for ways of attacking king and minister. Anything was suitable as a stick to beat that hateful combination. Attacks ranged from the lowest scurrility to the loftiest appeals to principle. Bute was attacked as a Scotsman, a foreigner, and the tale put about that he was the lover of the king's mother. At the other extreme, disaffected Whigs began to formulate novel constitutional theories that would enable and justify their return to power. They began to flirt with forces other than the oligarchic; they began to appeal to more popular sections of society. And here they gave a twist to the oligarchic-democratic dichotomy. For given what had happened in the seventeenth century it was difficult, if not impossible, for the monarchy to link up with the democratic forces to present a united front against the oligarchy. It was correspondingly easy, however, for the Whig aristocrats to put themselves forward as the saviours of the nation in the Glorious Revolution, and the natural bulwark of the people. But it was only flirting with the people, only using them, and essentially the Whig oligarchy was entrenching itself against the threat posed by the young sovereign.

Yet to make George III solely responsible for this polarization would be a misrepresentation of the situation as absurd as the attempt to make him into the tyrant responsible for the loss of the American colonies. George III was more the catalyst, acting on a situation that was ripe for change. For there were new forces at work about mid-century that, even without the new king, would have called for fundamental readjustment. One of the most significant pointers to the emergence of a new order was the Wilkes phenomenon.

John Wilkes burst into public notoriety in 1763. The offspring of middle-class parents, he had been taken up by Lord Temple, a leading Whig, and set up as editor of the *North Briton* journal. In 1763 the king's throne speech announced the terms on which Britain would terminate the victorious Seven Years' War; a major provision of the peace was the retention of Quebec and the return to France of the rich Caribbean sugar island of Guadeloupe. Wilkes chose to attack these terms in issue number 45 of the *North Briton*, and in so doing violently antagonized the ministry, which decided that he should answer for his temerity. The Secretary of State issued a general warrant (i.e., a warrant that named no names) for the arrest on a charge of seditious libel of all those connected with the publication of number 45. Such prosecutions had been common enough in the past, but on this occasion the ministry had overreached itself.

Wilkes was a disreputable character, and the aristocrats who delighted to use him as a means of embarrassing the government were careful to keep their distance. But he had an effective pen, a superb wit (what could match his instant rejoinder to the peer who prophesied that he would die either on the scaffold or of the pox that 'It depends, my lord, on whether I embrace your principles or your mistress'?), and the fascination to draw people to his cause. He was not without courage, and was eager to resist the government.

At the trial several grounds were put forward for Wilkes's release. The judge, Charles Pratt, later Lord Camden, a friend of the leading politician, Lord Temple, agreed that since Wilkes was a Member of Parliament he could claim immunity from arrest. He ordered Wilkes released, to the delight of the crowd. Once at liberty Wilkes immediately took the initiative and sued the authorities for the trespass and loss he had suffered when the law officers broke into his premises to look for incriminating material. Pratt again presided and, holding that general warrants gave such a discretionary power to the executive as to be 'totally subversive of the liberty of the subject', found for Wilkes and awarded him the large, punitive damages of £1,000. The illegality of general warrants was confirmed in the later case of *Entick vs. Carrington*, which grew out of the same seizure of number 45 and those connected with it. Thus a series of heavy blows had been struck against the executive power. The release of Wilkes was an embarrassment to the government, and his winning of damages was an even greater one. The sweeping power of general warrants, a potent means of controlling dissidents, had been denied. And finally it had been made clear that Secretaries of State did not have the authority to issue warrants but had to obtain them in the normal way by application to the judicial authorities. Here was a further blow to the prerogative that the executive was now claiming to exercise.

The government could not let matters rest with Wilkes at liberty and in receipt of damages. The House of Commons had the power to expel any member who, it was felt, brought the House into disrepute. Wilkes's private life, and in particular the obscene *Essay on Women* that he had had a hand in writing, were enough for the Commons to vote his expulsion. Deprived of his immunity he would be open to arrest and trial on the original charge of seditious libel, but this time on an ordinary warrant, and also on the new ground of obscenity. But before the expulsion could take place, Wilkes had slipped away to France.

This was by no means the end of Wilkes, however. A few years later he returned to England and challenged authority by declaring his candidature for a Middlesex seat in Parliament. His campaign was the occasion for a great outburst of popular support. Wilkes was overwhelmingly successful. The Commons declared him incapable of taking his seat. At the re-election Wilkes again headed the poll. Again the Commons refused to seat him. This occurred four times in all, until eventually the Commons declared that his defeated opponent 'ought to have been elected'. This confrontation, and the trials and imprisonment to which Wilkes was subjected on the old charges, served to inflame popular passions. Rioting took place, troops fired on the mob, and London, which adjoined Middlesex and was the hot-bed of discontent, rang to the shout of 'Wilkes and Liberty'. And if for the moment the authorities had succeeded in keeping a critic out of Parliament, in the long run they failed to prevent the voters choosing their man. For in 1782 Wilkes had the satisfaction of having the record of his expulsion from the Commons expunged from its journal. A second victory against the executive had been won, the right of the voters to be represented by the man of their choice.

There was yet a third issue in which Wilkes played a major role in weakening executive power. The oligarchic House of Commons buttressed its pretensions by denying the non-parliamentary classes any detailed knowledge of what went on within its doors; no newspaper reports of debates were allowed. But in the period of the Wilkes excitement newspapers were ready to risk legal penalties by breaking the law. In 1771 the authorities decided to make an issue of this illegal practice and ordered the arrest of the offending newsmen. Wilkes, by this time an alderman of London, was able to use his authority and that of his fellow London officials to force a confrontation with Parliament.

The case was not a clear-cut victory for either side, but the government burnt its fingers so badly that it never again attempted to deny the public's right to know what its representatives were doing. A further victory for the freedom of the press had been won as a result of Wilkesite agitation.

In all this the Wilkesite agitation must be seen as a tremendous demand for the rights of Englishmen, as a dramatic assertion of principle. It was less of a practical program. But a little later England did produce a political movement that indicated that more positive forces were at work, and that has been described by a leading historian as England's abortive French Revolution. This was the County Associations movement of 1779–85, which centred upon Yorkshire, whose 16,000 freeholders made it by far the biggest of the English counties, and which established an off-shoot in the London district of Westminster, whose 9,000 voters made it easily the biggest of the borough constituencies. But this movement and others connected with it will not be analyzed here. They have been mentioned merely to round out the picture of a polarizing society, dramatized by the fact that in the 1780 election half of the contested seats were fought on an Association, i.e., party, basis; this, as will be seen later, was revolutionary indeed and emphasized the tensions within English society.

What lay at the root of this tension was a change in the nature of English society. Wilkes and the County Associations were significant more as symptoms than anything else. It is the reporting of debates that especially gives the clue to what was happening, for it underscores the fact that a new surge in middle-class pretensions was taking place. The mob that chanted 'Wilkes and Liberty' might be composed in the main of the lower orders, but what significance there was in the froth was middle-class. This can be seen clearly in the founding in 1769, at the height of the 'Wilkes and Liberty' outburst, of the Society of the Supporters of the Bill of Rights. It was the forerunner of many similar societies in the next few years, for instance the County Associations themselves, and the Society for Constitutional Information, 1780, which emerged in London as a central co-ordinating organization linked with the Association movement. Small, closed oligarchies do not need impersonal organizations to seek out and bring together like-minded individuals—they are already known to each other. But a widening political nation needed new methods of reaching out and communicating, and these the political societies provided.

The accelerating entry of the middle classes into a fuller share in the political life of the nation was accompanied, and made possible, by other changes. An altered law of libel was one such. A bourgeois society is modern; traditional methods give way to more rational ones, choice among alternatives is encouraged. But choice means discussion, even dissension. Now this is hardly possible in any situation where the law of libel, and particularly that of seditious libel, is structured as it was in the eighteenth century. This law, which had been laid down in the last years of the Stuart régime, made the definition of libel a matter for the judge; the jury was called upon to decide merely the fact of publication, and once this had been admitted or established there was no further question of guilt. It was easy for the authorities to secure verdicts, therefore, and political discussion was cramped by a fear of consequences. The old fixity of libel trials began to be challenged in the 1750s, and by none other than Charles Pratt. Further challenges followed over the next few years, including one from a prominent Wilkesite lawyer. It was symptomatic of the Enlightenment century that the view began to gain ground that since values were relative, what once might have been considered libellous might no longer warrant the same description. Therefore, it was felt, the question of libel should not be one of law, but rather one of fact. And if it became a question of fact then the decision should be in the hands of the jury, not of the judge. Such thinking finally prevailed and was embodied in the Libel Act of 1792, which fittingly was carried in the Lords by the forceful intervention of Charles Pratt, now Lord Camden.

Modernization calls for a choice among the institutions of society. Eighteenth-century British society, while much more open to choice than, say, the French, still possessed a rigid framework, best exemplified in the Anglican monopoly; Wilkes, for instance, being excluded as a Dissenter from Oxford and Cambridge, attended the Dutch university of Leyden. Now, just after mid-century, fresh attacks were to be made on such monopolies in favour of increased pluralism.

It was not that the plight of Dissenters was getting worse. Far from it; since the Hanoverian succession their position had been improving. Their Dissenting Academies, alternatives to the Anglican universities and public schools, were able to continue, though technically they were illegal, and to contribute men of superior education and talents to society. Since 1732 the three main Dissenting denominations, the Congregationalists, the Presbyterians, and the Baptists, had had a formal organization to represent them, the Protestant Dissenting Deputies. This was so well received that it had the right to approach the throne itself and make representation to the Crown; for this reason the New England Puritans kept in close touch with the Deputies, who on occasion presented petitions from Connecticut and Massachusetts to the king. Above all, the Dissenters were eased by the very British device of annual indemnity. From 1727 Parliament each year passed an Act that relieved from penalty those who had assumed office to which by the operation of the Test and Corporation Acts they were not entitled.

What happened from the 1770s on must be seen, then, as a new spirit among the Dissenters, a new accession of confidence and a determination to do away with anomalous legislation. That there was a new attitude abroad with respect to religious tests may be confirmed by reference to what was happening within the Anglican Church itself. In 1771 a group of Anglican clergy met at the Feathers' Tavern in London and got up a petition to Parliament. In this they called for a relaxation in the requirement that Anglican priests subscribe to the Thirty-Nine Articles, a statement of belief dating from the Reformation. The Lords rejected the request, but that it had been made, and that it had carried in the Commons, indicated the challenge to the old fixities. It was also an encouragement to the Dissenters to press ahead with their own campaign.

Dissenter demands peaked between 1787 and 1790 with an assault on the Test and Corporation Acts. The Commons vote of 1787 rejected the proposal 176–98, but by 1789 the gap had closed to 122–102. However, in 1790 the bill was rejected by 294–105. What was responsible for this dramatic swing back to the former oligarchic stance was, of course, the impact of the French Revolution. This Revolution, the most amazing of all those included in the Atlantic Revolution, was responsible for giving the polarization of English society another twist. But before saying something about the French Revolution, it remains to round out the examination of the democratic tendencies by looking at those in Britain's colonial possessions.

But it is not in North America that this examination must begin. Closer to home was Ireland, which in the second half of the eighteenth century was passing through one of the most turbulent periods of its history. Already by this time Anglo-Irish relations were poisoned. The Irish crown had been won by England in 1152 and since then there had been little peace between the two peoples. From that time on, victorious English commanders had been granted land in Ireland confiscated from the defeated natives. Repeated Irish attempts to undo these arrangements, usually by backing a claimant to the English throne, had only given the English further opportunities to repeat the confiscation on bigger and bigger scales. The seventeenth century saw the increasing estrangement of Ireland. James I settled loyal Presbyterian Scots in

Ireland, especially in the northern province of Ulster; Cromwell savagely subdued Ireland at mid-century after it had backed Charles I, and made an example of the town of Drogheda by slaughtering its entire population; William III finally defeated James II in the Irish Battle of the Boyne in 1690, where once again the Irish provided the English pretender with an army. And this last combination of Catholicism and nationalism having been defeated, the total subordination of Ireland to England was pushed through.

Economically Ireland was ruined for the benefit of England and in accordance with the dictates of Mercantilism. A prime example of this was the killing off of the once flourishing Irish woollen industry by prohibiting exports. Agriculture was in a deplorable state. Much of the land was owned by members of the English aristocracy and others who preferred to live in England; they were absentee landlords who had severed any connection with their tenants so that there was not the slightest vestige of that *noblesse oblige* that humanized landlord-tenant relationships to some extent in England; the use of agents meant the fastening on to the peasantry of an unscrupulous class of people whose aim was to increase the rent yield in the short run with little thought for the long-term consequences. And under such treatment the Irish peasantry failed to develop any initiative, any interest in the improvement of the land. Indeed in many instances the tiny size of their plots, and their want of capital, quite prevented any attempt to break the vicious circle in which they were trapped; instead they sank to a disastrous dependence upon a single crop, the potato, and already by the first half of the eighteenth century famine was devastating Ireland. Taxes had to be collected at gun point, and the countryside was ravaged by savage peasant bands that took instinctive revenge against the possessing class, its agents, and its wealth. The tradition of Irish agrarian outrage had already been formed.

The legal subjugation of Ireland was equally pronounced. As far back as 1494 the Irish parliament had been deprived of all genuine life, for in that year, in the wake of an attempt to back the losing side in an English succession squabble, Henry VII had passed an Act that stated that bills of the Irish parliament would become law only when approved at Westminster; this Act was known as Poynings' Law after the name of the king's deputy in Ireland at the time. Besides this, the Irish parliament was much more of a sham than the English. There was no limit to its term, a parliament being elected on the accession of the king and continuing for the rest of his life. Whereas England had some controls on the number of placemen in parliament, there were none in Ireland. Two-thirds of the Irish revenue came from hereditary sources that the parliament could not control or question. Finally in 1719 the subordination of the Irish parliament to the English was made unambiguous with the passing of the Declaratory Act, which in addition to spelling out the superior-inferior relationship, made the final court of appeal in legal cases not the House of Lords of Ireland but that of England. Further to be noted was the lack of habeas corpus in Ireland, and the fact that Irish judges did not have the tenure given to their English counterparts by the Act of Settlement. In short, the power of the executive was supreme, and it was the English executive that in the last resort had the controlling power.

In addition to the economic and legal injustices there were the religious. The established Church of Ireland had been fastened on to the country during the sixteenth century. But only a small minority of the population belonged to this denomination, perhaps only half a million out of an eighteenth-century population of four and a half million. It suffered from the decay that marked its sister church, the Church of England, with the further drawback that Irish loyalty to it was weakened by the English habit of using Irish bishoprics as patronage to reward English connections. Bitterly opposed to the Church of Ireland were the million or so Presbyterians, concentrated for the most part in Ulster. Since they had been brought over as a means of pacifying the country and because they were known for their loyalty and industry, they were outraged when their religion was slighted and when their economic activities were crippled by Mercantilism. During the eighteenth century many of these Scots-Irish emigrated to America, taking with them their sense of betrayal and fear that once again England might seek to destroy them.

But the vast bulk of the population was Catholic, three million or so barely tolerated beings. They had no vote, of course, and could play no part in civil society. But this was normal at that time. What was abnormal in the case of the Irish Catholics were the additional penal laws designed to keep them beyond the pale and in a condition in which they could be no threat to the Protestant succession. No Catholic was allowed to lease land for more than thirty-one years; no Catholic was to own a horse worth more than £5; any son turning Protestant was to inherit all the father's property to the exclusion of all other Catholic children. Catholics in Ireland were treated as barely human, and where possible were completely ignored. In the early part of the eighteenth century this beaten people was content to remain cowed, but by the end of the century a new assertiveness began to spread.

The crucial point at which Ireland began to change was again about mid-century. As in England, the reforming efforts of George III upset established ways and triggered off a series of readjustments. In 1767 he sent over a new Lord-Lieutenant, Lord Townshend, with orders to end the corruption of the Irish system and to break the power of the oligarchs who used parliament for their own narrow ends. One result of Townshend's energetic action was the Octennial Act, 1768, which by limiting the life of an Irish parliament to eight years did something to weaken the oligarchs' hold. But more was needed to tame them adequately, and Townshend found that the way to fight their patronage was by the use of superior Westminster-based patronage. Another result of his efforts, then, was to bring British control of Irish affairs more blatantly into the open, and in reaction Irish sentiments were encouraged. A Patriot party in the Irish parliament was in existence in the 1770s.

As in the English case, however, the royal initiative must be seen as catalyst, not as cause. About this time Irish wealth was increasing, and despite handicaps agricultural rents and commercial profits were going up significantly. The capital, Dublin, was taking on its Georgian air as a new prosperity rebuilt it in style. This mood of improvement, and affluence even, was felt in social and political spheres. As London had thrown up its champion, so too did Dublin produce Charles Lucas, who was described by Townshend in 1768 as 'the Wilkes of Ireland'. Lucas was a chemist, and later, after study at Leyden, a doctor; clearly he was not from the natural ruling class and indeed not even from the upper-middle class, the eighteenth century having a very proper idea of just how far down the social scale a doctor stood. He had first come to public notice when he championed the Dublin council against the claims of the inner group of city magistrates, the aldermen. Later he was returned to the Irish Commons as the very popular representative of Dublin. Lucas was never the figure Wilkes was, and accomplished nothing. However the fact that he could become a popular focus indicates the changing style of Irish politics at this time.

The broadening of the political process was revealed even more clearly shortly after Lucas' day. When the American troubles began the people of Ireland were much involved. There were the family links that spanned the Atlantic. There were the constitutional links that, many thought, bound Ireland to the American cause, for both societies were treated colonially by Britain at a time when increasing maturity demanded some alternative relationship. But if political consciousness was revived, it was not unanimously directed against Britain. When

troops were drained from Ireland for service in America, Britain's inveterate enemy France threatened once again to use Ireland as the back
door into England. The critical attitude to Britain was tempered overnight, and all over Ireland bodies of volunteer troops were formed to
replace the regulars. But political discussion still ran high.

It might be, as a bow in the direction of established notions, that
these volunteers were commanded by the landed aristocracy, but overwhelmingly the membership was middle-class—the doctors, lawyers,
traders of the towns, and the middling kind of landowners of the
countryside. And the Irish Volunteers were Protestant, given to holding
their parades on the anniversaries of victories over the Catholic Stuarts.
They were formed as much by the need to preserve law and order, i.e.
to protect property from the depredations of the lower orders, as by a
patriotic desire to help Britain. That their export trade had suffered by
the disruption caused by hostilities and especially by the decision of the
rebellious North American colonies not to buy British goods was a
further spur to these middle-class volunteers to come together.

And this is the best way to look upon the Volunteers. They were
military organizations and they did wear uniforms, hold parades, and
go on manoeuvres. But the units were small, closely knit, and as suited
for political education and action as anything else, especially necessary
at a time when political machinery and newspapers were still so rudimentary. Their further development bears out this interpretation. Even
after the American war had ended, the Volunteers kept up their organization. Indeed they called conventions and debated further reform
until this urge petered out in 1785. They took a particular interest in
trying to obtain free trade with England, and having convinced the
government at Westminster, were robbed of their victory only by the
obstruction of the English merchant interest.

But before this the Volunteers had a great victory to their credit. In
1782 the Irish parliament had recovered almost all of its original
autonomy. The Patriot Party, fired by the example of the Americans,
guided in the Commons by the middle-class orator, Grattan, and backed
by some 50,000 Volunteers, confronted a Britain defeated in America
and isolated in Europe, and won the repeal of Poynings' Law and the
Declaratory Act. Ireland was now independent except in matters of
imperial concern such as foreign policy and trade. The new parliament,
known as Grattan's Parliament in honour of the major architect of the
new order, began the direction of a resurgent country. The economic
revival continued and quickened; Irish national aspirations were as-
suaged if not wholly satisfied; even the religious bitterness began to

lessen, so much so that by 1793 Irish Catholics were no longer denied the vote on the grounds of religion, though Catholics could still not sit in the Irish Commons. Of course, it was the upper- and middle-class Catholics who benefitted, and the direction of affairs was still in the hands of the Protestant, i.e., Church of Ireland, Ascendancy. Even so, the grant draws attention to the fact that once again the demands of modernization had encouraged a move towards pluralism. All in all, then, the polarization of Irish society had been resolved into a stability that later generations would remember as a 'golden age'.

That the mid-eighteenth century was a decisive turning point was even clearer in the case of North America. From 1756–63 Britain and France had been locked in the Seven Years' War to decide which of these two expanding imperial powers should have the primacy. It was, by the standards of the day, a desperate and at times savage war, and the eventual British victory was dearly bought indeed. Huge sums had been involved, which had more than doubled the British national debt. If taxes in Britain were not to be raised to a level that would endanger the government, some way would have to be found of making the entire empire contribute to the costs of maintaining it. The solution that suggested itself, and that in fact was long overdue, was a tightening up of the mercantilist system, so that a more efficient administration would turn over more realistic sums to the authorities. The days when the Massachusetts' customs houses would collect £2,000 in duties a year but at a cost of £8,000 in salaries and expenses were to end. Yet such tampering could only lead to a wholesale rethinking of the colonial situation. A further cost of the war, and another ground for rethinking relationships, was the transfer to Britain of the lion's share of French possessions in North America. There was the question of what to do with Quebec, the most developed of the French possessions and the one most strategically placed to affect the fortunes of the existing British colonies. Was Quebec to remain an anomalous civilization, or to be assimilated to the British way? And then there was the problem posed by the ending of a French threat on American soil. Until 1763 colonial pretensions had been kept in check by colonial dependence upon British protection. Now this check had been removed, and it became apparent that Americans would be less willing to fit in with the mercantilist scheme of things. At mid-century, then, the North American societies were in a state of flux, and the polarizing tendencies had the scope to develop.

But not within the French society of Quebec. That unit was too small, too immature, for there to be any great tendency to cleavage, and the pattern laid down by the former régime helped to retard the fragmentation of society. Indeed the fact that many of the officials of New France, and many of the wealthy who could afford to do so, chose to return to France, drew off many of the élite and so strengthened the homogeneity of French-Canadian society. Nor did British policy after the Conquest do much to alter this solidarity. The Royal Proclamation of 1763 did envisage an eventual anglicization of the population as more and more settlers from the south moved up to take advantage of the new opportunities, thereby swamping the French element. But this migration failed to happen and so the pattern of development was increasingly set not by mass pressure but by the attitudes of the British authorities. In these immediate post-Conquest years the personalities of the first two governors were crucial. James Murray and Guy Carleton were both aristocrats who had made careers in the army. Both were temperamentally opposed to the middle-class traders up from the colonies to make quick profits from the war situation, and even to their more acceptable successors who predominated after the conclusion of peace. Both chose to identify with the aristocratic elements that remained from the French régime, and favoured the Church and the seigneurial class behind whom, they assumed, the *habitants* would fall into line. This policy was made official in the Quebec Act that was finally passed in 1774.

Carleton had gone to London in 1770 and remained there until the Act was passed, keeping his eye on developments and obtaining much of what he wanted. In the newly defined colony of Quebec, which extended down to the junction of the Ohio and the Mississippi, English criminal law was to be imposed. But French civil law, which did not use juries, was to be retained, and since this civil law embraced land law, it meant the retention of the seigneurial system. And because it also embraced commercial law it restricted the growth of trade and commerce and so helped to maintain the status and power of the seigneurs. The Church was also looked after. Even before 1774 the British had turned a blind eye to the consecration of Bishop Briand, who had rewarded the authorities by an intense loyalty to his new allegiance and by strenuous efforts to keep his flock obedient to the British. Now by the Quebec Act the Catholic Church was recognized to the extent that it could demand tithes from the Catholic subjects of the colony; this was not establishment since there was no right to tithes from the non-Catholic population, but even so the Catholic Church had been given a status quite exceptional within the then British system.

It has long been clear that the older picture of a monolithically united and docile society quietly passing under British control has been too one-sided. Carleton's play to the Church and seigneurs had unwelcome repercussions. There is evidence, for instance, that some of the French-Canadian merchants were prepared to link up with their English counterparts and protest against the retention of French civil law. More significantly the retention of seigneurialism had irked the *habitants*, whose inveterate independence had been reinforced by the breakdown of continuity and certainty. When the Americans invaded in 1775 some *habitants* supported them, few rallied effectively to the British forces, and in the investigations that followed a majority of the militia officers were found wanting. And yet, when all credit has been given to a necessary work of historical revision, it still remains true that French-Canadian society was passive in tone. If the *habitants* would not fight for Britain in 1775, neither would they fight against it in any numbers. For all their miscalculations Murray and Carleton had done their work well—well enough certainly to reconcile French Canadians to a new régime and to retain their sense of solidarity. Protest in French Canada was to remain for some time of an instinctive, negative kind, a demand to be left alone as much as possible.

What polarization there was in Quebec was not along social as much as racial lines. The merchant class, increasingly dominated by English, Protestant elements, was incensed by the provisions of the Quebec Act. They had been promised in 1763 an English colony with English institutions. But now they were denied a law code adequate for their commerce, and in addition they were not to get the assembly that was the rule in British colonies. Carleton had argued that since the vast majority of the inhabitants was Roman Catholic and incapable therefore of voting or sitting in an assembly, the calling of one would be to give the colony over to a tiny Protestant minority. He preferred to rule as a strong governor aided by an appointed council, a system he thought would be more congenial to the mass of French Canadians anyway. But to his merchant critics this was impossibly reactionary; that there was in the Act no provision for habeas corpus seemed to be further evidence of an attack upon 'English liberties'. It must be added that the British instructions given to Carleton, in the light of which he was to interpret the Act, were at variance with a good deal of the Act itself; for example, Carleton was instructed to consider the introduction of jury trials in certain circumstances, and the addition of habeas corpus. But Carleton blandly ignored these instructions and wherever possible sought to apply the Act in the way that would do most to perpetuate the French identity. Thus he was able to short-circuit the British intention to make the Quebec system approximate by degrees to the prevalent British system, and thereby he helped to entrench a polarity in Canadian society.

But it was a polarity unlike that which marked England or even Ireland. In those countries the key development had been the politicization of social strata previously outside the political process, and their mobilization in formed groupings for the purpose of public debate. Such developments were impossible in Quebec, in part because of the inherited tradition, the a-politicalness of the *habitant* reinforced by the small scale of affairs lost against a background of huge distances and poor communications, the lack of literacy, and the absence of a developed press. But most of all it was because what criticism there was, was directed at an imperially backed executive by a tiny merchant body wholly dependent on that very same imperial authority and its mercantile system. It was this dependence upon Britain that had caused the Quebec merchants to rally to Carleton in 1775 in the face of American invasion. With no room for manoeuvre, with no real choice in the matter, there was no possibility of political development.

Much the same may be said of the Atlantic region of the British empire. Nova Scotia, a much more extensive area than today's province, and Newfoundland had been British since 1713, and Cape Breton Island and Prince Edward Island (then known as St John's Island) were added to the empire by the Treaty of Paris at the end of the Seven Years' War in 1763. All that France retained of her once mighty empire in this area were the two tiny islands off Newfoundland, St Pierre and Miquelon, and ill-defined fishing rights off the coast of Newfoundland. These eighteenth-century additions to the British empire at France's expense were undeveloped. Newfoundland's society was primitive in the extreme, for in accordance with mercantilist thinking the island was barred to settlers, the authorities preferring to keep it as a vital element of the fishing industry, a shore to be used merely in the summer months. Those who had established permanent settlement there were few in number and so completely ignored by British governments that only the barest skeleton of a civil administration existed. Cape Breton, thinly populated, was kept a part of Nova Scotia, but Prince Edward Island was erected into a separate colony in 1769. Its population was less than a thousand, but even so, in tune with British thinking, an assembly was instituted.

Only Nova Scotia had anything like an established society. New Englanders suffering from land shortage or wishing to take advantage of trading opportunities were an important section of the population, bringing with them a religious pluralism and a factious disposition that helped distinguish Nova Scotia from Quebec. But the main determinant of the colony's development was again the imperial authority. The hub of Nova Scotia was the huge military base of Halifax, and through this citadel-port flowed the imperial orders and government patronage that supported the economy of the region. The rest of the colony never broke free from the centralizing grip of this town, and when an assembly was given to the Nova Scotians in 1758 it was easily dominated by the Halifax merchant interest. When the Revolution broke out in 1775, therefore, the predicament of Nova Scotia was essentially that of Quebec. Some were sympathetic to the American cause, for after all many had but recently migrated from New England and still had friends and relatives there. A feeble rising, quickly crushed, did take place in 1776. But in view of the economic links with Britain and the actual presence of great naval and military might, the most that the non-loyal could hope for was a neutral status. And when it is added that, at the very moment when hostilities broke out, there took place a religious revival akin to Wesley's, led by one Henry Alline, which drew off into religious channels whatever disaffected energies there might have been in the colony, it will be seen that there was even less of a chance that a modern kind of politics would develop.

How different was the situation in those colonies soon to become the United States of America! That it was different might be gathered from the fact that these colonies *did* respond to the call to arms in 1775 and *did* join in a Declaration of Independence in the following year. Not, however, that this study intends to become embroiled in establishing the causes of the War of Independence; that vexed question may, fortunately, be put to one side. For a study that seeks to trace the unfolding of these three societies must be less interested in the totality of what actually happened than in pinpointing those factors that influenced subsequent development. In this respect the myths of the Revolution may well be more significant than the truth, a partial picture more revealing than all the details. As one historian of the Revolution has wisely warned, 'history is based on social psychology, though it is rarely considered from that basis since it is more easy to remember and list events than to recall emotions'. This section seeks, then, to capture something of the social psychology of the American people on the eve of separation.

In the introductory section of this book the claim was made that the British colonies in North America were by and large much more middle-class, much more open, much more imbued with Enlightenment attitudes, than was the parent society; to use Palmer's terms, they were much more democratic. It has also been noted how, in response to the cost of the Seven Years' War, an overhaul of the mercantilist system had been undertaken; what may be called, to use Palmerian terms again, an oligarchic reaction. This tightening-up struck at the wealth of many prominent colonists, who naturally protested against the changes. A prime example of such a measure and of colonial reaction to it, and containing within it the main outline of subsequent antagonisms, was the Stamp Act of 1765. When the stamp duties on legal documents and the like, duties that had been levied in Britain for many years, were extended to the colonies, there was a violent outcry and such difficulty in carrying on legal business that the Act had to be repealed the next year. But even before the Stamp Act Britain had been responsible for legislation that had hurt the economic ambitions of the colonists. The Royal Proclamation of 1763, which had promised English institutions to Quebec, had also dealt with the question of the trans-Appalachian lands. It was a problem that had been made urgent by the savage Indian rising under Pontiac, which had just decimated the forward settlements. The imperial solution for the western lands was to take them under the control of Westminster and to close them off from further colonization. The area was to be kept as an Indian reserve, which would cut down the likelihood of another rising and which would also have the advantage of preserving the fur trade. But as was mentioned above in reference to migration to Nova Scotia, many colonies were by now close to being overpopulated. More importantly, many influential members of colonial society had a financial stake in continued western expansion, for they held for speculative purposes huge tracts of land in the now forbidden zone. Especially in the case of Virginia, whose use of land was notoriously profligate (tobacco was a great exhauster of fertility) and whose indebtedness to London merchants was notorious, was this denial of expansion particularly disastrous.

But economic exploitation was not the only grievance against the oligarchy and it was certainly not the main ground on which the protests were founded. The main thrust of colonial complaint was that Britain was breaking the constitutional proprieties. It was an effective position to take. It could be represented that the mother country had no right to raise revenue in the colonies at all, since it was an essential part of English liberty and Lockean political philosophy that a people could be taxed only through a parliament in which they were represented. The cry of 'no taxation without representation' had, therefore, a plausible ring to it—but no more than plausible in an age when virtual representation (the view that although a farmer, say, did not vote he was still represented in the Commons by members elected by other farmers) was an accepted theory. The closing of the western frontier could be protested on the ground that the original colonial charters had envisaged continued expansion, to the Pacific if necessary; again this was merely plausible, since the Royal Proclamation had specifically recognized that colonial claims were not expunged and that at some future date the colonies might extend into the Indian zone after treaty with the tribes. A special complaint was directed against the tyranny of the royal executive in the matter of vice-admiralty courts, used in smuggling cases. Experience had shown that colonial juries, sympathetic to smugglers, would circumvent the efforts of an improved customs service by refusing to convict even in the face of incontrovertible evidence. The only way to obtain an adequate verdict, therefore, was to dispense with trial by jury by transferring the cases to vice-admiralty courts (in effect martial law) held under the authority of royal prerogative. But it was against prerogative courts that free Englishmen had gone to war with Charles I. And so it was hardly surprising that American interest in John Wilkes was intense, and that, for instance, the Sons of Liberty of Boston and the Assembly of South Carolina sent him tokens of respect when he was in prison for having defied the royal executive.

In ways like these the British actions could be attacked as unconstitutional interferences with liberty. But the vital thing about so much colonial reaction was the readiness to interpret such actions not merely as misguided but as evil, as part of a deliberate campaign to enslave the American people. Just as George III was subverting the constitution in the home land, so were his ministers destroying freedom in the colonies. It is not going too far to describe a major segment of American opinion as being infused with a conspiracy theory of history. For instance, disproportionate excitement was aroused on the very eve of the War when the terms of the Quebec Act became known; indeed it was added to the list of 'Intolerable Acts', on a par with the closing of the port of Boston, which also took place in 1774 in retaliation for the Boston Tea Party of the previous year (this was the occasion when American radicals hurled British tea into the harbour in an anti-imperial demonstration). It was not so much that the Quebec Act, by annexing the Ohio-Mississippi triangle to Quebec, reinforced the denial of expansion contained in the Royal Proclamation, but that Catholics had been granted toleration. Catholicism was the sign of slavery, as the mob cry of 'No Popery, no wooden shoes' made plain. And if it be objected that anti-Catholicism was normal at that time, and could even bring London to a standstill in the Gordon Riots at a date later than this, and that therefore it cannot be urged as a sign of conspiratorial-mindedness, it may be replied that the Gordon Riots were pure mob stuff, disapproved of by the authorities and indeed instigated by legal concessions granted to Catholics by the ruling class. In America, on the other hand, the prejudice against Catholicism continued far higher up the social scale and was much more representative of society as a whole. Furthermore, British policy since 1765, which is now known to have been a succession of blundering improvisations by frequently changing and unstable ministries, was seen by many colonists as a conscious, consistent plan to which the Quebec Act was merely the climax. Another way of stressing the general willingness to see evil everywhere at work is to point to the fear, again on the eve of the War, that an Anglican bishop would be appointed for the colonies. So long as the bishop was the Bishop of London, three thousand miles away, the prevailing Calvinism felt secure; to bring episcopacy any closer was to imperil the freedom of Americans and an indication of a plot to re-emphasize subordination and status.

Whether one concentrates on the fact of reaction to British policy, or on the nature of that reaction, it is clear that there was a deep and growing divergence between the two societies. And because colonial society was mature it was able to articulate its views about the crisis in imperial relations. The population was sufficiently large, its educational heritage and apparatus developed enough, to ensure a wide diffusion of books and newspapers. The actual emergence of political parties might have been slow, but that was only to be expected in a colonial setting where, in addition, no national forum of debate yet existed.

But that the potential for such organizations already existed seems plain. Two grounds for this statement may be given. On the eve of the War of Independence the formation of Committees of Correspondence throughout North America was a swift and easy matter, and the success with which they called attention to British tyranny and co-ordinated anti-British feeling was testimony not only to the fact of antagonism but also to its effective dramatization. And secondly there had been the Zenger case. As far back as 1735 a printer, John Peter Zenger, had been acquitted of libel against the ruling class when the past experience would have led everyone to expect a guilty verdict. Older historical accounts interpreted this decision as establishing freedom of the press for Americans. But although there was after 1735 a greater willingness to print material critical of the authorities, censorship and control did in fact continue; as late as 1769 New York produced its Wilkes when the printer Alexander McDougall was jailed for three months for criticizing the colony's assembly. Even so the Zenger case remains a landmark, relevant more to the idea of free debate than to an actual freedom to publish. For it was in this trial that the principle that libel was a matter of fact and not a matter of law, to be ruled on not by the judge but by the jury, was first adumbrated. It seems, indeed, that the Zenger case was known to Lord Camden and that it influenced him when somewhat later he began to move English law in the same direction. Here was an early instance of how in some ways America was to move ahead of the parent society.

There is evidence that polarization was not confined to that between imperial authority and colonial society, but that it was also taking place within colonial society. Indeed this was what might have been expected, and certainly there were many colonists who believed in a natural law of emerging oligarchies. All societies, and especially those closer to traditional norms, have a tendency towards oligarchy as the élite tries to perpetuate its pre-eminence by finding ways of handing on power to relatives and friends. Since North American society in the second half of the eighteenth century was experiencing land hunger, and the denial of economic opportunity under a tightened-up Mercantilism, this tendency could only have been intensified. On *a priori* grounds, then, one could expect that the 'openness' of American society would be modified in the direction of the more normal stratification of the *ancien régime*. But where is the evidence to support this empirically?

There are studies to show that oligarchic control in the colonies was becoming stronger in the generations immediately before the Revolution. But a more interesting way of illuminating this dimension of American society is to examine one of the most striking phenomena of the day, one that is being re-examined at the moment from a new perspective and applied to the Revolution in a new way—the Great Awakening.

The beginnings of a dramatic series of religious revivals that continued to roll in waves over North American societies throughout the eighteenth century and on into the nineteenth, and of which Alline's movement in Nova Scotia was but an episode, were to be traced in the 1720s, though an effective start was not made until the 1730s. A key figure was Jonathan Edwards, a Harvard-trained minister who from his church at Northampton, Massachusetts, began his revival in 1734. His importance was not merely in his preaching ability, in which anyway he was surpassed by others, but rather in his great learning and insight, which he communicated to his readers and to subsequent leaders, so that many in the revival may be termed Edwardians. The second great initiator was George Whitefield, the one-time fellow-worker with the Wesleys. In all Whitefield made seven trips to the New World, that of 1740 being the most impressive. His outstanding oratory gave to the revival an impetus that ensured its wider spread. Together, and backed by a host of lesser revivalist preachers, their call for a New Birth in religion was so effective that the decline in religious involvement was arrested, and so much interest whipped up that the existing institutions could not stand the strain. The Congregationalists split into the New Lights, who stressed the new illumination of Christ's teaching that they had experienced as a result of being reborn spiritually, and the Old Lights, who stuck by the quieter ways of pre-Awakening times. The Presbyterians similarly divided, the New Side confronting the Old Side. Other denominations were affected, too, if not quite so dramatically.

The conversion techniques of Whitefield and his kind, the demand for a 'converted' ministry where evidence existed of the preacher's rebirth, the insistence upon a *renewed* Christian life, the tendency to splitting, all make clear what was happening. Here was a reassertion of the sectarian side of Calvinism. It will be appreciated why it was the Congregationalists and the Presbyterians who were hardest hit. Those denominations were hybrids, something between true churches and true sects. Remember that Presbyterianism had been the church in Scotland, but merely a sect in America, while Congregationalism had begun as a sect in England but by right of 'prior discovery and occupation' had established itself as a church in much of New England. Now under stress as part of a society in transition, this hybrid was breaking apart. The sequel to the Great Awakening showed this clearly enough. As the implications became clearer there took place a realignment of allegiances. Those who owned to the sectarian leanings tended to slip away to those denominations where theology was played down but where sectarian tone predominated, and so in the aftermath the Baptists and Methodists were the gainers. At the other end of the spectrum were those who, disapproving of the sectarian enthusiasm, moved over in other directions; some joined the Unitarians, that most unenthusiastic branch of Dissent that repudiates anything so mysterious, so magical, so unreasonable as the Trinity and that, worshipping God alone, denies Christ any divine attributes; others opted for a church, and joined the Anglicans, and it was this accession in their numbers that gave point to Calvinist fears about a North American bishop.

Society's polarization was reflected in religious developments, then.

Not surprisingly, the sectarian 'outs' were to be found in the newer rural areas, and in the towns among the lower orders. And in the words of Alan Heimert, who has done some of the most interesting work on the significance of the Great Awakening, these sectarians elaborated a 'critique of the business ethic which remained at bottom a lament for society's departure from its pristine natural equality'.

The Great Awakening may be used, then, to draw attention to a change in the social climate of colonial America. But two further points may usefully be made about it. To begin with, this manifestation of sectarianism may be compared with others, say with the contemporaneous one of Methodism. The astonishing thing about this American sectarianism is the very pronounced way in which it was in tune with the new ideas of the time. Earlier in the introductory section it was stated that there are often progressive implications in sectarian movements, even if these are overlain by more backward-looking elements, or, as in the case of the Methodists, by a reactionary, Tory streak. But here was much more than implication. On so many points the revivalists were centrally in the Enlightenment tradition, so that alongside the enthusiasm so deprecated by Locke and especially by the continental Deists went a pattern of thinking that those *philosophes* could not but have agreed with. Spokesmen like Edwards were open to the latest ideas in science and technology, and were especially keen on the coming science of chemistry. Their thinking was inductive and their religion experimental; how often did they insist that the fact of rebirth was something to experience, and see in practice; how often did they urge that the consequence of rebirth was not a private matter but public, not contemplation but doing good? A forward-looking orientation was strong, for as Edwards himself wrote, 'There is need we should forget the things that are behind, and be reaching for the things that are before.' Nowhere was the modernity of the Great Awakening more clearly seen than in its attitude to man's position in society, a tremendous contrast to what in the opening section was referred to as 'the fragmentation of totality' that is most pronounced in the feudal, Catholic scheme of things but that tends to persist in any structured institution, even in the Old Side Calvinisms. Heimert nicely contrasts the outlook of the 'legal' preachers, that is, the more traditional and staid, whether Anglican or Old Side Calvinist, with the outlook of the evangelical enthusiasts. He writes, 'The duties which such "legal" preachers urged Americans to perform were appropriate only to the more static society of the previous century. Evangelical religion divested Americans of this quasi-feudal intellectual heritage by defining virtue not as a variety of deportments that differed from class to class and calling to calling but as a "temper" essentially the same for all men, regardless of station. The new Calvinism thus made it possible for an individual to cope with the ethical problems inherent in an expanding economy and a mobile society.' The thrust, then, of Great Awakening preaching was not to detail the content of virtue appropriate to any particular social rank, but to describe an approach that could be applied to any of the changing roles that a fluid society called upon its members to fill.

Thus the Great Awakening was an odd imposition of Enlightenment style upon enthusiasm. And the resulting tension may be noted, for it is one that will be met with again; on the one hand there is a backward longing for a departed golden age, yet on the other a forward-looking search for a new adjustment.

The second interest of the Great Awakening for the purpose of this study is its relationship with the Revolution, and through that, with the evolution of the new nation. The initial effect of the revival was to disrupt the existing loyalties of colonial society. Until the Great Awakening loyalties had been intensely local; even in 1754 the Albany Conference proposals for a union of some kind between the British colonies in North America had been wrecked on the rocks of local particularism and mutual jealousy. Part of the reason for this was that individual colonies and their religions had been very closely bound together, each set off against the others. But with the revival, and with the readjustment of religious adherences, more and more did this particularism break down; more and more did Calvinists see themselves as part of a grander union. And since in their sermons their preachers developed the notion of America as the promised land, contrasting it overtly with decadent Europe, they also by implication developed the notion of America contrasted with the separate colonies. A *national* emphasis pervaded their thinking, and paved the way for a national political consciousness. The stress on brotherly love that was a hallmark of sectarian style was particularly potent in spreading the idea of unity.

Once having formed larger loyalties, this manifestation of sectarianism went on to prepare the way for revolutionary activity. The anti-rich sentiments inseparable from sectarianism were well to the fore, and could be channelled against the un-Awakened Calvinists, the Anglicans, and eventually against the imperial authority itself. In a more constitutional way this impulse emerged as a demand for liberty. These sectarians were opposed not only to hierarchical Anglicans but also to the more established kinds of Calvinism. Like any other new-comers they were at a disadvantage against entrenched privilege; consequently they raised a cry for more freedom so that all denominations could compete equally. A plea for disestablishment eventually widened to become a generalized claim for, quite simply, liberty. And once again it was easy to direct this claim against the imperial authority. Then, too, there was the fact that this sectarianism, like others, dwelt on the coming millennium, which could not be too far off. It would arrive after some apocalyptic clash with evil, and given the prevailing thinking in the colonies this was for many a confrontation with the British. It was significant that when the Stamp Act was passed New Light mobs in Connecticut were at the forefront of the physical destruction of the stamps, and that their clergy were sympathetic to such activity; and that again in 1774 they mobilized at the news of the Quebec Act. The climax came in the same year that Boston's port was closed, when the revivalist disciple of Edwards, Joseph Bellamy, headed a New Light host ready to march to the defence of Boston against Anti-Christ in the person of the British admiral.

Having examined such evidence Heimert is convinced that 'the uprising of the 1770s was not so much the result of reasoned thought as an emotional outburst similar to a religious revival'. But exactly what Heimert is saying should be carefully noted. He writes of 'the uprising of the 1770s', an awkward phrase when one would have expected the more normal 'American Revolution'. But the more awkward had to be used, for it draws attention to the fact that an emotional outburst was responsible for the motive power of revolution, the drive that brought people to the point of resistance to authority and eventually to the clash of arms. It says nothing about the revolution when considered as a completed, successful movement, giving birth to ideas and institutions that governed the evolution of a new society. That there is nothing incompatible between emotional motivation and reasoned conclusion should be evident from what has been said of the Great Awakening itself. It was perfectly possible for revivalist preachers, fanatics to their opponents, to hold to many of the Enlightenment norms; after all enthusiasm is a term that has reference to psychological style, whereas Enlightenment norms have reference to intellectual content. Thus when the froth of war had settled there was no insuperable difficulty in allowing an instinctively Enlightenment solution to emerge.

Yet at the same time the revision that Heimert has offered is most suggestive. In 1835 the French observer De Tocqueville published his classic *Democracy in America* and drew attention to the potential danger of a mass democratic society, unchecked by any independent institutions within it, where public opinion could emerge as the worst tyranny of all. This observation has been repeated at intervals since then, and today is expressed in the oft-heard claim that American society is one of the most conformist in the world. And it finds an echo in Palmer's book, where he notes that the American Revolution was much more intolerant towards its victims than even the French Revolution was; his argument is not convincing, and the comparison may not stand up, but that he makes the point at all is a salutary reminder of an aspect of the War of Independence too often glossed over. And that aspect may be judged by considering the fate of the British Loyalists, as will be done shortly. This streak has to be explained, and Heimert offers an explanation that reinforces earlier thinking in the same general direction.

In the opening section reference was made to Acton's conclusion about Calvinist thinking on deviance. Reference was also made to the fact that in that religion there was a tendency to a self-righteous, intolerant attitude towards others. Heimert notes that during the Great Awakening this conception of righteousness was re-emphasized, and also given a twist by taking the decisions on godliness out of the hands of the ministers, the élite, and giving them over increasingly to the congregations at large, the people. There emerged a view of society where 'men . . . should act as their brothers' keepers'. Thus if Calvinist thinking was largely responsible for the uprisings of the 1770s, it was also responsible for building into the American style at a crucial, formative period a leaning towards intolerant mass conformity, and for intensifying a tradition that will be traced out in the pages that follow.

Upheaval, then, had been the common experience of the North Atlantic communities from about 1750 onwards. In all this there had been no guiding hand, no uniformity of manifestation. But a trend to what Palmer calls the democratic revolution does seem to be discernible. It was weakest in Quebec, and almost as faint in the Maritimes, and given the extreme colonial dependence of these societies and their lack of a political tradition, this was only to be expected. In Ireland, where colonial status had been imposed on an already existing national identity, the trend was appreciably stronger. In Britain it was pronounced. Strongest of all, however, were the manifestations in the British North American colonies that were to become the United States of America. That this was so is doubly interesting. These societies were colonial and so might have been expected to come somewhere further back along the spectrum, say between the Maritimes and Ireland. That they did not underlines the fact that these societies were colonial only in a formal sense. Their size, population, developed economies, above all their intellectual maturity marked them as ready for a superior status. Indeed resentment against being considered colonial seems to have been a powerful concomitant of the sense of nationalism developed by the Great Awakening and a potent reinforcement of the readiness to risk rebellion.

The second interest lies in the nature of the democratic revolution in America and in Britain. In America the upheaval was due to the fact that there the norm was democratic openness and that increasing oligarchic control, both within society and from without, was resisted as an interference with the natural order of things. This pattern had a lasting effect on the outlook of the American people, helping to form an instinctive distrust of authority as such. In Britain, on the other hand, the norm was oligarchy, and the rising wave of democracy had to struggle against it for recognition. There was, then, no such readiness to look upon authority as such as evil. Rather the aim was to capture, or at least to infiltrate, that authority and thus be in a position to use it positively for good. This basic difference will crop up throughout what follows.

✻ ✻ ✻

The democratic revolution was never more than a trend, so that even when it was in full spate there were instances of oligarchic challenge. By the 1780s there were signs that the challenge was beginning to prevail. This swing of the pendulum was first to be noted in Britain.

There in the early eighties the promise of reform proved unsubstantial. It is true that in April 1780 Mr Dunning successfully moved a resolution in the Commons to the effect that 'the influence of the crown has increased, is increasing, and ought to be diminished'. It is true that a group of Whigs, especially Edmund Burke, followed up this anti-executive sentiment two years later with a series of Acts, together known as Economical Reform, that cut down the patronage at the disposal of the crown and so gave some teeth to Dunning's resolution. But the impetus to reform had already weakened and was on the point of disappearing. The immediate cause of the backlash, and which was responsible for making the County Association movement such a nine days' wonder, was the outbreak in June 1780 of the Gordon Riots, a week of destruction for London that began as an anti-Catholic crusade but that soon became an indiscriminate looting of the city. But another cause was the American situation, which by 1780 was already a lost one to many people; moreover since 1778 France had gone to war with Britain on behalf of the United States, and Britain was isolated against Europe. While some were eager to use the defeats by America as reasons for change at home, many were on the contrary led to believe that this was not the occasion for any tampering with the constitution. Thus when in 1785 the new Prime Minister, William Pitt the Younger, found that his modest proposals for the reform of parliament met stiff resistance in the Commons, he backed away from the task and showed no especial eagerness to take it up again; as it turned out, and as will be explained, developments were to ensure that reform would not be seriously considered for another half century. But perhaps the most significant development of the eighties and the best indication of a change was the attitude of the London merchants. This class of men, of tremendous power in the eighteenth century as the controllers of the capital city of the leading power, had traditionally been at odds with government—any government, it did not matter which; after all, Whig ministries in the eighteenth century, for all their countenancing of trade, were still too aristocratic, too landed, to be sympathetic to the traders. But in the eighties this inveterate hostility was replaced by a novel compatibility between government and merchants, an accommodation that owed much to Pitt's deliberate courting of these interests.

This new-found oligarchic confidence was to be seen in the new attitude shown towards the remaining North American colonies. Some readjustment would clearly have been required in the wake of the loss of thirteen colonies, the most economically developed of them all. But there was an additional reason for coming to grips with the problem. Not all the inhabitants of what was now the United States of America had been enthusiasts for the Revolution. As in most such convulsions, the majority had had no strong feelings. Indeed so lacking in unanimity was the colonial reaction that there was a sizeable minority that looked for a British victory. As the war drew to its close in 1782–83 there were many opposed to Independence who had so compromised themselves that they could not, would not, remain behind in the new country. Some 100,000 chose to emigrate. Of these some went to Britain, some to the West Indies, and eventually some trickled back to the United States. But perhaps some 40,000 emigrated to British North America, and it soon became evident that their coming would call for changes to accommodate them.

But these migrants, the United Empire Loyalists of Canadian and imperial history, are important not only for their impact upon colonial arrangements. They had an influence upon the evolution of Canada in a deeper sense, for they were an important formative stock, even claiming to be the founders of British Canada; after all, the total British stock of British North America before their arrival was well short of 40,000. So imposing, in fact, has the position of the Loyalists become that recent scholarship has had to be devoted to revising their myth. Who, then, were the Loyalists, and what values did they impart to the new societies?

The Loyalists were not particularly aristocratic, a leaning one might have expected in those attached to the crown. High-born and wealthy families were to be found among them, it is true, but they were a small minority. For it seems that of the Loyalist emigrants the wealthier and better connected preferred to make for Britain or the long-settled and sophisticated West Indies, and that only the relatively lowly chose to move into British North America. Thus the lists of Loyalists coming north include large numbers of farmers, shopkeepers, craftsmen, and so on. Nor were they, as might have been expected from the affinity of crown for mitre, overwhelmingly Anglicans. All manner of Dissenters were included, and Quakers and other pacifists who had not supported the Revolution were also present. All in all the Loyalists were a mixed group where no one stratum or religion stood out.

Yet this is not to say that there was no common pattern. Loyalists tended to come from areas that were relatively backward and in fear of dominant neighbours, dominant both economically and socially. Thus the 'Regulators' of North Carolina, an association of backwood farmers who since 1768 had been struggling with the established seaboard interests and had to be put down in pitched battle in 1771, became Loyalist in the Revolution. Similarly with religious groups; Dissenters in Anglican Virginia tended to Loyalism, whereas in Puritan New England it was the Anglican who became the Loyalist. Ethnic minorities tended to look to the British crown, perhaps for protection against what they sensed was the uniformity demanded by Revolution. Loyalists were local minorities, and as such were fearful of change. As a leading historian of these people has put it, 'One feature all American Loyalists had in common was that they preferred the known ways to the unknown.'

Did the Loyalists bring with them an ideology? Did they represent, within this context of oligarchic-democratic polarization, a principled attachment to an older political philosophy in opposition to the Revolutionists' more up-to-date practices? There have been those to think so. It has been noted that some Loyalist spokesmen were prepared to go back beyond Locke for their ideas. Charles Inglis, for instance, the Loyalist who became the first Anglican bishop of Nova Scotia and incidentally the first colonial Anglican bishop ever, found his justification in Hooker, the Anglican divine who died in 1600 and whose ideas were pre-Lockean and indeed still medieval; another Loyalist, Jonathan Boucher, went so far as to resurrect Filmer. But while this might have been true of a few intellectuals, the mass of Loyalists seem to have differed in no significant way from the Americans they left behind. As much evidence can be produced that they supported Locke as that they repudiated him. But the test would seem to be the reaction of those who went back to Britain, and there experienced a society that despite modernization was still very medieval in tone. By and large these Loyalists felt ill at ease, and obliged to face the fact that after all they were American.

Yet the fact that the Loyalists in Canada did not bring with them an ideology that marked them off as un-American did not mean that they could not develop one. They had been expelled from their home, which was now a republic, and so did not wish to call themselves Americans; never having come face to face with the real British society they were not forced to come to terms with their own Americanness. They were in danger of succumbing to an identity crisis, which, however, they avoided by stressing their Britishness and their loyalty to the crown; the tie with the imperial authority began to be emphasized, so initiating a tradition that was to last all through the nineteenth century and on into the twentieth. In this way their tendency to paternalism was grafted on to the paternalistic treatment of the French that already existed in British North America. And it was further reinforced when the British authorities provided provisions to the Loyalists to get them through the first cruel years, and also compensated the Loyalists for their losses. The American term for Loyalist is Tory; as things turned out it became a meaningful one.

The reader may be wondering why it was necessary to deny that the Loyalists brought their Toryism with them, and to insist that it was developed in their Canadian exile. In a certain context the distinction is crucial, however. For any intellectual baggage brought from the States meant a loss of that baggage from the States. Thus to say that the Loyalists took their ideology with them is to suggest that the Americans expelled that ideology along with them. But the argument presented here is that the Americans, far from expelling Toryism, did not have any, and that those who left were essentially the same as those who remained. This reading of the situation will be seen to be vital when theories of development are discussed in the last chapter.

Having now said something about the Loyalist style, their impact on existing institutions and balances may be described. The vast bulk of this 40,000 went by boat, mainly from New York and Boston, directly to Nova Scotia. Most of this migration of more than 30,000 settled in the area about Saint John. There, conscious of their identity, suspicious of the original Nova Scotians whose loyalty in the late war had been decidedly questionable, dissatisfied with the competence of the governor, they petitioned the imperial authorities to have a new colony created for them. This was agreed to, and the colony of New Brunswick came into existence in 1784.

There was good reason for this, in that with poor communication between Saint John and Halifax there would have been difficulty administering the new area from the old capital. But there was another reason for the decision. The British government was convinced that a policy of 'divide and rule' would increase the ease of controlling British North America and of avoiding for as long as possible any such development as had just taken place in the thirteen colonies. Further evidence of this policy may be seen in the Maritime region. It was decided that Prince Edward Island would continue to enjoy its independent status, despite its failure to grow significantly. But in addition Cape Breton, which was so tiny that an assembly could not be justified and which had to function under a governor and council, was separated from Nova Scotia to become another colony, a status that it retained until 1820 when it was once again merged with Nova Scotia.

It was essentially the same in Quebec. Here there was the additional problem that the influx of some 7,000 Loyalists, mainly English-speaking and used to English-type institutions, reinforced the existing demand for an end to French law. Over the next several years there was to be a continuing migration of land-hungry farmers from the United States into Canada. These people are referred to as 'Late Loyalists'. But they assimilated to the genuine Loyalists, and their impact was essentially the same as the latters'. A leading Loyalist who became Chief Justice of Quebec, William Smith, added fuel to the fire by his determination to question the post-1774 régime. His legal decisions, such as permitting English methods to operate in civil law cases where both the parties were non-French, cut the ground from under the Quebec Act. Eventually in 1791 the British Parliament passed the Constitutional Act. The old colony was split into a French-dominated Lower

Canada, the St Lawrence up to and including Montreal, and an English-dominated Upper Canada, the region westward and about Lake Ontario in particular. In the former, the French civil law and land-holding systems were maintained, with the provision that future land grants could be freehold; this last was recognition of the fact that Vermonters were slipping across the border and settling the Eastern Townships, and that given their Anglo-American heritage they would find seigneurial land-holding a grievance that might, at some future date, become the occasion for trouble and an appeal for help back across the boundary. In Upper Canada English civil law and freehold were to be the norm.

Common to both reconstituted colonies, however, was a new institutional framework. The principle on which it rested was made explicit by the minister responsible for the act, William Grenville, cousin and friend of the Prime Minister, Pitt. Grenville acknowledged that his scheme was 'to assimilate the Constitutions of that Province to that of Great Britain'. And by this he meant that he would avoid the systems of the old empire whose main defect and the one responsible for the urge to Independence was that 'the Aristocratical part of [their] Constitution was but ill supplied'. Thus in the Canadas the upper houses, the Legislative Councils, were built up in authority and prestige. To approximate them as closely as possible to the House of Lords, their members would be appointed for life, and provision was made, though it was never used, for the establishment of an hereditary class from which to staff this Council. There were, also, to be Executive Councils, advisory bodies but again selected by the governor and responsible to him alone. Finally, there would be an assembly. This was necessary since the cost of maintaining the colonies, a charge that fell overwhelmingly on Britain, was proving excessive, and it was intended that increasingly the colonies contribute to their own support; and since Britain in 1778, as part of a belated attempt to conciliate the rebellious Americans, had promised never again to tax a people, the only way of raising a revenue was to institute an assembly. It was hoped that the monarchical and aristocratic elements had been so built up that there would be no danger from an assembly. But as a further safeguard against popular forces, two kinds of land reserves were created; a crown reserve of one seventh of the land was to be set aside, the proceeds from which were to provide a civil list for the executive and so lessen its dependence upon the assembly; and a clergy reserve, again of one seventh of the land, was set apart for the benefit of the Protestant Church, a form of words that was to cause trouble since it was claimed by Anglicans to refer to them alone but by the Presbyterians and Methodists, who were becoming increasingly strong with the heavy British migration after 1815, to include them as well. But either way, the import was the same; religion, a check to too much democracy, was to be given state aid, a provision in stark contrast to that just a few miles to the south where the complete divorce of church and state had just been insisted upon.

But it must not be thought that in the newly independent United States of America there was unambiguous democracy; the same broad swing towards the other end of the spectrum was taking place there, too. Indeed, given the nature of Independence, it was a most pronounced swing.

The break from British allegiance had been announced in July 1776 in the Declaration of Independence, largely the composition of Thomas Jefferson. There, fused together in a classically eloquent statement that has guaranteed its ability to mould opinion across the generations, were two very different appeals; the first was to British principles, to the right of a people to resist a tyrannous king, and, in the manner of the Bill of Rights of 1689, his actual infringements of their liberties were listed; the second was to the more abstract rights of man in the tradition of the Enlightenment. Together they amounted to a trenchant assertion of the democratic impulse, a summing up of the polarization that had taken place in imperial relations.

But this polarization, remember, had been accompanied by another within colonial society. Independence would, by itself, have demanded new state constitutions. There was, however, an additional reason for the urge to rewrite the colonial charters. While Britain had exercised authority she had managed, more or less successfully, to control the social tensions within the different colonies. Now that that restraining hand had been removed, these tensions flared forth with a new virulence, and the opportunity was taken to reorder social as well as imperial relationships. Of course there were differences in the new constitutions from state to state, from those of Connecticut and Rhode Island, the two corporate colonies already so republican that only minor changes were felt necessary, to that of Pennsylvania, where there had long been tensions between the established areas and the newer, western regions peopled overwhelmingly by recent Scots-Irish immigrants and where the revolution in the constitution was most striking. Even so, there were trends in common.

In general the assemblies, the democratic element in the constitution, gained at the expense of the governors and the upper houses. Indeed in some instances the rise of the assembly was very marked. In Pennsylvania, for instance, the governor, thought to be too much of a monarchical figure and a potential tyrant, was replaced by a board of twelve popularly elected commissioners, and the upper chamber was entirely swept away since it was felt that the people could be adequately served by the assembly. If other states did not go this far, they took care to limit the executive's veto, at least, and to strengthen the people's representation by widening the suffrage (though some went the other way on this point), increasing the number of representatives, and holding annual elections.

Constitutional change was accompanied by social change. The land laws of British America favoured freehold, but there were here and there relics of an older, more feudal system. Quit rents were an example. These were payments, often small and often not collected or collectable but nevertheless legally payable, that were attached to some lands and were intended to help defray the costs of administration. At the Revolution the tendency was to sweep away even these light encumbrances in favour of an even more outright ownership of the land. Entail was another feudal reminder. This was the legal device whereby land could be so tied up that the owner became in effect the user only, entitled to a life's interest in the profits of the land but obliged to hand the estate itself on undiminished to his heir; in turn, the heir would be restricted in his control of the estate, and so on through the generations. It was a system designed more for the family than for the individual, and one that preferred certain, traditional profits over possible, greater ones. It too was abolished in favour of the free disposition of land more in tune with the improving, speculating climate of the colonies. Primogeniture was yet another legal system abolished in most areas at this time, the law that gave the eldest son the inheritance ahead of his brothers and sisters and that was more in tune with feudal, hierarchical, and static notions than the times called for. And in addition to these property reforms, there was the disestablishment of the churches. It did not take place all at once, and Massachusetts had an established Congregationalism until 1833, but there was a crucial change in thinking on this point best exemplified in Jefferson's *Statute for Religious Liberty* passed in Virginia in 1786, which enacted 'that no man shall be compelled to frequent or support any religious worship, place or ministry whatsoever'. Taken together these changes, even if often only symbolic, indicate a fruition of the elements of modernity—openness, pluralism, democracy—that had been implicit in the colonial experience.

The same impulse that gave rise to the Declaration of Independence and to the rewriting of the state constitutions was responsible for the character of the Articles of Confederation. To co-ordinate the war effort it was clear that some federation of the colonies would be necessary; but it was a minimal union that was finally ratified in 1781, though work on these Articles had begun mid-way through 1776. There was no intention on the part of the states to give up any of their sovereignty. All decisions were to be unanimous, for instance. There was no common executive, and the central authority was denied any taxing power, or the right to levy troops, or the ability to establish national courts. There were those who expected the Articles of Confederation to lapse with the conclusion of peace in 1783, and in many ways they might just as well have done so. It was a standing grievance with the Loyalists that they could never get any satisfaction from the states for their claims, although this had been included in the peace treaty, and the national authority could do nothing but point to its lack of sanctions against the individual states as a reason for not taking action. Now the significance of this minimal union must be seen against the common presupposition of the eighteenth century about forms of government. It was axiomatic that only small, homogeneous states could be democratic, and that as soon as they grew bigger and their social composition became more complex there was a need for more aristocratic, even monarchical, systems. Any proposals for a more centralized union, and there were such proposals in 1776, were seen as examples of what monarchical Britain herself had been attempting since 1763, and were viewed with horror.

But as the eighties progressed, more and more dissatisfaction began to be shown towards the system of government and the functioning of society. Increasingly people began to feel that the balance had tipped too much in the democratic direction. Benjamin Franklin noted that 'We have been guarding against an evil that old States are most liable to excess of power in the rulers, but our present danger seems to be defect of obedience in the subjects'. The facts seem to bear him out. A breakdown in law and order characterized too much of American society, and the rebellion led by Daniel Shays in Western Massachusetts 1786–7 was only the most dramatic episode in a continuing series of lawlessness. There was a growing feeling that the state constitutions would have to be revised, as happened in Pennsylvania in 1790. But the most promising method, it was thought, of saving the Revolution and especially of rebuilding American standing in the eyes of Europe lay in reforming the Articles of Confederation and erecting an effective government that could control the situation in a way that the states obviously could not.

A meeting with this end in view at Annapolis in 1786 failed when only five of the states attended. But the following year at Philadelphia all but Rhode Island sent delegations and the work was begun that finally issued as the Constitution of the United States of America. Opinion on the revision was sharply divided between those who wanted to move in the direction of aristocracy—a group known as the Federalists, which had for a mouthpiece the essays of that name composed by James Madison, John Jay, and above all by Alexander Hamilton—and those who stuck by the democratic spirit of 1776 and were basically content with the Articles of Confederation, and who were known as the Antifederalists. After the debate was over, and the Constitution ratified in 1789, it was clear that the Federalists had carried through a revolution.

To begin with, in contrast to the earlier confidence in democracy that had given increased powers to the assemblies, the Constitution marked a return to the more orthodox eighteenth-century doctrine of the separation of powers. The legislature was to be balanced and checked by the executive and judiciary. The President was to be given great executive power. It was he who was to select his ministers, judges, and ambassadors (though subject to ratification by the Senate); he was to be commander-in-chief of the armed forces; he was to be given the treaty-making powers (though again subject to ratification by the Senate); the veto was restored to him (though it could be overridden by a two-thirds majority of the legislature). But the swing of the pendulum was indicated not only by this extensive return of powers to the chief executive officer but also by the way in which the presidential office was hedged about. Care was taken that the popular forces should be kept a suitable distance from the Presidency. Election was not to be direct, but through a college of electors, and in the early days of the Constitution many of these were elected by the state legislatures. Although a four-year term was set, there was nothing to prevent the successive elections of the same person, and so was dropped the idea of rotation in office, one of the eighteenth century's favourite devices for preventing the emergence of the 'elected king'. And while the impeachment of the President was permitted, the machinery was such that it is almost impossible; only one attempt has ever been made, and that failed. The federal judiciary was also made strong and buttressed against democratic clamour. The judges were to hold their commissions, as in England, 'during good behaviour', which meant in effect for life; they had recovered the independence denied their state colleagues by so many state legislatures.

The structure of the legislature, Congress, was in line with this swing away from democracy. The lower house, the House of Representatives, was to contain the representatives of the states, and these representatives were to be proportional to the population; this was an arrangement that pleased the large states and Virginia in particular. These representatives were to have a two-year term, and all were to be elected at the same time; in this way the House, the democratic element, would always be in close touch with popular sentiments. The upper house, the Senate, was to consist of two members from each state, a provision that made possible a compromise between the large and the small states. The senators were intended to act as a check on the popular House, and accordingly the mechanism of their election was very different from that of the representatives. They were not to be elected directly by the people, but by the state legislatures; in this way a screening process similar to the Presidential Electoral College was set up. Senators were to sit for six years, making them less dependent on the whim of fickle public opinion, and moreover only one third were to retire at any one time; in this way the Senate would never become the new, inexperienced body that the House so often could become. All in all, then, the Constitution was the work, as Richard Hofstadter has written, of men who 'had a vivid Calvinistic sense of human evil and damnation . . . [who] did not believe in man, but . . . did believe in the power of a good political constitution to control him'.

So great, in fact, had been the swing of the pendulum that, then as now, there were those who saw evil conspiracy at work to rob the people of their democratic gains. The circumstances surrounding the Philadelphia meeting, it could be claimed, were suspicious. Many of the leading radicals of the day were missing from the meetings; Jefferson, for instance, was in Paris as ambassador to France. Indeed so changed was the country's leadership in the dozen or so years since Independence that only six signatures were common both to the Declaration and to the Constitution. The deliberations in Philadelphia were held in secret and the details of what was said did not leak out for many years afterwards. Then it must be remembered that the meeting had been called to amend the Articles, yet the final product could not be called an amendment by any stretch of the imagination. Any change should have been unanimously agreed to, but it was agreed that nine out of thirteen would be sufficient. Any change should have been ratified by the states via their legislatures, but the Constitution was ratified by the people at large. These last points have encouraged some to brand the proceedings as illegal, and to press on to a very conscious formulation of the conspiracy theory.

In its most developed form this conspiracy theory was the work of Charles Beard, whose *An Economic Interpretation of the Constitution* appeared in 1913, and of his disciples, notably Merrill Jensen, whose *The Articles of Confederation* was published in 1940. This school will draw attention to the fact that there existed a class of rich people who were not happy with the way American society was developing under the Articles. Some wished to develop industries, which in the face of competition from established societies, especially Britain, meant a need for a protective tariff. The Articles of Confederation did not give the central authority power to raise a tariff wall about the thirteen colonies, however. The army officers were another group that inclined against the Articles, since while they were in force it had not been possible to pay the officers on the conclusion of hostilities with the bounties that they had been led to expect. Nor did the Articles contain any mechanism to prevent the states, which by and large were under the control of popular agrarian forces, from passing legislation that favoured debtor as against creditor classes. The expanding state societies (and the population rise in the eighties was perhaps proportionately the greatest in any decade in American history), still debt-ridden from the war, were in need of greatly increased credit. They were accordingly favourably inclined to the issue of paper money to supplement the more normal gold and silver. But the tendency for paper money to lose its value was much more pronounced than that of hard money, and the situation was one of rampant inflation. This of course benefitted the large number of farmers whose recently acquired farms carried heavy mortgages and embarrassing taxes; with money losing its value the fixed mortgage and tax payments became lighter every time. But equally this state of affairs penalized creditors, who found that their profits from interest were being wiped out. Some states even went so far as to interfere with existing contracts, modifying them in favour of the debtor classes. Shays's rebellion grew out of this environment, in fact, for in the mid-1780s Massachusetts, at last moving to halt the emission of paper and return to hard money, caused farm payments to shoot up overnight, and so provoked resistance. Finally the Beard school will make much of the inability, under the Articles, to settle the war debt. To pay for the Revolutionary war great amounts of paper money had been issued, which had lost value as its redemption became more and more remote. Much of this depreciated paper, argued Beard, had been acquired by a speculative class. Now if the new central government would agree to assume the old debts, and agree moreover to redeem the old promises at par, then these speculators would make a tremendous windfall profit. It was Beard's contention that over fifty per cent of the delegates at Philadelphia held war paper, and that their work for a new Constitution was in great part motivated by a self-seeking desire to enrich themselves. Today there are few to accept such an interpretation; the criticisms of R.E. Brown in *Charles Beard and the Constitution* (1956) and of Forrest McDonald in *We the People: The Economic Origins of the Constitution* (1958) have been too devastating. But the popularity of that thesis was testimony in part to the completeness of the revolution between 1776 and 1789.

Already in the eighties, then, the earlier democratic tendencies throughout the North Atlantic communities had been checked, and the swing towards aristocracy begun. The nineties were to see this tendency intensified. For then there took place the shock of the French Revolution. In 1789 the economic collapse of France, which had overextended itself in backing the American colonists against Britain, led to the calling of the Estates General for the first time since 1614. As in England in 1640 this was to open the floodgates of pent-up criticism. It was also to release the energies of new ideas and of new classes of men, which had been germinating within the confines of the *ancien régime*. Absolutism was swept away, and an uncertain constitutional monarchy took its place. Quickly the restraint and solidarity of the first days broke down. The anti-clericalism that had been so much a part of the French critical tradition blossomed, the Catholic Church was despoiled, and the Worship of the Supreme Being was instituted to take its place. The King attempted to flee from a situation that was becoming intolerable, and to seek foreign aid for an absolutist restoration; he and the royal family were intercepted on the way to the border and returned to Paris. By this attempt monarchy had lost what respect still lingered on, and on the 10th August 1792 France became a republic. Meanwhile physical violence was increasing. The September massacres in Paris in 1792 prepared the way for the execution of the king in January 1793 and for the Reign of Terror later in the year when the guillotine was used as a method of government, striking such fear into Frenchmen as to force them to support the national war effort. For by this time France was ranged against almost the whole of Europe, a war in which Britain had become involved in February 1793. From this point until 1815, first against the Revolution and then from 1799 against Napoleon, the struggle was waged by Britain almost ceaselessly. The effect of such a long drawn out, desperate world war was, of course, calamitous and distorting. But at the same time the response to such abnormal strains did reveal in a stark way something of the essential characteristics of these societies.

In Britain the initial reaction to the Revolution was favourable. It was the common estimation that France was at last to enjoy the constitutional blessings that had been England's since 1688. After all, was not the Revolutionary slogan 'Liberty, Equality, Fraternity'; had not the feudal system been abolished; had not the Church been put in its place; had not the king agreed to share power with the nation? This estimate was particularly prevalent amongst the Dissenters, who just at this time were mounting their campaign for the repeal of the Test and Corporation Acts, and was to be seen in the Revolutionary Society, founded mainly by Dissenters in 1788 in honour of the centenary of the Glorious Revolution, or in the sermon the Dissenter Dr Richard Price preached in 1789 on the anniversary of Dutch William's landing in England. To support the Revolution in France new societies were founded. The existing Society for Constitutional Information received a new lease of life, and was joined in 1791 by the aristocratic Friends of the People. More significant perhaps was the appearance in the same year in Sheffield, an industrial centre dominated by the metal trades, of a radical society drawn not from the natural ruling class, not even from the middle class, but from the lower orders. Early in 1792 the same kind of organization was set up in London, where the shoemaker Hardy, drawing upon existing artisan organizations and using their system of weekly penny subscriptions, established the London Corresponding Society. In addition to co-ordinating activity with the provinces, the Society began the political education of the lower orders by disseminating tracts.

But already the French Revolution was beginning more to frighten than to attract. The earliest critic was the extraordinarily prescient Edmund Burke who, stung by Price's sermon, published the brilliantly prophetic *Reflections on the Revolution in France* in 1790. His criticism was very significant. For Burke had a fine record of supporting reform causes—witness his attack upon George III's use of patronage in 1782 —and in particular he had been in favour of the American cause. But in this case, some fifteen years later, he took what seemed to be a very different line. It was not that Burke was mellowing with age and losing his youthful radicalness. Rather he detected the fundamental difference between the two revolutions. That of the Americans was not truly a revolution; the colonists having come to maturity were ready to develop the existing British ways in directions suited to their own particular setting. In this, nothing was denied other than the imperial authority. But the French were seeking to deny their very being. Confronted by a situation that Burke agreed was intolerable and would have to be changed, they had refused to return to the traditions of French consti- tutionalism. Instead they had torn down the past, pretending to be able to start again from a *tabula rasa*; that they soon replaced the week by a more sensible unit of ten days, and reordered and renamed the entire calendar, that they swept aside a thousand-year development of the life of the provinces, Normandy, Brittany, Burgundy, and a host of others, and replaced them by the artificial, uniform, and colourlessly named modern *départements*, bore out what Burke had foreseen. Such attempts, he argued, were recklessly utopian; they were not true to the laws of *organic* development and so were bound to fail. It was a classic statement of the conservative case, the need for change by evolution rather than by revolution.

Even while on the intellectual plane attitudes towards the French Revolution were being revised, action on the more immediate, physical level was taking place. The mob was being turned against radicalism. The most notorious instance was in Birmingham where in 1791 the establishment inflamed the mob with the cry of 'Church and King' and set it to sacking the house of one of the leading Dissenters of the day, a friend of Price, Joseph Priestley. He himself was not harmed but his laboratory, instruments, and records of experiments that had given him a world-wide reputation in chemistry were destroyed, and almost immediately afterwards Priestley left England for America, where he died.

The declaration of war in 1793 naturally intensified these critical tendencies. The Whigs, traditional defenders of liberty, began to grow cool towards the Revolution. One by one their leading Parliamentarians crossed over to support the Prime Minister, Pitt, until finally their leader himself, the Duke of Portland, joined what was increasingly being seen as the patriotic party. And in Parliament the mood hardened against anything that smacked of change. A motion to reform the composition of Parliament, moved in 1797 by Charles Grey, later the second Earl Grey, was resoundingly defeated. Defeat was only to be expected, however, for long before this the government had embarked on a severely repressive policy. In 1794 habeas corpus was suspended, soon afterwards acts were passed to redefine treason, and to control meetings and the press; in 1799–1800 the Combination Acts were added to prevent workmen's agitation for higher wages and improved conditions. Trials of leading reformers were mounted, including Hardy, the artisan founder of the London Corresponding Society. Though the government failed to convict in England, it was much more successful in Scotland. There radical ideas were much more widespread and effective (perhaps the result of a Presbyterian environment, and especially of its stress upon literacy—certainly the average level of education in Scotland was much superior to that in England), and the determination of the judges to convict much stronger. Indeed the most notorious judge, Lord Braxfield, declared during one trial that 'Two things must be attended to that require no proof. First, that the British Constitution is the best that ever was since the creation of the world and [second] it is not possible to make it better'. The result was a collision that was savage indeed. At least one hanging took place, and several people were ordered transported to Australia, a sentence in many cases equivalent to death. In all this the reality of an armed rising against the state was non-existent; even so, the aristocratic revival had been transformed into a panicky conservative reaction.

The situation was much the same in Ireland, though there the results were much more tragic. Even while the condition of the country was improving under Grattan's Parliament, views critical of the position of Ireland were developing. On the one hand the imperial authorities, and especially the Prime Minister, Pitt, were beginning to wonder if the quasi-independence of Ireland was not too great a threat to the security of the empire. After all the Anglo-Irish relationship was one of shared sovereignty, a foreshadowing of Commonwealth developments that would not mature until much, much later, and anomalous in the eighteenth century with the stress upon the strong state. On the other hand there were sections of Irish society that felt that the reforms of 1782 did not go far enough. Representative of this new wave was Wolfe Tone. His father had been a coach-builder and farmer, in other words the family was not a member of the natural ruling class, not even of the upper-middle class. And not only was Tone not a member of the natural parliamentary class, more significantly he did not choose to attach himself to a patron (as Burke had done in England, coming in on the coat-tails of the Marquis of Rockingham) in order to break into the charmed circle. Then too his attachment to deist and Enlightenment ideas set him further apart from such politicians as Grattan, and made him impatient with the Protestant-dominated parliamentarianism of 1782. Increasingly he gravitated towards a position hostile to the Ascendency and eventually to favouring republicanism. He took a leading part in the foundation, in 1791 in Belfast, of the Society of

United Irishmen with the aim of bringing together Catholics and Dissenters in order to defeat the Protestants and break free from the British connection.

The French Revolution reinforced both trends. The war situation renewed perennial fears that France would use disaffection in Ireland as a means of attacking Britain from the rear, and so the urge to bind Ireland more tightly to the empire became stronger. At the same time the United Irishmen saw the French Revolution as a crucial stage in the unfolding of democracy that had marked the last decades and that was destined for further advances. Their catechism, couched in symbolic language for the political education of initiates who were illiterate and traditionally minded, read in part as follows:

Q. What have you got in your hand?
A. A green bough.
Q. Where did it first grow?
A. In America.
Q. Where did it bud?
A. In France.
Q. Where are you going to plant it?
A. In the Crown of Great Britain.

And more practically they saw the chance of using Revolutionary dynamic and actual aid to carry through their own liberation. Tone himself went to France, by way of the United States, and encouraged the French to fit out an invasion force. But two attempts to land French troops and supplies in Ireland failed, the first in 1796 on account of bad weather, the second in 1797 when the invasion fleet was defeated at the battle of Camperdown. The preparations for a rising had gone too far, however, for it to be put off. In 1798, in scattered and ineffective engagements, the Irish rose against their rulers. The repression was complete and brutal, and despite a faint revolutionary echo in 1803 led by Robert Emmet, the Irish resistance was thoroughly broken. Tone himself was captured, and rather than be hanged as a traitor he committed suicide.

Yet the situation was too dangerous to be left like this. Pitt was determined that Ireland should be united with Britain. A massive campaign of bribery was undertaken in the Irish parliament to get the members to vote their own dissolution. This was carried through in 1800, Ireland being granted one hundred seats in the Commons and thirty-two representatives in the Lords at Westminster. Naturally this loss of identity, especially coming hard on the heels of recent gains and the destruction of the 'golden age', were bitter blows to Ireland and further poisoned Anglo-Irish relations.

But this was not all. As part of the deal for Union Pitt had let it be understood that acceptance of the Bill would mean the *quid pro quo* of full Catholic emancipation, that is votes for Catholics in Britain as well as in Ireland and the right of Catholics to sit in parliament. This was only an understanding, however, and was not a part of the Act of Union itself. In Britain and among the Irish Protestants resistance to this concession was intense, but the crucial negative came from George III, who could not bring himself to weaken the Protestant religion he had sworn to uphold in his Coronation Oath. His views having become known, Pitt dropped the proposal and resigned the Premiership. Here was additional ground for feeling betrayed by perfidious Britain.

Nor was this the only religious development of the time that boded ill for the future. Irish Catholic confidence was mounting on the eve of the Rising; had not Catholics in Ireland been given the vote in 1793? Indeed their new-found aggressiveness was frightening to the Protestants, and encouraged them in their turn to become aggressive. In 1795 a minor skirmish took place between the two forces, and in the aftermath the Irish Protestants founded the Orange Order, named for the House from which Dutch William came, an organization that was to have tremendous influence in the years to come. It was, it should be noted, not yet Presbyterian dominated, for the Dissenters were still anti-Protestant, so much so that their citadel, Belfast, today the capital of pro-British sentiment and loyalty to Westminster, was the leading rebel city in this period. But as the years passed and the identity of Irish nationalism and Catholicism became ever tighter, the Presbyterians increasingly dominated the Orange Order; today Presbyterian rather than Church of Ireland sentiments characterize the Order.

The colonial situation in British North America was not nearly so explosive; on the contrary the French Revolution and its associated wars had the effect of strengthening British control and of intensifying the aristocratic cast of mind. For British North America was too distant from the main European theatre of operations to make the situation as critical as it had been in Ireland. There was a minor scare in 1796 of French landings in the Maritimes, and two years later a United Irishmen rising there aborted. But these were minor. Indeed so booming were the colonial economies thanks to the war situation that there was not the resentment on which revolutionary appeals could fasten, so that by and large the British authorities could afford to leave these still tiny societies to their own devices.

What impact there was affected the Canadas. Lower Canada was evidently an area where the French might stand a good chance of embarrassing the British and even of recovering the colony. That memories of the old loyalties were not dead was indicated when some of the militia cried out 'Vivent les François'. An agent was recruited by the French, one Henri Mezière, a young man born in the colony in 1772 and schooled on *philosophe* writings. But such signs of disaffection never amounted to anything. Mezière was not particularly able and when he finally arrived in France was unable to convince the authorities to provide effective intervention in the colony's affairs. And without any firm leadership, either from France or from the United States, which still had not given up completely on 1775, the discontent of the *habitants* was fated to remain muted. And anyway the revolutionary tendencies were soon to be suffocated by a counter-revolutionary wave. One result of the French Revolution was the emigration of thousands who could not make their peace with the new order; many of these, of course, were Catholic priests. Some forty-five of these made their way to Lower Canada. Not only were they a welcome addition to an under-staffed clergy, not only were they a welcome infusion of talent into a deficient pastorate, they were also a tremendous reinforcement of the devout religiosity that had originally marked the colony. They and the existing hierarchy, of course, preached that the Revolution was the work of Anti-Christ, that France had succumbed to godless reason, and in so doing they intensified the existing anti-Enlightenment tradition in Lower Canada. French-Canadian links with France, never especially strong, were almost completely severed as, faced with a choice between religion and the motherland, the *habitants* chose religion.

In Upper Canada the impact of the French Revolution was tangential indeed. A major aspect of the war, especially in its Napoleonic phase, was the use of economic weapons to force a solution. Napoleon attempted to destroy Britain's ability to fight and to pay subsidies to her European allies by declaring the continent of Europe closed to British shipping—the so-called Continental System based on the Berlin Decrees—and followed this up by ordering that any shipping coming from British ports be confiscated. In retaliation Britain declared, by Orders in Council, that neutral shipping trading with the enemy was required to call at British ports and be licensed there by the authorities. The United States, like other neutral powers, was caught between the two systems; any of her ships trading with the Continent were liable to be seized by the British, unless they had called at a British port for a license, in which case they were liable to be seized by the French. In addition the

United States was antagonized by the claims of both countries to search neutral shipping. When this happened, Britain tended to claim many Americans as British and to impress them in the Royal Navy; France tended to make the same claim about nationality and to imprison them as enemies.

The United States smarted under this treatment, and after trying vain expedients to bring an end to such harassment, declared war upon Britain. The obvious target, and one with the added advantage of killing two birds with one stone by satisfying the expansionist sentiments of South and West, was Upper Canada, a colony almost totally devoid of troops and overwhelmingly peopled by recent American arrivals. In 1812 the war finally broke out with the invasion of the colony.

It was an inconclusive war, and both sides were eager to terminate it at the first opportunity. The Treaty of Ghent, 1814, stopped the fighting and changed very little. But the war had a tremendous importance nonetheless. The failure of superior American manpower to seize a tiny outpost of empire consolidated the Loyalist myth and entrenched an intense anti-Americanism. It became politic for all inhabitants of the colony, whether Loyalist or American, whether they fought for Britain or against (and there were many of the latter kind), to claim to have been loyal and to be devoted to the Crown. Moreover the imperial authorities began to look to ways of keeping the republican contagion at bay. The first traces of assisted emigration from the British Isles to Upper Canada took place on the conclusion of peace, and legal devices to keep Americans out were explored. In the case of this colony too, then, the trend was towards an even greater identification with an aristocratic imperial identity.

In America itself reaction to the French Revolution was extremely mixed. On the eve of the Revolution there was already in the United States a growing divergence of opinion on which reaction to the events in France could graft itself. The debate on the Constitution had given rise to an embryonic party system, the Federalists against the Anti-federalists. In the years that followed, this division was perpetuated— the Federalists (who were broadly but not identically connected with those involved with the Constitution) and the Democratic-Republicans (an awkward name in view of more recent American party development and doubly so since sometimes the one and sometimes the other of its terms are used alone). Both initially responded favourably to the events of 1789. After all France had been the saviour of the newly independent republic of 1778 when the two had signed a treaty of alliance and French aid and naval power had been the cause of British defeat. But the Federalists were instinctive believers in order, who inclined to view Britain with a good deal of affection and respect. The Democratic-Republicans, more thorough-going repudiators of the British past, execrated this Federalist attitude. Thus when the French established their republic, and especially when war with Britain was declared, the two parties did not have to hesitate long before making their identifications.

Upholders of the French Revolution enjoyed popular support in the early days, but as time went on initial approval gave way to questioning and eventual hostility. One reason for this was the ineptitude of the French ministers and agents. Following the setting-up of the French Republic an ambassador, Citizen Genêt, was sent to America, the first republican ambassador from France to be received anywhere. Genêt, young and inexperienced, had grandiose schemes for reconquering the French possessions in North America, including Canada for whose recovery he recruited Mezière. But like Mezière he was not up to the demands of a delicate position. Misled by the warmth of his reception in the United States, the adoption of republican cockades, the renaming of streets, the use of the appellation 'citizen', and so on, he thought to be able to dictate to the government and to presume on the terms of the treaty of 1778. Genêt overreached himself badly and one by one alienated the leaders of America. Rather later, in 1798, an even worse débâcle took place in Franco-American relations. New representatives to France failed to be received. Eventually it was put to them that the distribution of bribes and the provision of loans would smooth their path. This was reported to the President of the United States, John Adams, who in turn communicated the affront to Congress and so to the people; in that report Adams referred to the French agents as X, Y, and Z, and for this reason the affair has become known by those three initials. Its effect on public opinion was profound, completing growing disillusionment with the French Revolution. War with France became a distinct possibility.

What helped the change of sentiment was the belief, which had been gaining ground since 1794, that the French Revolution was godless. It has been pointed out how in America the Enlightenment had always played down the deist aspect, and how the drive to republican independence had been in great part religious. Now the preachers, like those in Lower Canada and elsewhere, were beginning to identify Revolution and Anti-Christ. The mood of the country hardened against republican excess, against 'democrats, mobocrats and all other kinds of rats'. In this condemnation were included not only Frenchmen but also the Irish population, most of whom were suspected of belonging to the Society of United Irishmen. And against such potential dangers the Federalists hastened to pass, in 1798, the Alien and Sedition Acts. These acts gave the government greater powers to control freedom of speech and recent immigrants, the qualifying period for naturalization being increased from five to fourteen years. If not so severe as the British legislation, the Alien and Sedition Acts marked a step in the same direction of reaction.

❊ ❊ ❊

To stress broad similarities in the developments of the three societies is a useful and necessary exercise. Yet more worthwhile is a comparison that shows more precisely the degree to which any one society was committed to a particular trend. It is this latter task that this section will now attempt. And it will take the form of a dichotomous analysis. For at this period the British North American societies were not mature enough to contribute a style of their own. In all essentials they followed the imperial pattern. From time to time they were leavened by doses of Americanism, though this last, while always at work and destined to play a part in the evolution of a Canadian identity, was yet minor. Thus it is justifiable to contrast the British with the American way.

A striking characteristic of British society in this period of change and adjustment was the degree of continuity exhibited. This was the case not merely with reference to surface phenomena, to the fact, for instance, that while America and France were declaring themselves republics and Ireland and the British North American colonies were being changed constitutionally, Britain made no essential alteration in its form of government. In a much deeper sense was it true, and what was noteworthy was not the fact of a democratic wave followed by one of reaction, but the weakness of the first and the ready acceptance of the second. The Wilkesite movement posed no real threat, and its lack of genuine challenge was nowhere better shown than when Wilkes himself defended the Bank of England during the Gordon Riots and shot down the mob. The County Movement was even less of a danger. Its program was decidedly tame and old-fashioned, calling for the addition of one hundred county members to the Commons (county members, it was thought, were more independent than others, given the relatively large electorates), annual or at least triennial parliaments, and a curtailment of crown patronage; they were, in fact, nothing more than the backward-looking ideas of middling gentry seeking to recover something of their fancied influence. Essentially the same judgement may be passed on the most notable reform actually enacted in this period—the Economical Reform of 1782, a vain attempt to restore the pristine, and mythical, independence of the House of Commons.

What meaningful radicalism existed was thin indeed. The Westminster group of 1780 did put out a program that went much further than the proposals from the County Movement of rural Yorkshire. But that program was so far ahead of its time, and so out of tune with eighteenth-century society, that it was not until the 1840s that the same proposals next came before the public in a realistic way; even then the time was not ripe for their adoption. Hardy's following, the lower classes, represented a force of the future, but this, too, was premature. And even these more modern radicalisms were still tinged with older residues. It was the mark of the eighteenth-century enlightened reformer to make his appeal to the reason of his individual listener; the aim was to *convert* those in authority. Thus their organizations were merely the coming together of like-minded people, the pooling of resources for the publishing of some tract. There was as yet no grasp of the more up-to-date notion of organization, the generating of larger pressures that would *oblige* the authorities to make alterations. There was no middle ground between humble petitioning and desperate rebellion.

Reform, then, was either old-fashioned or weak. The *status quo* was popular. What was significant about the 1790s was the ready collapse of reform. Admittedly the repression was savage. But such action may have two consequences; it may lead to a collapse or to a heightening of the critical forces. That it so quickly led to the former says much about the relative strengths of the established and critical attitudes, and justifies the comment of an early historian of this period that 'In its war against radicalism the government was supported by the mass of public opinion'.

A determination to resist too great a degree of change must not be interpreted as a rejection of all change, however. Radical changes were, in fact, taking place, but they were beneath the surface or only half-understood by those responsible for them. It was an organic evolution that was occurring, the very recipe that Burke was even then prescribing. The structure of government was in flux, and parliament was changing out of all recognition.

It was pointed out in the introductory section how the static medieval notions had lingered on into the eighteenth century, for example the belief that parliament's work was essentially negative and lay in the elimination of abuses, or the assumption that law was fixed for all time and had merely to be declared. But in the changed conditions of the late eighteenth century such static ideas had to give way to more dynamic ones that would permit accommodation. It was in this period that the practice (one cannot say belief, since the process was too unconscious for that) began to gain ground that parliament was an illimitable body, the source of final power, and so capable of decreeing anything. Not only was the ever-expanding concept of indivisible sovereignty, current since the late sixteenth century, squarely located in parliament, but the even more novel idea was grafted on that in addition to being supreme over competing powers such as king or church it was also uncontrollable by any sanction whatsoever. This novelty was summed up by the very influential *Commentaries* of Blackstone, the greatest legal authority of the day and, by virtue of his professorship at Oxford, the moulder of the minds of many of the country's eventual rulers. Parliament, he wrote, had 'sovereign and uncontrollable authority in making, confirming, enlarging, restraining, abrogating, repealing, reviving and expounding of laws, concerning matters of all possible denominations, ecclesiastical, or temporal, civil, maritime, or criminal. . . . It can, in short, do everything that is not naturally impossible; and therefore some have not scrupled to call its power . . . the omnipotence of parliament.' The view was taken in Britain that what was legal was constitutional, that is, whatever had been duly passed by both houses of parliament and assented to by the monarch could not be contraverted or appealed against.

Accompanying this emergence of what today is termed its omnicompetence (it is said that an Act of Parliament can make a man a woman, and vice versa, something that Blackstone guarded against in his qualification above) was a more modern grasp of its main area of concern, the public business of the state. Then, as now, the executive was the king's, the ministers were His Majesty's Secretaries of State, and so on, the judges' commissions expired on the death of the sovereign and new ones had to be granted by the new ruler. But now the executive is the monarch's only in name. Then it was reality, as was indicated by the method of paying them out of the royal Civil List; that grant might be voted by parliament but once voted parliament had no control over its disbursement. It was Burke's Act of 1782 that began to alter this arrangement, for statute now laid down certain principles that were to govern the payments from the Civil List. The details are not important here; the principle had been established that the legislature could interfere with the executive in a crucial area. (It should perhaps be noted that Burke was not intending to establish a new principle; the whole program of Economical Reform, remember, was directed at cutting down what was thought to be growing executive interference in the independence of parliament.) Further changes in the concept of the Civil List followed. In 1802 the distinction was drawn between the charges that were domestic (the upkeep of the royal palaces, the food bills, and so on) and those that were public (the payment of ambassadors, say). Finally in 1830 the Civil List was reduced when the state rather than the king took responsibility for the public charges.

Parliamentary control over executive spending was a step towards a more efficient control of the energies of the state. Parallel with this development went an overhaul of the administrative system, a further step towards a modern bureaucracy. The departments of state were expanded and reorganized. For instance, colonial affairs were separated from those of the Home office, which had handled them until the close of the eighteenth century. This was not all gain for colonial matters since they were now to be handled by the War office, but the gain to the Home office was great. This department, now unencumbered by colonial concerns, was free to develop a new positive approach to social problems, to the business of law and order for example. The nature of the bureaucratic staff was also changed. To begin with the public capacity of an official had not been adequately distinguished from his private one. It had been usual for officials to make no distinction between their own money and state money committed to their care; they might even use state money and draw the interest on it for the time between collection and accounting. Now it was decided (again by an Act for which Burke was responsible) that special government accounts should be opened at the Bank of England for these state funds. Until this period few officials had been paid salaries. Rather they had been paid by fees, each member of the public who took advantage of a bureaucrat's time and expertise paying him directly for that service. This was not only an inefficient system, encouraging officials to multiply stages and to drag out proceedings so as to increase the opportunities of charging for services rendered; it was, even more significantly, symbolic of a feudal attitude to office not so very different from that of the French *Parlementaires*—office was a freehold belonging to an individual and not a function of the state. That judges until 1826 were paid by fee could only encourage the idea that they were private arbiters rather than the interpreters of the state's rulings. Another bureaucratic change that took place at this time was the central collection of funds from which set amounts, determined from time to time by parliament, could be disbursed to run departments and pay salaries. The Consolidated Fund, established in 1787, replaced the previous system whereby the yields of specific taxes were appropriated to the support of particular services. Clearly the old system lacked flexibility, and was more suited to a static than to a dynamic society.

If parliament was to be the agency through which social change was to be mediated, it was imperative that parliament reflect the needs of the entire community. It was this that was responsible for the attack on virtual representation mounted by the radicals, for instance in the Westminster program of 1780 to enlarge the electorate. As mentioned above the time was not yet ripe for a frontal assault upon virtual representation, and this demand was stifled in the eighties and effectively killed in the nineties. But in one particular area thinking about representation did move to keep pace with new conditions. As part of their demands some radicals called for the binding of M.P.s to the instructions of the constituents; this had been a feature of the Wilkesite movement, for instance. This democratic demand was often accompanied by a demand that the candidate be a resident of the constituency he was fighting. But such calls were not really suited to a modern society. They threatened to elevate local concerns at a time when national problems were pressing; they marked, in fact, a return to the medieval requirements that had worked in a traditional, fixed society. The attempt to make M.P.s delegates from local communities was raised in a very salient manner in 1774. For in the election of that year the voters of Bristol attempted to obtain assurance from their member that he would take instructions from them. The candidate was Edmund Burke, however, and he seized the opportunity to deny the delegate theory of representation. 'Authoritative instructions,' he said, 'mandates issued, which the member is bound blindly and implicitly to obey . . . are things utterly unknown to the laws of this land, and which arise from a fundamental mistake of the whole order and tenor of our constitution.' In the same year parliament showed that it was in accord with this essentially aristocratic as opposed to democratic conception by finally abolishing the medieval requirement of residence, thus belatedly sanctioning a practice that had long existed.

This omnicompetent parliament, increasingly the forum for national debate, was further changing in two important ways. It was ceasing to be dominated by the monarch, and was beginning to be responsive to public opinion. This term, which is heard everywhere today, is surprisingly modern, and indeed public opinion cannot be said to have existed in Britain before the reign of George III when, as already indicated, significantly larger sections of society were politicized. A dramatic indication of these changes occurred in 1782. In that year the Prime Minister, Lord North, found that his supporters no longer had confidence in his conduct of the American and French war. A majority could no longer be created for the king's minister, and George III had to accept North's resignation and the succession of the Marquis of Rockingham, a leader he would never have chosen had he been in a position to make a real choice. This was revolutionary.

Indeed the entire two years of instability that followed the resignation of North further underlined the extent of the change that was taking place. Rockingham died soon after taking office and was succeeded by the Earl of Shelburne. He chose to announce a program he would follow. Here was revolution again, an attempt to appeal to the nation beyond the narrow confines of parliament. And then early in 1783 Shelburne, having made peace on terms that public opinion did not approve, was defeated in the Commons. He resigned. The original revolution had been repeated. The king, much against his wishes, was obliged to entrust the government to a coalition of North and Charles James Fox, whom the king detested. This was to rub salt in the wound!

The Fox-North coalition was not destined to last. Its defeat occurred late in 1783, and did so when George III encouraged the Lords to reject a crucial bill that the ministry had sponsored. This ability of the king to bring down a ministry he did not like is a useful reminder that the change of 1782 was not clear-cut, and that change in the British constitution is not smooth and unambiguous but rather a slow adjustment by fits and starts. That the king could now in late 1783 and 1784 entrust the government to the man of his choice, William Pitt the Younger, and maintain him in power in spite of overwhelming adverse votes in the Commons, and that when parliament was dissolved in 1784 it was in order to hold elections in which royal backing was decisive in building a majority for Pitt, are confirmations of the fact that the monarch's influence was still vast. But to claim that this showed that the eighteenth-century system had been dented in 1782-3 but not altered is to go too far. Pitt was in tune with public opinion and dependent on it, and if it was true that without royal backing he would never have been prime minister, it was equally true that the king could have built a majority for no one else but Pitt. Royal backing and public opinion both played a part in 1784, a watershed in British constitutional development.

If the monarch was ceasing to play such an undisputed role in the direction of state affairs, there was a vacuum forming that had to be filled. Here there was a radical departure, but one that was disguised behind the use of an old name and where an existing institution was given new life and purpose. This was the development of the cabinet.

Kings had always had their groups of advisors. But as with almost all such institutions the tendency had been for these groups to increase in size and hence lose in effectiveness. This had been true of the Privy Council, which still exists but does so largely for ceremonial reasons, inclusion in that body being a convenient way of recognizing public worth. By the late seventeenth century another group, small and more efficient, had grown up alongside the unwieldy Privy Council, known from its confidential accessibility to the king as his Cabinet Council. This too had grown and had thrown off yet another inner cabinet, which was the one that would come to dominate British government down to the present. It may be noted, however, that the evolution of an inner, inner group did not cease there; under the pressure of World War I a War Cabinet of but five people was set up, though this was dismantled at the end of the war.

But the cabinet of the early eighteenth century was hardly the modern institution. The ministers were very conscious of the fact that they were the king's ministers and dependent on him. Even if the first two Hanoverians, foreigners and uninterested in any discussion of British affairs, decided not to preside over the cabinet, and even if George III declined to reverse this convention, the theory that each minister was responsible for his own department and to the king alone was still accepted. As one observer wrote towards mid-century, 'According to our constitution we can have no sole and prime minister: we ought always to have several prime ministers or officers of state: every such officer has his own proper department; and no officer ought to meddle in the affairs belonging to the department of another.' The structure of the cabinet, then, was extremely loose, and there was no notion of what today is referred to as cabinet solidarity, the idea that all members are assumed to be in agreement with the publicly announced program and that should any member be fundamentally opposed at any point he ought to resign. Members of eighteenth-century cabinets were considered free to speak and vote against their colleagues.

Yet the facts were working against the theory. All groups tend to throw up leaders, and throughout the eighteenth century the need for leadership was getting stronger. The business of government was growing in volume, complexity, and interdependence; the war of 1776–83 was a particular case in point. And when George III began to withdraw from the extremely active role that he had assumed on his accession, the need for a prime minister became overwhelming. This occurred in the eighties. George III had seen his system crash in the crisis of 1782–4. In 1788–9 he was to suffer the first of his bouts of insanity; not only was he unable to function as the head of the executive, but on his recovery he did not have the same interest in the day-to-day running of public affairs. And finally this was the period of Pitt's dominance. Indispensable as the king's leading minister, increasingly powerful as the articulator of emerging middle-class aspirations, buttressed by public opinion, and the rock of salvation against the rising revolutionary tide, Pitt was modern enough and bold enough to take the pejorative term prime minister and make it an accepted part of the constitution, the head of the new-style cabinet. This revolution in government was signalled in 1792 when Pitt got the king to remove the Lord Chancellor, who was not in agreement with cabinet policy and spoke against the ministry in parliament. Just over ten years later Pitt underlined the change when he spoke of 'the absolute necessity there is . . . that there should be an avowed and real Minister, possessing the chief weight in the council, and the principal place in the confidence of the King. In that respect there can be no rivalry or division of power. That power must rest in the person generally called the First Minister, ... If it should come unfortunately to . . . a radical difference of opinion, . . . the sentiments of the minister must be allowed and understood to prevail. . . .' In this further way, then, the executive had been brought within the ambit of the legislature.

Yet another revolution was taking place in British government at this time. Public opinion operating within a parliamentary system means the emergence of a party system. It has been noted how in the debate over the exclusion of James II and the Settlement of the Crown in the Protestant line the excitement produced two antagonistic groupings, the Whigs and the Tories. Any meaning that these two terms had in the reigns of William and of Anne disappeared in those of the Hanoverians. In part this was because the Tories had been too identified with a possible Stuart restoration, and the Jacobite risings of 1715 and 1745 to that end had served to confirm the suspicion that Tory meant traitor; thus by the mid-eighteenth century all those wishing to play a role in government took care to call themselves Whigs. But there was a deeper reason, too, why party had not developed. If government was the king's government then any criticism smacked of treason; in attacking a minister one was attacking the head of state, almost the state itself. There was accordingly a great reluctance on the part of the 'outs' to act as an opposition, as a formed organized opposition. Political understanding was not yet sophisticated enough to grasp the truth that criticism could be other than self-seeking and destructive of the nation's unity. But this pre-modern outlook was on the point of changing.

The key figure in this was Edmund Burke. A section of the Whigs, seeking a means of recapturing office, used the intellectual Burke to establish a ground on which they could fight. To this end Burke developed a new definition of party. It was:

> Party is a body of men united for promoting by their joint endeavours the national interest upon some particular principle in which they are all agreed. For my part, I find it impossible to conceive, that any one believes in his own politics, or thinks them to be of any weight, who refuses to adopt the means of having them reduced into practice. It is the business of the speculative philosopher to mark the proper ends of government. It is the business of the politician, who is the philosopher in action, to find out proper means towards those ends, and to employ them with effect. Therefore every honourable connexion will avow it is their first purpose, to pursue every just method to put the men who hold their opinions into such a condition as may enable them to carry their common plans into execution, with all the power and authority of the state.

Such a definition may be read today as self-evident and unexceptionable; when it was written in 1770 it was revolutionary. Not that the new understanding caught on immediately. But when in the next decade the Whig Club was founded to bring young aspiring politicians to the notice of the leadership, and when their rivals started the Constitutional Club in retaliation, the faint beginning of modern political organization may be discovered.

A party system had been justified, then. But the structure of the system had to be worked out. In contrast to later continental developments, which established multiparty fragmentation, Britain adopted a two-party system. There were several reasons for this. There was the ready-made choice of party names, Whig and Tory. The very shape of the Commons' chamber, a narrow oblong, has been held to have been a factor, by encouraging a division of opinion down the middle. But most important was the existence of a key question to which response tended to be black-white and emotional rather than reasoned and complex. This was the question of change itself, epitomized in the reaction to the French Revolution. On an issue like this, one was either strongly for or strongly against. Pitt came to be the rallying point of those who believed the British constitution to be in danger, and Burke of the *Reflections* their intellectual spokesman. What came to be called the Tory party (sometimes distinguished as the second Tory party, the first being the Anti-exclusionist grouping of the late seventeenth and early eighteenth century) emerged as the party of law and order. The rump of the Whigs, left under the leadership of Fox after the majority had followed Portland into Pitt's camp, was left to uphold the dimming but never wholly extinguished light of reform and liberty. Much later their day was to come again. But here a meaningful party system, based on competing values and ends yet in sufficient basic accord for dialogue to take place, was being born, and the two-party tradition being established. A modern structure, flexible but disciplined, had been created.

Britain then represents a paradox, a society clinging to established ways and old forms and yet effecting a revolution and fitting her society to the challenges of the modern world. By contrast the newly founded United States of America seems to be much more clearly modern. From the Declaration of Independence on, the modern Enlightenment presuppositions shine through. That document itself contains ringing assertions of self-evident truths 'that all men are created equal, that they are endowed by their Creator with certain inalienable Rights, that among these are Life, Liberty and the pursuit of Happiness'. And the forms of government established then and over the next few years amply fulfilled the requirements of the Declaration and of its spirit. All governments were to be republican, a form guaranteed by the Constitution. At a time when Europe was overwhelmingly monarchical, when indeed Sweden reverted after 1772 to monarchy after a long republican experiment, the choice of a republic was a bold affirmation of the Enlightenment belief that kings and priests were inherently tyrannical. So at the same time governments took care that priestcraft should be minimized; a crucial article of many state constitutions and eventually of the federal government was that religion should be a private and not a public matter, and in view of the British retention of the Test and Corporation Acts long after this date, this again was a bold step to take.

Similarly in tune with the Enlightenment outlook was the belief that society was contractual. Indeed the American adoption of Locke was much more thorough-going than it had been in his native England. There the view prevailed that the ruler was in some way outside society, separated from the people, and that the contract was between these two essentially distinct parties. And given the fact that England was part of a traditional on-going society where the ruler had in fact constituted a separate code of existence, this formulation of the contract theory was as much as could have been expected. But a century later in America, which had never known the reality of sacred kingship, the notion of the ruler as apart from society was harder to maintain. For

Americans, then, the contract was formed among the people themselves, and was not so much a device to negate tyrannical proclivities as a positive measure for the conduct of a better life.

A practical testimony to the American belief in equal, contractual government was provided in 1787 by the North-West Ordinance. The lands of the old North West, lying between the Mississippi and the Ohio, were American, but as yet they were sparsely settled. Eventually they would fill with people and the question of their relationship to the existing United States would become acute. Foreseeing this, the Americans planned the stages by which an area would qualify for statehood —it was fixed at 60,000 free inhabitants—and so for entry into the union as a complete equal with the other states. Even though the situation was so very different one compares this with Britain's fumbling equivalent towards Ireland and the retreat from Grattan's Parliament, or with the almost contemporaneous Constitutional Act for Canada.

This logical development of Enlightenment thought, the sovereignty of the people, was nowhere better shown than in the American invention of the founding convention. As the states worked on their new constitutions, more and more they felt the need for some mechanism adequate to validate such a solemn undertaking. The early use of the existing state legislatures seemed defective, for with their tendency to see tyrannical developments everywhere, too many Americans suspected that the legislators had become a class apart and that whatever they enacted would be tainted with vested interest. Eventually the idea was hit upon that a special body representative of the people should be elected for the set purpose of debating and ratifying the proposed constitution. Once this function had been discharged the convention should cease to exist, for now the founding fathers would come under the constitution and be answerable to it like any other member of the republic. This in fact was the method selected when it came to the ratification of the federal Constitution, the state legislatures being by-passed in a more direct appeal to the people.

It was certainly true that by superimposing such edifices upon the already existing open society, the United States was able to mobilize tremendous resources and develop a dynamic that soon impressed the rest of Europe as a distinctive style of life. In many ways the United States was fitted to take advantage of modernity as few other societies were or have been. And yet alongside much that was modern went a surprising amount of what can only be described as medieval.

If the optimistic, Enlightenment side of American political philosophy was summed up in the Declaration of Independence, the pessimistic, medieval aspect was revealed in the Constitution. The two documents have both been canonized and made central to the American experience, though they pull in opposite directions and help to account for that special tension that distinguishes American history from those of Britain and Canada. Just how the Constitution represented a reversion to older ways must now be outlined.

The most obvious example of reversion was in the return to the theory of the separation of powers. At the very time that the model—Britain—was moving towards a further blurring of any separation of powers, and long after the formal separation called for in the Act of Settlement had been given up by the Regency Act, America entrenched a triple division into legislative, executive, and judicial branches of government. The Watergate affair has recently re-emphasized this fact, for until the very last minute it seemed that Nixon could continue safe from the reach of the people's representatives behind the protection of executive independence. As it was, the American political system came very close to bogging down completely.

This modern illustration brings out the negative aspect of the Constitution, the way in which, in the language of the eighteenth century, a system of checks and balances may restrict a government. A further aspect of restriction in connection with the Constitution is the accompanying doctrine of judicial review.

Examples of this doctrine could be found in the pre-Constitutional period, but its full emergence and acceptance was the work of a slightly later period, and notably of the dominant Supreme Court judge, John Marshall. Marshall was appointed Chief Justice in 1801 and remained in that office until 1835. In the course of this long tenure he had occasion to pass on several crucial issues, and his judgements, delivered with great forcefulness, affected the subsequent course of American legal and constitutional development. The key decision for the doctrine of judicial review was that in *Marbury vs Madison*, 1803. The defendant Madison had, as newly-incumbent Secretary of State, refused to deliver to the plaintiff a commission as justice of the peace that the outgoing President, John Adams, had signed. Marbury brought the action to enforce delivery of the commission, basing his claim on the provisions of an Act of Congress of 1789. But Marshall, repudiating the recently triumphant British doctrine that whatever is legal is constitutional, roundly declared that the provisions relied upon had been unconstitutional and so were merely pretended law. Lying behind this approach was a medieval-style appeal to the eternal law, superior to legislated law.

A third way in which the Constitution could have a restrictive effect upon the development of society was the willingness of many politicians to approach it from what is known as a 'strict construction' point of view. According to this interpretation the Constitution is to be read with a strict regard for what is explicitly authorized in that document, and if a proposed measure cannot find that explicit authorization, then it is automatically unconstitutional.

Such an approach would seem to be so restrictive as to lead to stagnation. One factor that helped avoid such a development was the widely held view, particularly among strict constructionists, that the Constitution was not the only social agency to which Americans could appeal. There were also the states, which, many people felt, retained a good measure of sovereignty and which had a contractual arrangement with the federal government. Indeed the Constitution itself was seen as a compact, and did furnish support for this interpretation; as the tenth amendment, the last of those in the original batch ratified in 1791, put it, 'The powers not delegated to the United States by the Constitution, nor prohibited by it to the States, are reserved to the States respectively, or to the people.' And even greater than the actual power was the sense of state identity, so powerful that until 1800 at least a reference to 'my country' should be interpreted to mean 'my state' rather than 'America'. Ever since the earliest days states' rights has been a doctrine that has continued to run through the American experience. Most recently it has been invoked by segregationist governors in the Deep South. Its appeal in the early years may be judged by the response to the Alien and Sedition Acts. Whereas in Britain much more thorough-going repression was by and large accepted, in the United States the Acts were met by a barrage of criticism; in particular two sets of resolutions, one adopted by the legislature of Kentucky and the other by that of Virginia, were circulated, both reasoned statements attacking the reactionary legislation and both based on the principle that a federal law that infringed upon a state's rights might be disallowed by that state since the federal government was a compact in which the states were parties. Incidentally this localism, so typical of the older outlook, was also to be seen in another way. Even while Burke was repudiating delegate democracy, and parliament was abolishing residence requirements, the Americans were moving the other way. Binding instructions to members of the legislature were common, and close ties between representative and constituents were insisted upon. Even to this day localism is much more a feature of American politics than of British.

In these various ways, then, the drive to modernity was threatened in America. But not denied completely, for that drive was strong enough to ensure that ways were found to circumvent the restrictions. A major agency for dynamic change, and one particularly noticeable in the twentieth century, has been the presidency, inexorably gathering unto itself more and more powers, constantly exercising more and more leadership; in charting this development the historian Arthur M. Schlesinger, Jr., entitled his book *The Imperial Presidency*. And secondly, there has been the preponderating tendency to apply not a strict but a loose construction to the Constitution. Loose constructionists take the line that anything not explicitly disallowed by the Constitution may be implemented by the federal authority. This interpretation had been favoured by the Federalists, and especially by Alexander Hamilton, Washington's Secretary of the Treasury. Hamilton, as will be seen in the next chapter, was keen to build a strong industrial nation, and favoured a strong executive that would use all possible powers, including those merely implied in the Constitution, to pursue an aggressive policy of growth. It was an approach that received decisive support in the case of *McCulloch vs Maryland*, 1819. Part of the decision hinged on the question of whether the second Bank of the United States, federally chartered in 1816, was constitutional, for the Constitution did not expressly confer upon the central authority the power to charter a bank. It was found that the Bank's charter was sound since, as it was put, 'Let the end be legitimate, let it be within the scope of the Constitution, and all means which are appropriate, which are plainly adapted to that end, which are not prohibited, but consist with the letter and spirit of the Constitution, are constitutional.'

The restrictive qualities that stemmed from the Constitution, then, were tempered in practice. That they yet persisted was due to yet another kind of medievalism that characterized the development of the new nation. But whereas the examples of medievalism so far given have been institutional or formal, this one is more mythical, part of a pervasive feeling in American society from the first days down to the present. The centre of this myth was the third president of the United States, Thomas Jefferson, about whom coalesced the elements of a particular political style. And there is no doubt that Jefferson has entered the consciousness of the American people as few other presidents have, and it is this fact that makes the naming of Archie Bunker's black neighbour Jefferson such a rich and exquisite irony, as will, it is hoped, become plain. While Jefferson was president for only two terms, 1801–9, he was succeeded by two like-minded men, James Madison, 1809–17, and James Monroe, 1817–25. Thanks to this quarter century of continuity the Jeffersonian tradition became firmly embedded in the American consciousness.

The eponymous hero of this tradition has been met with already. The main composer of the Declaration of Independence, he was, as might have been gathered from the introductory part, soaked in the Enlightenment outlook; for him Bacon, Locke, and Newton formed a 'trinity of the three greatest men the world has ever produced'; in his own eyes one of his greatest triumphs was the disestablishment of religion in his own state of Virginia; a major interest was his part in the founding of the University of Virginia as a rival to the traditionalist, classically oriented College of William and Mary, and in developing a more modern, practical curriculum that stressed modern languages and professional training; a lasting tribute to his belief in education may be seen in the Library of Congress, formed about the nucleus of his own library; although a slave-owner himself he looked to the day when slavery would be abolished. Absent in France from 1785–9 he missed the debate on the Constitution. He accepted that document but significantly with two reservations; he was not happy with the possibility of re-electing a president, and he was in favour of adding a Bill of Rights. Both these points are indicative of a basic Enlightenment fear of government as such. Indeed, on hearing of Shays' Rebellion, did he not observe that 'A little rebellion now and then is a good thing, and as necessary in the political world as storms in the physical'? But with the actual working of the Constitutional government he was not in agreement. The Alien and Sedition Acts were the final proof that the Federalists would have to be defeated. It was, in fact, Jefferson who wrote the Kentucky Resolutions and Madison those of Virginia. The Antifederalists began to form about Jefferson. The choice of party name, Democratic-Republican, was indicative of their beliefs and an especial attack upon Hamilton, Jefferson's *bête-noire*, who was accused (falsely) of harbouring monarchical tendencies. The election of 1800 was to be a crusade to return America to the path of righteousness.

All this was indicative of Enlightenment leanings. So too was the Jeffersonian response of Madison when in 1811 he was given the opportunity of demonstrating his beliefs in the strict interpretation of the constitution. His predilection for states' rights he had shown in 1790 when he authored the Virginia Resolutions; now as President he could go further. In 1811 the twenty-year charter of the first Bank of the United States, a child of Hamilton's loose constructionist thinking, came up for renewal. Madison allowed the Bank to die. But the most telling way of rounding-out the Jeffersonian-Enlightenment anti-power, anti-privilege complex is to stress the cult of simplicity that this tradition practised.

An extremely important point to grasp about the American Revolution was its moral content. It must be understood that for many Americans, especially those who had been affected by the Great Awakening, the real significance of the Revolution was the rediscovery and re-emphasis of virtue. This was, in fact, the real meaning of the term republican, not so much a form of governmental structure as a quality in the people themselves, an absence of monarchical pomp and of mobbish appetite alike that would support a free, virtuous government. Jeffersonians showed themselves, in small but significant ways, true to this tradition. Jefferson took care to walk to his Inauguration rather than ride in an aristocratic coach, and afterwards returned to his simple boarding-house; Madison was proud of the fact that his Inauguration clothes were home-spun American and not from foppish Europe; the diplomatic corps in Washington soon tired of republican simplicity and ceased to attend Jefferson's banquets. That folksy, populist side of American life that last surfaced with Lyndon Johnson was entrenched in this Jeffersonian period.

All this was fully compatible with a society evolving towards modernity. Indeed had it been otherwise the Jeffersonian style could not have become so much a part of the American tradition. And yet behind these manifestations of modernity were others of a far different kind. Jefferson's thinking was rooted in the past in a way that would have amazed the French Enlightenment philosopher and ardent champion of progress, Condorcet. Jefferson had an odd attachment to the anglo-saxon past and tended to see the Norman Conquest of 1066 not as a means of bringing England into fruitful contact with the continent and the beginning of an energizing mix of cultures, but as the destruction of a free society by a conspiracy of power-seekers. Even more surprising in one steeped in the Enlightenment tradition that was so modernly urban was the mystique that he attached to the land. For all his interest in science and technology, his real attachment was not to industry and commerce, which he distrusted, but to agriculture and the free yeomanry that it supported. His references to the farmer were fulsome; 'God's peculiar deposit for substantial and genuine virtue' was but one of the many tributes that he paid to the farmer, the essential element in any virtuous republic. Land had always bulked large in the American consciousness, and in view of its vast and spectacular extent this was inevitable. But Jeffersonian attitudes added a further, emotive aspect to this and ensured a nostalgic attitude towards the agrarian golden age that would eventually feed into the 'Western' romance, the main arena for American creativity. Here then was a second tension present in American society that was not present in the British—a pull between the forward-looking technological promise and the backward-looking agrarian myth. For Britain, for all its attachment to tradition, is in some ways more consistent in its modernity, capable of taking the past in its stride. Consider the fate of their two leading agrarians, the American and British. The American champion, Jefferson, was a president, no less. But the British champion, who can name him? He was in fact roughly contemporary with Jefferson, William Cobbett. In his day he enjoyed a measure of popularity but he soon dropped from the folk consciousness of the ordinary man; he never became a mythical figure like Jefferson.

The appeal of the agrarian golden age, dominated by middling, self-sufficient farmers among whom were no serious divisions to disturb the pastoral calm, was helped by the existence in American life of yet another medieval trait. Medieval society had been one where a mono-lithic orthodoxy prevailed and where pluralism could not be conceived; any significant diversity could only appear to be heresy. The coming of modernity has meant the spread of pluralism, however. Now in many ways America was, and is, a very pluralist society. The multiplicity of religious denominations springs to mind, as does the early and impressive spread of newspapers. But in other ways America can be surprisingly non-pluralist. What may be called the American tendency towards ideological totalitarianism must now be sketched, and when it has been it should become clear why the Jeffersonian myth could fit so neatly into such an environment.

The already existing leaning to conformity in American society that has been mentioned above was intensified in the early national period. An early hint that this was to be so was provided by the fate of the United Empire Loyalists. Whether one believes they represented an ideologically defeated minority, or whether one accepts that they were essentially the same as the victorious majority, is in this context beside the point; the fact remains that they were a large body of dissidents lost to the new country. One remembers Palmer's point about American vindictiveness towards these Tories and realizes that because of this intolerance there would be many more, besides the emigrés, opposed to the new ruling class who would be obliged to remain silent. That there was an absence of any real opposition to the prevailing thinking at this period may be confirmed by looking at Federalist arguments. In arguing for an aristocratic Constitution of checks and balances they realized the impossibility of talking openly of the need to control the people. Instead they spiked the Antifederalist guns by seizing the appeal to the people and claiming it for themselves. The three separate branches of government, they argued, were not representative of three different orders of society, as in England, where the people could control only the legislature. In the United States, they claimed, all branches of government were the people's. And was it not the Federalists who called for ratification of the Constitution to be carried through by the people, assembled in special conventions expressly for that purpose? Did not Jefferson himself accept the Constitution, and was not Madison, a later Jeffersonian, a contributor at an earlier period to the *Federalist*? It was only later when the Federalists began to *use* power in a certain way that Jefferson and others moved over to the counterattack. But more than anything else the history of the Federalist party reveals the consensual character of American politics. The Federalist party was in power until 1800. In that year it was defeated and never recovered, and although Federalist candidates were to come forward for a few years yet, the party was dead. It was the suddenness and completeness of the Federalist defeat that is striking and that may be pondered. Jeffersonianism was one special application of this drive towards unanimity. The longing for a simple, undifferentiated past was a clear declaration of this urge to ideological solidarity.

Britain and America differed, then, in that the former tolerated ideological diversity whereas the latter distrusted it. But ideological diversity was a basis for Britain's developing party system. This would seem to imply that the United States was not to enjoy party politics. But as may be seen from Federalist–Antifederalist confrontations down to today's struggles between Democrats and Republicans, party has been a constant feature of American politics. Is there then a contradiction here, or is there an explanation for what is really only an apparent gap between premise and conclusion? The solution will lie in an understanding of the meaning of party in the American context.

A prime source for this understanding is issue ten of the *Federalist*, an issue, written by Madison, published 23 November 1787. The first interest of this discussion lay in the fact that Madison used the older eighteenth-century term, still redolent with pejorative connotations—'faction'—instead of the more modern 'party' that Burke had adopted in 1770. That in fact Madison believed faction to be an evil he made quite plain in the definition he provided: 'By a faction, I understand a number of citizens . . . who are united and actuated by some common impulse of passion, or of interest, adverse to the rights of other citizens, or to the permanent and aggregate interests of the community.' Given such a definition the problem was that of controlling the evil. Madison realized that it would be impossible to remove the causes that gave rise to faction, since this would be to demand an end to liberty or to make all men and their views identical. He concluded pessimistically that the 'causes of faction are . . . sown in the nature of man'. The only solution, then, is to control the effect of party. The way to do this is to ensure a multiplicity of competing groups that would tend to cancel each other out and so achieve a kind of balance. How different is this negative, reluctant attitude from that of Burke! And how different was subsequent practice in the two countries. British parties have always been at bottom ideological clashes, whereas their American counterparts have been rather coalitions of widely differing sub-groups held together by the pragmatic need to obtain and retain power. The point has often been made that the campaign statements of the two contrasting party systems differ profoundly. In Britain they are *programs*, statements of basic political commitment; in America they are *platforms* put together of specific *planks*, statements of immediate, concrete goals. So different are these conceptions that it is tempting to say that whereas in Britain one engages in *politics*, in America one engages in *politicking*.

Finally it may be claimed that the American tradition is medieval in that its national being is built upon fixed, absolute positions. Earlier the salience of the Declaration of Independence and of the Constitution was mentioned, but then attention was drawn to the tension between their implications. But now the coincidence of their appeal must be insisted upon. Because of their compact form, their classic and majestic language, but even more because of their very essence, these two statements have come to dominate American development in a way totally unknown in Britain. Very frequently surveys of American history will include in an appendix the Declaration and the Constitution, and key passages from them are expected to be known by literate Americans. A British survey would be at a loss to know what to include in such an appendix; who would be able to understand Magna Carta, or even the more modern legalism of the Bill of Rights; more importantly, who could *respond*? The Americans, in short, are a people of the Book.

This attachment to a fundamental text has given rise to responses that are particularly American. For instance many Americans have felt that these documents, especially the Constitution, have exercised a tyrannical sway over subsequent developments, preventing sufficiently flexible responses. Americans have been prone to books with such titles as *Our Constitution: Tool or Testament?*, and the title *Our Living*

Constitution was a clear statement of the author's position. At the same time Americans have been forced to acknowledge the gap between promise and actuality in a way few other people have had to do. In all societies the gap has existed. In most, however, the gap has been blurred and the contradiction has not been too glaring to too many people. But in America the rights and the reality of man have been highlighted in a dramatic fashion. Thus in the Declaration one may read that 'all men are created equal' but in the Constitution that the population of any state 'shall be determined by adding to the whole number of free persons . . . three fifths of all other persons' (i.e., negro slaves). The results of such inescapable contradiction have been paradoxical. On the one hand such a situation can give rise to the feeling that the system is corrupt, if not hypocritical. And if the feeling does not go quite this far, it may produce an uneasy suspicion that something, somewhere, is not quite right; the American reading public has shown itself avid for books that will account for the flaw in the system, and Charles Reich's *The Greening of America* is merely the latest in a long line of masochistic self-critiques. On the other hand it can give rise to a belief that the highest ideals having been proclaimed it is impossible to lose sight completely of that beacon, and that men will turn again and again towards it and so eventually be guided upward. The truth is that both responses are possible, and the American reform movements that will be met with later in the book will show this overlap. But it has meant that American development, torn between promise and actuality, has oscillated more violently than has the British.

❊ ❊ ❊

This section has dealt with the dimensions of the new societies, concentrating upon developments in the institutional framework. These were, of course, but the tip of the iceberg, and what has yet remained out of sight must now be brought to the surface. The next section will deal with the way in which the economies of these societies were affected by industrialization, further fragmenting the original unity. The treatment will not be narrowly economic, however. The unfolding of these societies must be traced in their total response to the pressures of industrialization, and the varying conceptions of, say, education should be included. But clearly the starting point will be the Industrial Revolution itself.

3

The Impact
of
Industrialism

The phrase 'the industrial revolution' has a long history going back at least to 1827, and it is so firmly entrenched in the language that its replacement by some other term is unthinkable. This is unfortunate, however, since on two counts the phrase can be misleading.

To many ears the word 'industrial' has the connotation of 'mechanical'. What is summoned up to the mind is a catalogue of key mechanical inventions, the textile machines such as Hargreave's spinning jenny of 1765, Arkwright's water frame of 1767, Crompton's mule of 1779, and the steam engine of Watt in 1776, and the improvements in transportation, which culminated in 1829 with Stephenson's railway engine the *Rocket*. The danger in such thinking is that it encourages the belief that the industrial revolution was simply the expansion of scale that became possible once mechanical means had supplanted mere muscle power. In other words such a way of interpreting the phrase 'the industrial revolution' concentrates too heavily on the *quantitative* differences and tends to ignore the *qualitative* changes that were involved. As will be shown, the post-industrial revolution society was not merely the old writ large, the same only bigger and better; it was altogether different, a new civilization even.

And there is a second danger involved in dwelling on 'industrial' and reading it as 'mechanical'. In concentrating on a list of inventions, it is easy to fall into the error of assuming that these inventions were the reason for the industrial revolution. In turn there is the further danger of seeing these inventions as a series of lucky accidents, in that geniuses just happened to be around and just happened to invent the machines that were needed. Such thinking is common among students; but it is a classic instance of putting the cart before the horse. The saying 'Necessity is the mother of invention' is a useful reminder of the way in which such processes operate. The fact was that in Britain by the last quarter of the eighteenth century, when the industrial revolution first began, there had been a long history of complex political, economic, demographic, intellectual—in short, total social—change that prepared the ground for the industrial revolution, and indeed that may be said to have called it into existence. The inventors then, far from being the cause of the industrial revolution, are better seen as the consequences. A good example of this truth is seen in the early stages of the industrial revolution. Richard Arkwright is commemorated in Nottingham, where he set up one of his first workshops to house his waterframe—an invention that mechanically spun a superior cotton thread—by a major thoroughfare named after him. But Arkwright was not the inventor of the waterframe—that work had been done a generation earlier—but the businessman of genius who when the times were ripe could apply the invention and make it pay a dividend where previously others had been ruined.

This totality of change justified the use of the word 'revolution'. But even so this can be misleading too. The trouble with 'revolution' is that the change it implies is normally marked off in time with reasonable precision; there is usually a clear-cut distinction of before/after, an *ancien régime* and a *nouveau régime*. However, the more research done on the industrial revolution, the less tenable becomes the older view of a sudden break occurring in Britain about 1760. Now the beginnings of the industrial revolution are being pushed back to the upheavals of the seventeenth century or even of the sixteenth. Nor is the question of a terminal date any easier. The industrial revolution, it is now realized, has never ended. If in Britain a certain sense of completion could be felt about 1850, that was merely the rounding out of the first phase of a still continuing process. What had come to fruition was simply the steam-power stage of the industrial revolution. Within a few years of 1850 a second stage, built on electricity and the internal combustion engine, was to begin. And while this stage is not yet over, there are signs, made urgent by the Middle East crisis of the seventies, that the third stage must be hurried in, that in which atomic power provides the energy. An understanding of the stages of the industrial revolution is important, therefore, because each stage posed significantly different problems for society and demanded significantly different solutions. Even in this crude sorting by motive power this can be seen. For instance the effect of steam power is to concentrate industry and workers, since it is not technically feasible to operate machines at any great distance from the source of power; the internal combustion engine and electricity have had a dispersing effect, however, and readers may like to consider what might have been the pattern of modernization had electricity preceded steam. They may also care to note that the present change from petroleum to atomic power will be dwarfed in consequence by the increasing reliance upon computer technology. But perhaps even more important than an understanding of the individual stages is an understanding of the fact that there are stages at all, that the industrial revolution was not a one-time revolution but is rather a continuously unfolding process with a logic and drive of its own. The reality of the industrial revolution has encouraged modern man in his belief that change is the norm, that the transition from one stage to another is not the occasion for relaxed acceptance but for the conquest of new goals. As the American poet and essayist, Ralph Waldo Emerson, announced in 1870, 'Invention breeds invention', or as a recent oil company put it on Canadian TV, 'In this country nothing stays the same longer than it takes to improve it'. There is nothing of the final apocalypse about this revolution.

The industrial revolution then, narrowly understood, was but an episode in a wider series of transformations. That this was so may be further illustrated by glancing at three similar but distinct developments that took place in the eighteenth century.

One of the most dramatic symbols of a new climate in socio-economic matters was the founding in 1694 of the Bank of England. Banks had been known for many years in western Europe, but they had been uncertain institutions with no dominant role in the economy. The founding of the Bank of England was the sign of a new order. A private institution, it was yet so closely connected with the government of the day (that of Dutch William, remember) that its solidity was much more impressive than that of earlier banks. From the beginning it had that aura of respectability that still persists to this day and that made it possible for the Bank to play a crucial role in the financial development of the country. It was true that banking technique was still rudimentary, and that local banks were deficient, not to develop until the industrial revolution called them into effective existence. Even so the Bank of England, and the growing use of bills of exchange about this time, which took the place of cumbersome cash transactions but which also served as a means of expanding credit, indicated a financial coming of age.

Accompanying this evolution was the growth of the London Stock Market. By the early years of the eighteenth century investment in stocks and shares had developed to such a pitch that it was becoming impersonal; that is, individuals with money to invest but knowing nothing about the companies and their businesses were matched by promoters who needed capital on a scale that their friends could not or would not provide, and both sides came together through the medium of brokers on the Exchange. At first it was an unstable institution, treated without caution by a public new to investment and prepared to risk wildly. The result was the South Sea Bubble smash of 1719–20. An investment fever gripped society, and the price of stock was bidden up astronomically; one in particular that rose dizzily was that of the South Sea Company formed to trade in the South Pacific, and it was this company that gave its name to the entire mania. When confidence in ever-rising prices could no longer be maintained, the market duly crashed, and the bubble fortunes burst and evaporated. But what is important to note is not the crash but the recovery. The stock market was so necessary to Britain by this stage of its development that this shock was not permanently harmful. By 1773 the Exchange had its own permanent premises in the City, as the commercial section of London was and is known. And equally important is the comparison with France. There too, at the same time, an investment fever gripped high society—the Mississippi scandal. But the shock to French society was much more serious, and distrust of the risk-ridden stock market persisted throughout the *ancien régime* and even beyond; much more attractive to French investors were the venal offices, state funds, and land. It may also be noted that the Bank of France was not founded until 1800, when Napoleon established it.

This financial revolution in Britain was not readily visible, and affected directly only certain small sections of society. But it did represent an extension and a deepening of the new attitude to money and money-making—that the aggressive pursuit of financial gain in an efficient and purposeful way was not wholly incompatible with the life of a gentleman. A much more evident and dramatic instance of this changed attitude was to be seen in the agricultural revolution that took place a generation or so before the industrial. The impact of the agricultural revolution was more impressive than that of the financial for two reasons. On the one hand, land was one of the best indicators of the medieval outlook. As was pointed out in connection with the seigneurial system in New France, the older scheme of things prized land not so much for its economic returns as for the prestige that it conferred, less for the rent it produced than for the tenants it supported. That the British landowner should change his approach to his broad acres was, then, a clear sign that new standards were making inroads. And on the other hand, the great majority of the population was engaged in agrarian pursuits. By and large this majority still practised an agricultural technique that was almost unchanged from medieval times. Thus the potential for change was vast, both in terms of method and in terms of the numbers likely to be affected. Some idea of the magnitude of the transformation may be gained by an account of pre-revolutionary agriculture, which employed at mid-eighteenth century some three million out of a population of some six and a half million in England and Wales. (The inclusion of the more purely agricultural Scotland and Ireland would raise the agricultural proportion even higher.)

Agriculture, which must adapt itself so nicely to the changing nature of climate and terrain, must be one of the most difficult of all pursuits to sum up, and any overview of agriculture systems must be even more of a caricature than such summaries usually are. Clearly the agriculture of the moors of Cumberland will be quite unlike that of Kent's market gardening or of Bedfordshire's heavy ploughland. And even within counties, even between two neighbouring villages, there would be vast differences of technique and attitude, for this was a time when customary methods inherited over centuries marked community from community as from foreigners. But at the risk of great distortion it may be said that the main agricultural area of England, the midland arable plain, was farmed according to the open-field system.

The first thing to surprise a modern observer about an open-field village would be the preponderance of arable land. Some land had to be left as waste (that is, in its original state) as a source of wood for building and for fire, and as a place to pasture animals, a fact that throws light on the level of farming at that time. Some land would be set aside as pasture, but such grazing land was a luxury and winter feed was always in short supply, so much so that the majority of beasts had to be slaughtered in the fall and the meat salted away. The bulk of the land was arable, devoted sometimes to wheat but as often as not to the inferior grains—rye, oats, barley. This concentration on grain, and the dependence of most people on bread, bread, and bread again, shows how close the average pre-modern person was to subsistence; actual famine might have been scarce, but shortages were normal, and only an unremitting concentration on grain could give the peasant a feeling of security. The second surprise would be the absence of any clearly marked individual holdings. Rather the entire arable land of the village would be seen to lie in two or three large fields. Technique was so poor that to avoid the danger of over-cropping and soil exhaustion, one field at any time would stand in fallow. This meant that in a two-field system 50 per cent of the land was unproductive, and in the more advanced three-field system 33 per cent still lay idle. The only hedge or fence to be seen would be a temporary affair put up around the growing crop to keep out the beasts, which grazed in common where they could, until on a fixed day, the harvest being in, the fence would be dismantled and the animals allowed to eat the stubble. And a third surprise would come when the attempt was made to identify any individual's land in the village. An individual would hold his own land, but hardly ever would it be in a compact block. It would be scattered over the different fields in several strips; they would differ in size and shape depending on the lie of the land, division between heirs, and so on, but notionally they were oblongs of 220 yards (a furrow-long, today's furlong, and the reason why athletes in the British Commonwealth run races in multiples of that distance) by 22 yards (a natural unit of length to a peasant, and the length of a cricket pitch; its proper name is a chain, subdivided into 4 rods, poles, or perches, each of which is a peasant's name for an ox-goad and an everyday measure to him), which oblong is one acre in area and the amount of land that an average ox-team under average conditions could plough in a day—again a revealing statistic on pre-modern agriculture. Many of these strips would go to make up a peasant's holding, for instance one Richard Derby of Buckinghamshire possessed twenty-four strips of land, in all twenty-six and a half acres.

Even from this cursory account the appalling inefficiency of the arrangements can be appreciated. Poor technique meant an over-concentration on grain, which meant a lack of animals, which meant a lack of manure (and artificial fertilizers did not appear until the phosphate revolution of the 1840s), which meant a lack of pasture, which meant an over-concentration on grain, and so on. The pre-modern farmer was trapped in a vicious circle of fertilizer deficiency that he found almost impossible to break. Then too the open fields and communal agriculture meant that everything had to proceed at the pace and in the way set by immemorial custom, which is to say, not far above that of the slowest. Individual initiative was all but impossible, as was improvement that depended on controlled experiment; for instance, it was not possible to breed animals for improved strains so long as the communal grazing of herds was the rule. And finally there must have been a significant loss of efficiency in the use of small, scattered strips; if nothing else, the time lost in travelling from one to another must have been appreciable.

Even before the eighteenth century change had been taking place. Thus piecemeal improvement had managed to raise the grain yield (harvested grain to seed) from the pathetic medieval figure of about 4:1 to a much more respectable 10:1. But it was in the eighteenth century that the pace of improvement suddenly quickened and the breakthrough to a new kind of agriculture took place. Largely this was the result of the systematic application of advances that had been known for some time but used only locally or on a small scale. Thus Coke of Norfolk achieved fame by his popularization of rotation, the cycling of crops on the same ground so that one crop puts back into the soil what previous crops have taken out. The introduction of turnips as a field as opposed to a garden crop was an essential component of the rotation system, and in addition to cleaning the ground was an invaluable source of winter feed and a basis of a new livestock industry. The marling of land was undertaken, as was the draining of heavy soils, though this last had to wait for its real application until the coming of cheap tile in the mid-nineteenth century.

Especially important in making the switch to modern farming was the enclosure movement. The advantages of throwing all the village land together and then reportioning it so that each member of the community could hold his land as a compact block were evident, and the trickle of enclosures that had been taking place since medieval times became a stream in the 1760s and 1770s and rose to a flood during the French Revolutionary and Napoleonic wars, when fears for national survival coupled with a series of bad harvests drove up the price of grain and encouraged a torrent of enclosing. While some enclosures were the result of private agreement, the favoured method in the eighteenth century was to obtain an Act of Parliament authorizing the change. The figures indicate the trend; the 1740s saw but 38 acts, but the next decade witnessed 156 and the next no fewer than 480. By 1801 a General Enclosure Act was passed to simplify the process, and it helped to ease the passage of many of the 2,000 odd enclosures that took place between 1793 and 1815.

In the long run these improvements in technique, and especially the enclosures, were of immense benefit to society. They enabled the land to support the vastly increased population of Britain, which in the eighteenth century alone increased by some 70 per cent, and to do so in a way that improved rather than undermined the health of the people. For instance it was only after enclosure became the norm that there was any commercial application possible of Robert Bakewell's pioneering efforts at livestock improvement, a development that saw the average weight of sheep brought to London's Smithfield Market increase from 28 pounds to 80 pounds; the move away from a staple bread diet would not have been possible but for the interrelated techniques of turnips, rotation, enclosure, and scientific breeding. Naturally in the short run the effects of these changes could be disastrous for individuals. Undoubtedly many suffered cruelly. And the widespread and savage risings of the agricultural labourers in 1830, with their rick burning and destruction of threshing machines, do indicate the extent of the suffering. The classic picture of a peasantry despoiled by their landlords, who used their dominance of the Houses of Parliament to give legislative sanction to their depredations, was provided by J.L. and B. Hammond in their book *The Village Labourer*. Recent work, however, has tended to exonerate many of the enclosers, their agents, and their parliamentary commissioners from the worse charges; on the whole, and given the standards of the day, they seem to have been fair to the villagers whose land they reapportioned. And certain it is that the old picture of wholesale rural depopulation, of large-scale forced migration to the cities, cannot stand. The proportion of people engaged in agriculture may have begun to fall, for society was diversifying, but the absolute number of people on the land increased throughout the eighteenth century and indeed down to the middle of the nineteenth. For enclosed farming demanded hedging and ditching, turnip cultivation was very labour-intensive in an age before mechanization, stock-breeding required more and superior outbuildings; all these and others besides added to the possibilities of rural employment. Thus it is important to grasp the way in which this long-term improvement in agriculture was carried through. The landlords in most cases were not increasing their revenues by the simple method of cutting wage costs, thereby making windfall profits. Rather they were prepared to spend considerable sums of money in the rationalization of an age-old business and to wait a considerable time before the gains would become apparent. It is this long-range investing mentality that is to be noted, and that marks the crucial break in attitudes to land and money-making.

A final point to be made about the agrarian revolution is the way in which this new approach was so frequently initiated or participated in by the ruling class. Many of the aristocrats took an active interest in the running of their estates, and often were the first in their areas to champion a new technique. Turnips were so advocated by Townshend that he has gone down to history as 'Turnip Townshend'; but it is vital to know that he was Viscount Townshend and an outstanding political leader of the early eighteenth century. The standing of agricultural improvement in Britain as contrasted with that in France is nicely made in the following example. At the time when Marie Antoinette, the Austrian wife of Louis XVI, was playing at being a milk maid, having a complete model farm built at Versailles and the washed and perfumed animals driven in for her and the court ladies to play with, George III was so genuinely interesting himself in agriculture as to deserve the familiar name given to him of 'Farmer George'; he did indeed write an agricultural column under the pseudonym 'Ralph Robinson'.

But perhaps the most pervasive sign of the new socio-economic climate was a negative one—the decline of the medieval approach to work organizations and the regulation of labour. As mentioned earlier, the accepted notion was for the authorities, either the natural ruling class working through the J.P.s or the élite of the work force working through the guild masters, to control the structure of economic life in minute and paternal detail. Thus the hours of work were regulated, the rate of pay was specified, and even prices were kept in line by reference to a theoretical, absolute standard that measured, not market fluctuations in supply and demand, but rather the intrinsic worth of the article. At their more formal meetings, the Quarter Sessions, the J.P.s would establish the prices of those peasant staples, the quarter loaf and a gallon of beer. More than anything else the apprenticeship system brought out the essence of the older, medieval notions; anyone wishing to practise a craft was bound apprentice to an acknowledged master, and for the duration of the apprenticeship the relationship was that of son to father in all but the very narrowest of definitions—for instance the master was responsible for the moral welfare of the apprentice as much as for anything else.

It has been noted how in colonial America such regulation early ceased to have any *raison d'être*. Increasingly in eighteenth-century Britain the same development was taking place. More and more were the justices failing to set prices, more and more were guilds failing to insist upon their monopolies, their right to control entry to the crafts, and the methods of production within them. But there was this difference. Whereas in America the passing of guild control was a smooth, unnoticed affair, in Britain there was a considerable body of support for its retention. The most notable instance of such a counterattack was that mounted by the workers themselves, mainly in the textile industries, in the opening years of the nineteenth century; in 1813–4 the climax came with the presentation to parliament of a petition in favour of apprenticeship signed by some 300,000 workers. But this stand, like that in favour of wage and price regulation, failed, and 1813–4 saw the official repudiation of the basis of the medieval system when Queen Elizabeth's Statute of Artificers, 1563, was repealed.

The building of a modern financial infrastructure, the creation of an improved agriculture, and the abandonment of attempts to control the methods of work, indicate that a profound and total change was taking place in the sphere of economic life. But in the last quarter of the eighteenth century the pace of that change suddenly and dramatically increased, and growth became the most striking phenomenon of the age.

In manufacture it was best seen in the textile industry and above all in cotton. The first faint beginning of expansion had been the flying shuttle of John Kay, 1733, but it was not taken up to any great extent for another generation. This was a primitive extension to muscle power that enabled a weaver to throw the shuttle over a greater distance and so weave cloth double the size of the old. In time this upset the balance between weavers and spinners, and the next necessity was some means of increasing the output of thread. It was provided, first by Hargreave whose jenny was a hand-worked device for multiplying the threads that could be spun at any one time, and secondly by Arkwright whose waterframe was a mechanical spinner that not only increased output but produced a stronger thread than hand-spinning could manage. A few years later Crompton combined these two novelties in the suitably named 'mule', which made possible a thread as fine as the jenny's and as strong as the waterframe's. By these means spinning caught up with weaving and the next invention was the mechanization of weaving. The power loom of Edmund Cartwright, patented in 1785, was the answer. What this cycle of challenge and response meant was made clear by the figures for raw cotton imported into the country; at mid-century Britain imported some three million pounds, in 1771 some four and three quarter million pounds, in 1781 almost five and a half millions; but by 1789 it had shot up to thirty-two and a half and by 1802 to over sixty million pounds.

The application of power was equally dramatic. Steam engines of doubtful efficiency had been in use for some time, those of Savery and Newcomen dating from the years about 1700. The improved version of

James Watt, first patented in 1769 but only significantly applied after Watt had entered into partnership with the businessman Matthew Boulton of Birmingham, was so superior that steam power began to be applied to all manner of undertakings. The former dependence on waterwheel power, which had meant building works beside swiftly flowing rivers, could be given up, and industry began its spread over new areas of the country. Now power could be taken almost anywhere, and the criteria for industrial sites increasingly became the availability of mineral deposits.

For another key area of expansion was the metal trades. Iron production had been stagnant in the eighteenth century, since many of the forests were exhausted and the charcoal used in smelting the ore was in short supply. Britain's dependence on Swedish iron was great and embarrassing. The use of coke in place of charcoal was pioneered by the Darby family from the beginning of the eighteenth century, though like Kay's shuttle some time was to pass before it caught on and became general. Iron produced in this way contained impurities, however, and a method of eliminating these had to be found before such iron could be put to the more demanding uses. The puddling process, credited to Henry Cort in 1784, solved this problem. Dependence on foreign supplies ended. Iron increasingly took the place of wood and stone in construction (John Wilkinson, an early iron-master, chose to be buried in an iron coffin), and even more importantly opened the way for products that would have been impossible without a supply of abundant and cheap iron; the railway is a case in point.

And railways were perhaps the epitome of the industrial revolution. They were the climax to a transportation revolution that had paralleled the industrial revolution itself. Improvements in communication, so necessary to bring in the increased raw materials and to distribute the finished products, had begun with a wave of turnpike building about mid-century. These were private enterprises, sanctioned by Act of Parliament, whereby a company would build an effective road and charge the public for using it. At a time when the ordinary roads were abominably bad the turnpikes were a great step forward. But within a few years they were overshadowed by the mania for canal building. The signal for this craze, and the proof of the savings that could be effected, was the opening in 1761 of the Duke of Bridgewater's canal from Worsley to Manchester. This modest 'cut' of but seven miles immediately reduced the price of coal by half. But by the early nineteenth century the turnpikes and canals were no longer adequate for an economy that had seen such dramatic expansion. The early steps towards railway transportation were brought to a successful culmination in 1829 when Stephenson's *Rocket* performed so well in the Rainhill Trials for the projected Liverpool-Manchester railway, which duly opened in the following year. Once again the expansive effect of a single break-through was dramatic; before the railway opened some 500 people a day travelled between the two centres, but with the railway this imme-diately rose to 1200, and at half the cost in half the time. Within an amazingly short time, well within the generation, the main outline of a national railway network had been completed, and there emerged a truly national economy and consciousness in place of the earlier regional self-sufficiency.

Nowhere, however, was the fact of expansion more startling than in the sheer increase of population. Precise statistics began only in 1801 when the first official census was taken—a suggestion that one be taken in 1753 was rejected as 'totally subversive of the last remains of English liberty', an instinctively traditional dislike of quantifying that the new mentality could only slowly overcome—but sufficient is known of the broad outline of eighteenth-century population figures for a clear trend to be observed. The population of England and Wales at the beginning of the eighteenth century was about six million, had increased by about a million at mid-century, and by 1801 stood at something over nine million. In 1821 it was over twelve million and by the middle of the nineteenth century was almost eighteen million. Thus in the century or so of the industrial revolution the population of England and Wales had much more than doubled. Indeed the mid-eighteenth-century popu-lation had doubled itself in about fifty years, whereas the last doubling before 1750 had taken some two hundred and fifty years. Scotland had experienced an increase similar to England, and Ireland, where there was an incredible and dangerous reliance upon the high-yielding potato, was even more dramatically affected; there the four and a half millions of the late eighteenth century had shot up to eight and a half millions by the mid-1840s.

The relationship of this population increase to the new movements in agriculture and industry is not clear, and a debate continues to rage over it. On the one hand there are those who maintain that the increase in population was the independent variable that made possible and called forth the economic transformations, that for instance it was the challenge of more mouths to feed that called into existence the response of more efficient farming and more inventive industry. On the other hand are those who claim that the improvements of the eighteenth century were the cause of the population increase; they point to the improved quantity and variety of food that became available, to the increased use of light, easily washed cotton fabrics in place of the heavier woollens, and other such changes as the keys to a healthier, longer-living, and more fertile stock. There is no need here, however, to decide between these two viewpoints. What has to be grasped is that, whether cause or effect, the new outlook and in particular the industrial revolution was the essential development that permitted population growth to be maintained without check and that permitted the vitality of the population to be maintained and eventually improved. For in earlier times populations had increased, only to be checked by disease and the self-defeating pressure on static resources, so that they sank back to their former levels or even dropped below them. And where this did not occur it meant a catastrophic decline in living standards. Present-day India is an example of this kind of development. But there was an example within the North Atlantic community itself—Ireland, which did not or was not allowed to develop an advanced, sophisticated economy. Instead it was obliged to support a population locked into the cycle of subsistence agriculture and even worse, and was unable to break through to a higher level of economic activity as Britain had done.

To suggest that the industrial revolution and its accompanying change of mentality was a prerequisite for the long-term improvement of the material basis of society is not, of course, to deny that there were dislocations produced that were disastrous in the short run, or that even in the long term there were lasting problems. The cost side of the transformation was a heavy one indeed, and some of the major items on this side of the ledger must now be given.

One of the first costs to be experienced was in the area of work organization; in short, the factory was substituted for the domestic system. The textile industry, the first to be transformed by the industrial revolution, well illustrates the substitution. Under the domestic system the weaver was a self-employed artisan working at home and drawing upon the help of wife and children. The loom may well have belonged to the weaver, though increasingly throughout the eighteenth century the ownership of the loom was passing to a merchant capitalist who then rented it back to the weaver. In other words the crucial distinction between those who possessed capital and those who did not was already forming. This merchant capitalist was the individual who made his rounds of the weaving district, supplying the weavers with the raw materials they needed and then taking back the finished product; it was this control that enabled the merchant capitalist eventually to expropriate the weaver's means of production. Thus although many weavers might be linked by dependence upon one merchant capitalist, the scale of day-to-day working was small; even when the manufacture was not as purely domestic as in the above example but was more of a guild, the same held true, for the work cells would be but a handful of men, and the relationship, remember, a paternal one of master and journeymen over apprentices. And these essentially family work units were animated by the traditional approach to work, by today's standards a hit-and-miss affair indeed. There was a traditional cloth to be produced, in a traditional length of time. Beyond that the rest was up to the producers. Work was often a spasmodic affair then, long bouts of hard work succeeded by long spells of idleness, agricultural work (for the rigid separation of town and country had only just begun and few weavers would not possess some land or interest in land), and dissipation at the 'wakes' (fairs). In all this, the weaver could maintain that he was his own master.

The spread of mechanized methods, and above all the introduction of steam power, altered this system out of all recognition. The superior amounts of capital involved encouraged the pooling of machines in one spot under the control of some commercial leader. This new breed of textile industrialists might not at first employ as many workers as the older merchant capitalists dealt with, for large factories had to wait a while until advances in steam power had been taken a good way. But however many they employed the basis of work and the relationships involved were quite different. In new departures, untrammelled by tradition, a ruthless pursuit of greater gain could be practised. No longer, for instance, could the workers be allowed to pace themselves. No owner of an expensive steam engine could allow his machines to stand idle, wasting a good head of steam, until the workers chose to report for work. No worker could disrupt the continuous process by taking a break when he fancied. Rather a factory had to be run in unison, the men disciplined to work to the rhythm of the machines. Now none but the factory owner could pretend to be self-employed, and the older terms master/apprentice or master/servant began to give way to the modern employer/employee. And it was a hatred of becoming a mere employee that marked so many of those caught up in the switch from pre-industrial to industrial society. By the 1840s, for example, the plight of the handloom weavers was desperate indeed. The competition from the factories had reduced prices so that the only way they could make even a wretched living was to work incredibly long hours. For them to give in and enter the factories could only have meant a gain, both in pay and in time, yet they fought such a solution for as long as possible.

What they objected to in the factories was loss of their freedom and the imposition of a hateful 'discipline'. For this reason factory employers liked to employ women and children; not only would they work for less money, but they were more amenable to the new discipline.

But factory discipline was much more thoroughgoing than mere punctuality and regular shifts. The autonomy of workers was broken down in other ways too. Here the best documented example comes not from the textile industry but from the pottery works of Josiah Wedgwood in Stoke. To him was due not only the ringing of early morning rising bells, a primitive system of clocking-in, and the rewarding of punctuality, but much more besides. Before Wedgwood's day a worker would have been responsible for a great variety of tasks in any working day, for instance moulding cups, saucers, and plates, decorating others, and glazing yet others. For Wedgwood this approach was too amateurish, and resulted in a small output of inferior wares. His new system, which practised that division of labour that Adam Smith was a few years later to praise so highly, broke the work up into separate processes (coarse ware from fine; cups from saucers; etc.) and trained up workers to be experts in just a few of the processes, say affixing the handles to cups. Similarly controlled was the design that a worker was permitted to apply; in future there was to be no scope for individual expression, each decorator being required merely to copy as exactly as possible what the artistic director had decreed. Wedgwood was very open about what he was attempting; it was, he wrote, to 'make such *machines* of the *Men* as cannot err'.

Such a spelling-out of the meaning of discipline points to a further consequence of the factory system. It helped to wreck that balance that ought to exist between production and consumption, and to give the priority to the former when it should belong to the latter. The salient fact of the factory system (as indeed of the entire transformation of the eighteenth century) was the ability to increase output; society began that obsession with sheer production that has lasted down to the present's unthinking admiration for crude Gross National Product figures. But this balance-wrecking was not quantitative only. More important, perhaps, was the way in which discipline destroyed man's capacity to consume aesthetically. The ideal of the older industrial system had been the craft master, one who delighted in his work and was capable of high technical and aesthetic results, and what he made could be enjoyed by the consumer. Factory discipline destroyed this ideal and substituted the unthinking automaton. Given Wedgwood's prescription, it was not surprising that nineteenth-century factories wanting workers should have advertised merely 'hands wanted'. And the things produced by mere hands were shoddy.

Caught up with this debasement of humanity was another consequence of factory discipline, industrial man's changed concept of time. Time had acquired a new precision. And so pervasive had this become that the only way of recovering a sense of pre-industrial time is to go altogether outside the western-industrial heritage. Consider, for instance, western-industrial man's sense of what constitutes punctuality compared with, say, the far-eastern. In the North Atlantic community an appointment for three o'clock, for example, would mean a meeting at exactly that hour; a few minutes leeway, perhaps five or even ten minutes would be allowed, but after that embarrassed apologies would be in order. Diplomats and similar people going to live in the Far East, however, have to be warned that to make an appointment for three o'clock may mean one's opposite number showing up at five or even later. A precise sense of time is no doubt a useful acquisition; unfortunately it has not stopped there but has spilled over into other facets of life with less acceptable results. The clock has become tyrannical, the human rhythm has been sacrificed to non-human ends. The reduction of man to a sheep-like bustle will be familiar to those who have had the good fortune to have seen Charlie Chaplin's *Modern Times*.

The adjustment to factory discipline, used in the widest sense, was a first cost of the industrial revolution. A second was that exacted by urbanization. Pre-industrial revolution society was overwhelmingly agrarian. London, it is true, was already by the end of the eighteenth century a vast concentration of over 850,000 people; but London was unique, and that was the ground for the fear that its size struck into most observers—Cobbett called it 'the great wen'. After London the size of towns fell off greatly, Manchester with some 90,000 being the second largest, and indeed only one sixth of the population of England and Wales lived in centres of over 20,000 inhabitants at the opening of the nineteenth century. And not only were towns small, they were lacking in a distinctively urban atmosphere. As was pointed out in connection with the pre-industrial weavers, the interpenetration of agrarian and industrial activities was pronounced, and it still remained true that the rural areas set the tone for the vast majority of the towns.

But throughout the nineteenth century this picture changed with dramatic swiftness, so that by the end it was the towns that were dictating to the rapidly shrinking rural areas. Already by mid-century the proportion of the population living in towns of over 20,000 had risen to one third. More striking yet was the emergence of the 'big league', cities of more than 100,000 people; at the time of the first census only London was in that league, but by 1837, when Queen Victoria came to the throne, five others had entered, and by the close of the century there were no fewer than twenty-four members. And it was on this class of city that the attention of the age focused, and particularly in the boom period after the end of the Napoleonic wars; on Liverpool, which between 1801 and 1831 grew from 82,000 to over 200,000; on Leeds, which increased from 53,000 to over 120,000; and above all on Manchester, the cotton city, up from 90,000 to almost 240,000. By the time of the last nineteenth-century census, 1891, just fractionally under one third of the population of England and Wales was living in the 'big league' cities. The implications for society of this kind of transformation were awesome.

Part of the problem lay in adjusting to the sheer speed of this growth. The challenge of housing such rapidly increasing populations was a daunting one, and if in some cities public-minded landlords responded successfully, it was more frequently the case that the response was insufficient. The opportunities for quick gains were too tempting, the lack of means to control such tendencies so widespread, that all too often the result was deplorable housing. Houses were crammed into the available space and huge numbers of row houses were built on the back-to-back principle, which meant that in each dwelling there were interior rooms that received no direct sunlight and had no possibility of through draughts for ventilation. Most were so jerry-built as to lack damp-courses, with the result that walls so suffered from rising damp that no wallpaper would adhere to them (such houses still exist, and the very hovels condemned by Engels in 1844 are still occupied in the 1970s in Manchester). Sanitation was usually inadequate and sometimes all but totally lacking; in certain parts of Manchester, for instance, there was but one toilet for every 212 people. The very worst was the cellar accommodation; no less than a sixth of Liverpool's population, many of them Irish immigrants, were living literally underground existences in the worst period of the city's growth. Of late there has been a move to play down the physical horrors of early nineteenth-century city life by pointing out that rural housing was often deplorable, and by noting that urban housing received disproportionate comment because it was a novel, concentrated phenomenon. The caution is a useful one, putting one on guard against the romanticization of rural life that became all too common once the rural reality began to be threatened. Even so, this defence of urban conditions is hardly convincing. Urban life in the industrial revolution was so unhealthy that towns were devourers of people; they could not reproduce their own populations let alone add to them, and that they grew at all was due to migration from the surrounding countryside. As the *Report on the Sanitary Condition of the Labouring Population of Great Britain* showed in 1842, there was a striking difference when the average age at death in Manchester was compared with that of Rutland, an agricultural county. In the former city gentry and professional people might expect to live to 38, in the latter county to 52; tradesmen could expect 20 and 41 years respectively, and the lower orders but 17 and 38. In Liverpool the figures were even more appalling; gentry 35, tradesmen 22, and lower orders 15!

This was urban blight considered physically. But there was an equally important spiritual side to be considered. Even when efforts were made to build impressively, there was too little concern to build for overall beauty and amenity. The new towns were ugly, marked by rows of mean houses monotonously laid out on grid-iron patterns. They were disfigured by factories and workshops unrestrained from polluting the area with their wastes and their clamour. The land set aside for recreation was niggardly and usually too long delayed—Manchester, for example, did not get a municipal park until 1844, some two generations after its modern growth. The splendid municipal buildings such as Leeds Town Hall, erected to symbolize the achievements of trade and manufacture, were insufficient to offset the overall drabness that still to this day characterizes for the majority of their inhabitants the towns of the industrial revolution.

These problems were technical, and were in great part to be solved in an acceptable manner and within an acceptable time. But the urbanization of society also brought with it other problems that were not merely technical and whose solution was not to be so straightforward. For urbanization is not merely or even mainly quantitative; it is qualitative too. Urbanization produces a mentality that is opposed to that of the previously dominant agrarian society, and must struggle with it. Something of this new mentality must now be outlined.

Urban man is a rootless man. Naturally care must be taken when making such statements. On the one hand it is being realized that the rural society of pre-industrial times was never so static, so unchanging as the older accounts would suggest; as Laslett writes in his *The World We Have Lost* of one village he has studied in detail, 'something like 50% of those living in Cogenhoe in 1628 were not there in 1618'. And on the other hand it is clear that after the first shock of urban experience had passed, new institutions emerged to provide meaning in people's lives. But even so two points may be made. First the degree of mobility was much increased; after all, the greater part of the early urban increases was made up of migrants—migrants from only a few miles away, perhaps, but still migrants. Nor was it merely a question of geographical mobility. The new society was a market society; goods were produced in response to impersonal demand, and economic life was marked in a totally new way by the phenomenon of boom and slump. In boom times industries were eager to attract additional hands by paying high wages to lure them away from their competitors, but in slumps they were ruthlessly prepared to cut them adrift. Occupationally, then, the new society was much more mobile than the old, and moving between jobs became an accepted part of life for more and more people. And secondly the links that bound this new society together had to be of a new kind. The scale of the urban experience, the heterogeneity of the cities, the speed with which they grew, the lack of institutions adequate to handle the inevitable problems, meant that there could be no automatic slotting into an existing framework; a new one would have to be *constructed* and the *contractual* basis of relationships would be much more in evidence. At the same time the individuals that went to make up the new institutions were seen as much more homogeneous than before. And here is a striking paradox. Because the city brought together such heterogeneous elements it was no longer possible to agree upon a stable norm; in the midst of such flux all were reduced to their essentials and the new norm emerged, the atomized individual.

One way of spelling out the rootlessness of isolated urban man will be to look in some detail at the political organizations typical of the urban-industrial environment, and this will be done in the next section. Here the more generalized change, as it affected the style of thought rather than the content, will be noted.

Pre-urban society was held together by what may be called negative propaganda. Propaganda is an essential part of all social functioning, though it is only in the twentieth century that its use has been pushed to such positive lengths as to include explicit brainwashing. Propaganda was rarely so positive in the pre-urban environment. At times, perhaps, the clergyman (and for the vast majority this would be an Anglican priest, Dissenters being less than 10 per cent of the population on the eve of urbanization) would speak openly on the need for submission to the authorities; at times the J.P.s would take advantage of their legal role to make wider ranging pronouncements. But more generally than this most of the people would instinctively follow the lead of the gentry without the need for any explicit guidance; they looked to squire and parson not because they had thought the relationship out, not because they recognized them as more intelligent or better educated, but simply because they knew them as gentry. It is this instinctive quality that justifies the description negative propaganda. It was so instinctive, so pervasive, that it seemed not to exist. Indeed it revealed itself only on the rare occasions when its monopoly was challenged; then, for instance, a too aggressive Nonconformist would be harassed by invoking the anti-Dissent legislation that remained on the statute book; the 'Church and King' mob that was turned against Priestley was an extreme example of this, and one that incidentally shows that Birmingham in the 1790s was not yet infused with the spirit of urbanism. This older method of binding followers to leaders (subordinates to rulers would have been truer to the old conception), this kind of social cement, is normally referred to as influence. And influence was dying in the new urban world. One of the last formal applications of influence came in 1818, a time of crisis amid the dislocation caused by the ending of the Napoleonic wars. Parliament, recognizing the unrest endemic in the towns, and seeking to allay it, voted the enormous sum of £1m for the building of additional Anglican churches.

But even while this forlorn hope was being pursued, the new type of cement was making its appearance—opinion. Whereas influence is a total attitude, given once and for all, opinion is the thinking of the moment in response to a particular issue. The distinction may be dramatized by claiming that influence is the product of the deductive mind, opinion of the inductive; in the case of influence there is a mental set and from that mental set different ways of dealing with particular problems as they crop up are worked out, while in the case of opinion a single problem is identified and a solution put forward. Clearly, political organizations based on these different principles will be totally unlike. In traditional, influence-based groups the leader and his followers are bound together by what is essentially a charismatic relationship, the followers trusting that the leader will just simply know how to respond when the challenge comes. This irrational linking makes it difficult for a genuinely influence-based party to operate, since the appeal to potential supporters tends to be of the 'take it or leave it' kind and there is a distrust of and unwillingness to undertake organization as such. In those groups based on opinion, however, the link that binds leader and led is only the coincidence of opinion, it is a relationship put together for a limited end and when that has been achieved the link is automatically dissolved (and in the next section something will be said of one striking example of this very dissolution; here may be merely noted the Association of Working Men to Promote a Cheap and Honest Press, founded early in 1837 and disbanded a few months later when the duty on newspapers was reduced from 4d to 1d). Of course few organizations were single-minded, for opinion on one issue would overlap with that on another and in this way a party as a federation of compatible opinions would be built up; for instance those working for better housing will presumably be keen to work with those advocating more recreational facilities. This difference had been highlighted about 1770 in British politics in the debate between men and measures; Burke, despite his modernity in advocating party, could not make a clean break with the politics of influence, for he repudiated 'the Cant of Not men but measures, a sort of charm by which many people get loose from every honourable engagement'.

But once again it was urbanization that accelerated the emergence of opinion, and this it did in a variety of ways. To begin with it was a process that almost overnight destroyed the agrarian world, the seed-bed of the traditional social relationships; for example, the rootless urban populations never developed that habit of automatic church attendance and all that went with it that characterized so much of pre-industrial life. This negative work of breaking down old patterns was vital, but urbanization was more than merely negative. Urban living posed a host of problems, just those issues, new and striking, that called insistently for solution along piecemeal lines; prison reform, factory inspection, housing were discrete problems demanding technical solutions for which opinion could be mobilized with reasonable ease. And then the urban setting was one that encouraged the emergence of organizations to give force and direction to these opinions. The urban dweller, in comparison with his rural counterpart, had a livelier mind, a more flexible outlook, and even (after the worst of the early stages was over) more leisure and purchasing power to devote to his opinions. The greater size, wealth, and resources of the city made it possible to mobilize opinion in a newly effective way. Newspapers, already seen as a key indicator of a growing middle-class outlook, showed a sudden spurt in numbers and influence in the fifty years after 1780; particularly noteworthy was the tripling of the provincial press, which began to rival that of London, the very influential *Manchester Guardian* dating from 1821 for instance. Cities made possible public libraries; libraries had existed before this, of course, but they had been aristocratic or quasi-aristocratic, requiring high entrance fees and subscriptions. The new public libraries of the industrial cities were supported by the public and enabled a far bigger proportion of the population to benefit from literacy. A new class of reader was made possible and in turn a new style of thinking about society was born. Clubs of all kinds, from those of the well-to-do and devoted to trade, intellectual, or social pursuits, through to those of the workers. Both trade unions and, more significantly in the first three quarters of the nineteenth century, the fraternal orders such as the Oddfellows, began to multiply, all training their members in the arts of organization and administration. Whatever their immediate purpose, the effect of club life was to politicize—in the widest sense—the outlook of the members. And a special mention should be made of one particular kind of club. The Dissenting chapels, whatever their religious function might be, also had a social function. And it is noteworthy that during the urban-industrial revolution the Nonconformists, who had always been strong in the towns, began a dramatic rise in numbers and influence. This was brought out very clearly in 1851 when the only religious census of nineteenth-century Britain was undertaken. Most shocking to contemporaries was the overall decline in church-going; this was most pronounced in the big-league cities where less than 10 per cent were attenders. The biggest loss, however, was among the Anglicans who were a decided minority in the big cities. The Nonconformists, on the other hand, made up some 40–50 per cent of attenders. In part it was to be expected simply because sectarianism is a response to dislocation. But it was also because their polity was much more in tune with the requirements of urban living than was the Anglican. These Dissenting congregations, and especially the Methodists, were so successful in organizing their members that later secular organizations consciously copied their techniques. And this kind of organization was, of course, the antithesis of the Anglican patriarchal-influential kind.

The two costs discussed so far, those caused by the change in work organization and those in living patterns, were closely connected. Both were characterized by the new impersonal scale of things that dwarfed the familiar intimacy of pre-industrial society, and both were marked by the increasing fragmentation of life. There was a third area where this process was to be seen, and one where the costs of transition were to be particularly heavy. The structure of society and men's thinking about that structure were changing.

Previously there had been few qualitative differences between, say, London and Derby, Kent and the Pennine uplands of northern England; what differences there had been were rather of a quantitative kind, a matter of degree. For essential difference one had to go, like Samuel Johnson, to the Highlands of Scotland, or possibly to Wales. And of course Ireland was quite apart. With industrialism the possibilities of tension between regions multiplied, and northern England in particular began to seem a nation apart from the dominant south. But in fact the fragmentation of Britain's unity never went much beyond possibility. Wales, Scotland, and Ireland did become very peripheral, and as time went on were lumped together as the 'Celtic fringe'; only recently, with the discovery of North Sea gas, has Scots separatism become threatening. The rest of England, however, was sufficiently evenly affected by industrialism to remain one entity.

This was not so, however, when social unity rather than geographical unity is considered. The concentration demanded by industrialism threatened to destroy the unity, the homogeneity, of traditional society. The traditional theory of society held that it was composed of orderly gradations from king to labourer. There were no discontinuities in this chain, for each rank shaded imperceptibly into the next. Each rank had its place and its specific duties (what was required of a duke was not necessarily required of a yeoman), and the harsh realities of life were smoothed by the sense of *noblesse oblige* that animated social relationships. Naturally actuality did not correspond exactly to this ideal. But there was enough correspondence for the theory to maintain the field. As a result tension was diffused and localized, and on most occasions the natural ruling class was able to contain resentment. When containment was not possible the protest was violent, instinctive, and anarchical, for given the theory there was no ground for meaningful dialogue. The industrial régime destroyed this complex arrangement and with it the theory. For the effect of the new organization was to concentrate more than merely motive power and populations. It also concentrated economic power. Domestic craftsmen might own their means of production, but factory hands clearly did not. An agricultural labourer before the agrarian revolution might own no land yet still have an equitable interest in the village economy based on custom, but after improvement he would be simply a labourer, dependent solely on an employer. Before urbanization many would have clung to their claim, however perversely, that they were free; buried in the big city, few could continue to believe the myth. Language began to reflect the change coming over society. In place of ranks and orders people talked increasingly of classes, the middle classes being spoken of just before 1800, the working classes just after. At first, it should be noted, the word was used in the plural, for the monolithic quality of these blocks, essentially the possessors of capital and the non-possessors, had not become fully clear; in 1792 Tom Paine, the supporter of republican America and France and critic of the British government, had had an inkling of the dichotomy when he wrote of 'two distinct classes of men in the nation, those who pay taxes, and those who receive and live upon taxes'. But in a short while the singular established itself, and the host of the working class faced that of the middle class, with both opposed to the aristocrats, the natural ruling class. But in the main the split was a simple one between the possessors and the non-possessors, the haves and the have-nots. It was a tension captured by the young politician and future Conservative Prime Minister, Benjamin Disraeli, when in a novel written in the Hungry Forties he described England as being composed of 'two nations'. In the post-Napoleonic war period, class became a fact of British life. The day of the Association Movement of the 1780s, based upon the freeholder (i.e. corporate rank independent of economic means) and structured by counties (i.e. traditional units that did not correspond with economic regions), was utterly passed.

* * *

What has been outlined so far has been industrialization and the broad transformation it caused in the country of its origin, Britain. Its impact was not the same everywhere, and North America differed sharply in its pattern of industrialization. It is now necessary to explore the emphases that marked the process of industrialization in the United States and in Canada, and that differentiated them not only from Britain but from each other.

Today North America must be counted as materially the most favoured part of the world. The United States and Canada, in addition to being among the richest industrially, are in the fortunate position, shared only by two other countries, Australia and the Argentine, of being able to produce more food than they consume; in other words, their impressive industrialization has not been one-sided, as has Britain's. And their superiority to Britain translates starkly into hard figures; in 1970 Britain's per capita domestic product was $2,128 compared with $3,676 for Canada and $4,734 for the United States. Britain's pioneering lead has long been eroded.

These figures speak so eloquently that one is tempted to say that the eventual North American triumph was inevitable, and there are two other and different reasons for saying this. To begin with there is the material argument. North America had been peopled by those steeped in the traditions and developments described above, and at the crucial time of industrial take-off, the late eighteenth century, the North Atlantic community was very much a reality. And then, too, the physical advantages in America were enormous. Its huge spaces were lavishly endowed with resources of all kinds, many in forms that were convenient for exploitation. Nor should population be ignored when considering the material factors. The population of North America increased by leaps and bounds during the nineteenth century, that of the United States from something over 5 million in 1800 to 76 million in 1900, and that of Canada from less than a third of a million to 5 million in the same period. (Britain's increase had been from 12 million to 38 million.) In itself an increasing population is a factor aiding economic growth, for it encourages expanding demand while yet acting to prevent wages from reaching too high a level. But more than this, the North American increase was in large part the result of immigration, the best way, from the point of view of economic growth, of adding to a population. In this way the host country gains a high proportion of ambitious, upwardly mobile individuals, most of whom are in the prime of life, that is, old enough not to be a charge upon the nation's education resources and yet not so old as to impose on the medical-charitable services.

And secondly, there is the realization that North America has been much more thorough-going in its commitment to the entrepreneurial ethic than has Britain, as people say, 'more go-ahead'. If anyone should doubt that this was true even in the nineteenth century, then consider the contrasting national exhorters of upward mobility, the chroniclers of the 'rags to riches' saga. The British high priest of this cult was Samuel Smiles, whose *Lives of the Engineers* pointed out how the great men of the day were frequently self-taught individuals who had risen from the poorest ranks through the application of *Duty*, or *Thrift*, or *Self-Help* (all titles of other books by Smiles). As their titles indicate, these were dry calls to duty, and the readership, while large, would not be vast. But Smiles's American counterpart, Horatio Alger, wrote novels with such catchy titles as *Helping Himself: or Grant Thornton's Ambition*; *Risen from the Ranks: or Harry Walton's Success*; and *Strive and Succeed: or the Progress of Walter Conrad*. That they appealed to a wider audience and continued to be read for far longer than Smiles's works is indicated by the fact that Alger sold in all seventeen million copies, making him one of the world's bestselling novelists.

Britain may have been the first to become a modern industrial state, but it must be acknowledged that by the latter part of the nineteenth century countervailing trends were becoming dominant. If not the actual triumph, then at least the strong persistence of the older ways is the striking thing about modern British society.

The middle class was captured by the aristocracy. The fusion of the two was aided by the fact that the British aristocracy had always been flexible and for long had been imbued with the entrepreneurial spirit—witness, for one, the Duke of Bridgewater of canal fame. And if the aristocracy was prepared to move some way towards the middle class, the middle class was more than ready to accommodate itself to aristocratic ways. The fact that the crown, on the advice of the prime minister, could confer nobility on a successful middle-class person was an aid in the assimilation process, and certainly the House of Lords was growing throughout the nineteenth century. Intermarriage, of course, had always been a way of infiltration. But such instances as these were merely the tip of the iceberg. More revealing was the way in which successful businessmen were deserting sectarian religion and joining the Anglican Church; a notable example of this was the four-times prime minister, William Ewart Gladstone, son of a Scots Presbyterian slave trader. Another way in which middle-class values were deserted was the purchase of a country estate and the taking on of the role of lord of the manor, responsible for the tenantry and the well-being of the county; Gladstone again, on his Hawarden estate, showed this vestigial patriarchalism.

Accompanying this middle-class shift went an equivalent switch in money-making. The entrepreneurial skills began to recede, and the art of financial manipulation, considered a more genteel form of amassing a fortune, began to take its place. The controllers of business became less concerned with continued innovation, and it became a matter of concern by the end of the century that such newer industrial powers as Germany and the United States were forging ahead of Britain in the application of new processes. Britain was relying to an increasing extent on what are called 'invisible exports', the provision of financial services such as the insurance business, the provision of capital to foreign countries, the merchant marine; Britain, in fact, was becoming a *rentier* nation.

But perhaps the best indicator of the way in which Britain was prepared to move some way, but not all the way, towards a more efficient utilization of its intellectual resources and so fit itself for a technological civilization, was its attitude towards education. Any society committing itself to industrialism will have to change its educational system. The relationship between social change and education was brought out clearly in the eighteenth century in Britain. The traditional education system was firmly under the control of the established religion, and Restoration legislation made teaching an Anglican preserve; something has already been said of this state of affairs, which sent John Wilkes for example to Leyden rather than to Oxford or Cambridge. The Dissenters set up illegal schools, the Dissenting academies, which by the eighteenth century were well-established and produced outstanding men—Defoe was one such. Of interest in this context is the marked modernity of their curricula. When Oxbridge still clung to Latin as the language of instruction, the academies used English. Whereas at the universities the subjects studied were the traditional ones such as classics, theology, mathematics, and philosophy, in academies more stress was put on the useful subjects such as modern languages, book-keeping, penmanship, and so on.

By the early nineteenth century the Anglican monopoly had been successfully challenged by Nonconformist commitment. This state of affairs was epitomized in the foundation in 1811 of the National School Society under Anglican control and in 1808–14 in the British and Foreign Schools Society under Nonconformist auspices, two organizations that directed their attention to the need for education in the newly emerging urban centres. This connection of education and religion has never been entirely obliterated in England. A concomitant of modernization is secularization, and this has happened in English education. But it took a long time, and traces of the older conception remain. The very first state grant to education in England in 1833 was channelled through the two societies above. The major Education Act of 1870 continued the existing religious schools, though it erected a parallel secular system alongside them. The equally important Act of 1902 perpetuated this dual system by making it possible for religious schools to receive support from public funds. The present English compromise is for the religious body to build the school and for the local education authority to see to the running expenses, teachers' salaries, etc. It may also be pointed out that Anglican privilege was long maintained at Oxbridge, the final abolition of Anglican favouritism not coming until 1871.

Just as slow to operate in England was another facet of a modern educational system, the role of the state. The very first state grant to education in England was as late as 1833, and was a tiny £20,000, and by mid-century it was only up to £5 million—and this at a time when the navy estimates alone were running at £9 million a year. Equally slow was the decision to make elementary education compulsory, a necessity in any modern, mobile society. The first step in this direction was taken in 1870 when authorities were permitted to make attendance compulsory, but they were not forced to do so until 1880. Then too, there was the failure to maintain the early lead in technical and useful education; the Dissenting tradition became attenuated, and by the last quarter of the nineteenth century it was being recognized that England was lagging in such areas, notably behind Germany.

The failure of the state quickly or fully to establish its control over education and the vanishing lead in technical education were not isolated problems. Their essential connection may be seen by looking at the key nineteenth-century educational development in Britain, the reform of the public schools. This is a term puzzling to North Americans. It refers to the ancient, usually medieval foundations that by the eighteenth century had become boarding schools for the aristocracy. They were expensive and exclusive, and the North American term for such schools, private schools, is a much more exact description. At the opening of the nineteenth century these schools were in a deplorable state and ripe for reform. The outstanding example of such a reform was that mounted by Dr Thomas Arnold, headmaster of Rugby 1828–42; it is his régime that is immortalized in the novel of Thomas Hughes, *Tom Brown's Schooldays*. Arnold, a convinced Anglican of low church or evangelical leanings, transformed the boys from ill-mannered bullies into dutiful high-principled Christians (or at least a crucial number of them). Organized sport was encouraged, since the rough-and-tumble was considered good preparation for the hard knocks ahead in the game of life, and this amalgam of sport and piety gave rise to what was known as 'muscular Christianity', a powerful weapon in the maintenance of the second British empire. What Arnold had done was to apply middle-class values to the aristocracy, and so successfully that a rash of new public schools were founded during the nineteenth century. But it is important to note that the upper-class ethos was not given up. Again the parallel with *ancien régime* France comes to mind; Louis XIV could never decide between *gloire* and efficiency and in the end the former prevailed. It was so in the British public schools. Despite early modernizing of the curriculum, the classics remained prestigious, and by the end of the nineteenth century the public schools were upholding a code that was rapidly passing away.

Above all English education was non-modern in that it failed to make the best use of the intellectual resources of its people. Despite a series of reforms, notably the Acts of 1870 and 1902, education was still class education; the great bulk of the working class had to be content with cheap elementary schooling, which they left at age 12 (in 1899) knowing the three Rs; the middle class had their secondary/grammar schools; and the upper-middle and upper classes had the public, fee-paying schools. The universities were the preserve of the élite, and expanded but slowly. Oxford and Cambridge retained their pre-eminence; they were joined by University College 1828 (the first secular university and the nucleus of London University), and by Durham 1832; but no real expansion took place until the beginning of the twentieth century, when the new cities opened universities—Leeds, Liverpool, Bristol, and so on. Finally the lack of opportunities for women may be noted. Cambridge provides a good example of discrimination in this respect. Although women were allowed at Cambridge in 1873, and were allowed to sit for the examinations in 1881, it was not until 1947 that they were permitted to take the actual degree and so become full members of the university. But then Cambridge did not vote to establish sociology as a discipline until the 1970s!

In America the indices of modernization in education are much earlier. State involvement in education has a long history. As far back as 1642 Massachusetts had ordered townships of a certain population to see to it that a school be established. By 1837 Massachusetts had evolved a comprehensive system of public education operated under a state board. And it was Massachusetts too that pioneered compulsory schooling, and its Act of 1852 was a generation ahead of England's in years and twice that perhaps in terms of industrial development. (That Massachusetts should lead in so many instances should not prove any surprise.) Very revealing was the provision in the North West Ordinance of 1787, which set aside one section in each township (i.e. 1/36th) for the support of a common school. This beginning was followed up in the Morrill Land Grant Act of 1862, which granted 30,000 acres for each Congressman in the state for the support of higher education. Private education has never had the salience in America that it has in Britain, in the 'public schools'. Similarly modern was the commitment to secularization. Although early education was religious, and there was a spate of university founding on a denominational basis during the Great Awakening, the secular basis quickly became the orthodoxy. Indeed as early as 1779 Jefferson, whose work in connection with the University of Virginia has already been noted, moved for this kind of system in his state. That was a little premature, but was yet prophetic. Today in America what religious schools there are must receive all their operating costs, plant, and salaries from the denomination. And finally it goes without saying that the curriculum in America has always been more suited to an industrial society than England's. The University of Virginia contrasted with the College of William and Mary was an early national instance of this; that the Morrill grant was conditional on fostering agriculture and the mechanical arts was a more modern instance; that today the universities of Minnesota and Wisconsin offer a Bachelor of Mortuary Science degree is surely the climax.

A further point may yet be made. The open nature of American society meant that education was always much broader than in England. It led to the view that the highest education was not something reserved for an élite but was the birthright of all. This may be illustrated in a variety of ways. Consider, for instance, the refusal to discriminate in naming post-secondary institutions in America; from the highest to the lowest they are universities or at least colleges. In England, on the other hand, university is an exclusive title; alongside, but crucially marked off and enjoying considerably less prestige, are the Polytechnics (more industrially oriented), the Colleges of Education (only recently entitled to grant degrees), and Colleges of Further Education (a catchall of offerings). Or consider the far greater number of institutions of higher education in America; about mid-nineteenth century in the United States there were over 180 colleges, and even allowing that some of these would not be classed as colleges or universities in England, the disparity is enormous. Consider again how as early as 1830 Oberlin College pioneered co-education. And consider, too, how in American popular speech 'school' has become ambiguous; it may mean both high school and university. In other words few people see any qualitative difference between school and university, the one succeeding the other automatically. No English student would blur the distinction.

Mass education has been accompanied by a changed role for the university. In the English tradition, derived from the medieval foundations, the university was a society within, or even a little apart from, the main society. It was often referred to as an ivory tower. Such a position meant that it could look upon itself as a community of scholars, controlling its own affairs and being responsible for its own standards. To put it in institutional terms, the university was faculty-run. And the intellectual counterpart of this was the pursuit of knowledge for its own sake. American universities had broken with this by the eighteenth century. Initially it was because they were denominational and anxious to see to it that their specific qualities could be preserved. Accordingly trustees from the denomination came to exercise a dominant role in the life of the university, and the board of governors was established. When circumstances changed in the nineteenth century this pattern persisted, however. For given the directed, practical slant in American life, it was much more efficient to have control vested in businessmen and other representatives of the larger society than in academics. This ethos may be seen intellectually in the fact that all

disciplines in American educational establishments have been prized
not so much in themselves but for their capacity to be useful, to be
applied. It has been pointed out, for instance, how in American elementary and high schools women teachers are much more numerous
than in English and European schools—it is not only that women
teachers work for less but also that men, in the American view, are too
busy doing real things in the real world and therefore do not become
teachers.

Britain's embracing of industrialism was ambiguous, then. But after
all, such a response seems to be the norm; the newer groups having
become the successful ones turn conservative. It has been noted, for
instance, in the case of the old and new nobility in the *ancien régime*
of France, where arrival led to fusion. The point about North America
is that the withdrawal from entrepreneurship has been much less
marked. The absence of an aristocratic ethos may be noted to account
for this. From the earliest days the aristocratic life-style had been difficult to maintain. The Episcopalian Church in the United States, the
Anglican Church in Canada, have never had the same establishment
quality as in Britain. The land has always had different connotations
there, so that if a North American buys a country estate he does not
assume the role of squire (except perhaps in the south); rather it is as a
pioneer that he likes to imagine himself.

Then, too, the constant immigration has had its impact in impeding
aristocratic emergence. In any society waves of newcomers, not bred to
the outlook of the society and lacking instinctive deference to people
and values, must prove inimical to an aristocratic order. But in an industrializing society this must be even truer and must magnify the attractions of the entrepreneurial style. And this for two reasons. Immigrant
groups begin at the bottom, discriminated against and almost outcasts.
The industrial world offers them a means of proving themselves and
the opportunity of upward mobility. The succeeding efforts of different
groups to gain acceptance and status means constant reinforcement of
the middle-class ethic.

Secondly, the drive to industrialism remained strong in North America because immigration, vast though it was, was yet taking place in
an area so huge that it dwarfed even these millions. From colonial times
onward, labour had been in short supply in North America. Even before
the coming of industrialism this shortage had dictated resource use and
had entrenched an outlook that was to persist. In Britain, where land
was scarce in relation to a plentiful supply of labour, it was essential
to use the land carefully, working it in an intensive manner; after all

this is the essence of the agricultural revolution. But in North America, where scarce labour was dear labour and where the land was abundant, it made sense to farm extensively. Newcomers from Europe were appalled at the wasteful manner of using the land, working a plot until it was exhausted and then moving on. But after a while these same critics found that it made sense to operate in this fashion. Unfortunately it encouraged a habit of mind that in other endeavours was more reprehensible; in the timber trade the wastage was incredible, both from timber cut but not used and from frequent forest fires. At the same time high labour costs have been a constant spur to mechanization. It is no accident that the British improvements to agricultural machinery did not include the reaper and binder or the combine. These crucial breakthroughs were American. The same was true in industry. The need to economize on labour led to early American inventions in light engineering and above all in assembly-line mass production. Wedgwood had gone a good way in this regard, but when Eli Whitney —the same who invented the cotton gin—early in the nineteenth century produced fire-arms of standardized, interchangeable parts he did something that British and European experts had claimed was impossible. Henry Ford's production of cars was right in this tradition, as was Taylor's Scientific Management, a movement about 1900 that systematized all stages of production even down to specifying how a labourer should move. But once again there was another less praiseworthy side to this high cost of labour; there was a tendency to cut quality. In the 1830s this was seen when British locomotives proved too heavy for the American tracks, which were lightly built for a short life of quick returns, and was still to be noted in the early twentieth century when British foundry workers in Montreal found that their practice of finishing *both* sides of manhole covers was costing them pay.

The North American entrepreneurial spirit, then, was untrammelled by any countervailing ethos, and was able therefore to develop its thinking about enterprise to much starker conclusions than in Britain. As a twentieth-century president, Calvin Coolidge, was to put it, 'The business of the United States is business'.

Yet those who dwell on the superior physical endowments of North America, or on its more aggressive entrepreneurialism, should also note the long delay in the industrialization of that continent. That the United States did not explode industrially until the second half of the nineteenth century may be seen from the following statistic. Before 1860 the total number of patents issued in the life of the republic was 36,000; but between 1860 and 1890 some 440,000 were granted. A second statistic will make much the same point. A key indicator of industrial success will be the point at which industrial production exceeds that of agriculture; in Britain this had taken place about the 1820s, but the U.S.A. had to wait until about 1880—and Canada until after the First World War. Just why this lag should have occurred will become clearer when the evolution of these economies has been sketched.

North American societies were from the beginning mercantilist colonies. Their function had been to serve the mother country, and in accordance with mercantilist teaching there had been no move to build up secondary industries, indeed the reverse had been true. What had been insisted upon was primary industry, the exploitation of the natural resources of the country for the benefit of the imperial power. To this end raw material was sent eastwards across the Atlantic in exchange for manufactured articles. One of the earliest products to be exploited had been the cod fish of the Newfoundland Banks, demanded by England and France and exported also to the Mediterranean countries. The southern colonies produced tobacco on a large scale. In the north, via the outlets of the St Lawrence, Hudson's Bay, and the Hudson River, fur was exported in great volume. In time this was superseded by timber, from the St Lawrence and also from New Brunswick, for during the Napoleonic wars Britain's normal source of supply, the Baltic region, was closed to it. In turn wheat, from the United States as well as from Canada, displaced timber, becoming one of the most important exports towards the end of the nineteenth century. But perhaps the greatest of all these specialties was cotton, produced in the southern states. It was of later prominence than tobacco, for it was not until the very end of the eighteenth century that it began to boom. Then it did so because the British textile revolution made huge demands for raw cotton, and this incentive encouraged the invention of the cotton gin (by Eli Whitney in 1793), a mechanical device that made possible the speedy separation of cotton fibre from the seeds. Until the invention of the gin, separation had been the bottleneck in the industry, with output per man per day about 6 pounds; with the gin output rose to some 800 pounds. What this meant to cotton production may be judged from the surge in exports, which jumped from 20 million pounds in 1801 to 1,768 million pounds by 1860. At this rate cotton dominated the south to the point that it was a monoculture.

Now all these products are basically similar, and collectively they are known as staples. And staple trade has well-marked consequences for the producing society. First, it tends to perpetuate sparse settlement.

Of course North America at the opening of the nineteenth century lacked a dense population and urban concentrations. The rural predominance was overwhelming; in the United States, suddenly doubled in size in 1803 when Jefferson purchased Louisiana, Philadelphia had some 70,000 inhabitants, New York about 60,000, and Baltimore, Boston, and Charleston about 25,000 each; in all some 4 per cent only lived in towns of over 2,500. And in British North America urbanism was even less of a reality; Montreal and Halifax each had about 10,000 inhabitants. The way in which a commitment to a staple militated against settlement was well seen in connection with Newfoundland where, in the interests of the cod fishery, settlement was actively discouraged by the British government. It was also seen in connection with the fur trade. Too great a density of population would interfere with the fur-bearing animals, and anyway the canoe transport suitable for carrying skins out and supplies and trade goods for the Indians in was not suitable for the bulkier cargoes of settlers. Cotton, which devoured land, also led to sparse settlement, and the urbanization of the south soon lagged behind that of the north. And there was the further discouragement to urbanization in that plantation life favoured self-sufficiency with a minimum of buying in from the outside. Timber, mineral extraction, and wheat are also inimical to dense settlement although, to avoid sending ships empty from Britain to North America, the timber trade filled them with emigrants and so contributed to population growth. Even so, the aim for many in the New World was to acquire a family farm, and this too helped to disperse the people over a wide area.

A further consequence of staple trade is the continuing colonial subordination of the producing society to some more advanced power. Staple trades are large-scale and call for centralized organization and large amounts of capital. For example the fur trade needed trading posts and trading parties far away in the interior, and had to reckon on the fact that the trade cycle, from the departure of the brigades to the final sale of the furs, was a long one. Then, too, the demand for furs was not a constant one, changing fashions in Europe being capable of making all the difference between success or failure. The tendency, then, was for control of the fur trade to pass into fewer and fewer hands, and to get further and further away from those in the field and increasingly into the hands of the middlemen. Cotton was very similar—the fluctuations might not have been so marked, but the other problems were there. It was a crop that tended to exhaust the soil very quickly, and so plantation owners were constantly having to acquire new land; it was a labour-intensive crop and required the ownership of large numbers of slaves, a heavy capital burden, especially since in bad times slaves could not be laid off like factory hands. Cotton producers tended to be in debt, and the control of their economy by outsiders was always marked; originally it was British capital that was used, but in time northern state money, especially New York's, tended to take over. Thus it is frequently the case that beneath a façade of apparent strength and prosperity staple producers are in a weak and vulnerable position. At the same time the tremendous profits that it is known can be made in successful years tend to keep staple producers in that field and to discourage diversification. The over-reliance on cotton is a thing of the past, but that on prairie wheat has marked the present time. In short, staple economies tend to be vulnerable and too dependent upon forces beyond their control. This dependence may be illustrated by British reaction to the loss of the old North West (the triangle lying between the Ohio and the Mississippi, land that Britain might have continued to hold had it pressed hard enough) at the conclusion of the War of Independence in 1783. Britain was confident that its established fur traders, based in London, would have sufficient control of the markets to retain the control of the trade even after the title to the area had passed to the United States.

If staple economies were ever to break free from such colonial-like positions it would be as the result of determined effort. Official recognition of this need dates, in the case of the United States, from the very earliest days. It has already been noted how politically the early national period was marked by the struggle between Jeffersonian Democratic-Republicans and Hamiltonian Federalists. That dichotomy was paralleled by one between Jeffersonian agrarians and Hamiltonian industrialists. Hamilton matched his strong centralism in politics with an aggressively nationalist economics that stressed self-sufficiency and industrial growth. His appointment as Secretary of the Treasury in Washington's first administration in 1789 gave him a position from which he could put his ideas into practice. The First Bank of the United States, 1791, was part of his drive; the Report on Manufactures, submitted to Congress in the same year, was a second major element. The Report called for extensive government aid in establishing industries, bounties were to be paid to encourage certain products, inventions were to be rewarded, and above all a tariff was to be erected to exclude foreign wares and allow the infant industries of the United States to grow to the point where they would be able to stand unaided against their competitors. The Tariff Act of 1792 was enacted to do just this.

Paradoxically, however, it may have been Jefferson rather than Hamilton who did more for the industrialization of America. Despite Hamilton's urging, Americans were still too keen to invest in trade and commerce, or in land speculation, leaving industrial undertakings alone. But this continuation of colonial patterns was disrupted by the Napoleonic wars and especially by Jefferson's response to the strains. Faced by a Britain and a France that alike claimed the right to interfere with neutral shipping, and a Britain that impressed American sailors on the grounds that they were British, Jefferson sought to retaliate by depriving both countries of the benefits of trade with America until they learnt their lesson. Accordingly in 1807 Jefferson had the Embargo Act passed to prohibit the export of any goods from America and the sailing of ships from American ports. When in 1809 Jefferson was obliged to repeal this Act he substituted the Non-Intercourse Act, which allowed trade with all countries but France and Britain. Under the impact of these two measures American trade came to a standstill. Those who were not ruined sought alternative outlets for their capital, and there was a spate of industrial investment in these years and immediately afterwards.

British North America was precluded from using official energy, via a protective tariff, to break free from a staple economy. For these British colonies were still part of a mercantilist system, subordinate to the overall design of the imperial trading area. Not until much later, when Britain had dismantled the mercantilist controls, would British North America, by then Canada, be able to strive for an industrial society behind a tariff wall. The first significant tariff (as opposed to a tariff for revenue) had to wait until 1879 when the National Policy was inaugurated.

Of course official determination was not the only force making for industrialization; indeed, it may not have been the determining factor at all. Much more crucial was the determination shown by individuals and institutions to make the leap from a primary industrial level (including the carrying trade) to a secondary. Without a doubt this spirit was best exemplified in the north eastern United States.

At the conclusion of the War of 1812 this area enjoyed no well-marked economic primacy over others in North America. The situation, in fact, was fluid, and primacy would go to whichever area could tap the wealth of the west—for this was the period when the trans-Appalachian west was being opened up. The key to the transportation necessary to make western settlement possible and attractive was water routes; in the pre-railway age, land transport was ruinously expensive, it being possible about 1815 to move a ton of freight 3,000 miles across the Atlantic for $9 but only 30 miles overland within the United States for the same price. It seemed, then, that the wealth of the west would fall either to New Orleans, the port on the Mississippi, or to Montreal, the outlet from the St Lawrence. The attraction of the former was that, thanks to the Louisiana Purchase, it lay within the United States; its drawback was its distance from Europe. The latter was much more conveniently situated in this respect, but was a British possession and in addition was icebound for half the year. Thus the north east, and especially New York, was encouraged to try to wrest control of the mid-west from its natural outlets. In 1817 New York mounted its tremendous challenge and began the construction of the Erie Canal. This undertaking joined the Hudson River, which emptied into the Atlantic at New York City, to Buffalo on Lake Erie, and there was also a branch to Oswego on Lake Ontario. By 1825 it was possible for goods to travel by water between the mid-western interior and an Atlantic port open year round and conveniently situated for Europe. When it is realized that in 1817 New York state had a population of only one million, the magnitude of the risk-taking involved will become apparent.

Even so, New York was not to rest content with this *coup*. The city went on to take risks, in the best tradition of aggressive entrepreneurship, to consolidate its hegemony over many other parts of America. Thus it was New York that regularized and popularized the auction system. Before 1817 British and other European goods had been dumped in American ports only to wait for long periods until buyers could be found. New York broke with this uncertain practice by encouraging regular auctions at which buyers and sellers could be reasonably certain of doing business; the price to the seller might be somewhat lower than might have been obtained by waiting for the best buyer, but the certainty and volume of sales more than compensated for this. European agents came to prefer New York for its facilities, then. Similarly go-ahead was the decision of the New York Black Ball line to institute regular Atlantic sailings in 1818. Previously ships had sailed only when they had a full cargo, but the Black Ball fleet scheduled regular departures, full cargo or no. The losses at first were eventually outweighed by the vastly increased business that the line attracted. Once again there was nothing automatic about this; it was a far-sighted gamble, the quintessence of the entrepreneurial mentality.

British North America could show nothing on the scale of New York. But within its own context Upper Canada stood out above the other colonies for its entrepreneurial energy. The Maritime region was prosperous, mainly on the profits of the carrying trade based upon the Bluenose schooner, which delivered American-produced foodstuffs and lumber to the West Indian islands. But the Maritimes did little to add secondary industry to this carrying trade, and in time prosperity was to become a memory. Lower Canadian *habitants* were wedded to the land, where they practised a slovenly agriculture; in many years they were unable to produce enough to be self-sufficient. But Upper Canada never wavered in its determination to take advantage of the St Lawrence, and in this the merchants of Montreal joined them. Indeed the Montreal interest in the St Lawrence as the grand avenue for wheat and flour exports to the imperial market was much stimulated in the early nineteenth century as the fur staple of that river died. Increasingly bitter competition in the interior between fur merchants based in Montreal, the North West Company, and those of the Hudson's Bay Company, which exported and imported through York Factory on Hudson Bay, ended in 1821 with victory for the latter. Montreal needed the alternative of grain, as well as that of timber.

But the wheat staple was crucially different from the fur staple. Wheat was a bulk product whose volume-to-profit ratio was low, whereas the reverse was true of fur. The canoe, which had been adequate for getting the furs to the St Lawrence, would have to be replaced by bigger boats. At the same time the up-river traffic would have to change, since European immigrants farming the land, the sellers of wheat, had very different demands from the Indians, the sellers of furs. But more efficient boat transport was prevented by the obstacles to navigation, the rapids and waterfalls. The need for canals became crucial in the early 1820s when it was seen how successful the Erie Canal was becoming. The result was a spate of canal building on the St Lawrence, beginning with the Welland, which was completed in 1829. Unfortunately the canal program did not proceed smoothly. The usual difficulties of undertaking such works in an economy still very much a pioneering one were compounded by the political division of the region. The pressure for canals came from the grain producers of Upper Canada and even more vocally from the Montreal merchants. From the *habitant* of Lower Canada came resistance to such expense and a refusal to contribute to the costs. It was not until 1848, by which time Upper and Lower Canada had been reunited, that the chain of canals was completed.

By 1848, however, canals had had their day. This was particularly true of a system like that of the St Lawrence, where for six months of the year traffic was halted by ice. The railway, which could be used year round, was especially advantageous in such a setting. Canadians and especially the Montreal interests took up the challenge. Allying with New Englanders who resented the dominance of New York's port, they undertook a railway from Montreal to Portland, Maine. This line, giving St Lawrence produce an outlet to an ice-free port, and one that was closer to Europe than New York itself, was completed in 1853. This network was then extended westward from Montreal to reach Sarnia, in order to tap the wheat at source. The entire line, the Grand Trunk railway, was completed by 1860. All told, the railway mileage of British North America amounted to over 2,000 miles by this date, and the St Lawrence region, especially Montreal and the area to the west, was the main beneficiary. Like the achievement of north-eastern states, though on a smaller scale, it was an heroic development, the realization of great gains from small beginnings.

It should not have escaped the attention of the reader that the ending of staple economies in, say, Upper Canada or the north-eastern United States did not mean the total abolition of staple dependence in North America. What it meant, in fact, was merely a change in the identity of the superior trading partner. In Canada, for instance, the flowering of the Laurentian region, and in particular of the future Ontario, was simultaneously laying the foundation of resentment of both east and west against this 'have' part of the country. Regionalism, and the jealousy of the 'have-nots' against the dominant 'haves', was in fact to be an enduring aspect of the industrialization of North America.

The most striking example of this development came in the United States in connection with the southern states. More about this sectional clash will be said in the following chapter; here the economic aspects of disagreement will be noted.

As the demand for cotton increased the southern economy became dependent upon that crop to an ever greater degree. But even while this was happening the north was diversifying and becoming industrial. Southern resentment against the fact that the balance, roughly equal at the opening of the century, was tipping in favour of the north was fanned by the response to the tariff. As over the years the tariff wall was built higher, southerners argued that their region was being discriminated against. Like any other staple producers they were obliged to sell their products on the world, i.e., unprotected market where prices were bidden down to the lowest level. At the same time they were obliged to buy in the home market where prices were kept artificially high. This resentment peaked in 1828 when the tariff was raised to unprecedented heights, the so-called 'Tariff of Abominations'. Emotions became so heated that the appeal of the Virginia and Kentucky Resolutions was felt again, and the leading southern statesman of the day, John C. Calhoun, led his state into a defiance of the national government. In 1832 South Carolina declared that the tariff was not to be borne, and that in self-defence South Carolina would 'nullify' the offending federal legislation. In the end the issue was settled by compromise, but this resurrection of states' rights had dramatized the sectional tension that increasing industrialism was causing.

It is important, therefore, that the North American economies had their origin in the staple trades, since it points to basic differences between their development and that of Britain. It was not merely that they lagged behind in the process of industrialism. They also experienced tensions of a kind not found to any great extent in Britain, those based on regional antagonism. For as already hinted, British 'have-not' regions were almost completely destitute of economic leverage against the dominant area; until North Sea gas there was no staple to correspond to, say, cotton. So great were the tensions in the United States, and north and south were moving along such different tracks that they were becoming foreigners to each other well before the Civil War broke out in 1861. This may be illustrated by considering railway building in the United States. That country, being one of great distances, was ideally suited for the early and rapid spread of railways, and by the 1840s the United States trackage of over 3,000 miles was much greater than the combined European total of less than 2,000. But it was a striking fact that despite the railway's ability to unite distant and disparate areas, the northern and southern networks remained distinct and made contact at one point only, Bowling Green, Kentucky.

Earlier it was noted that if differences existed between North American industrialization and Britain's, there were also differences within North America. The experience of Canada was significantly different from that of the United States. Remember, for instance, that when Britain's per capita domestic product of $2,128 was compared with that of the United States at $4,734, Canada's fell between at $3,676. Remember, too, that if British industrial production surpassed agricultural some half a century ahead of the States, it was a whole century in advance of Canada. The continuing lag of Canada behind the United States makes a mockery of Prime Minister Laurier's boast that the twentieth century would belong to Canada.

In accounting for this lag, the material disadvantages of Canada as compared with the United States clearly play a big part. Already it has been pointed out that the St Lawrence, the key to so much development in the formative period, was a siren. On the one hand it seemed to promise so much that generation after generation was led to trust in it; on the other, its favours were to be given but grudgingly and only after the expenditure of ruinous amounts of capital. The vast sums poured into canals fastened the weight of heavy fixed costs on to the Laurentian region, and the chances of eventually recouping any benefit were blighted because no sooner were the canals completed than the railway upstaged them. But there, too, the same dilemma had to be faced. Without railways there was no future for an industrial Canada. But given the vast and difficult terrain and the initial lack of settlers and traffic in any significant density, the fixed costs had to be out of all proportion to the receipts. It was an impossible position.

The hardness of the land has been inescapable. The wealth locked into Canada has required far greater effort to release than comparable resources in the United States. Immigration, so crucial to the growth of a new society, has avoided Canada, and again the hardness of the land was a major determinant there. In the two generations after Waterloo there was heavy immigration from Britain and Ireland, most of it to Upper Canada, which by mid-century had overtaken Lower Canada in population. But when compared with the numbers going to the United States, it was a tiny trickle; between 1815 and 1865 a total of some 1.17 million arrived in British North America from the British Isles, but during the same period the British Isles sent some 3.6 million to the United States, and this comparison ignores the fact that there was heavy non-British/Irish immigration into the United States, which was missing in the case of British North America, and it ignores the fact that those who arrived in British North America but who ended up in the United States were many more than those who passed in the reverse direction. And it is also true that the relatively small population of British North America was thinly dispersed. The point has been made that in the early period of United States history the Appalachians had served as a dam, bottling settlement up and forcing the pace of economic differentiation within the settled area. But from the earliest days the northern areas, the future Canada, had thrown their peoples across the continent.

However, when every allowance has been made for these material disadvantages, one may still wonder if Canada would have done much better, materially speaking, had it not suffered from such drawbacks. Even by the time of the War of 1812 it was being acknowledged that the British colonies were not developing economically as rapidly as the United States, a state of affairs borne out by the fact that the inhabitants voted with their feet, causing a net outflow from the British system.

From the earliest days of New France it had been evident that if anything were to be accomplished in such a setting, local and individual initiative would have to be supplemented by central encouragement and direction. This tradition had been reinforced in the case of the Maritimes, dependent upon the Halifax naval base or on the imperial handouts for the Saint John United Empire Loyalists, and also in that of Upper Canada. From necessity and habit, then, British North Americans were content to operate on a lower key than their neighbours to the south. Their refusal to become so aggressively venturesome may be illustrated by a glance at two institutions of crucial concern to any industrializing society.

The first institution is banking. So many comparisons between the two economies of the United States and Canada break down because the given physical advantages are so different. But banks, an essential part of any modern economy, are almost completely free from the physical background, and consequently mirror far more closely than usual the economic mind of the societies. The banking system of both societies was derived from Britain, whose Bank of England dated from 1694. In 1791 Hamilton began the Bank of the United States, and in his tendency to look to Britain not surprisingly patterned his Bank on the London Bank. When a good few years later British North America established its first bank, the Bank of Montreal, in 1817, it looked (and the choice is significant) to the United States. What is interesting is that British North America held fast to this Hamiltonian-British heritage, but that quite soon the United States had repudiated it. In the first place the Americans found Hamilton's conservative centralist system too cramping. The result of Hamiltonian-British practice was what is known as branch banking, that is, a few major units are chartered and they establish branches across the nation; thus today, and especially after a series of mergers, in Canada there are the Big Five and in Britain too there are the Big Four. Thus by the 1840s British North America had less than twelve banks, but the United States well over seven hundred. What this points to is the centralism and bureaucratic control frequently to be found in Canada, but suspect in the United States. And in turn this indicates Canadian addiction to the routine, the tried and trusted, and the American urge to challenge and innovate. This point is confirmed by the second way in which the Hamiltonian-British tradition was repudiated by Americans. Part of that tradition was the requirement that a bank be chartered, that is the legislature of a state should confer both a seal of approval and a quasi-monopoly on the bank corporation. In many American states the experiment was tried and persisted with of 'free banking', that is, allowing any institution to operate as a bank and refusing to recognize any by charter; it was a clear instance of an attachment to equal opportunity and *caveat emptor*. In British North America that experiment was tried, but only from 1850–66, and even then the chartered banks operated alongside. In this experience, then, Canada has remained between the United States and Britain, and rather closer to Britain in fact.

The same may be said about that second key institution, education. Indeed, in the case of French Canada, there was an attachment to a system that even Britain was leaving behind. From the beginning education in Quebec had been religious. Of the fifty or so educational institutions that are known to have existed under the French régime, only one was not religious; that was the School of Mathematics and Hydrography established in 1665, mainly to train pilots for the St Lawrence, and even that passed to the Jesuits in 1708. After the Conquest attempts were made to erect a less religious system, and the estates of the suppressed orders, notably those of the Jesuits, were spoken of to this end. But ecclesiastical resistance was too great and by 1824 the attempt had been abandoned; in that year an act confirmed the church's control of education, and by giving the church the right to public taxation at the parish level it in fact gave the church an authority greater than that which it had enjoyed under the French kings. The British element did establish its own institutions, capped in 1821 by the founding of McGill University. But the French Canadians held aloof, countered in 1853 with the foundation of Laval (the descendant of the Seminary of Quebec of 1686) and stuck by the narrow classical curriculum that had always characterized the province's system. The élitism that had moved a Jesuit director in the seventeenth century to declare 'It is far more worthwhile to have only a few students, and that they be good ones', remained characteristic, too. So markedly different was French-Canadian education that when the Union of 1841 came into effect and rejoined Upper and Lower Canada under one legislature, and far-ranging reforms were undertaken in that decade, no attempt was made to assimilate the two systems.

But in the other British colonies there was a struggle between the older and newer conceptions. For instance many of the early universities were denominational; King's College, Nova Scotia, 1802 (now a part of Dalhousie University) was Anglican; Mount Allison was Methodist; Acadia, Baptist; Queen's, Presbyterian. But the newer ones were increasingly state ventures, and this was the norm when the west was finally settled. A clear case of collision between the two outlooks was seen in the battle over the University of Toronto. It was chartered in 1827 as King's College and was to be under Anglican auspices (though it must be admitted that blatant Anglicanism was to be restricted to the Divinity School). But to many even this smacked of establishment arrogance, and a campaign to revoke the charter was begun. In 1849 the revocation took place and the university became non-sectarian. A compromise position was hammered out however in 1853, by which the non-sectarian university retained the endowments and the right to examine and grant degrees, but by which sectarian colleges might affiliate to the university and hope for some financial aid. Eventually the rising costs of universities strengthened the state element at the expense of the denominational, and so the Canadian institutions of higher learning have approximated more and more to the American pattern. This trend may also be seen in the board control of universities, and in the requirements for graduation, the older British pattern of a course of study being replaced by broader and broader elections of separate courses, the completion of say, fifteen (a proposal now under discussion at the University of Manitoba would say *any* fifteen) being enough for a degree. And the percentage of eligible students attending university in Canada is much closer to the American figure than to the British.

High-school development has been in the same general direction. Religious education long persisted in Newfoundland, but before the close of the Napoleonic wars Nova Scotia and New Brunswick had opted for the New England pattern of state control. Upper Canada again showed the clash between the two possibilities. In 1846 a reform was carried through under Egerton Ryerson, the leading Methodist of the day. From America he drew the idea of public schools controlled by elected boards with authority to spend public money. But from British (more exactly from Irish) experience he drew the notion of some accommodation for religion; time was to be set aside each school day for instructional visits from clergymen who would instruct children of their own denomination. However the next few years saw the abandonment of this basically secular system. Mounting Catholic pressure in the fifties (it was a world-wide phenomenon, and in the Canadas was exacerbated by the large French-Canadian bloc and increasingly large numbers of Irish-Catholic immigrants) gained separate, that is, publicly supported Catholic schools in 1855 and 1863, and despite fluctuating fortunes the question of separate schools continues to bedevil

Canadian politics to this day. It is another sign that Canada was not so prepared as the United States to pursue efficiency and modernity.

The issues discussed here have been very general, and it is time, perhaps, to look at these changing societies in more concrete terms. By looking at the major movements for reform it will be possible to see how the new industrialisms were taking shape in additional detail.

4

Varieties
of
Liberalism

The nineteenth century, especially the earlier portion, was a period of reform and social hopefulness. A standard treatment of English history from 1815 to 1870 (Ll. Woodward's volume in the Oxford series) is simply entitled *The Age of Reform*, while a comparable work on American society down to the Civil War is Alice Tyler's *Freedom's Ferment*. On every side could be found individuals and groups striving to eradicate abuses and to build a better society. Organizations existed to fight slavery or prostitution or illiteracy, to control excessive child and female labour and to regulate the hours of work, to press for improved drainage schemes and recreational facilities, to win votes for women and to reform the political system, even to usher in instant utopia through the establishment of communes. But no matter how diverse the specific aims, most were united in being part of one broad stream of reform, liberalism. Here was a philosophy that from the early nineteenth century on so completely dominated the three North Atlantic societies that fundamental opposition to its tenets was unusual. This chapter, therefore, must begin by outlining the main elements of the liberal creed.

Liberalism was an amalgam whose formation early in the nineteenth century was made possible by the industrial revolution. Without the sweeping changes caused by industrialism, liberalism might have remained a speculative creed and never have become the practical force that shook the old fixities to their foundations. Growth and innovation became the order of the day, and writers such as Smiles and Alger celebrated the rise of the new men, the new types, and the new values. Yet the presuppositions of the new order could not be found in mere fact, however much the fact of the industrial revolution was necessary to precipitate and establish the new *Weltanschauung*. The philosophy of liberalism was rooted in two existing outlooks, that of the Enlightenment and that of sectarian religion.

The economic aspects of Enlightenment thinking, which were compatible with the facts of the new industrialism and so were taken up, were to be found in the ideas of Adam Smith, the Scottish Enlightenment philosopher whose classic *Wealth of Nations* appeared in 1776. Just as Locke had taken as his starting point individual man, so too did Smith. But whereas the former had assumed political man, driven by a need to involve himself in the political process, the latter postulated economic man, an entity driven by the need to maximize his wealth. This was to be achieved by buying cheap and selling dear, and there were two ways by which this could be done.

The first was to insist upon specialization. Concentration would mean efficiency and the possibility for a manufacturer to produce, i.e. to buy labour from his workmen, cheaply. The last chapter pointed out in a slightly different context Wedgwood's attempts to specialize the production of china; Smith's own example was nail production, for if a workman attempted to make the entire product himself his output would be but a handful a day, whereas a team of men each performing one repetitive stage could turn out thousands. But specialization could be applied in rather different ways, too. Consider for instance the hypothetical example given in chapter 1, the need for Britain to import grain and the probability that a Dutch freighter would submit the most competitive bid. Smith would argue, give the contract to the Dutch shipper; the British competitor will either have to reduce his prices by becoming more efficient, or else go out of business, in which case his capital will be obliged to find more suitable employment elsewhere. British coin will go abroad, but this will be a short-term loss, for the ensuing cheaper grain, and the more efficient use of capital, will mean lower production costs and the eventual larger sale of British goods. By letting capital and inventive skill find their own level, the optimum division of labour will be discovered. If this will mean Britain's becoming the workshop of the world, then let her grain production die. Thus Smith was quite prepared to contemplate regional dependence upon the goods that could be produced most efficiently there.

The example just given points to the second mechanism insisted upon by Smith for maximizing wealth. Economic man could be sure of buying cheap only if all potential sellers were allowed unimpeded access to the market; any interference by the authorities, then, was to be resisted, no matter how well-meaning. And by the same token economic man could be sure of selling for the best price only if all potential buyers were allowed freely into the market. The value of any good, therefore, was to be fixed not by any paternalistic government or guild but by the autonomous action of the market itself; supply and demand were to be the only arbiters. It was thus that the market acquired a novel, symbolic centrality in society. In particular it should be noted how value had now become democratic; the value of anything was determined by the votes that were given for it.

What lay behind such thinking and marked it off from the older mercantilism was a revolutionary open-endedness. Smith was assuming a dynamic quality totally missing from mercantilism. At bottom, mercantilism was a science of exchange; there was an instinctive belief that there was a finite stock of goods in the world, so that what one gained another had to lose. This was why using Dutch shippers for Britain's carrying trade was so heinous—any profit to the Dutch was an equivalent loss to Britain. But the new economics was one of production; it accepted the notion of an ever-expanding amount of goods, so that more for one might allow more for another as well. Just as the *philosophes* had demanded that man be released from his traditional shackles in order to flourish, so did Smith demand that the economy be freed in order to expand.

Not surprisingly, the new economics took as its slogan 'laissez-faire'. The fuller phrase 'laissez-faire, laissez-passer' (which may be translated 'leave things alone, let them happen') had been coined in the mid-eighteenth century by the forerunners of Smith, the French school of Physiocrats who had numbered in their ranks the *philosophes* Turgot and du Pont de Nemours (a later emigré family whose name in slightly different form has become well known in United States business). Physiocracy itself had not amounted to much, but its slogan was exactly right and quickly passed into general currency. And it was exactly right in drawing attention to the strength and weakness of the new economics, a quality that it shared with the general Enlightenment background from which it sprang. Laissez-faire drew attention to that delight in testing an economy by its evident, tangible results. Here may be seen the fragmentation of the whole that had been implicit in the Enlightenment preference for 'how' over 'why' questions. Smith was like Newton and Locke in recognizing the limited scope of what he was doing, but once again, in the hands of later developers, this insight was lost sight of. Laissez-faire economics became notorious for ignoring the purpose of accumulation; it was enough to show that the total output was increasing to prove that a course of action was justified. Economics, it may be said, had become an autonomous discipline.

Laissez-faire was one slogan of the new economics. Another, and more salient at the time, was free trade, and it was fitting that when Manchester, the capital of the cotton kingdom and the epitome of the new urbanism, decided in a burst of civic and middle-class pride to erect a splendid building for public occasions, the building should have been called the Free Trade Hall. The original thrust of that slogan was clearly economic, a call for the abolition of all tariff barriers between nations as an essential first step towards the construction of the perfect market. It was also a call for the ending of all regulations restraining the methods of work; if upholders of the older guild approach argued that without regulation standards would suffer, they were met by the response that if the public did not want shoddy goods then they would not buy them and so producers of such goods would go out of business —in other words the market would autonomously regulate quality as well as price. Of course in all this free trade was in part a mask for self-interest. Free trade, meaning an end to tariffs, was attractive to Britain; it was the first country to industrialize and by the mid-nineteenth century was in a position to scorn rival attempts to sell manufactured goods in Britain, and yet it wished to sell its own products abroad at the lowest, i.e. unprotected, price. Significantly Britain was the only member of the North Atlantic triangle to pledge wholehearted adherence to the new doctrine and accompany the abolition of mercantilism by the removal of all tariffs; both the United States and Canada kept their protective walls. And free trade, meaning an absence of governmental regulation, was naturally appealing to hard-headed businessmen eager to make their fortunes.

But free trade was not merely self-interest, not merely economic even. Liberalism was also a genuine commitment to a world better and freer in every way. At the bottom of Smithite economics lay the doctrine of the natural harmony of interests. Smith had recognized the paradox of making economic man, self-interested as he was, the basis of a social theory. It must be admitted that his resolution of the paradox was perfunctory, a bald statement about economic man to the effect that 'by directing [his] industry in such a manner as its produce may be of the greatest value he intends only his own gain, and he is in this, as in many other cases, led by an invisible hand to promote an end which was no part of his intention'. Yet however shaky the basis of the natural harmony of interests, it was widely and strongly held. A belief in cosmopolitan brotherhood was an outcome of this attitude. The economy of the entire world was seen to be interdependent, and wars that prevented the proper operation of the market were expected to become a thing of the past. It has already been mentioned that an attachment to free-trade doctrines could lead to a less selfish attitude than formerly to territorial acquisition. By the Treaty of Versailles in 1783 the old North West, remember, had been allowed to pass from British possession to American. The minister responsible for this development was Shelburne, an early disciple of Smith, who argued that no matter who had political sovereignty over that area, the produce would go to the centre most economically suited to take charge of it and that could most fitly provide the manufactured goods needed in exchange, and this centre would continue to be Britain. That the present Canadian boundary is so far to the north may be put down in large part to early laissez-faire thinking.

Another aspect of this cosmopolitanism, and one that brings out the wider implication of free trade beyond the mere economic, is the attitude to the free transmission of ideas. Here the Enlightenment's willingness to be critical of accepted beliefs and the more specifically laissez-faire attachment to the market mechanism blend in a striking fashion. Liberalism placed great value on pluralism. Just as no physical impediment should be placed in the way of products, but each allowed into the market place so that its real value might be assessed by the demand for it, so too there should be no intellectual impediments to the free flow of ideas, the value or truth of which was also to be assessed in the 'market'. It should be appreciated that such an attitude to truth was essentially as democratic as was the attitude to price; all ideas were to be treated initially as equal, and only the 'votes' of the 'buyers', also to be seen as equal, would determine which were to be considered correct. Like the belief in a dawning age of peace, it stressed the fundamental rationality of affairs, and so contributed to that pervasive cosmic optimism that was abroad.

Finally this side of liberalism was still further entrenched by the open-ended attitude alluded to above. The dynamic quality that Smith saw in the economic process spilled over until it informed every aspect of society, until it came to characterize life itself. Just as man was learning how to construct bigger and more powerful steam engines, so too was he learning to understand more and more of the world; improvements in sanitation design would be paralleled by those in social engineering. A major assumption was that liberalism meant Progress—and the capital letter is justified since so many saw it in quasi-religious terms. It is no accident that this 'steam intellect society' produced in 1859 *The Origin of the Species*, in which Darwin made open-ended evolution a dominant element of consciousness.

The second source for liberalism's creed, and also a potent source for its driving force, was sectarian religion. In America the Great Awakening had petered out by the end of the eighteenth century, but with the new century and especially after the War of 1812, a series of revivals again swept the country. Frequently organized about the camp-meeting, a kind of religious fair to which the scattered populations of the outlying districts would be attracted, they kept sectarian zeal at fever pitch. New York state was so frequently and so deeply affected by wave after wave of revivalism that it became known as the 'Burnt-over district'. And it was a movement that spanned the entire spectrum of sectarianism; at one extreme were the Unitarians, the most intellectual and rational of the Calvinist family, who denied the divinity of Christ, while at the other were the Millerites, a group of millennialists who confidently expected the end of the world and the second coming of Christ in 1843. Between these extremes pullulated a vast multiplicity of sects, a hallmark of American religiosity.

In Britain the same broad development of sectarianism took place, though not on such an extreme scale, and it was significant that whereas earlier Britain had made a gift of Whitefield's revivalism to America, from now on Britain was to look to America for its revivalists. British sectarianism in the nineteenth century, despite progressively more extreme schisms from the original Methodism, was generally in the direction of increased sobriety, and it gravitated towards a middle-of-the-road position. That sectarianism there was more centralized was indicated by the fact that the Anglican Church itself threw up a wing, the Evangelicals, which approached the sectarians very closely, and it numbered in its ranks many from the establishment. All told, the sectarian impulse was very unified in Britain, and it was summed up as the 'Nonconformist conscience'.

For a time it looked as though British North America would take on an American tone when it came to sectarianism. At the very opening of the nineteenth century American-based or -trained preachers were flooding across the border and bringing with them the camp-meeting. This tinge was never completely lost, but after the War of 1812 Americans were in disfavour, and as British migration picked up, the balance tipped towards a more sober style. A touchstone of this swing is provided by the Methodist experience in Upper Canada. Originally the Methodists in that colony were from America, and were imbued with American notions. But in 1824 it was felt that this link was a disadvantage in a loyalist setting, and so an independent Upper Canadian Methodist Conference was set up. It was, however, still affiliated with the American parent. But in 1828 this link was broken. Even so, the official classes were not happy, and in 1833, thanks to imperial backing, the main body of Upper Canadian Methodism agreed to merge with the British Wesleyans; it was at this time, and in the wake of this development, that the political about-face by these Methodists, mentioned in chapter 1, took place. But however tamed, sectarianism in British North America remained extensive and influential, quite dwarfing the churches.

The strength of sectarianism was of the greatest importance for liberalism. That there is an affinity between sectarianism and expansive capitalism has been noted, and so here was additional motive power for liberalism. But sectarianism also brought content to liberalism. It was part of the Christian scheme, after all, to help one's fellow man. Thus the various reform movements were frequently staffed by those whose concern was religious. In Britain the lead against the slave trade, finally outlawed in 1833, was taken by the Evangelical Anglican, William Wilberforce, and the leading fighter against excessive hours of work was also an Evangelical, Lord Ashley (later the Earl of Shaftesbury). In British North America the prominent reformer, George Brown, was a staunch member of the Free Kirk (the secession from official Presbyterianism that took place in 1843; the Free Kirk corresponded to the Evangelical wing of the Anglican Church), and it was this religious commitment that drove Brown to reform and especially to his work for the 'underground railroad', the escape route used by fugitive slaves from the southern states to British North America. And in the United States many, perhaps most, of those working to end slavery were religiously motivated, a tradition that has lived on in, say, Martin Luther King, Jr.

Then, too, sectarianism was democratic, and this was a key element in liberalism. The general ways in which sectarianism tended towards democracy have been touched upon in chapter 1. Here it may be added how in Britain political developments emphasized this commitment. The Test and Corporation Acts were still on the statute book until 1828. The long campaign to have them abolished had schooled the Nonconformists in politics, and once formal discrimination had been removed Nonconformists flocked into national and local politics determined to press for further reform. As late as 1902 Nonconformists had an issue on which to fight and over which to raise a plea for democracy; in that year an Education Act entrenched public support for denominational schooling and perpetuated Anglican favours, and in protest against such a denial of democracy, as they saw it, several Nonconformists chose to go to jail rather than pay the assessments. Similar patterns marked Canadian sectarian history. There was a long history of struggle against Anglican privilege; for instance, it was not until 1831 that Methodist ministers were given the right to perform marriages, while in Upper Canada a long feud continued over the division of the Clergy Reserves. In the United States, of course, such struggles were unnecessary. But there the identity between sectarianism and democracy did not need the spur of formal discrimination to strengthen it; as an observer wrote at mid-century, 'Men are free, and claim the right to think for themselves in religious as well as in political matters'.

One final remark must be made about the religious component of liberalism. So far that creed has appeared as a sunny doctrine. But the Calvinist roots of sectarianism injected something very different into the amalgam. The dour side of Calvinism, which has already been touched upon, reappeared in liberalism as a tough-mindedness that in realistic fashion qualified much of the optimism derived from the Enlightenment tradition. Liberalism might believe in open-ended progress and might be democratic. But it still pointed out that the way upward was difficult and that not all would make it to the top. Life was a hard struggle in which many might go to the wall and only a concentration upon the sterner qualities would enable one to avoid the many pitfalls that trapped the unwary. The gains promised by liberalism were not automatic, but were to be won only by unremitting toil and application.

In summary, then, one may say that liberalism was an ambivalent philosophy. It postulated a world built upon freedom in which progress would be the norm, and at the social level its outlook was decidedly optimistic. At the same time, however, there was grave doubt about the ability of the individual to rise to the opportunity and to take advantage of the possibilities. And of course, while there might be basic agreement on the philosophy in the broad outline noted here, there was a great deal of room for disagreement on the degree to which any element could or ought to exist. This disagreement was particularly noticeable among the members of the North Atlantic community, as will now be demonstrated. That discussion may be structured about the following three questions; how thorough-going was the commitment to democracy? how real was the commitment to the free expression of opinion and the existence of pluralism? and how optimistically was the future prospect seen?

※ ※ ※

Evidently liberal democracy may be pushed to extreme conclusions. Its 'live and let live' presuppositions may be extended even to the anarchical, and several liberals almost came to that resting place. But such extremes could not be taken up on any appreciable scale, though the United States showed that it was prepared to go a good deal of the way.

American experiments with democracy in the first half of the nineteenth century may be conveniently summed up as Jacksonian democracy. Like all summaries it is misleading, since President Andrew Jackson was in power only from 1829–37, and he was by no means solely responsible for the changes that took place even within that period. But it is not an impossible summary, for Jackson was so in tune with the major thrust of the entire period that he epitomizes a very important side of the American consciousness. Marvin Myers, whose *Jacksonian Persuasion* is one of the best books on the phenomenon, restates the mid-nineteenth century finding that only Washington himself has given his name to more places in America than Jackson, a simple but effective test of his appeal to his fellow Americans. Analyzing that appeal will say much about the American brand of liberalism.

That the United States was in flux at the opening of the nineteenth century, and so ripe for an extension of democracy, may be indicated by the changing socio-economic relationships. The dominance of agriculture was being challenged and urbanization was slowly taking place. The strike of carpenters in Boston in 1825 and those in Philadelphia in 1827 point to the emergence of a crucial number of wage earners with interests of their own to protect. In 1827 unions in Philadelphia came together in an association. In 1828 a Workingman's Party was in existence. That a major plank in its platform was the need to modify the debt laws was indicative of the changing environment. The existing laws of debt prescribed imprisonment as the penalty, and in a traditional, static society this was not wholly unreasonable—in normal times few would need to go into debt and failure to discharge it would be due to culpable shortcomings. But in the newer, mobile, impersonal society debt had to be seen as the norm and it had to be recognized that inability to discharge it might have more to do with the trade cycle and the state of the money market than with personal failings. In the new society imprisonment for debt would be simply counterproductive, removing a potential contributor from the economy. The importance given to education in the Workingman's Party platform is a further indication of the climate of change.

But change was even physical. The United States was expanding rapidly in this period. In the first twenty years of the nineteenth century no less than eight new states were established and admitted to the Union. Such expansion made for a second kind of fluidity and provided incentive and the possibility for new departures. Beginning from scratch, the new states could structure themselves in tune with the prevailing sentiments, and once their example existed it became possible for them to influence the older states; Connecticut in 1818, Massachusetts in 1820, and New York in 1821 were states that revised their systems in the light of changing outlooks.

Jacksonian democracy was characterized by a thorough-going egalitarianism. In formal political terms this was strikingly so. The new state franchises, and several of the reformed older ones, were extremely wide (by European standards). By 1824 only three states out of the twenty-four then in the Union did not have what amounted to adult white male suffrage. Another indicator of a shift towards a more egalitarian politics was the attack on the electoral college. It will be remembered that as a buffer against popular passions the Constitution had decreed that the president was to be elected by an electoral college. The choosing of these electors had been left up to the individual states, which had chosen to use their legislatures as the means of electing their members of the college. Now, in the opening years of the nineteenth century, state after state altered the requirements to permit the members of the electoral college to be elected on a popular basis.

But a key development in national politics perhaps best reveals the way in which a generalized mood for change was sweeping America at this time. Choosing a presidential candidate had been done by the caucus, that is by a relatively small group of inner politicians. Thus, for instance, the Federalist members of Congress would agree among themselves (with possibly some advice from prominent Federalists not in Congress) on whom to put forward; the Democratic-Republicans would do likewise. But the caucus of 1824 was the last to select candidates in this manner; indeed it cannot be said to have succeeded, for the Democratic-Republican nominee was in fact challenged by three other candidates all from the same vague Democratic-Republican grouping. From now on the nominating convention was to be the machinery for generating a presidential candidate. This was a very American device, the counterpart to the earlier ratifying convention; both were ways of returning to the people their original powers and of cutting out the middle men, the manipulators. In practice, it must be confessed, the nominating convention did not fulfil these hopes, for such large un-structured gatherings easily fell under the control of a hard core of professional politicians who staffed the key committees. But the impulse was in many cases to return power to the people, and it was in these terms that its use was advocated in the 1830s until it became an integral part of American politics.

Before leaving the political side of Jacksonianism a concomitant of mass politics ought to be noticed. In the Jacksonian period larger and larger numbers were politicized and encouraged to vote. It is a remark-able thing that American voter turn-out is often so low; it was particu-larly true in the period after the excitement of the Revolution had worn off, when frequently less than 25 per cent of those eligible would turn out. But in 1828 no less than 56 per cent of the electorate voted; in 1832 it was over 55 per cent. Now such numbers needed a new kind of politics. The days of a calm, reasoned appeal to the better elements had gone; now sloganizing, the simplification of issues, became necessary. Jackson himself was dubbed Old Hickory in testimony to his upright strength and with the suggestion that he would be the broom to sweep away corruption. Vituperation of the lowest kind became usual, and it was alleged for instance that Jackson had been living in sin with his 'wife'. Nowhere was this new-style politics better shown than in the election of 1840, when Martin Van Buren, the Jacksonian president from 1837–41, was defeated by William Harrison. That election proved that 'the making of the president' was not a twentieth-century inven-tion. A nonentity without a platform, Harrison could yet be sold to the voters. And significantly the way to do this was to stress his military prowess (he had been victorious over Tecumseh's Indians in the battle of Tippecanoe twenty-nine years before), his humble origins in a log cabin, and his simple style.

For here was a second way in which the egalitarianism of American democracy was brought out in Jacksonianism, a style so influential that even the opponents of the Jacksonians had to subscribe to it. Jefferson-ian simplicity was deepened during the Jackson years. Jeffersonianism had always stood for the simple, the unadorned; in its vocabulary 'democratic' meant the absence of aristocratic foppery as much as any-thing else. Jefferson had indicated this in his objection to titles and to ceremonial towards which the Federalists had always leaned. Jackson continued this tradition, nowhere better seen than at his inauguration, when the White House was invaded by all manner of people not normally admitted to such lofty settings; to many this disregard for distinctions marked a new stage in the reign of the mob. But then such action might have been predicted of the man. He was not from the usual political classes, he was not even a gentleman like Jefferson. Jackson was an adventurer from the newly emerging west, who had used raw Nashville, Tennessee, as his springboard; in his time he had been a school teacher, merchant, slave owner, self-educated lawyer, racehorse owner, land speculator, duellist, and victorious general over the British in the battle of New Orleans, 1815. Here, then, was a very different political animal.

Egalitarian politics and style were accompanied by an egalitarian distrust of bureaucracy. When Jackson entered office in 1829 he showed his antagonism to the idea of specialization by dismissing some ten per cent of the federal civil servants; they were opponents of Jackson, their replacements were Jacksonians, and what was being practised was simply the 'spoils system'. Of course this kind of thing had existed as long as politics itself, but not only was the scale of Jackson's dismissals greater than anything previously known, but he had the temerity to defend what he was doing. Jackson remarked, 'The duties of all public officers are . . . so plain and simple that men of intelligence may readily qualify themselves for their performance'; in other words, since expertise was not necessary and since almost any citizen was capable of doing the job, the rotation of officeholders could only be of benefit by bringing new blood into the bureaucracy and preventing the buildup of vested interests. To this day there is a gap between American expertise when applied to a business or a technological venture such as putting a man on the moon, in which fields American knowhow is proverbially efficient, and when applied to a governmental agency, say the Post Office, where inefficiency is the rule.

Finally, Jacksonian egalitarianism may be encapsulated by sketching the biggest political issue of his presidency. It was the question of the Second Bank of the United States. It will be remembered that Hamilton's First Bank, a central bank designed to act as regulator of the economy and as a watchdog over the other banks, both state and private, had been allowed to expire with its charter in 1811, and that a Second Bank had been established in 1816, the needs of the economy triumphing over the Jeffersonian misgivings of Madison. The charter of 1816 was also for twenty years, and so would run out in 1836. Those in favour of the Bank, headed by its very able and determined director, Nicholas Biddle, decided that it would be wiser to seek renewal of the

charter sometime before 1836, and accordingly began a campaign to
that end that culminated in the summer of 1832. When Congress
granted what Biddle and the Bank wanted, but Jackson vetoed the Bill,
it was clear that the election of 1832 would be fought over the Bank
issue. It was a bitterly contested election, in which the Jacksonian wing
of the Democratic-Republican party (stressing the 'Democratic' qualification and often referred to simply as 'The Democracy') defeated the
other wing of the Democratic-Republicans (known during the 1828
election as National Republicans but increasingly thereafter as Whigs),
and the Bank was killed. Opposition to the Bank was, then, the touchstone of democracy as understood in the United States in the 1830s and
an important clue to the mind of America.

There were many reasons why the Bank was unpopular. Much of
the opposition to the Bank was for the usual reasons; for example those
with interests in certain state or private banks were opposed to the
Bank's superior power and ability to curtail their speculative business.
And in a more principled guise there was the opposition from those
strict constructionists who felt that the Bank was unconstitutional and
was usurping functions that ought to be left to the states. And then
others could disagree on principle with the banking policy pursued by
Biddle; for instance Jackson himself believed that the Bank's ability,
by granting or withholding credit, to expand and contract the economy
had the effect of robbing the ordinary man, and Jackson's devotion to
'hard money' led in 1837 to the 'specie circular'; by this act, public
lands were to be sold for cash or specie only, a restriction that went too
far and helped precipitate the slump of that year.

All these objections played their part in the Bank war; of major
interest here, however, is the way in which the egalitarianism of the
day was affronted by the Bank. Pure Jeffersonian agrarianism might
have been tempered by an increasing devotion to industry, but much
of America still wished to cling to a simple method of production in
which small-scale operations would compete on a basis of equality.
Against this, however, was a trend in economic organization, developed
earlier and to a greater extent in the United States than in Britain,
towards the emergence of the chartered corporation. Early capitalist
ventures had been individual affairs or, at worst, partnerships; either
way the principals who owned the capital ran the business, were personally involved, and could argue that any success that they enjoyed
was the result of their own efforts. But the eagerness of Americans of
even modest means to invest and the need for capital led to the emergence of the corporation, an impersonal organization of many investors

whose sole connection with the business was the financial one, the day-to-day control of that business being in the hands of managers. Now this was bad enough, since mere money was taking the place of superior enterprise, creditism was succeeding capitalism. What was worse was the fact that too often these corporations were given monopolistic favours by charter. There was the feared aristocratic tendency, in the sense of exclusive privilege, entering American life. Against this danger Jacksonians raised their cry 'Equal rights for all, special privileges for none'. And of course the Bank, the federally chartered but yet privately owned super-corporation, was a splendid symbol of a development that threatened to destroy the Republic.

A further aspect of this kind of danger should be noted. The Bank was not only exclusive, it was also mysteriously so. Its officials, more clearly than in the other areas of the economy, were specialists. This, given American, especially Jacksonian, assumptions, was bad enough. To make it worse was the special characteristic of banking. It was a technique that was so remote from the lives of ordinary people that there was an aura of magic about it; even today the operation of the world money market presents this image to the average man, who apprehensively refers to the 'gnomes of Zürich' who control his economic fortunes in a way he does not understand. In the United States of the 1830s, an important result flowed from this way of thinking. That tendency towards conspiracy thinking that has been touched upon earlier was reinforced. The bankers at the centre were seen as malevolent figures working secretly to make their fortunes on the ruin of the ordinary man.

The Bank issue had a symbolic importance for American democracy. Opposition to the Bank united all those who hankered after the older America of simple and evident values that even then was felt to be disappearing. That typical American longing for departed innocence was intensified during the Jacksonian period; it was an odd accompaniment to a future-oriented thrust towards egalitarian democracy.

❊ ❊ ❊

Jacksonianism found few echoes in Britain. There the dominant application of liberalism was that derived from Jeremy Bentham. That philosopher began writing in the 1770s, taking as his starting point the French *philosophe* (mentioned in chapter 1) Helvétius. This time Bentham fed the Enlightenment tradition back into Britain, but with twists of his own. As the starting point of his system Bentham proposed the only self-evident fact, that man is a creature who wishes to seek pleasure and avoid pain, and that his self-interest in maximizing pleasure and minimizing pain is the guide to the individual's conduct and eventually to that of society. (Clearly Bentham's formulation is that of Adam Smith but made more abstract.) Given this fact, it becomes possible to evaluate any course of action in much the same way as an economist evaluates profitability; in place of considerations of abstract justice, the test becomes that of efficiency—will this proposal best preserve man and increase his well-being? *Utility*, the usefulness of anything, was to be the yardstick, and the individual, the point of departure for Bentham as for Smith, was to decide between two alternative courses of action by quantifying the pleasures and pains that each course would bring; these were to be totalled, the pains of each course were to be subtracted from the pleasures, and these two resulting figures were to be compared; the higher figure indicated which course was to be chosen. But if the individual was the point of departure, it was still true that man lived in society and that an unregulated pursuit of individual happiness would end in harming others. The solution to this problem was merely to extend the 'felicific calculus' to all actions and to make the guideline 'the greatest good of the greatest number'. Utilitarianism was a philosophy tailor-made for the age of double-entry capitalism.

Bentham himself was too extreme, both in person and in his writing, to attract much attention. Not until about 1810 did he secure a following, and even then his disciples watered down the original rigour of his approach. Yet this group was very influential, and John Stuart Mill, the son of one of Bentham's original disciples, James Mill, became the most representative figure of British liberalism. Utilitarianism was diffused by this key group, known as the Philosophic Radicals, especially through its organ, the *Westminster Quarterly*, founded in 1823.

What made the Philosophic Radicals such a representatively British-, as opposed to an American-, style group was their championing of a limited democracy; theoretically 'the greatest good of the greatest number' might seem to promise egalitarianism, but in practice it came to mean middle-class direction. The basis of Jacksonian democracy was a belief in natural rights; the individual had certain inalienable rights and the corollary of this belief was an almost anarchical freedom for each to pursue his own ends. Bentham, however, had repudiated such unprovable abstractions. As he wrote on one occasion 'Natural rights is simple nonsense, natural and imprescriptible rights nonsense upon stilts'. More directly, he referred to the Declaration of Independence as 'a hodgepodge of confusion and absurdity'. Instead his concentration upon total actually measured benefit made possible the entry of collectivism quite out of place in the American scheme of things. Certain individuals will have to take action for the good of the other individuals —and given the period, given the triumphs of laissez-faire capitalism, who better to take this action than the middle class? After all, was not this the time when a Lord Chancellor, Henry Brougham, could declare that 'by the people . . . I mean the middle classes, the wealth and intelligence of the country, the glory of the British name'? This adulation of the middle class, with its implication that aristocracy had ceased to matter and that the working class did not count, must now be estimated.

It may be estimated, first, by looking at the political change that corresponded with the American widening of the franchise, the establishment of the nominating convention, and so on. The British equivalent was the great Reform Bill of 1832.

The years since Waterloo had been years of great strain in Britain. The long-term problems caused by a changing socio-economic system had been compounded by the dislocations occasioned by converting from a war- to a peace-time economy, and also by developments in Ireland; there a resurgent Irish Catholic nationalism, led by Daniel O'Connell, had challenged the still-continuing discrimination against Catholics, and thanks to his efforts Catholic Emancipation—allowing Catholics in Britain and Ireland to hold state office and to vote—was carried in 1829. This, coming hard on the heels of the repeal of the Test and Corporation Acts in 1828, put a final nail in the coffin of the Tory party, the party of church-state identity, which had been in power almost continuously since 1784. The pre-modern belief in the identity of church and state had crumbled, and its collapse served notice that a long overdue reordering of politics was at hand.

In 1830 King George IV died. Parliament, the king's parliament, died with him, and new elections were necessary. Against a background of extensive rioting a Commons was returned that gave power to the Whigs, and Earl Grey, who had been prominent in the reform movement of 1793, was asked to form a ministry. This done, he brought in a bill to reform parliament. It achieved a majority of one, which was too precarious, and so Grey asked for and received a dissolution. At the new elections of 1831 the Whig majority was increased. This time the Reform Bill was lost in the Lords. Grey accordingly resigned. The Duke of Wellington, the Tory leader and the ex-Prime Minister under whom Catholic Emancipation had been passed, was unable to form a ministry, however. The king had no other choice but to return to Grey, who was now in a position to bargain. He received the promise from King William IV that, in the event of Lords opposition, enough Whig peers would be created to drive the bill through. The Tory peers, when informed of this promise, withdrew and the bill went through in June 1832.

The Reform Bill did two things. First it redistributed seats so that some notice was taken of population densities. One hundred and forty-three seats, like the notorious Old Sarum, were suppressed and were allocated to the more populous counties and the new urban centres; Leeds, Birmingham, and Manchester, for example, were given representation at this time. Secondly the franchise was extended. In the counties, in addition to the forty-shilling freeholders, those adult males paying rent above a certain figure (it varied) were given the vote. In the towns the old hodgepodge of qualifications was replaced by that of ten-pound occupation, that is, the vote went to those adult males occupying premises worth at least £10 annually.

In the long run the Reform Bill was revolutionary. The absolute distinction between voters and non-voters based upon freehold had given way to a relative distinction based upon wealth, and whereas the former had a logic about it the latter was arbitrary; thus with time it would be found that there would be no logical stopping place until all had been given the vote. But at the time the striking thing about the Reform Bill was its restricted character. There was no clear break with the old, and the distinction between urban and rural, rapidly becoming meaningless, was maintained, indicating that the older conception of representation, that communities not individuals were represented, was not yet dead. Above all, it was restricted to the middle class. The total electorate, still minuscule compared with America's, increased from a mere 435,000 to but 650,000 out of a population of 16.5 million. Not surprisingly the radical papers sent up howls of disappointment when the terms of the Bill became known. And the lag behind the United States was indicated by the slow way in which the franchise was widened. A further installment of reform took place in 1867 when the urban ratepayers were given the vote, and in 1884, when the same principle was extended to the rural areas. Even so, full adult male suffrage did not come until 1918. That the vote was given grudgingly and gradually in Britain was nicely illustrated in the case of women's suffrage; in 1918 those over 30 were allowed to vote, and women did not cast votes equally with men until 1929.

The Reform Bill indicated a middle-class triumph in formal political terms. Perhaps an even greater triumph was the middle-class assault upon the restrictive mercantilism that still prevailed in Britain. The

Reform Bill had been essentially the gift of the aristocratic class and amounted to a technical change. But here was the middle class seeking to swing national policy from one pole to another by initiating a national propaganda campaign, the Anti-Corn Law League.

During the Napoleonic wars the need for Britain to be self-sufficient in grain had led to a great extension in acreage and production. The end of the war threatened to ruin many and so in 1815 the Corn Laws were passed by an unreformed parliament dominated by the landowners; by the Corn Laws foreign grain was denied entry until the home price had reached 80 shillings a quarter—a quarter being eight bushels. Such legislation annoyed the middle class. They argued that protection kept the price of bread artificially high, and this at a time when the bulk of the ordinary person's diet was bread. More self-interestedly they could note that artificially high bread prices meant their having to pay wages higher than would otherwise be the case, and also that if Britain took foreign wheat the wheat-producing countries would be in a position to absorb her manufactures in return. In 1820 formal protest against the Corn Laws took place when the Petition of Merchants was presented to the House of Commons, a petition that rehearsed the by now classical argument of Adam Smith. By 1836 the Philosophic Radicals had mounted agitation against the Corn Laws as part of a general assault upon all protectionist legislation. But in 1838 a new organization was founded in the capital of free trade, Manchester, and an epic movement known as the Manchester School was launched.

From the first the Anti-Corn-Law League was dominated by two men, Richard Cobden and John Bright. Together they epitomized mid-nineteenth-century Britain. The former sprang from a long line of yeomen, that dying breed of small, independent farmers. In 1815 peace had destroyed the family holding and Cobden turned to the textile trade, first as a traveller and then, moving to Manchester in the year of the Reform Bill, as a manufacturer. Always cosmopolitan in his outlook, he visited the United States, which impressed him greatly and which helped precipitate his free-trade views (since he saw that eventually Britain would be threatened by American industrialism and so would have to increase its manufacturing specialization to meet the challenge). Bright was a Quaker, son of a Rochdale mill owner. Never so intellectual as his colleague, Bright was a superb platform orator who learnt his biblically based technique in the anti-church-rates agitation of the early thirties. Like Cobden he was such an individualist and devoted laissez-faire exponent that he opposed any legislative interference with the hours of work. Indeed he was the more extreme of the two, for his opposition to the state went to the extent of fighting any state role in education.

To these two, more than to any others, was due the great impact of the League. Some there were, naturally, who were convinced by the facts. But great causes do not rely on rational persuasion alone. The driving force behind the League was something essentially Nonconformist, and in particular Methodist, which was the combination in the two leaders of brilliant organization and a grasp of the law together with a moral fervour that was at times nakedly religious. The League was consciously modelled upon the Methodist structure (though it must be said that Wesleyan Methodists hung back from actual participation in the movement), with local cells being kept closely tied to the organizing headquarters. Full advantage was taken of the introduction in 1840 of the modern postal system of speedy, cheap delivery based upon pre-paid stamping in order to keep in touch and to disseminate propaganda, publicize meetings, and so on. A more direct way of influencing opinion was by returning M.P.s committed to repeal. To this end some of the League's extensive funds were used to multiply freeholds, that is to acquire freehold land, which carried the right to vote, and break it down into the minimum units of 40 shillings and 'sell' these holdings to sympathizers; in this way enough new voters could be added to swing an election. In parliament Cobden, a master of the facts and statistics, Bright, and others hammered away at the government and at entrenched mercantilist thinking. It was all a model of efficient, rational expertise.

And all the while the religious appeal was present. Usually it was just beneath the surface, a subliminal force awaiting the cue provided by a biblical turn of phrase. But occasionally it could appear openly. Thus in 1841 the League sponsored a conference of ministers of religion, which was well attended; of the 645 in attendance Congregationalists, Baptists, and Presbyterians totalled 510, but there were no Anglicans. And Cobden himself paid tribute to the part that religion, in effect Dissent, played; 'It is fortunate for me,' he wrote, 'that while possessing a strong logical faculty . . . I have religious sympathy which enables me to cooperate with men of exclusively religious sentiment . . . the success of the free trade struggle . . . has been more indebted to the origin of veneration for its success than is generally known.'

It does not matter that repeal, when it came, was not wholly the result of massive League pressure. The Tory Prime Minister, Sir Robert Peel, was independently moving in that direction. And his willingness to act was turned into determination when in 1845 the Irish potato crop failed, ushering in the great famine that was to kill a million and force the emigration of many more. Amid such catastrophe the repeal of the Corn Laws took place in 1846. What is vital is that the League had given classic expression to middle-class aspirations, and that, by seeming to have done so much to destroy traditional impediments, had given the middle class a tremendous confidence in itself. When three years later the Navigation Acts, main pillar of mercantilism, were abolished; when in 1860 the Chancellor of the Exchequer, Gladstone, virtually wiped out the remaining tariffs; when in the same year an agreement guaranteeing unimpeded trading between Britain and France was negotiated by (fittingly) Cobden; it seemed that the victory of the Manchester Free Trade school was complete.

The Anti-Corn-Law League was a good indicator of middle-class style, because such an important part of its success was due to bureaucratic expertise. The stress upon the bureaucratic virtues, in fact, was widely marked in liberal Britain and contrasted sharply with the American attitude. At the very time when rotation in office was being championed by Jackson, the Benthamites were urging the merits of open competition for filling the civil service, and were advocating its increasing professionalization. Their triumph came in 1853 when the Indian civil service replaced patronage by competitive examination as a method of recruitment, in 1855 when this method was partially applied to the British civil service, and in 1870 when patronage was finally ended. The United States did not move in this direction until 1883.

The operation of bureaucratic 'do-goodism', a kind of middle-class paternalism that is particularly British, was well seen in two key reforms that followed in the wake of the Great Reform Bill. In 1834 the Poor Law Amendment Act was passed. It was clear from the rapidly rising costs of poor relief that the existing system was not working; relief costs of £1.5m. in 1775 had become £8m. by the end of the Napoleonic wars, and although by the time of the Reform Bill the price of bread had fallen 33 per cent, relief costs had only dropped to £7m. But there was in truth little system in the poor law. It had grown haphazardly since Elizabethan times, based upon the notion that people belonged to the parish in which they were born and if they became destitute should be returned to that parish, which then had the responsibility of caring for them. It fitted a traditional society. The method of caring most prevalent in the 1830s was that known as the Speenhamland system. It had begun in 1795 when the J.P.s meeting in Speenhamland in Berkshire agreed to supplement the wages of poorly paid workers by paying out of the parish rates sums of money depending on need and number of dependents. This typical piece of paternalism was copied by parish after parish, though it was never officially fostered and never became a national policy. It was well-intentioned, but for evident reasons did not work effectively. It was against the lack of uniform, efficient rationality that the new poor law was directed.

The driving force behind the new system was a leading Benthamite, Edwin Chadwick. Under the Poor Law Commission, Boards of Guardians were established throughout the country; for this purpose the too-restricted and out-dated parishes were replaced by larger territorial units. The Guardians were to operate on a new principle. In place of the 'outdoor' relief offered by Speenhamland, 'indoor' relief was henceforth to be the rule; that is, recipients would be required to leave their homes and enter the workhouse. Additionally, these workhouses were to be run on the lines of 'least eligibility'. By this Chadwick meant that conditions would be one degree less pleasant than those of the poorest not on relief. To the end, then, of encouraging work and of discouraging idleness, the poor law régime was made severe indeed. Husbands, wives, and children were segregated within the workhouse, and work was deliberately made monotonous; silence was rigidly enforced. As one Assistant Commissioner stated, 'Our intention is to make the workhouses as like prisons as possible . . . our object . . . is to establish there a discipline so severe and so repulsive as to make them a terror to the poor and prevent them from entering.'

A year later the reform impulse turned to local government. The existing town corporations were generally small bodies of the local establishment perpetuating their power by co-option. The Municipal Corporations Act replaced these by town councils elected by the ratepayers. In this way the middle-class concept that those who pay for anything should have a voice in how that thing is administered (the equivalent of the 'household' franchise) was applied at the local level.

Both measures had some characteristics in common. In both there was centralized control, the Poor Law Commissioners being paralleled by the Treasury control that was exercised over the boroughs' financial transactions. And in both, centralization was tempered by local initiative, the Guardians and the Councillors being local men elected by those who knew them. In both, professionalism was prominent. It was not merely that the background to the new measures was the Royal Commission, a full, detailed inquiry into the facts, beloved of the Philosophical Radicals. It was not merely that the principle of election began the process of downgrading the J.P.s, who were on the Boards of Guardians *ex officio* but of course no longer in sole, undisputed charge. It was that once set up the new organizations leant heavily on the specialist. The Guardians and the Councils were to appoint salaried administrators, full-time professionals.

These developments, almost exactly contemporaneous with Jacksonian democracy, reveal very different emphases. To round out the contrast something may be said about the representative figure of British liberalism, the counterpart of Jackson himself, William Ewart Gladstone. In his long public career—he was in parliament from 1833 to 1893—he moved in an increasingly liberal direction. Originally a Tory who was against the Reform Bill, he became a Peelite in the 1840s as the country moved towards free trade. In the vital position of Chancellor of the Exchequer he was able in the 1850s to complete the sweep of Cobdenism to the climax of 1860 when his budget removed almost all tariffs. His dismantling of privilege was to be seen in his championing of civil-service reform, and in the abolition, during his first premiership, of the buying and selling of army commissions; particularly noteworthy were the educational reforms that characterized Gladstonianism—the 1870 Act, which set up the first national system of schools alongside the existing denominational ones was an example, as was the opening of Oxford and Cambridge to members of all creeds in 1871, and his abolition of the duty on paper, in effect a tax upon knowledge, should be added here. His opposition to influence was seen in his extension of the franchise (that of 1867 was a Conservative measure that stole Gladstone's crusade, but that of 1884 was a Liberal measure), and in the passing in 1872 of a ballot act to make voting secret. Above all there was Gladstone's attitude to Ireland, the supreme example of his liberalism. He was successful in disestablishing the Irish Church in 1868 and in passing Land Acts in 1870 and 1881 to improve the condition of the Irish peasant. But his championing of Home Rule for Ireland was not so successful. Bills to this end in 1886 and 1893 were lost, and caused the breakup of the Liberal party as a significant section broke with Gladstone, took the name Liberal Unionists, and eventually fused with the Conservatives.

Yet for all this Gladstone was no Jackson; the democracy he represented was always very different. Jackson was the man of the people who became a mythical figure. Gladstone's patrician quality always kept him aloof. Although he drew his strength from the Nonconformist conscience (of the 85 Nonconformist M.P.s in 1880 only one was not a follower of Gladstone), he was himself a High Anglican; although he represented the progressive forces in British life he was attached to the aristocracy such that his first cabinet of 1868 contained seven peers and eight commoners, and that not one of his four cabinets included a member of the lower classes (the first working-class minister was John Burns in 1905). His distance from the ordinary man, as from Jackson, comes out starkly and even poignantly in the following episode. The working men of York sent this testimonial, redolent of religiosity, to him in 1864: 'We thank you from our inmost souls. We look upon you as a powerful and consistent advocate of our cause, and may God long preserve your life. That you may continue to be the sound and impartial statesman—the friend of the poor, seeking simple justice to all—is the fervent wish and desire of the workingmen of this ancient city.' Gladstone merely noted 'My desire was simply to frame that answer so as to discourage a repetition of like addresses elsewhere'. It would seem, then, that his increasing liberalism was motivated not so much by instinctive, wholehearted commitment as by a curious mixture of sheer logic and a sense of which way the tide was going.

Somewhere between these two poles of egalitarian democracy and democratic paternalism came the democracy of British North America. Its flowering there was complicated by two factors, however, and something will have to be said of the special circumstances. The first was the position of Lower Canada.

The French Canadians were conscious of being a nation apart, 'la nation canadienne'. What marked them off from the mainstream of the North Atlantic triangle's liberalism was their Catholicism rather than their language. Catholicism as a social fact, rather than as a private matter, was still an aberration in the North Atlantic community. It is easy to overlook the continuance of anti-Catholic feeling into the nineteenth century. The repeal of the Test and Corporation Acts and the passage of Catholic Emancipation did not change prejudices overnight, and when in 1851 the newly aggressive Papacy announced that it was openly re-establishing the Catholic hierarchy in Britain under a provocatively titled Archbishop of Westminster, there was widespread opposition. This sense of outrage was communicated to Upper Canada. There Irish Protestant immigration had been strong, and its Orange Lodge had become an extremely powerful force in provincial politics; naturally its members were prominent in criticizing papal aggression. But even more moderate forces were caught up in the excitement. George Brown, Presbyterian editor of the leading reform paper in British North America, the *Globe*, campaigned mightily against Catholic pretensions. And it must be confessed that Brown had some justification for his stance. Catholicism, never so wholehearted in its embrace of industrialism as Protestantism, was particularly stand-pat in this period. In 1840 Ignace Bourget became Bishop of Montreal. Bourget was an ultramontane with a streak of the royalist in him. Using a well-developed press, and leaning heavily upon the Jesuits whom he re-established in Canada in 1843, Bourget was able to make his brand of Catholicism a dominant force in French-Canadian life. He was not afraid of open links with politicians and an open role in politics, and he thus broke with the existing practice of the hierarchy of working behind the scenes. Bourget's kind of thinking became a main element in the political mentality known as the *bleu* outlook, a conservative, traditionalist viewpoint that was characteristic of Lower Canada. There was little sign that French Canada wished to break with its traditional ways; the élite much preferred the professions of law and journalism to that of commerce—when it did not go into the Church—and it was significant that French Canada remained attached to its seigneurial system, which if it stood in the way of money-making helped to preserve the family, and also that year after year French Canada would defeat the attempts of Upper Canada to repeal the laws against usury, i.e., uncontrolled or market rates of interest. When in 1806 *Le Canadien* was founded, the first newspaper to speak for the emerging French-Canadian identity, it made a point of coupling its strictures on the English-speaking Montreal merchants with attacks upon the New England mentality, which it saw as sordid and material; to this end the verb 'yankifier' was coined as a term of abuse.

That the *bleu* tradition was dominant did not mean that no alternative existed. There was a liberal tradition, that of the *rouges*, but it was weak and crucially different from that of Britain or America. Given the absence of a native Lockean-derived tradition, and given the dominance of the Church, it was almost inevitable that the opposition should look more to the French revolutionary tradition. Belatedly some French Canadians were becoming aware of the 'natural rights' philosophy, and by 1834 (and the time lag is significant) banners could be seen in Lower Canada inscribed 'Vive le peuple souverain, la liberté, l'égalité'. But such liberalism was always restricted to the intellectual minority, it had few roots in the wider society to anchor its more extremist growths, and so it took on a strident, shrill anti-clericalism more in keeping with continental than British or even American liberalism. The leading *rouge* newspaper, *L'Avenir*, founded in 1847, made much of attacks on the Church.

Catholicism might have been the bigger distinguishing badge, but the French fact had its significance too. The determination to maintain their French identity, to ensure *la survivance*, meant that even *rouges* were sometimes keen to stress aspects of traditional ways that they might have been expected to attack. Thus seigneurialism was actually upheld by some proto-*rouges* on the ground that it was distinctively French-Canadian. And in a wider sense that cosmopolitanism that was such a feature of liberalism was often missing from the *rouge* crusade, which all too often was devoted to the maintenance of French-Canadian particularism. All told, then, liberalism in Lower Canada was a strange and weakly growth.

The second complication applied to British North America in its entirety; it was colonial. This status mattered on two levels. There was, first, the constitutional consequence, the absence of socio-political homogeneity. What this means may be seen by recapitulating the constitutional development of Britain. Although there was formal distinction between king, Lords, Commons, in practice there was no distinction. Lords and Commons were staffed by identical types, for the latter were elected by a very narrow franchise that permitted the maintenance of the rule of the natural élite. Since Queen Anne had last used it in 1708 there had been no use of the veto power, and even covert interference was becoming a thing of the past. In fact the last occasion on which a monarch had interfered with the ministry's wishes, that is, the wish of the group enjoying parliamentary confidence, was in 1839 in the Bedchamber crisis. In that year the incoming Tory Prime Minister, Sir Robert Peel, asked the young Queen Victoria to dismiss her ladies-in-waiting who, being married to Whig statesmen, might prejudice the Queen against him; the Queen refused, Peel declined to form a ministry, and the Whigs, though they did not command the support of the Commons, carried on for two awkward years. Even so this was a minor affair, little interfering with the easy flow of parliamentary business.

But in the colonies it was very different. There homogeneity was lacking. The governor, who represented the crown in theory and the imperial government in practice, was drawn from the aristocracy of the mother country; in choosing his Legislative and Executive Councils he chose men as near to the aristocratic stamp as possible, and in many cases the two councils were synonymous. Against these elements of the colonial constitution was arrayed the Assembly, and here the analogy with Britain broke down. The much wider colonial franchise and the lack of deferential habits, together with the example of North American democracy, meant a tendency for the Assembly to be in deadlocked opposition to the other branches. This state of affairs was endemic throughout British North America, and even backward Newfoundland, which only received representative institutions in 1832, had to have its constitution suspended from 1840–42.

Colonial status also mattered on the intellectual level. These colonies as yet lacked political traditions, and were in fact engaged in constructing traditions for themselves. In this condition they were open to the attractions of more firmly established ways. And two ways in particular competed for the allegiance of British North America, the British monarchical form of liberalism and the American republican model. Just how precariously balanced was British North America between these alternatives was dramatically indicated in 1849. These colonies, and in particular the St Lawrence region, had grown and prospered under the protection of British mercantilism, and the continued profitability of the staple trades in grain and timber seemed to depend on continued preferential tariffs in Britain. Overnight this preference disappeared when in 1846 the Corn Laws were repealed and in 1849 when the Navigation Acts were abolished. Under this shock the Montreal merchants, English-speaking bourgeois in a sea of *habitants*, who had been the rock of support for the British connection, reversed their position completely and in 1849 put out the Annexation Manifesto in favour of linking up with the republic. Further to point up the anomalies possible in such a setting, the *rouges*, the normal enemies of the English-speaking Tories, were the French Canadians pressing for annexation— a strange 'alliance' indeed! Annexation may have been an extreme instance, but it did dramatize the pull of the United States and its effect upon British North America. That it continued was seen in the attempt to extend Reciprocity when it expired in 1866; this was the agreement for free trade in natural products between British North America and the United States, which had begun in 1854. And that the pull was not restricted to economic matters will become clear.

The peculiarities of the British North American setting having been noted, the working out of its brand of democracy may now be traced. The first real opportunity to observe it came in the late 1820s. It was a time when even small out-of-the-way colonies could not ignore the pressure towards reform. In the republic to the south Jacksonian democracy was coming to the boil. At the same time British reform was creating a fluid situation and suggesting novel alternatives. From both centres immigrants and mails were bringing new outlooks to British North America. And on top of this the thirties was a period of strain culminating in a bad harvest in 1836 and a trade depression in 1837, which has been identified as the first slump to affect the entire North Atlantic economy. It was in the St Lawrence region that these impacts were most powerfully felt; there interaction with American practices was easiest and most frequent; to that part of British North America was immigration heaviest; there the effect of bad harvest and slump was most acutely felt. The Maritime provinces, though caught up to some extent in these currents, were not driven to such extremes.

Disaffection in the two Canadas had targets for its wrath ready to hand. In both colonies the real direction of affairs was in the hands of small oligarchies, what was known in Lower Canada as the Château Clique (from the seat of the executive) and in Upper Canada as the Family Compact (though in fact there was no unusual degree of intermarriage between its members). Given the facts of a colonial setting, both these groups could present a very élitist and indeed reactionary face to society, a tendency reinforced by the fact that the governors were military men (the Canadas after all were the outposts of empire and vulnerable to attack). It was easy, then, for opposition to take an egalitarian tone based upon an appeal to natural rights.

The Lower Canadian Assembly under the leadership of Louis Joseph Papineau indicated its leanings in this direction when it passed bills for the more democratic organization of parish vestries (an anti-clerical motion), for an elective upper house, and for a constitutional convention. All these were rejected by the Legislative Council, but a bill for a Schools Act largely patterned on the New England model was actually put on the statute book. This kind of Enlightenment-American thinking was summed up in the *Ninety-Two Resolutions* passed by the Assembly in 1834.

Much the same was happening in Upper Canada. The counterpart there to Papineau was William Lyon Mackenzie, a Scots immigrant. A visit to America in 1829, when he met Jackson, convinced him that republican virtues were superior to monarchical, and this was the message that he trumpeted in his newspaper, the *Colonial Advocate*. His creed, which was never clear but comes over best in the *Seventh Report*, 1835, a document of the Assembly, and in the draft constitution that he prepared for the province, itself an American notion, was a version of Jacksonianism; he was against sectarian education, preferring the secular form even then triumphing in the United States; he was opposed to entail, primogeniture, banks, and the sheer cost of royal government. His support was drawn mainly from the American elements and from the western, outlying portion of the province. What he seems to have wanted (he was far better as critic than as builder) was the direct democracy possible in small-scale, unsophisticated communities.

Thus in both Upper and Lower Canada there was a groundswell of interest in American reforms and republican institutions. But it was not extensive. In 1837 risings broke out in both provinces. However Mackenzie could muster only a few hundred supporters for a march on Toronto, and that tiny force was contemptuously dispersed; he himself was forced to flee into American exile. In Lower Canada the rising was more serious and pitched battles took place, but in the end the rebels were defeated and cowed; Papineau was likewise forced to exile. A second rising, and continued harassment and invasion from sympathetic northern states throughout 1838, were never too serious, for while there were undoubtedly those who would have welcomed the American-style changes but were not prepared to come out into the open, it is safe to conclude that the majority did not wish to move in that direction. The other British colonies in North America repudiated the risings and contributed to their suppression. The rebellions did, however, intensify British willingness to try alternative arrangements for the Canadas. The imperial authorities sent Lord Durham to North America in 1838 to investigate, and his *Report* appeared in 1839. In part thanks to his suggestions, but in greater part thanks to independent testimony, it was decided to re-unite the St Lawrence region. In 1841 the new colony of Canada (divided into Canada East and Canada West, but usually referred to as Lower and Upper Canada) was established.

As Aileen Dunham wrote in her study *Political Unrest in Upper Canada, 1815–36*, 'The rebellion was not a climax, but rather an anti climax, accidental rather than inevitable . . . ' . For even while a few were advocating Jacksonian-style remedies, others more representative of the colonial situation were working out solutions more congenial to the British tradition. And not in the Canadas alone, for the Maritimes, too, were feeling their way to a new constitutional order. This was the implementation of responsible government.

Responsible government is the transition from royal to cabinet government; the cabinet, chosen from the party enjoying the backing of society as revealed in the elections to the lower house, continues to govern until it loses that confidence; the executive power is thus dependent on, i.e., *responsible* to, the legislature. And while it has that confidence the monarch is obliged to accept its recommendations. As indicated above this doctrine had emerged in Britain by the time of the first Reform Bill and was taken as fully established by the failure of the

Whig ministry after the Bedchamber crisis. In the colonies a proto-cabinet did exist, the Executive Council, but there was no method by which this could be related to and made dependent on, i.e., *responsible* to, the legislature. Where Britain had made sure, by the Regency Act, 1707, that there would be interpenetration of executive and legislative membership, colonial practice kept the two bodies quite distinct.

And there was a further bar to the acceptance in the colonies of responsible government. Demands for the principle had been made from at least 1828. In that year William Baldwin, an Irish immigrant to Upper Canada and a member of its Assembly, wrote to the British Prime Minister, Wellington, advocating 'a provincial ministry . . . responsible to the provincial parliament, and removable from office by his majesty's representatives at his pleasure and especially when they lose the confidence of the people as expressed by the voice of their representatives in the assembly'. The Lower Canadian Assembly declared for responsible government, and New Brunswick under imperial prompting moved in effect in that direction by bringing members of the Assembly into the Executive Council. But apart from Upper Canada the clearest statement of the principle came from Nova Scotia. There the leading reform politician was Joseph Howe, and it was under his leadership that the Assembly declared for responsible government in 1837.

Nothing could be done, however. In 1837 Lord John Russell, a leading Whig cabinet member, responded to Canadian agitation by condemning responsible government in the *Ten Resolutions*; after the rising he re-iterated his conviction by pointing out that under the proposed new system a governor would be 'no longer a subordinate officer, but an independent sovereign'. Lying behind such observations was the fact of colonialism as it then existed, mercantilism. Since the British empire was one gigantic trading system it would be impossible to allow any portion of it to wreck the overall policy by pursuing its own ends. Only in the late 1840s, as Britain went over to free trade, was the change possible. The first victory for the new system came in 1848 when the Nova Scotian Assembly met after an election. The existing ministry was defeated in a vote of confidence and the governor called upon Howe and the Reform party, the group with the backing of the House, to form a new government. In Canada the triumph of the new principle was even more dramatic. For in 1843 the Canadian equivalent of the Bedchamber crisis had occurred; the governor had refused a request from the Lafontaine-Baldwin government (this was Robert Baldwin, son of William) that in future he make crown appointments only on the advice of the ministry, and the Executive Council bar one member felt obliged to resign. Now in 1848 the new governor, Lord Elgin, promptly asked the leaders of the party victorious in the election to form a government. And then in the following year Elgin was given the opportunity to reveal his commitment to the new principle. A bill was presented for royal assent that undertook to compensate Lower Canadians for losses suffered as a result of the 1837–8 troubles. The English-speaking Upper-Canadian loyalists objected to the terms of this Rebellion Losses Bill, arguing that it legitimated treason, and they expected Elgin to refuse his assent. But assent he did, since a governor in a colony was now largely the figurehead that the monarch in Britain was.

This balance of competing forms of democracy was maintained in the years of mid-century. A pardoned and somewhat disillusioned Mackenzie returned to champion direct and simple forms of democracy, and to express distrust of responsible government. He and other old reformers were joined by newcomers to form the Clear Grits—a title referring to their alleged purity and simplicity, grits being unground oats. They favoured the American style of liberalism—elective officials, cheap government, secular education. But in time this Americanism was tamed to a great extent by the leader of reform in Canada, George Brown, whose *Globe* was the voice of Upper Canada's liberalism. This Scotsman had been glad to leave New York, which was so anti-British, and he never accepted the idea of universal suffrage. But the best opportunity to gauge the proportions of egalitarian and paternal democracy in the Canadian tradition is provided by Confederation, the union of British North America as Canada in 1867.

For a variety of reasons, local and imperial, economic and military, it was felt possible and necessary to strengthen the British colonies in North America by bringing them together in one entity. At first only Canada (Upper and Lower Canada, joined in the Union of 1841, reappeared as Ontario and Quebec respectively), Nova Scotia, and New Brunswick could be induced to opt for Confederation, Prince Edward Island and Newfoundland not choosing to join until 1873 and 1949 respectively; Manitoba, carved from the Hudson's Bay Company lands, entered in 1870, and British Columbia in 1871, while the remainder of the west, organized at first as a territory, entered as the provinces of Saskatchewan and Alberta in 1905. Yet the basic pattern of Canadian democracy was laid down in the constitution of 1867, the British North America Act, and in the atmosphere in which the statesmen, the Fathers of Confederation, worked.

There was a clear determination to stick to British modes. Thus from the start there was no appeal to the people. Negotiations were begun and carried on by governments, and governments, moreover, that had not been elected to carry Confederation. There were no constitutional conventions, not even a referendum after the event. When a suggestion was made for testing public opinion in Canada it was authoritatively replied that 'It would be unconstitutional and anti-British to have a plebiscite'. The closest to this kind of appeal to the people came in New Brunswick, where a general election took place in 1865. The pro-Confederation forces were defeated. But imperial pressure was exerted and by 1866 a second election had returned a government once more favourable to the idea of unity. It may also be noted that the Senate, the upper house, was not elective, but appointive (and by the federal authority, not the provincial). And finally to drive home this point about distrust of the people, the way the original movers of the constitution organized the North West Territories (proto-Alberta and Saskatchewan) in 1875 is crucial. Almost a century earlier the United States had laid down in the North-West Ordinance the way by which a territory was to become a state, a model of belief in the people's ability to make their own institutions and govern themselves. But Ottawa continued to control its territories in a paternalist way and showed much less confidence in the ability of the people on the spot to manage their own affairs. For thirty years the North West was kept in a colonial relationship with the rest of Canada.

And secondly Confederation was British in not being based upon written, absolutist positions as had been the case in America; thus the drive towards a thorough-going democracy was muted. It is true that the enabling legislation was a written document, the British North America Act, 1867. But that was only a part of the constitution of Canada, for it was accepted that Canada continued to enjoy the existing British constitution, that is, an unwritten constitution. Significantly there was no Bill of Rights to accompany Confederation. And it may also be observed that Confederation took the form of an imperial gift bestowed on the colonists, and that the dependent attitude was kept up for many years to come; to take but one example, Canada went to war in 1914 simply and automatically as a member of the British empire. This continued paternalism-colonialism, psychologically so inimical to egalitarianism, is all the more striking since the work of Confederation was so overwhelmingly a Canadian initiative and undertaking. Finally, it may be pointed out that the new Canada was almost called the Kingdom of Canada, and only an imperial unwillingness to affront the United States changed it to the Dominion of Canada. The original title would have been a fitting symbol of the repudiation of egalitarian democracy.

※ ※ ※

The second dimension of liberalism to be examined is the degree of commitment to free trade, not in the narrow economic sense (for it has been mentioned how while Britain opted for the removal of tariffs the United States and Canada built protective walls about their economies) but in the wider sense of pluralism, the freedom to follow alternatives. Of the North Atlantic triangle, the country with the biggest commitment to pluralism was evidently the United States; from the revolutionary Patrick Henry's 'Give me liberty or give me death', the rhetoric of America had been in favour of choice. It is this attitude that has underpinned the perennial appeal of states' rights, and that is appealed to by, say, the American Medical Association when it objects to any measure of collectivist medicare.

Certain it is that American history has been shot through with an extensive and principled adherence to pluralism. But attention ought to be drawn to the fact that behind the many instances of pluralism and behind the pervasive rhetoric there also lies extensive distrust of choice and a drive towards conformity. It has already been suggested that politically this has been so in America, and now that observation may be amplified.

The expulsion of the United Empire Loyalists had been an earnest of things to come. Soon after 1800 a further instance of a dislike of diversity was seen. The Federalists disappeared almost overnight. The Jeffersonian Democratic-Republicans were so dominant that political division almost ceased, and a newspaper of the day could apply to the period a title that has stuck—the Era of Good Feelings. James Monroe, who became president in 1817 in succession to James Madison, could announce that 'The existence of parties is not necessary to free government'. Politics began to be a series of faction fights between wings of the same party. Even when by 1836 the Democrats were opposed by the Whigs, or when by 1856 they were opposed by the Republicans, the same was essentially true. Unlike the split between Democratic-Republicans and Federalists, which was based upon a genuine alternative political philosophy, the more recent splits were lacking in substance. There was basic agreement on the ends to be pursued, and the only disagreement was over the tactical questions of 'how soon' or 'how fast'. All too often and to a greater extent than in Britain the parties were simply names given, almost by chance, to groups of office seekers.

A different kind of political intolerance may be seen in the growing divergence between north and south and in the eventual Civil War and its aftermath. In the last chapter the disparity between these two regions was underlined, and even in the absence of the explosive issue of slavery conflict might not have been avoidable. For a long time a series of compromises kept north and south balanced. In 1820 Missouri was allowed in as a slave state only when it was agreed that in future slavery should not be permitted in states north of 36'30", and when Maine was permitted to enter as a free state, for in this way parity in the Senate would be maintained. In 1850 a slightly different compromise was arranged; California became a free state and in return the south was gratified by a tightened-up Fugitive Slave Law. In the 1850s the question of slave or free in the territories was turned over to the territorial population, a buck-passing device by Congress based on the expectation that the more northern territories would be settled by 'free' settlers while the more southerly would be dominated by those favouring slavery. Incidentally the process provided ammunition to those who feared the ability of the people to arrange their own institutions; in Kansas both sides rushed 'settlers' in, and fanatics fought guerilla wars to decide whose constitution should prevail. What happened in 'Bleeding Kansas' in 1854 was a foretaste in fact of what was to come.

The possibility of compromise was breaking down, a situation dramatized in 1857 when the Supreme Court ruled in the *Dred Scott* case. It concerned a slave of that name who had been taken with his master from his home state of Missouri to the free state of Illinois for several years before being returned to Missouri. The question was whether residence on free soil made Scott free. The Court made plain what many had assumed but had refrained from spelling out, that negroes were not citizens of the United States and so could not sue, and that since negroes were property and since no citizen could be deprived of his property without due process (the Fifth Amendment) the provision of the Missouri Compromise outlawing slavery north of 36'30" had never been constitutional. Not only did this ruling bring to boiling point those who opposed slavery on religious-moral grounds, but it raised the spectre, remote though it might seem, that the southern ways might penetrate and even dominate the north. This could be such a frightening prospect because the south's culture was so very different from the north's and there was little willingness on the part of the north to tolerate this alternative society. Just how the south differed should perhaps be briefly sketched, and something said of *The Mind of the South* (the title of the excellent study by W. J. Cash).

The separateness of the south became possible only after the boom in cotton had taken place. The south had always been thinly settled and unsympathetic to urbanism, in part because of the temptation to depend on staple products like tobacco, rice, and indigo, and in part because the excellent river system of the tidewater region permitted the diffusion of population with adequate communication. The coming of cotton, which demanded vast acreages, intensified this scattered and self-sufficient economy. It was further entrenched by the use of slave labour. Cotton cultivation was simple repetitive work that poorly motivated hands could be driven to do, and so encouraged the use of slaves. And since the slave trade had been outlawed in 1808 the supply of slaves had to be produced in the south itself. This meant slave families, which in turn meant slaves over and above those suitable for field work. They could be put to work, however, on the plantation in other capacities, making it a closed household economy. And in slack periods even prime fieldhands, who could not be laid off like northern wage labourers, could be put to productive use elsewhere in the plantation economy. The result was a kind of paternalism, a reversion to an earlier system given up in the North Atlantic community with the possible lingering exception of Quebec, in which the plantation master stood as father to his extended black family.

It may be true that extensive plantations were unusual in the south. Only eleven owners had more than 500 slaves, only one sixth of the population owned at least five, and fully two thirds of southern whites owned no slaves at all. Despite this, paternalism became the norm; even the poorest white farmer, desperately trying to maintain his self-esteem by clinging to a belief in his superiority to the negro, would attach himself to the natural leader of his locality, who in turn would link up with the natural leader on the next level, in a way that was almost feudal.

Hardly surprisingly, the values developed in the south were those fitted to an earlier age, more suited to the Cavalier, in fact. Thus personal bravery and a mastery of field sports were admired (it is significant that in the Civil War the southern soldier proved himself superior to his opponent until eventually ground down by better staying power and organization, exactly the same pattern as in the English Civil War when Royalists confronted Cromwellian Ironsides); devotion to the ideal of pure womanhood was required—but was coupled with a more down-to-earth practice; there was an obsession with honour, so that duelling persisted after it had disappeared in the north; gambling was a passion; there was an impatience with formal justice, so that lynch law was common (it would seem that in the pre-Civil War period only about ten per cent of such executions were of negroes—slaves were too valuable). This life style was even matched by an ideology. In 1854 George Fitzhugh published *Sociology for the South*, where with beautiful consistency he called for the restoration of the apparatus of paternalism, primogeniture, entail, an adherence to a Catholic social outlook—he even invoked Filmer. The south had become an anachronism, but the north was not prepared to tolerate it. And equally the south could not accept criticism of itself. Opponents of slavery were driven out, and when the returned southern exile, Hinton Helper, bravely published *The Impending Crisis of the South*, showing how slavery poisoned the atmosphere and led to southern backwardness, he was outlawed. Intolerance finally led to the Baptists and Methodists splitting into separate northern and southern organizations, followed after the Civil War had broken out by the Presbyterians, Lutherans, and Episcopalians.

Something of the same kind of response may be seen within the ranks of those opposed to slavery. The north was never unanimous in its attitude to slavery, and many in the north were happy to leave things as they were and ready to look upon the critics as troublemakers. In 1835 Boston was the scene of riots sparked off by anti-slavery speakers and this was by no means an isolated instance. The first martyrdom of the anti-slavery crusade came in Alton, Illinois, a free state, when in 1837 Elijah Lovejoy was murdered for his newspaper stand against slavery. The dominant strain was the negative one known as Free Soil, the determination that all future additions to the United States should come in as free states, slavery being therefore restricted to the existing south. Abraham Lincoln, the Republican president and author of the Emancipation Proclamation, was himself in this tradition; on one occasion he made it plain that 'I am not, nor ever have been, in favour of bringing about in any way the social and political equality of the white and black races: that I am not, nor ever have been, in favour of making voters or jurors of negroes, nor of qualifying them to hold office, nor to intermarry with white people.' It is also clear that he was reluctant to interfere with existing slavery; he was delighted when the south, by firing on Fort Sumter in April 1861, branded itself as the aggressor and enabled the north to take the line that it was fighting to conserve the existing Union. But within the ranks of those opposed to slavery as such there were many extremists whose style was peculiarly American. These were the abolitionists.

They date as an effective force from 1829, for that was the year when the most spectacular (though perhaps not the most effective) abolitionist, William Lloyd Garrison, came out for that doctrine in opposition to the previously dominant method of dealing with slavery—the colonization movement for shipping negroes back to Africa. What he and his supporters wanted was immediate emancipation of the negroes, a sudden total transformation of their status and fortunes. His newspaper, *The Liberator*, which, said the first issue, did not intend 'to think or speak or write with moderation', later carried the slogan that the Constitution was 'a covenant with death and an agreement with hell', a belief that eventually led Garrison to demand the destruction of the Union and its reconstruction without the slave states. A most dramatic assertion of this side of abolition (and a caution to those who refuse to recognize that there is nothing new under the sun) was Garrison's burning of the United States' Constitution. Given these traces, it was not surprising when William Seward, the Republican politician, spoke openly of what many had felt obscurely, that in such matters as slavery, and in particular when it came to the application of the Fugitive Slave Law, there operated a 'higher law' superior to and in opposition to the Constitution. This kind of thinking even received formal state sanction; in 1854 the Wisconsin Supreme Court released an editor who had interfered with federal officials retaking an escaped slave under the Fugitive Slave Act, and upheld the validity of its decision for five years until the federal Supreme Court struck it down. Significantly, the state court had invoked the authority of the Jeffersonian tradition for what it was doing by drawing attention to the Kentucky and Virginia Resolutions.

What the abolitionist stood for was that American trait in evidence from the very beginning, a tendency towards antinomianism, a conviction of righteousness so intense that the law ceases to bind. It is a streak that comes out very clearly in the case of John Brown, who has been immortalized in folk song. He first burst into notoriety in 1856 when in the struggles over 'Bleeding Kansas' he led a party of abolitionists against upholders of slavery and massacred five of them. Three years later he led another group to the capture of Harpers Ferry, a federal arsenal, with the aim of arming the slaves and touching off a slave revolt. It was for this act that he was executed, so becoming for many a martyr to the cause.

That this total attitude, this black-white approach, was a pervasive one was seen once the war had broken out. The Republican party, a party put together from Free Soilers and other anti-slavery workers together with industrialists opposed to southern style, threw up an extremist wing known as the Radical Republicans. They showed the same tendency to look for sudden and total change. Thus Lincoln's mild proposal for the readmission of a seceded state after 10 per cent of its voters had pledged loyalty to the Union was repudiated by them, and the attempt was made to raise the figure to 50 per cent. When after Lincoln's assassination in April 1865 Andrew Johnson became president and pursued the same line, the Radical Republicans prevented representatives of the south from taking their seats in Congress. It was Radical pressure that added to the Thirteenth Amendment (the abolition of slavery) the Fourteenth (recognition that negroes were citizens), and the Fifteenth (the right of negroes to vote). It is fair to point out that southern resistance to change was marked (opinions after all do not change overnight, least of all after crushing defeat), and that the Black Codes passed by southern states on the war's end effectively perpetuated discrimination. It is also fair to point out that Radical opposition to Johnson, which culminated in the only impeachment proceedings ever instituted against an American president (it failed by one vote), was aided by his own poor political sense and personal qualities. But it is equally fair to point out that Radical intransigence had been in evidence before the south showed its provocation; for instance Lincoln's 'ten per cent plan' had been put forward, and resistance had been forthcoming, even before the war had ended. From the first the Radical thrust had been to remake the south apocalyptically with no attempt at letting the very abolition of servitude work its effect on society. This is not to say that a gradual policy would necessarily have been any better than the one pursued, but it is to underline the widespread refusal to consider a gradual policy.

In fact, northern attempts to remake the south failed. Despite the Amendments, despite the military occupation of the south from 1867 to 1877, despite the passage of Force Acts to give teeth to the Amendments, and indeed perhaps because of them, the south continued to see itself as a section apart and the negro as inferior. The south was reminded of its degradation by the presence of jumped-up carpetbaggers (northern politicians who rushed south with nothing but a carpetbag of possessions and got themselves elected to office in the political vacuum of war's end) and scallawags (renegade southerners who took part in northern-sponsored politics). Secret societies, of which the Ku Klux Klan was merely the best known, arose to terrify the negro into obedience. The south went solid for the Democrats, an enduring factor in United States politics down to this day. And by 1890 the states were busy introducing 'Jim Crow' laws to legitimize the discrimination against negroes, making voting, for instance, depend on passing a literacy test administered by a hostile white official. With the backing of the Supreme Court, which in *Plessy vs. Ferguson* in 1896 found that the provision of separate but equal facilities did not infringe the Fourteenth Amendment, the continuity with the old had been re-established. Perhaps it was worse, for now southern defence of its ways was embittered and paranoic, self-consciously frozen.

These examples of a tendency towards conformity, and its accompanying belief that such conformity may be imposed overnight, have been political. The discussion of north-south incomprehension, however, did touch upon more social dimensions. To round out this discussion additional examples of social intolerance may be adduced.

An example that nicely bridges the political and the social was provided in the Congregational debates over Bleeding Kansas. In 1856 Senator Sumner of Massachusetts spoke out against the attempt to make Kansas a slave state, and during a speech that identified the southern settlers as 'hirelings picked from the drunken spew and vomit of an uneasy civilization', attacked all southern senators. Sumner's verbal violence was matched by physical violence when a few days later Representative Brooks, nephew of the insulted Senator, attacked Sumner in the Senate and beat him into unconsciousness. And if it is felt that it is unfair to take examples from the slavery issue, which after all was an exceptional problem, consider the Maine Prohibition law of 1851, the first but by no means the last American experiment to make people more virtuous by legislative enactment. Or the commitment to the 'melting pot' theory—that immigrants are to lose their individual qualities and fuse into an all-embracing Americanness. On the reasonable level this was to be seen in the American theory of the common school; in the unreasonable level as a distrust of anything alien. The Un-American Activities Committee may be a twentieth-century manifestation of this urge to conformity, but it existed in the mid-nineteenth too; the American Party (popularly called the 'Know Nothings' since it was a secret organization and instructed its members to reply to prying questions with 'I know nothing') was a sizeable force in the 1840s and 1850s, stressing nativism and fear of foreigners.

And this mention of nativism points to a final dimension of American failure to take fully to liberal cosmopolitanism. The conviction that America was purity in a sea of corruption, which went back to pre-revolutionary religious ideas, was kept alive in this period. In 1823 President Monroe promulgated the doctrine named after himself, that the New World was to be kept free from Old-World contamination and that the United States had a duty and a right to maintain this isolation, by force if necessary. The 1840s was the period when the concept of 'Manifest Destiny' was named, the belief that somehow the entire North American continent was divinely fated to be part of the United States republic. That urge to conquer Canada, which had been seen in 1775, 1812, 1838, and at other times too, was to the fore in the Oregon dispute of 1846 when American bellicosity pushed the boundary line north to the present forty-ninth parallel. Much of this expansionism was simple territorial greed, but the peculiar American quality about it was the dogmatic conviction that theirs were the only principles of government and that benighted Canadians would vote to join the Union if only they could be freed from British blinkers. British North Americans, however, did not agree, for they, like the British themselves, followed a very different interpretation of pluralism.

✖ ✖ ✖

At the outset it must be admitted that Britain never had to face an issue like the abolition of slavery, which so warped the American experience. Britain could face the question of slavery within the empire in a much more simplistic fashion. The only portion of the empire where slavery was widespread (apart from India where the masters were native Indians rather than British citizens, and South Africa where they were Dutch), was the West Indian islands, and here the owners were not resident but settled in Britain itself. Accordingly the British anti-slavery crusade, a powerful one and a model consciously followed in the early stages by Americans, never had to challenge an entire way of life in opposition to threatened change as was the case in the United States. The decision of the British government in 1833 to abolish slavery was one that could be accepted without too much trouble, especially since it was accompanied by compensation. It is also worth pointing out that the abolition was not an immediate one, for the bond of 'apprenticeship' kept the ex-slave and master together for several years after 1833.

But the judgement may be ventured that even had Britain been faced with a problem comparable to America's, the reaction and the solution would have been different. For as indicated above, the rejection of pluralism was long entrenched in the United States and widely diffused. As early as 1835 the French observer de Tocqueville had identified in his *Democracy in America* the probability of the tyranny of the majority. His was a reaction congenial to the British at all levels. His friend John Stuart Mill was fully alive to the danger, and with a sideways glance at the United States had observed, 'No society in which eccentricity is a matter of reproach can be in a wholesome state.' And Mill was appalled by the attempt to legislate morality, and objected strongly to the Maine Prohibition law of 1851. These doubts about egalitarianism led to Mill's championing the idea of giving additional votes to the better educated and so on, and to advocating proportional representation so that minority viewpoints might be better heard. And this philosophic doubt about uniformity was paralleled by a practical determination to avoid it. Thus, as has been mentioned, British schooling continued to be fragmented, the state system alongside the denominational, the public alongside the private, the academically ambitious alongside the commercially practicable. But more indicative than anything else of British divergence from American patterns here was the existence of a genuine party system.

By the time of the Reform Bill the Whig party was being transmuted into the Liberal Party. The oligarchic upholders of an eighteenth-century kind of freedom were being permeated by a middle-class, Nonconformist view of freedom, and the resulting compound was a party that epitomized the dominant liberalism. But this Liberal Party, while dominant, did not have the field to itself. The old Tory viewpoint did not disappear. That reverence for tradition, and that loyalty to church and crown that Burke had championed so eloquently, was still very attractive. But it should not be forgotten that Burke was no reactionary, and that his system did call for change, so long as it was organic evolution and not revolutionary. Thus there was room within the Tory fold for principled men who were disgusted by the horrors of industrialism and urbanism. Most reformers, of course, had been attracted to the schemes of the Philosophic Radicals, but there were those who found the Benthamite approach too coldly calculating. These reformers found the Tory tradition of *noblesse oblige* a more appealing way of tackling abuse, and they could also draw upon the traditional guild principles of controlled methods of work as a means of preventing exploitation. Thus Toryism, far from being dead, received a new lease of life and was resurrected as the Conservative Party. And it is significant that this new title was announced in the *Tamworth Manifesto* of 1835 in which Sir Robert Peel put forth his program, ostensibly to his constituents but in fact to the nation. What is significant is that Sir Robert, the later dismantler of mercantilism, was the son of a self-made textile manufacturer, a new man whose natural home might have been expected to have been the Liberal Party.

A statesman like Peel could accommodate conservatism to the requirements of a new age. A generation later, Benjamin Disraeli was to perform a similar up-dating. In his longest premiership, from 1874–80, he carried through major social reforms (his Trade Union Act of 1875 was much more favourable to the working man than Gladstone's Act of 1871 had been) yet at the same time stressing the crown and the empire, a trend symbolized in 1876 when he had Queen Victoria assume the title of Empress of India. Thus a genuine alternative to the Liberal Party continued to be possible. In Britain, of course, many Conservatives were opportunists and cynical appropriators of Liberal planks. Even so, the Conservative Party always retained a core of principled politicians able to restate the philosophic case for an alternative politics. The impulse behind pluralism might have disappeared in the United States; it was not to disappear in Britain.

In British North America the issue about which pluralism revolved was essentially Lower Canada. At one point it looked as though the French-Canadian alternative would be crushed. This had certainly been an aim of the *Durham Report*. For Durham, although a Whig peer, was a radical, modern-minded man who had a great respect for the United States. He was appalled by Lower Canada and by what he saw as its feudalism. His union, then, was to be a thorough-going one that would eventually lead to the absorption of the French Canadians. Certain steps were taken towards this; the French language was not to be an official language and an ordinance enforcing English in Lower Canada was prepared. But this aim was soon abandoned. The language ordinance was never promulgated, and the proscription of French remained a dead letter; when in 1849 Elgin read the Throne speech in both French and English, the acceptance of French ways was signalled. It is true that in 1854 seigneurialism was abandoned, but otherwise the French way of life was maintained. For under the Union the French were able to use the political machinery to their advantage. Representation was frozen at an equal number from each section. The English members split into groups, but the French stuck together as a bloc, and in this way were able to dictate terms. A tribute to this effective mobilization of *bleu* sentiments was the reversal of Upper Canada's educational system; that system had been essentially a secular system of the American pattern, but under the United Canadian régime Catholic state-supported schools were introduced into the western half of the colony. The French and the Catholic facts, then, were resurgent by mid-century, and pluralism was gaining ground.

And so when Confederation was carried due notice had to be taken of such tendencies. Most delegates would undoubtedly have preferred a unitary system, but Lower Canada/Quebec made this impossible, and so a federal system was adopted. Within this framework the provinces were given control of important areas, especially of education. In particular the French and Catholic facts were recognized; French was to be an official language in the legislature and courts of Quebec and in the federal parliament and courts. Catholic (and other denominational) schooling was given protection. From the beginning it was clear that whereas the United States was committed to a 'melting pot', Canadians were determined on a 'mosaic' of styles. In passing it may be noted that the acceptance of monarchy as the symbol and cement of the new country facilitated this commitment to pluralism. For once allegiance has been sworn to the monarch, a subject (and this is especially true if he is a newcomer) has proved his loyalty, is under no compulsion to continue to prove his allegiance, and may therefore be free to maintain any other particularist loyalties he may wish. But an American, who has to demonstrate loyalty to a way of life, is under constant pressure to prove his continuing commitment; as has been pointed out, aggressive Americanism tends to be found among those whose migrant past is recent. This is, of course, not to deny that very real discrimination has been practised against immigrant groups in Canada; but however much performance has fallen short, the promise has been that of cultural pluralism. To put it very simply, Louisiana, despite its also having the civil law, could never maintain itself as the Quebec of the United States.

Pluralism was not to be allowed to slide into uncontrollable localism, however. The experience of the United States seemed to indicate the trouble that flowed from basing authority on the states and allowing the federal authority mere enumerated powers. The leading Father of Confederation, the Conservative John A. Macdonald, who became the first prime minister of the Dominion, was insistent that in Canada residual powers remain with the central authority so that the provinces were clearly subordinate. Care was taken that the lieutenant governors, the crown's representatives in the provinces as the governor general was for the Dominion, be appointed by the federal authority. Moreover the federal government was given the power to disallow provincial legislation. But while the main impulse in stressing centralism was the desire to avoid a civil-war-type situation, it should also be appreciated that a strong central executive was believed to be necessary to prevent the emergence of local tyrannies of totalitarian uniformity.

In these ways the formative Canadian experience approximated much more closely to the British than to the American pattern. Whether that approximation could be maintained, however, remains to be seen.

❋ ❋ ❋

The third and last dimension of liberalism to be looked at here is that referred to as the degree of optimism with which the future is contemplated. Although this term was derived from an examination of the religious component in liberalism, it should be made clear that this discussion of optimism does not focus upon any deeply metaphysical meaning of the term. What is intended, rather, is an idea of how the various societies visualized the upward progressive development of society and of the individual that liberalism postulated. Who would rise, and by what mechanism? These are the kinds of considerations intended here.

In the United States there had existed since colonial times a commitment to openness. This tradition reinforced and was reinforced by the sense of opportunity that the facts of industrialization, urbanism, and migration made possible. Amid the huge spaces and vast resources of America, which remained a reality well into the twentieth century, it was possible to maintain a belief in the possibilities of an Enlightenment-based individualism destined to manipulate the environment. It was plain that not all could be captains of industry, and it was notorious how wagon trains heading west towards opportunity would encounter a reverse stream of those who had failed. But sufficient people made good in Alger's sense, especially second-generation immigrants who could compare old- and new-world prospects. There was general subscription to the doctrine of success through 'unremitting toil and application', a doctrine known as Social Darwinism.

This outlook took its name from Charles Darwin, the popularizer of evolution. He had explained the evolution of species as a result of 'natural selection'; when living things press upon the means of subsistence, the weaker die first and fail to reproduce their kind, while the fitter individuals survive and breed similarly superior types. This idea was already in the air when Darwin wrote. Herbert Spencer, a self-educated railway engineer turned philosopher, was already close to this idea, and he seized upon the Darwinian theory and extended it to an explanation of society. His slogan was 'the survival of the fittest', which he and not Darwin coined, and he used it to explain and justify the evolution of society from medieval traditionalism, where group loyalties proved tyrannous and obstructive, to modern liberalism, where the individual was freed to develop himself and master the world. His was the most thorough-going defence of atomistic *laissez-faire*; contract, or the free play of the market, was the only law he acknowledged.

Spencer had a certain following in his own country, Britain, but he enjoyed his real vogue in America. There, either in person or through the writings of his disciples, notably Professor Sumner of Yale, he was tremendously influential. In the post-Civil-War boom the businessmen took him up, and the older outlook, that the state had a positive role to play in the economy and in society, all but completely disappeared. This is how John D. Rockefeller, Jr., applied Spencer's Social Darwinism to business life: 'The growth of a large business is merely a survival of the fittest. . . . The American Beauty rose can be produced in [its] splendour and fragrance . . . only by sacrificing the early buds which grow up around it. This is not an evil tendency in business. It is merely the working out of a law of nature and a law of God.'

Optimistic, or pessimistic? On the one hand the doctrine is pessimistic; it accepts as inevitable that many individuals will be sacrificed, and it tends to fatalism since there is really nothing that the authorities can do in the face of such cosmic impersonalism. But on the other hand it can seem optimistic; those who have the requisite qualities for toil and application can be hopeful of making it to the top, and can feel a deep sense of justification in each step that takes them nearer their goal. Like the Calvinism with which it so easily made contact, Social Darwinism could prove optimistically validating to the elect.

Above all, the optimism of Social Darwinism comes out when the equivalent theorizing in Britain is examined. Long before Darwin (indeed Darwin relied on this earlier work) *An Essay on Population* had been published by the Reverend Thomas Malthus. There he advanced the view that whereas the food supply was capable of being increased arithmetically (2, 4, 8, etc.), the population had a tendency to increase geometrically (2, 4, 16, etc.). Population tends to outrun the food supply, and in the absence of any restraint runs into periodic checks from war, disease, starvation. On this view life is a never-ending struggle for survival. And soon after 1800 this insight was used as a starting point by David Ricardo, who developed from it other disturbing conclusions. Ricardo argued that wages had a tendency to fall to mere subsistence level, that is, merely sufficient for the worker and his family to reproduce their kind; should wages be below this figure workers will die or fail to reproduce in the usual numbers, the worker-population will fall, and the fewer hands will be able to extract higher wages from the employers; should wages be above subsistence, however, the workers will breed at a greater rate, an increased labour force will compete for a fixed wage fund, and so drive wages back to the right level. This rigid doctrine was known as the 'iron law of wages'. Ricardo further held that the wage fund, at any given time, was fixed so that any increase paid to some workers would automatically mean a decrease to others. It followed from these two beliefs that any attempt by the authorities to intervene in the matter of wages was futile. *Laissez-faire* also meant freedom for wages and conditions to find their own market level, i.e., subsistence level.

Ricardo went on to draw a second conclusion that was perhaps even more disturbing. He developed a theory of rent that was revolutionary in its implications. An ever-increasing population demanded that more and more land be brought into cultivation, and as the good land was taken up, further and further recourse would have to be had to the marginal land. Imagine a parcel of this marginal land, land A, which on average yielded 50 bushels of grain a year and which was just adequate to support a tenant and his family. If one tenant could be found to live at this level, then all tenants could be obliged to do so. A landlord with land B, which produced 100 bushels, could withhold the land from the rental market until he found a tenant willing to pay to him the surplus 50 bushels as rent, the price of the privilege of being allowed to work the land. Now if rent is surplus produce, it is in the interests of the landlord to have that produce selling for a high price. But by the same token what was good for the landlord was bad for the two other interests, the workers and the capitalists, for if grain, say, was expensive, wages would not go so far or else they would have to be increased at the expense of profits. As Ricardo himself pointed out 'The interest of the landlord is always opposed to the interest of every other class in the community'. What Ricardo had done was to destroy the older view of society as a natural harmony of interests, where what was good for one was good for all. Now it was seen that society was composed of antagonistic sections. And if at first Ricardo's analysis was used by middle-class liberalism to attack the basis of feudal landowning power, it was not long before certain working-class thinkers turned the doctrine against the middle class. Liberalism in the Ricardian form could legitimize class, and class conflict.

The pessimism of the Malthusian-Ricardian outlook becomes apparent. Social Darwinism at least keeps alive the notion that society is one organism, and given a richly endowed and underpopulated America it was possible to believe that the whole of society would benefit even if some would benefit more than others. In Britain on the other hand resources were not plentiful and the population density was high, and the belief that what one section appropriated was thereby denied to another was readily accepted. It is significant that Ricardo's work appeared in 1817, just when the economy slumped. It was a major break with the Smithite doctrine of the natural harmony of interests, a doctrine that was not seriously challenged in the United States.

This difference may be highlighted by noting that modern British society and politics has been openly structured about class, whereas this fact has always been denied in the United States. In nineteenth-century Britain legislation could be put on the statute book with such titles as *The Artisans' Dwelling Act* (1875) and *The Workmen's Compensation Act* (1897). In the 1960s a plaque was to be seen in the double-decker buses of the industrial Midlands saying 'In the interest of other passengers, workmen are requested to travel on the upper deck'. Such open language can not be thought of in the United States.

The emergence of class in Britain took place in the period immediately after Waterloo, the very time when in the United States the Era of Good Feelings was setting in. The war had never entirely stopped popular protests, and in 1811–2 the Midlands textile areas had been the scenes of machine breaking as the Luddites, followers of the mythical General Ludd, demonstrated against growing industrialism (this structuring about Ludd indicates a pre-modern form of organization). But in the post-war depression the distress became national in scope, and merged with a demand for the political reforms long bottled up by the war effort. Late in 1816 a protest meeting at Spa Fields in London degenerated into a riot, and memories of the Gordon Riots were awakened. Despite the suspension of habeas corpus, troubles continued in 1817. The following year was quiet but in 1819 unrest was general. It culminated in the St Peter's Fields massacre. A large crowd in Manchester was dispersed by cavalry, eleven people being killed and hundreds injured; the event was nicknamed derisively 'Peterloo'. In 1820 the Cato Street conspiracy was uncovered, an attempt to blow up the entire government. This was the last of such violence for the time being, but the level of agitation continued high.

During these disturbances the working class was acquiring a consciousness of its own identity. A rising at Pentridge, Derbyshire, in 1817 was significant in that it was organized and led by the working men without any direction from their betters. And ironically the government repression aided the formation of this consciousness; in 1819 the Six Acts attempted to check large-scale protest and the ban on extensive meeting and petitioning was clearly directed against working-class agitation of the kind of Peterloo. But it was in the 1830s that a working-class consciousness really emerged. It was a time of economic uncertainty, and there was in 1837 a drastic slump (the same that affected America, and indeed the whole North Atlantic world, for only now had the economy become in effect one). But more significantly the feeling that the middle class was abandoning its erstwhile natural allies of the fight against aristocratic privilege was pushing the working class into a compensating awareness of their own identity. For instance, working-class disappointment when the limited nature of the Reform Bill became evident was great. And then there was the revulsion against the new poor law's workhouses—'Bastilles' as they were known to the lower classes who had an understandable horror of them. Against such instances of middle-class disdain new initiatives came from the workers themselves.

The attempt via the trade union movement, legalized in 1825 when the Combination Acts were repealed, was abortive; in 1834 the grandiose Grand National Consolidated Trades Union had been founded, a vast enterprise to unite all workers on the theory, derived from Ricardo, that society is not in natural harmony but is a mixture of warring classes and that the capitalists and landowners should be treated like the parasites they were. But in 1838 began a crusade that proved to be a much more effective means of channelling working-class consciousness. In that year a petition or People's Charter was drawn up.

The original impulse came from William Lovett, a cabinet-maker/shopkeeper who had organized the London Workingmen's Association, made up of artisans. This charter demanded six reforms; they were for annual parliaments, equal electoral districts, payment for M.P.s, no property qualification for M.P.s, secret ballot, and universal adult male suffrage, a list that indicates how far Britain had to go before it caught up with America; and remember the last demand was not granted until 1918. (Incidentally all the demands were eventually met, except the first, though the reduction in 1911 of a parliament's life from seven years to five was a step in the direction of keeping representatives close to their constituents.) It was Lovett's aim to collect so many signatures to his Charter that the government would be forced to grant the requests, though in fact its three monster petitions, claiming millions of signatures, were rejected by Parliament in 1839, 1842, and 1848. Such rebuffs were accompanied by internal dissension. Soon the dominant force in the movement was the Irishman, Feargus O'Connor, and his mouthpiece the Leeds-based *Northern Star*. Chartism split between Lovett-like 'moral force' proponents and those who upheld 'physical force', to which position O'Connor gravitated. Torn in this way, lacking leaders and organization of the stature of the League's Cobden and Bright, dividing its aims instead of single-mindedly pursuing one main one, the Chartist movement was eventually defeated and dispersed (dispersed is the right word, since some 500 leaders, mainly 'physical force' exponents, were driven into American exile; others went elsewhere). The Newport rising of 1839 achieved nothing but the loss of twenty-four Chartist lives; the 'Plug riots' of 1842, so called because the strikers knocked out the plugs of the steam boilers as a prelude to a complete stoppage of work, were no real threat to the system. That Chartism was a paper tiger was indicated when as early as 1854 John Frost, the leader of the Newport rising, was pardoned.

Chartism failed in the sense that its demands went unheeded at the time. But in a deeper sense Chartism had succeeded. It acted as a focus for working-class aspirations, and in Chartism's heroic struggles a separate consciousness was confirmed. In addition it must be said that it was a consciousness of a kind that would be compatible with the new industrial order. It was not merely a blind resentment, but a coherent alternative to the dominant ethic of the day. Nor was it a desperate longing for a departed golden age. There was this side to Chartism, of course, as to almost any protest movement, and in its declining years O'Connor turned more and more to back-to-the-land schemes. But on the whole Chartism accepted the industrial order, though demanding, naturally, a different method of control, and agrarianism was not effectively transmitted to later generations. It may be said, in fact, that Chartism ended the appeal of Cobbett; and it is noteworthy that Chartist land schemes had most impact in America, where the Chartist exile, Thomas Devyr, played an important role in the National Reform Association, a campaign that culminated in 1862 in the Homestead Act, the promise of western land as a right to the citizen. And finally it was an ideology that was flexible. Intransigent 'physical force' advocates were in a minority, and in large part their appeal was due to the terrible times and waned as in the late forties the economy picked up and moved towards mid-Victorian prosperity; then too the 'physical force' advocates tended to flee the country. Moral force was always more representative, and was the abiding lesson taken away from the collapse of Chartism.

In Britain, then, it was accepted that a 'we-they' dichotomy existed, and liberalism was accordingly qualified by a pessimistic sense that gains would have to be fought for, would have to be won from the other side. Karl Marx, who found many of his ideas in the works of British writers of the first half of the nineteenth century, spoke of the need to 'expropriate the expropriators'. It was a notion congenial to many in Britain but foreign to the vast majority of Americans.

One final comment on optimism-pessimism. It may be that in the long run it is the American outlook that is pessimistic, the British optimistic. Like the Calvinism of old, the American belief in a classless society puts a tremendous weight of responsibility on an individual's shoulders; if an American fails he is conditioned to believe that it must have been because he did not measure up, that it must be his fault. In Britain it has been possible to blame the system and to find refuge in the sub-societies of class. Today especially, as the general expansiveness that liberalism took for granted and that made it possible comes to an end, it may be that the British are psychologically better prepared for the mediating of tension than are the Americans. In an energy crisis Social Darwinism can look awfully pessimistic.

Where in all this would Canada go? Eventually that question would have to be asked. But not in this period, for as yet Canada was still basically an agricultural society. Not until the end of the century would Canada have to face up to the kind of situation that Britain and the United States had already gone through. But by then liberalism itself was coming under heavy fire.

5

The Challenge
to
Liberalism

Liberalism had enjoyed its heyday in the first two-thirds of the nineteenth century. Essentially a movement against privilege, it had shown itself to be driven by a sense of moral purpose and a calm confidence in the inevitability of its success. In a very real way it was a revolutionary movement, throwing overboard an inherited deadweight of tradition, and its keynote was the still novel demand for freedom. But its adherents did not see themselves quite in this light. Especially in the North Atlantic communities where a French Revolution had not been needed, they saw themselves rather as reformers, now quietly lopping off this excrescence, now soberly adjusting that institution; if there was any excess, and it could be seen most evidently in the American abolitionists, it was tactical rather than ideological. Any fundamental challenge to the order of things was defeated. In Britain, Chartism was a failure, particularly when set against the Anti-Corn Law League. In the United States the workingmen's parties of the thirties did not develop even to the Chartist level. And in British North America any such challenge was the weakest yet.

By the end of the century, however, liberalism was coming under heavy fire, and the old certainties were beginning to appear very shaky. What had happened was that, in an odd way, liberalism had proved too successful. This may be seen, for instance, in human terms. The early liberal drive came from outsiders. But before too long the liberal creed had enabled them to become insiders, either by making fortunes and buying into the establishment, or by entering the new-style politics, or with the intellectuals, artists, and professionals by having their values accepted by society. In Britain, where because of an entrenched aristocratic and traditionalist establishment the struggle had been greatest, the reversing of the pendulum was to be seen by the 1860s; individuals from the Liberal ranks began to join the Tories, large firms that traditionally had been Liberal changed their alliance, and when the thrust of Gladstone's legislation became apparent, especially that connected with Ireland, the drift towards Conservatism became a stream and led ultimately to a formal split in the Liberal Party.

The all-too-successful nature of liberalism may be seen in economic terms, too. The awful fact was that *laissez-faire* worked so well that it became self-defeating. The liberation of economic enterprise from state paternalism had promised tremendous gains, and initially did provide them, if not to the producer then at least to the consumer. But the competitiveness that lay at the bottom of this argument led eventually to the emergence of the single most efficient company in any particular business, and the end of that very competitiveness. In these developments the United States provides the best examples. There, in the post-Civil-War boom, the 'robber barons' perfected the trust and the holding company, monopolistic consolidations achieved between the survivors after ruthless struggle had weeded out the smaller fry; the classic early instance of this was Rockefeller's Standard Oil founded in 1870 and controlling virtually the entire American oil production by the end of the decade; the classic later example was the Northern Securities Corporation of 1902 in which Rockefeller oil and Morgan banking money were involved in what was essentially a railway conglomerate; in all, Morgan interests controlled a capital that was twice the assessed property value of the thirteen southern states. Not only did such monopoly offend against the individualism so important to liberalism, not only did it make a mockery of the self-help, upward mobility that was implicit in liberalism, it also attacked the liberal belief in the state. Liberals were never enamoured of the state—one of Spencer's best works was his *The Man Versus the State*—but they did allow it a vestigial role as 'policeman' or referee to see that the participants played by the rules. But concentration of power on the scale of the Northern Securities Corporation, entrusted to a handful of individuals over whom the democratic process had no control, was too much even for liberalism.

And liberalism's self-defeating success was to be seen in social terms. *Laissez-faire* had so expanded resources, including population, that it had produced the problems noted in Chapter 3. It was possible to ignore such problems only for so long; piecemeal reform could do something but not enough; by the end of the century the need for more effective action was pressing. It was not so much the mechanical, technical aspects that were proving awkward; such things as sewage disposal, transportation, and so on were things that the Victorian world could handle well when it put its mind to it. Rather it was such matters as unemployment benefits, or health care, or schooling adequate to the needs of an industrial work force and urban mentality that provided the problems. The liberal creed demanded individual self-help, but under the conditions of late nineteenth-century life this was an impossibility. For instance, in 1889 Charles Booth published the results of his investigations, *The Life and Labour of the People of London*, and established that almost a third of the people lived in such want that there was no possible margin for saving, no possible means of escaping into the middle class. What was worse was the finding at the turn of the century that under *laissez-faire* the inevitable progress was not in fact taking place and that the reverse was true; in the recruitment for the Boer War, 1899–1902, the British army was obliged to *lower* standards and even then had difficulty finding sufficient men: of 12,000 volunteers in Manchester only 1,200 were up to the reduced standards.

On top of this, the latter portion of the nineteenth century was one of prolonged depression. In 1873 occurred the great slump that lasted until 1896. Agriculture was particularly hard hit, as thanks to transportation improvements in railways, steamships, and refrigerated containers, huge portions of the globe became knit together in one vast market in which temporary overproduction was all too possible. It served to exacerbate the tensions that were beginning to be felt at the heart of liberalism, and it encouraged more and more people to respond as had the American writer, Henry George. In 1879 he published the best seller, *Progress and Poverty*, a book that by the standards of the time sold a tremendous number of copies in the United States, Britain, and Canada. Its solution, a higher tax on the increased value of land as the result of society's work in improving it (a typical American solution in that it identified one problem and suggested that one technical change would be all that was needed to usher in the millennium), is not of concern here. The significance of George was that he had begun with high hopes and had been disillusioned, and that he communicated this sense of contradiction, of frustration, to so many people. When he noted that although

the present century has been marked by a prodigious increase in wealth-producing power . . . and it was expected that . . . [it] would

> make real poverty a thing of the past . . . yet it becomes no easier for
> the masses of our people to make a living. On the contrary it is
> becoming harder . . .

he was speaking for the age. This chapter will deal with this mood of
doubt, and look at the most important methods advocated for dealing
with it.

❅ ❅ ❅

The very title of George's book highlighted contradiction. Other best
sellers of the period were similarly titled. In 1888 there was Edward
Bellamy's *Looking Backward*, a novel set in the 2000s, from which
point the absurdities of the present could be satirized; in 1894 Henry
Demarest Lloyd attacked corruption in *Wealth Against Commonwealth*.
These two authors, like George, were American. And it was hardly
surprising, for the contradiction to which their antithetically styled
titles drew attention was most pronounced in that country; there the
revolutionary rhetoric and the very prodigality of resources were standing reproaches to the reality, and especially to the open corruption
permitted by President Ulysses S. Grant. At the same time wealth in
America was flaunted in a manner not to be encountered elsewhere.
This was especially true of new wealth, which was not tamed or softened
in the way possible under the British social system. The generation after
the Civil War in America produced a 'Gilded Age', a boorish display of
extravagance that was not matched on the same scale in Britain. It is
fitting, then, to begin with protests in the United States.

The first large-scale protest came from the agriculturalists. While
industry was booming and being catered to by Republican administrations that raised the tariff ever upward, agriculture was suffering. This
was particularly true of the mid-west and the southern states where the
always vulnerable staples were produced. After the slump of 1873
prices began to fall, so much so that by 1890 it took three bushels of
wheat to buy what one had bought at the close of the Civil War. Deflation on such a scale was disastrous, but especially so for the farmers
and the communities dependent on them, for the average American
farmer of this period was a debtor on a large scale, having borrowed
heavily for land and machinery in the typical American belief that boom
times were coming. Thus every round of deflation increased the burden
of his debt charges. Resentment against eastern interests grew, for it
was there that the loan money was controlled and there that the high-
tariff industrialists were squeezing the staple producers in the way out-

lined in Chapter 3. And it was a resentment easily fanned by such books as George's—for there can be few contradictions more blatant than that of a farmer producing tangible plenty in the form of a bumper crop and yet being so reduced to poverty as to be sold up.

Farm organizations had been in existence since the end of the Civil War. They had been small, scattered, ineffective affairs, but by the late 1880s they began to coalesce into the 'Alliance' movement. In fact there were two Alliances, a northern and a southern, another indication of the imperfectly healed Union. That of the southern states did not play an important political role, for it was feared that a third party would weaken the solid Democratic allegiance that the south had adopted as a means of resisting Republican interference with its institutions. But the northern Alliance was prepared to become political and at its convention in 1892 in Omaha, Nebraska, launched the People's or Populist party into the presidential election. But it was always overwhelmingly a farmers' party.

In the presidential election of that year the Populist candidate (like almost all presidential candidates in this period, he was a Union general, James B. Weaver; for good measure his running mate was a Confederate major) polled over one million votes. Successes had been achieved in Congress and at the state level, and the prospects for 1896 looked good. And this was especially so when in that election the Democrat candidate, William Jennings Bryan, accepted Populist endorsement. For Bryan was himself from Nebraska and close to the mid-western farmers, and in addition was perhaps the greatest orator that America ever produced. The Populist-Democratic assault of 1896 was a tremendous crusade against the dominant Republicans, but in the end it fell short. Four years later Bryan, again representing both Democratic and Populist parties, came almost equally close to the White House. But by 1904 the alliance had come apart, and the independent Populist ticket drew but some 100,000 votes. After 1908, in which year the vote dropped below 30,000, it ceased to contest presidential elections.

In a formal way, then, Populism seemed to have little significance. But in a more generalized way Populist sentiments were to be found among the millions who voted for Bryan, and if politically that appeal failed it does not mean that it did not represent a major strand of American thinking. In fact Populist style was older than the 1890s, nor did it completely disappear with the 1908 election.

Populism was clearly rooted in Jacksonianism. One of Bryan's favourite slogans was the Jacksonian cry 'Equal rights to all, and special privileges to none'. The attempt to give the people a greater say in the government, which had been characteristic of the climate that ushered in Jackson, was repeated in Populist demands; thus they called for the popular election of senators (granted by the Seventeenth Amendment, 1913; until then, remember, senators had been chosen by state legislatures), the introduction of the initiative (whereby a motion approved by a stated percentage of the electorate had to be introduced into the legislature), and the referendum. The secret ballot was also demanded.

But the Jacksonian heritage was best seen in relation to finance. There Populism had two major planks. There was what was known as the 'subtreasury system'. This called for government to build and operate warehouses in which a farmer would be entitled to store his crops; at the time of storage no sale would take place but the farmer would be able to borrow from the government up to 80 per cent of the value of the crop, which sum plus interest and storage charges would be repaid when a sale had been made. The purpose of this scheme was two-fold. In the first place it would restore a purer form of *laissez-faire*; for now the producer was less at the mercy of the big buyers, and cushioned by the advance could pick his own moment at which to sell; in this way the booms and slumps of the market would be ironed out. And secondly it would inject additional purchasing power into the economy, each loan acting to inflate the money supply. And this state of affairs was one from which the indebted farmers would benefit.

The second financial plank was even more nakedly inflationary. This was the demand for 'free silver'. In 1873 silver, which like gold had been legal tender, was demonetized. Since then the discovery of extensive silver deposits in the mountain states and territories had sparked a campaign to have silver once more made legal tender. This campaign by the silver interests had been taken up by those who recognized the inflationary effect this would have and who approved of such an effect. Ever since the Civil War there had been a tradition of monetary reform that looked to an increased money supply as a means of invigorating the economy; the most noteworthy of these movements had been the Greenback party, which advocated a greater issue of paper money and in which Weaver himself had been prominent. These forces came together in the early nineties and by 1896 even the Democratic party went for silver, to be joined by Silver Republicans and the Populists; it was over silver in fact that Populists and Democrats had united behind Bryan.

Now both the subtreasury system and free silver are soft-money schemes—they repudiate the sanctity of gold and the fixed amount of purchasing power that gold dictates. And on the surface soft money

seems the very antithesis of the hard money that the Jacksonians demanded, say in the specie circular. But the contradiction is more apparent than real. In a simple age when farms were self-sufficient and
little actual money circulated, Jacksonians saw that hard money was
the best way of defeating the machinations of the bankers, those mystery men who, if not controlled, would manipulate the currency for
their own ends. But in the more complex economy of the nineties when
farms were bought on mortgage and their mechanization and specialization increased the demand for money in circulation even further, a soft-
money policy seemed the better way of undermining the monopolistic
gold power. And that this was a main concern was made plain at
Omaha when the delegates sang:

> They have stolen our money, have ravished our homes;
> With plunder erected to Mammon a throne;
> They have fashioned a god, like the Hebrews of old,
> Then bid us bow down to their image of gold.

The Populists did include demands for a federal income tax (also won
in 1913) and did call for government control of railways, telegraphs,
etc. (also made effective in the decade preceding the First World War).
But these forward-looking demands should not be exaggerated. The
main appeal of Populism was, like the Jacksonian, to a golden age in the
past uncorrupted by the bankers and professional politicians.

The demands of Populism are indicative of a mood, but even more
revealing, perhaps, was the style in which the message was presented.
The hatred of economic monopoly was accompanied by a distrust,
amounting to fear, of even the external signs of privilege. Thus Populist
speakers were distinguished for their homespun, down-to-earth, no-
nonsense style. There was Jerry Simpson, known as 'Sockless', 'Pitch-
fork' Ben Tillman, and 'Cyclone' Davis. Kansas produced Mary Lease,
who roused crowds to frenzy with her denunciations, climaxing in the
demand to 'raise less corn and more hell'; it must be remembered that
to the establishment a woman active in politics was unnatural, to say
nothing of the language used. And Bryan himself epitomized the Populist style; particularly important was his deeply felt fundamentalist
religion, a vital point of contact with his audiences. When in 1896 at
the Democratic Convention he secured the nomination, his peroration
blended pro-silver demands with Christianity in a perfect way—'You
shall not press down upon the brow of labour this crown of thorns: you
shall not crucify mankind upon a cross of gold.'

In this way, then, it is possible to trace Populist roots back through the nativism of mid-century to the original revolutionary impulse, itself so strongly Evangelical. It is an enduring strain in the American style, a tendency to take refuge in a self-righteous simplicity and to accuse the opponent of evil, not to say decadent, intentions. Those who have sensed this element in the American experience—the Puritan view of New France, the treatment of the Loyalists after the Revolution, the Jeffersonian attitude to the Federalists, especially to Hamilton, the Jacksonian suspicion of the Whigs, the Know-Nothing outburst, and, to leap down to the recent period, the McCarthyite witch-hunts—will find abundant possibilities for confirmation in the Populist experience. Their world view was shot through with conspiracy, a view that emerged most clearly in the works of their platform writer of 1892, Ignatius Donnelly; in addition to believing that

> A vast conspiracy against mankind has been organized on two continents, and it is rapidly taking possession of the world . . . it forbodes the establishment of an absolute despotism,

he held that Bacon had been the real author of Shakespeare's works. Indeed the readiness with which the Populist-Democratic campaign embraced pro-silver was an indication that, at bottom, many people were predisposed towards a conspiracy view. For that interpretation is essentially a simplistic one: the world is basically sound and any imperfection must be rooted in a small group who have seized control; that control may be broken equally simply by cutting out the one mechanism by which the artificial dominance is maintained. And currency manipulation is an ideal choice for such analysts. American history is full of such instances—the Jacksonian anti-Bank war, the Greenback crusade, and now the Populists are major examples; but the byways of history furnish many other examples, and in the 1930s a Roman Catholic priest, Fr Coughlin, kept this tradition alive over Michigan radios by attacking bankers and demanding the return of credit to the people. Canadians may note the success in 1935 in Alberta, the province most affected by American immigrants, of the Social Credit movement, a demand that the world could be put to rights by remedying mere bookkeeping errors.

Those who wish may push the argument further. Not only was Populism conspiratorial, but it was viciously so. Even if the leaders did not consciously do so, and even if they would have repudiated the idea, they were playing upon hidden fears and prejudices directed against the traditional out-groups. Populism was suspicious of the immigrant, and was resolutely against any involvement, even friendliness, with decadent Europe. Many commentators have professed to see barely disguised anti-semitism behind Populist writings. And it is true that the pamphlets against the gold-bugs (their term for financiers) would contain cartoons of bankers with stereotyped Jewish features, and that open references to Jews may be found. (Against this it may be noted that at that point in time the equation of Jewish and financial conspiracy was one that was automatically made. Little blame can be attached to many of those who simply accepted it.) And there were those who turned against the negro. The most notorious of these was Tom Watson, the Georgia demagogue who had been the Populist choice for vice president in 1896 and had been the presidential candidate in 1904 and 1908. In the nineties he had been the defender of negroes, but in the disappointing years after this Watson turned increasingly vicious, attacking Catholics and Jews, and above all negroes.

And finally there is Bryan himself, the Bryan of the declining years. The last occasion on which he came before the public was in 1925. In that year a schoolteacher named Scopes was put on trial in Dayton, Tennessee, for having taught the theory of evolution in his classes, thereby offending fundamentalist religion. Bryan, a lawyer, took part in the trial; he threw himself body and soul into the struggle to condemn the doctrine of evolution.

This late date indicates that Populism did not die completely with the second Bryan campaign in 1900. In many ways the elements of Populism lingered on. It has already been noted how several major Populist demands were accepted in the immediately succeeding period. This was especially true of measures for direct democracy. Certain states added to the initiative and referendum the device known as recall, a means of getting rid—at once and without waiting for the session to expire—of any representative who had ceased to mirror adequately the wishes of his constituents. Even more revealing of this continued Populist thrust was the adoption, first by Wisconsin in 1903, of the direct primary; before this reform the Republican nominee, say, for any office had been generated by the state Republican machine, but with the direct primary this device was taken out of the hands of the caucus and made the subject of a popular vote; Democrats and other groups would operate in a similar fashion. And then there was the extension of votes to women. This right had been granted in five mountain states by 1900, but it was extended eastward and by 1914 eight others were included, the farthest east being Ohio. In 1920, by the nineteenth Amendment, this right was secured to all American women. This faith in the people could also be seen in more subliminal ways. Even an ostensibly anti-Populist like President Woodrow Wilson could reveal his Populist leanings in this respect. This came out with special emphasis at the end of the First World War when, his plans for a just peace not finding favour with the European politicians, he took his campaign to the ordinary people of Europe and appealed to them over the heads of their elected leaders.

And Populist impulses were to be seen in less direct ways too. The enactment of Prohibition by the eighteenth Amendment in 1919 was part of the same fundamentalist-Populist crusade as the Scopes Trial. And conspiracy views, while muted, were still in evidence. Beard's *Economic Interpretation of the Constitution*, which has been mentioned above, was published in 1913, and it was by no means an isolated instance.

What disguised the continuing influence of Populism, and accounts for the separate name given to reform from 1900 to the end of the war —the Progressive Era—is the increased sophistication of the period. Whereas Populism had been overwhelmingly rural, Progressivism was urban. It has been pointed out how America lagged in urbanization, but by the latter part of the nineteenth century the problems of the American city were too big to ignore. In the half century or so between the Civil and World Wars the American rural population had increased about twice, but that of the towns by almost seven times. As the British observer, James Bryce, noted in his *American Commonwealth* (1888), city management was the big failing in the American system.

But it was not simply that the urban problems were demanding attention, and beginning to receive it. The towns and cities were able to foster a new kind of mentality. It is no coincidence that the expansion of American higher education, a truly great phenomenon, took place on the eve of the Progressive era; for instance the first American Ph.D. was awarded in 1861, and in its wake came a tremendous proliferation of higher degrees, professional faculties, and an emphasis upon research. This expansion at the upper level was accompanied by less dramatic but still significant efforts throughout the educational system, and in conjunction with the generalized effect of urbanism on mental attitude that was alluded to in Chapter 3, had a big impact on the general intellectual climate. This was the great age of journalism; daily newspaper circulation shot up from 2.8 million copies in 1870 to over 24 million by 1910. In the process the sober tradition of the days of limited circulation was challenged by a brash commercialism, and the phrase 'yellow journalism' became one to export to other English-speaking societies. Weekly magazines such as *McClure's*, *Colliers*, and *Hampton's* could reach perhaps a million readers a week. And it was soon discovered that the expanded reading public was avid for stories on the problems of the city and the economy. In the opening years of the twentieth century these papers featured investigative writers such as Lincoln Steffens, Ida Tarbell, and Upton Sinclair, who exposed the abuses, 'muckraking' it was called. It was a veritable crusade but one that, unlike the Populist, was driven less by a simplistic but burning sense of outraged morality as by an intellectual disgust at the way things were going. It was notable, for instance, that Progressive denunciations were not those of an Ignatius Donnelly or a Bryan but the result of painstaking, professionally trained intellectuals behind whose single article might be $4,000 worth of inquiry.

The same point may be made in connection with Wisconsin, one of the show states of Progressivism. What distinguished its leader, Robert La Follette, the state's governor and senator, who in 1924 ran for president as a Progressive, from Populism was not his demands; after all he was an exponent of direct democracy and was the godfather of the direct primary, a die-hard supporter of government supervision of communications, a bitter opponent of American involvement in the First World War and of Wilson's dream, the League of Nations. Rather the distinguishing mark was his style. He took care to match the old-line machines with one of his own, and far from being suspicious of intellectuals drew heavily for advice and ideas upon the University of Wisconsin, the first 'brains trust'. Wisconsin, for all its agricultural character, was taking on a sophisticated mentality more in tune with the urban environment.

And most importantly, the middle-class and upper-middle-class leadership of this movement must be stressed, a point that clearly marked it off from the lower-order character of Populism. On the face of it this tone, so important in sophisticating Progressivism, was unexpected. One explanation to account for it is that put forward by Richard Hofstadter in *The Age of Reform*. There he argues that the motive force for Progressivism came from those sections of society that were experiencing a status revolution; the old middle-class professions of church, business, law, and so on were declining in importance and in esteem as they were squeezed between the trusts on the one hand and organized labour on the other. But whatever the explanation, there can be no arguing with the middle- and upper-middle-class character of reform at the beginning of the twentieth century.

The setting was more sophisticated. And so too were the remedies urged by Progressives. Populist style was to call for further safeguards for the democratic process, to stress direct democracy, and to proliferate mechanical devices such as initiative, referendum, and recall. Progressives were not immune from this urge, but they tempered it by a realization that other methods might be needed. Thus after a series of experiments, the reform of cities was undertaken by combining democratic control with expertise, by having an elected commission supervise a professional manager (a belated recognition of a principle accepted in Britain in 1835). They went to work attacking specific abuses, and at the state level managed to do something to curb child labour and the hours of female employment, and to make a start on giving relief to disadvantaged groups—the injured, working mothers, etc. There was a determination to pass regulating Acts that were effective. As far back as 1887 the Interstate Commerce Act had been passed, and in 1890 the Sherman Anti-Trust Act, both designed to prevent the collusion that aided monopolies to maintain their position. But these acts were largely window-dressing; as a prominent plutocrat had remarked in opposing any repeal of the Interstate Commerce Act,

> The Commission . . . is . . . of great use to the railroads. It satisfies the popular clamour for government supervision . . . at the same time that that supervision is almost entirely nominal.

In the new century Progressive legislation was to have more teeth to it. In 1903 the Bureau of Corporations was set up to provide the information that would make trust regulation more meaningful. The Hepburn Act of 1906 was a reasonably effective method of curtailing railway power by giving the Interstate Commerce Commission the power to establish rates. And there were such acts as the Pure Food and Drug Act of 1906. Much still remained to be done, but a new departure had been signalled.

Implicit in such legislation was a further development that marked Progressivism off from Populism. There had been in Populism a concentration upon the legislative process: ensure the true representation of the people and all will be well. But Progressives had spotted that concentration upon legislative reform might not be suitable for a fluid society, and that executive action might be required. And as they learned that local and state regulation was often not the best way of coping with the trusts, which were national in scope, and as they saw the need for federal initiative, it was natural for these two demands to coalesce in a thrust to use the presidential authority to carry through a reform program. The climax to this drive was to be seen in the election of 1912.

It was an unusual election, and the reasons for it go back to the beginning of the Progressive period. In 1901 the recent Republican victor, McKinley, was assassinated, and the relatively unknown Theodore

Roosevelt became president. Of this complex man, whose real motives and ends are by no means evident, one thing at least is clear: he was a showman, a publicist who could sense the mood of the times and use it to boom himself. Within a short time he had made his mark by launching the prosecution of the Northern Securities Corporation under the Sherman Anti-Trust Act, an action that was successful. From then on and during his 1904–8 presidency Roosevelt was known as the 'trust buster', and Progressivism and the presidency were united in the popular estimation. In 1908 Roosevelt declined to run but picked William Taft as his successor. Over the next four years Taft continued the Progressive tradition and actually busted more trusts than his predecessor had in twice the time. Unfortunately he was not the self-advertiser that Roosevelt was, and seemed to be dragging his feet on reform. Roosevelt determined to wrest the Republican nomination for 1912 away from Taft, but the incumbent's control of patronage defeated his attempt, whereupon he bolted from the Republican party to run on a Progressive party ticket. The party became known as the Bull Moose Party since Roosevelt, asked how he felt, replied (in his usual braggadocio-cowboy style, for he knew the right myths) 'as fit as a bull moose'.

The Democrats were in need of new presidential material. In 1908 they had gone with Bryan, now a three-time loser. For 1912 they eventually picked Woodrow Wilson, an ex-president of Princeton University and since 1910 Progressive governor of New Jersey. The result was that the electorate was faced with three candidates with a claim to the title of Progressive, an indication of the pervasiveness of the mood, and with two who campaigned hard on the meaning of Progressivism—Taft's campaign was minimal only. The race was clearly between Roosevelt and Wilson, and its course and outcome provide a comparison that usefully illuminates the American mind.

Roosevelt was aided in articulating his appeal by reading a book published in 1909, *The Promise of American Life* by Herbert Croly. In that work Croly had produced a diatribe against the Jeffersonian tradition in American life, the tradition that venerated the people and held that all they needed was freedom in order to blossom forth in all their splendour. But, argued Croly, this was baseless and ignored the need for guidance and control of the people. Moreover in the economic context of the twentieth century it was absurd; trust-busting was largely a Jeffersonian reflex to destroy the conspirators and allow the ordinary businessman to flourish. In fact the drift to consolidation was inevitable and beneficial, it was the efficient ordering of business and the wave of the future. Clearly Croly saw himself in the tradition of Jefferson's arch enemy, Alexander Hamilton. In the hands of Roosevelt this thinking became the doctrine known as the New Nationalism, a call to recognize that the facts of modern life required a strong federal control of the economy and of the life of the nation in general.

The Democrats countered with the New Freedom. On the key issue of the trusts their divergence from the New Nationalism was clearly marked. A memorandum submitted to Wilson as an aid to clarifying the Democratic program noted that the New Freedom

> insists that competition can and should be maintained in every branch of private industry; that competition can be and should be restored in those branches of industry in which it has been suppressed by the trusts; and that, if at any future time monopoly should appear to be desirable in any branch of industry, the monopoly should be owned by the people.

It went on to observe that the New Nationalism

> does not fear commercial power, however great, if only methods for regulation are provided. We believe that no methods of regulation ever have been or can be devised to remove the menace inherent in . . . overwhelming commercial power.

It is pointless to demonstrate that Wilson had to hedge on this stand, remarking in delphic manner that 'I am for big business but against the trusts'. It is irrelevant to demonstrate that, as president, Wilson acted more in the spirit of the New Nationalism than of the New Freedom. What is vital is that the election was fought essentially on the choice between the two doctrines and that the electors voted almost 42 per cent for Wilson's brand as against just over 27 per cent for Roosevelt's (Taft picked up 23 per cent of the poll). No matter what the logic of the twentieth century demanded, the American people still clung to the Jeffersonian (and for that matter Jacksonian-Populist) myth.

Populism-Progressivism may not have been the liberalism of classic expression; their inward-looking sense of superiority that culminated in isolationism after the war was at odds with the cosmopolitanism normally part of liberalism, their equivocal attitude towards the negro did not sit well with liberalism's repudiation of all discrimination based on colour, their willingness to go along with state intervention was not in the Spencerian-Alger tradition. Even so their commitment to freedom, freedom in the sense of absence of restraint on individual initiative, was liberal enough. And they did accept the liberal institutions of the country; their demands for change, and especially for a more direct democracy, were desperate attempts to make the existing system work properly. Whether as much could be said of contemporary Britain is now to be seen.

※ ※ ※

At first glance it looked as though late nineteenth-century Britain was witnessing the rounding out of liberalism. There was an extension of many of the great liberal principles that had been laid down in the earlier period. The third Reform Bill of 1884 has already been mentioned, and now it may be added that this Act was accompanied in 1885 by a Redistribution Bill that (with certain exceptions) abolished the two- and three-member constituencies and made the single-member arrangement the norm, based on the 'one man, one vote' principle; this meant the almost complete erosion of the medieval notion that it was the community and not the individual that was represented at Westminster. Then there was the application of the principle of the Municipal Reform Act of 1835 to the rural areas, first by the County Councils Act of 1888, which finally ended the rule of the J.P.s (as a class, that is, not as officials), and then by the Parish Councils Act, 1894.

This formal opening of the political process to the people was accompanied by their eagerness to participate, not just in actual elections but in day-to-day organization and debate. Faint beginnings of such developments were noted in the period immediately before the French Revolution, when the pure oligarchic forms began to crumble. A second stage took place about the time of the first Reform Bill; in 1831 the Conservative Carlton Club was founded, in 1838 the Liberal Reform Club, both made necessary in a fluid society by the need to register potential supporters so they could vote. They were still semi-oligarchic, however, as their position in clubland indicated, but as the century wore on this narrowness was further broken down. A major development came in the wake of the second Reform Bill of 1867. In the interests of bringing representation closer to population, certain large cities were given an extra, third, member. But the voting system whereby each voter had as many votes as there were M.P.s to be elected was altered; in the interests of preserving pluralism it was decreed that voters would still have only two votes, and in this way it was thought to prevent either party from capturing all three seats. But in Birmingham the Liberals under the local leader, Joseph Chamberlain, spotted that by instructing the party faithful on exactly how to spread the two votes it should be possible to return all three Liberals. Such machine politics was so novel in Britain that a word for it was lacking. Eventually it was called the 'caucus', an American word. Finally Chamberlain was able to build up from these grassroots to form in 1877 the National Liberal Federation. The Conservatives were obliged to answer with the National Union of Conservative Associations.

The seal seemed to be set on liberalism early in the twentieth century when the Liberal Party scored a smashing victory in the 1906 general election, returning 401 members against the Conservative and Liberal Unionists' (now virtually one party) 157. Within three years the following measures had been enacted: in 1906 the provision of school meals for children, and medical inspection for school children were authorized; in 1908 the first tentative steps were taken towards a non-contributory Old Age Pension scheme, the miners' work day was limited to eight hours, and the Port of London Authority was established to bring order into the dockland chaos; in 1909 Labour Exchanges were set up to provide a means of bringing together, at public expense, those offering and those seeking employment, and the Trade Boards Act allowed the setting of maximum hours and minimum wages in certain trades, i.e., in the 'sweated industries' such as tailoring and lace-making. And then after a pause the Liberals returned to reform in 1911 with the National Insurance Act. Financed by contributions from employer, employee, and the state, this act did two things: it provided free medical care for all workers earning less than a certain amount each year, plus sick pay for work missed on account of illness; and it provided unemployment pay. This latter provision especially was a most advanced piece of social reform, and credit for it, as for much of the earlier legislation, must go to two young members of the Liberal ministry, Winston Churchill, a descendant of the Duke of Marlborough and son of a Radical Tory M.P., and David Lloyd George, a self-made Welsh nonconformist lawyer.

But like so many first glances, this picture of triumphant liberalism would be deceptive. To begin with this twentieth-century reform, which incidentally had not been the subject of public debate in the years before 1906, was at variance with the last full statement of the Liberal Party's aims. That had come in 1891 in the 'Newcastle Programme', named from the city in which the party was meeting, a program that Gladstone himself had endorsed. It called for a parliamentary life of three years as opposed to the then seven years (to bring the representatives closer to the wishes of the electorate), Home Rule for Ireland, the disestablishment of the Church in Wales and Scotland, and 'local veto', that is the prohibition of the sale of alcohol in localities that had voted themselves dry. The Liberals of post-1906 did not exactly ignore these planks. In 1911 the life of parliament was shortened—but to a compromise five years, and then largely because of the need to settle debts of minority groups that had supported them, the vast majority of 1906 being a thing of the past. In 1912 a Home Rule Bill was carried, due to go into operation in 1914 and made a dead letter by the outbreak of the war; here again the need to settle political debts was a big factor. And Welsh disestablishment was also voted for, but not implemented until after the war. But the Liberals' hearts were not in this kind of legislation, this negative legalism. They had turned to more positive, more social measures.

But were these liberalism? There was a growing realization that legislation of the Lloyd George type was perhaps too collectivist to fit liberalism's historic individualism, and that the limitations on adult labour and the setting of minimum wages were an interference with the operation of the market incompatible with traditional *laissez-faire*. It is true, as had been hinted earlier, that Britain, unlike America, had always allowed the state a role in the life of society, and that pure individualism, even as rhetoric, had been rare; such organizations of the 1880s as the Liberty and Property Defence League were minor indeed, attracting few of the leading figures of the day. And it is true that increasingly the Manchester-Cobden-Spencer tradition was giving way to that of Bentham-Chadwick, so much so that one of the most significant developments of the late nineteenth century was the growth of 'delegated legislation'; that is, parliament was content to legislate in broad terms, leaving it to the bureaucracies of the various government boards to fill in the details. (It is revealing of the British acceptance of the expert that no crusade for direct democracy arose against such developments, and that the potential danger of delegated legislation did not become a matter of public concern until as late as 1929 when Lord Hewart wrote *The New Despotism*.) But even granted such a tradition of positive state intervention, many felt that the liberal legislation after 1906 was a fatal departure from principle.

This dilemma at the core of the Liberal Party was of minor importance, however. Much more serious was the crisis of confidence in the broad liberal tradition. It was one thing to pass legislation that ignored the truths of *laissez-faire*; it was quite another to mount an open attack upon them. Yet this is exactly what the once Liberal Joseph Chamberlain did. Originally a follower of Gladstone, he had broken over Home Rule and become a Liberal Unionist. Soon after he began to identify himself with the wave of imperialist sentiment that was sweeping the world at this time, and in so doing repudiated his liberal cosmopolitanism. And then he saw that the British empire could more effectively be held together by granting colonial products a preference in the home market. To do this would mean abandoning free trade, something that even die-hard Tories had accepted after 1846. But since then Britain had lost her industrial pre-eminence and was facing more and more tariff walls—that of the United States was particularly high at this period. Thus when in 1903 Chamberlain denounced free trade in his Birmingham citadel, he was striking a welcome note. The campaign for tariff reform became an effective one, and had Chamberlain gone on to become the Conservative leader, as well he might, Britain might have declared for protection much earlier than it did. However Chamberlain suffered paralysis in 1906 and his career was ended; but under his son, Neville Chamberlain, Britain abandoned free trade in 1932.

Liberalism was also coming under fire in more generalized ways. A key assumption in liberalism was that public affairs were to be conducted rationally and soberly, with calm discussion between those holding divergent opinions until an agreed-on solution, in effect a compromise, could be evolved. This assumption was ceasing to hold. The very sanctity of parliamentary debate was being destroyed. The first crack in Westminster's decorum came from Irish causes. Ireland's continuing nationalist protest took a new form. After the 1874 elections it was clear that a group of Irish members under Isaac Butt was committed to Home Rule. In the next few years the group grew until it numbered in the eighties. And it was powerful because it was rich in funds contributed by Irish-American supporters, because after 1877 Charles Parnell, a brilliant organizer, took over as leader, and because the Irish party developed a monolithic unity. And this was openly used to delay parliamentary business. In place of reasoned debate the Parnellites used defiant obstruction, rising one after another to talk out bills. To prevent this, parliament was obliged to adopt in 1887 the 'closure' and the 'guillotine', two devices whereby discussion could be terminated by majority vote or by expiration of a time limit respectively.

Ireland, which continued to be a thorn in the side of Britain, provided further opportunity for revealing the extremism just below the surface. When it became clear that Home Rule was going to be granted to Ireland, the Protestant north, Ulster, determined to resist and to maintain the British connection. Focusing about the Orange Lodges, and rallying behind the leadership of Sir Edward Carson, the Protestant forces quickly exhibited their intolerance. Solidarity was shown by the massive endorsement of a petition, grandly but shrewdly known as the Solemn League and Covenant and named after the seventeenth-century Scots' undertaking against Charles I, and effectiveness demonstrated by the collecting of arms and the practice of military drill. The Conservative Party at Westminster egged Carson on. It was unfortunate that in 1911 the party received a new leader, Andrew Bonar Law; he was the son of a Presbyterian minister and had been born in New Brunswick, though the family had returned to Scotland when he was still young. His instinctive sympathies with Ulster led him into deplorable statements; in one message to Ulster he remarked

> Whatever steps you may feel compelled to take, whether they are constitutional, or whether in the long run they are unconstitutional, you have the whole Unionist Party, under my leadership, behind you.

The conspiratorial view, which has normally been so rare in British politics, made its appearance when Law sought to justify his stand by arguing that the Liberal Prime Minister, Asquith, had used 'force' to get a vote in favour of Irish Home Rule, and he drew a parallel with Stuart absolutism; 'King James II had behind him the letter of the law just as completely as Mr Asquith had now; he got the judges on his side by methods not dissimilar from those by which Mr Asquith had a majority in the House of Commons on his side'. By 1913 the rest of Ireland was arming to offset Ulster's threats. The Conservative Party still did not repudiate the Carson line, and gave support in 1914 when the army, at its Irish headquarters just outside Dublin at The Curragh, decided to obstruct the government; it was not, as it has become known, a mutiny, but a large number of officers did express their determination to resign if the army was ordered to move against Ulster. The Conservative Party was proving itself to be irresponsible.

Nor was Ireland the only issue on which the Conservatives could exhibit their unbalanced extremism. In 1909 Lloyd George brought in a budget to pay for the social reforms, and also for the extra battleships that the arms race with Germany demanded (the fact that a Liberal government was spending so heavily on armaments was yet another indication that the Cobdenite-Gladstonian days were over). In his so-called People's Budget Lloyd George proposed a supertax on large incomes, higher death duties, and taxes on land sales and the value of undeveloped land. The sting was in the last provisions, since it would require an up-to-date assessment of landed wealth and seemed to promise future assaults upon the establishment. The Conservatives, powerless in the Commons, used the Lords as they had done before to defeat unpalatable liberal legislation. But this time they had unleashed a constitutional crisis, since the convention was that the Lords could not reject a money bill.

Early in 1910 the government dissolved parliament and went before the people on the issue of the power of the Lords. The election kept the Liberals in power, but so increased the Conservative numbers that there was no clear mandate for the change. A bill to limit the Lords to the power to amend or to delay Commons' motions was brought in. Deadlock supervened, and late in 1910 the Liberal Prime Minister H. H. Asquith dissolved parliament for a second time. Again the Liberals were able to continue, but again only with the support of other groups. But they pressed on with the bill, letting it be known that the new king, George V, had agreed to create enough new peers to see its passage. Sufficient members of the Upper House were prepared to accept the inevitable for the threat to remain only a threat, and in 1911 the Parliament Act became law. The Commons now had legal recognition of its pre-eminence.

What was most significant about this crisis was the temper that was revealed. The Conservatives were frequently fanatical in their determination to resist; on one occasion they so forgot parliamentary manners that Asquith could not make himself heard and was prevented from delivering his speech. (The Liberals in revenge were no better, and silenced a Conservative spokesman.) The mood of wild unreason, so skilfully captured by George Dangerfield in his *Strange Death of Liberal England*, was a frightening coda to the liberal century.

More disturbing yet was the fact that what was happening in parliament was matched by the mood of the entire country. The sense of moral purpose that had animated the Liberal Party was vanishing. The Nonconformist Conscience had mattered as late as 1890. In that year Gladstone had been obliged to break his tacit understanding with Parnell when the truth of the latter's affair with Mrs O'Shea became public property; Gladstone himself had been aware of the fact, but now that it had become public he could not afford to antagonize the Nonconformists. Indeed the phrase the 'Nonconformist Conscience' was coined in the aftermath of the O'Shea divorce case. But within a very short while of this, the Conscience had become more of a liability than an asset. The temper of society was changing, and the Puritan virtues were increasingly out-of-date. The quick oblivion that attended the local-veto plank of the Newcastle Programme was an indication of the new mood. Another was the fact that Gladstone's successor was frivolous enough to patronize the Turf—indeed Lord Rosebery won the Derby twice running while Prime Minister. Yet another was the contrast between the two Liberal 'greats'; Gladstone had elevated politics, but Lloyd George, an adventurer, was to debase political life to an extent rare in Britain. And parties, no less than countries, get the leaders they deserve.

But undoubtedly the sign that British life on the eve of the war was badly sick, indeed illiberal, was provided by the suffragette movement. The demand for votes for women had had a long history, and J. S. Mill had made an important contribution to the cause. The politicians had made certain concessions to it; thus the Parish Councils Act of 1894 had permitted women to vote and to be elected to its minor offices. But this was not fast enough, and in 1903 the Women's Social and Political Union was founded. As time went on the militants under Christabel Pankhurst became more extreme. The disruption of meetings was succeeded by the chaining of themselves to railings, and then by destruction of property; windows were smashed, works of art defaced, letter-boxes set on fire, and several country houses, two railway stations, and the orchid house at Kew Gardens razed. Those arrested disrupted their trials—though it must be confessed that when one Olive Wherry threw a book at the magistrate and missed from a distance of six feet many a sceptic must have been confirmed in his belief in women's inferiority. The climax in attention-grabbing came in 1913 when Emily Davidson threw herself on the course during the running of the Derby and brought down the king's horse. Miss Davidson was killed and her funeral was turned into a huge demonstration.

Just as disturbing was the response of the authorities. Many of the women imprisoned went on a hunger strike. Forced feeding was tried, but the preferred solution was the 'Cat and Mouse' Act under which weakened prisoners could be released from jail to recover and then be re-arrested to complete another portion of the sentence. Bills that would have given the women what they wanted were defeated in parliament from 1910 on. When the vote was won for women it was only after the war had demonstrated that women could do many of the jobs assumed to be too difficult for them; facts had succeeded when abstract argument had failed, and then only in an atmosphere purged by the shock of war.

The standing of liberalism at the opening of the twentieth century was nicely summed up in a classic statement of the creed, L. T. Hobhouse's *Liberalism* published in 1911. Hobhouse, a fervent liberal who venerated Mill and Spencer though recognizing that their systems were in need of adaption, sensed that liberalism was being overlooked.

'We know all about you,' (people) seemed to say to Liberalism. 'Respectable platitudes, you go maundering on about Cobden and Gladstone, and the liberty of the individual, and the rights of nationality and government by the people. What you say is not precisely untrue, but it is unreal and uninteresting.'

British liberalism was indeed in crisis.

❈ ❈ ❈

Both in the United States and in Britain, then, the turn of the century had been a testing time for liberalism, marked by a swing away from the more political-institutional concern of the earlier nineteenth century to a more social-economic focus. This was not so in Canada. There was, it is true, a measure of interest in socio-economic reform. For instance the seventies saw a wave of working-class activity, and a rise in trade-union affiliation in particular; and if George Brown, the Cobdenite *par excellence*, held to the older outlook and fought bitterly against the typographers of his own *Globe* who were campaigning for a nine-hour day, then Macdonald, recognizing the future benefits to the Conservative Party of posing as the defenders of the artisan, could pass an act in 1872, modelled on Gladstone's of the previous year, to protect trade unions. Further concern for industrial peace was to be seen in the work of William Lyon Mackenzie King, later to be prime minister but before the war Deputy Minister and Minister of Labour, to oversee the economy on the lines of the American Progressives—that is, of the New Nationalist variety rather than of the New Freedom; it was King who was behind the Lemieux Act, the Industrial Disputes Investigation Act of 1907, which sought to discipline the use of the strike weapon. There was, too, the spread into Canada of the Social Gospel, the drive of Protestant denominations, and usually the sectarians, to grapple with urban problems by making a direct connection between Christianity and social work. This movement, which could be best seen in the 'settlement house', an oasis of Christianity amid the slums, from which were dispensed both food and morality, was to be found in Britain but was even more an American phenomenon. The two greatest names in the Canadian Social Gospel movement, Salem Bland and James S. Woodsworth, both Methodists, drew upon these two traditions in coming to their own conclusions. But significant though these and other instances of social-economic reform were, they were yet peripheral. For the main concern of Canadians in this period had to be the fleshing-out of the skeleton of nationalism that had been put together between 1864 and 1873.

However, before going on to show the dimensions of Canadian liberalism as revealed in the ways that its nationalism was developed, mention must once again be made of the apartness of Quebec. In that province there was still philosophical opposition to liberalism, and this gave a twist not only to developments within Quebec but also to those within the new Dominion itself.

The ultramontane views of a leader like Bourget were still in evidence. The *bleu* tradition even threw up an ultramontane grouping in politics, the 'castors'. The deep-rooted appeal of such an outlook was to be seen in the Guibord affair, which dragged on between 1869 and 1875. Guibord had been a member of the *Institut Canadien*, a *rouge* organization with anti-clerical overtones. Because of his membership in the *Institut* Guibord had been denied burial in consecrated ground. His family and associates began a court action to secure proper burial and eventually won their case. But the ultramontane forces had been able to whip up considerable popular feeling on their behalf that led to street fighting. Indeed, so suspect was the very word 'liberal' in Quebec in the first decade of Confederation that the provincial liberals attempted to give up that name; in the early 1870s they chose to go under that of the *parti national*. It required long effort, and above all the advocacy of the rising Liberal politician, Wilfrid Laurier, later to be prime minister of Canada, to convince the Church authorities that liberal did not necessarily mean a materialistic anti-Catholic philosophy (which was often the meaning on the European continent, a legacy of the French Revolution and of a continuing protest against conservative reaction), but was rather in the tradition of such good sons of the Church as, say, Daniel O'Connell. It was Laurier's speech to this end in Quebec City in 1877 that more than anything else symbolized the emergence of a viable Liberal Party and liberal spirit among the French Canadians. Yet at the same time it must be noted that ultramontane attitudes were not eradicated; they persisted and were to be responsible for some later peculiarities in French-Canadian developments.

That this was so was shown in the closing years of the nineteenth century when there again occurred that warping of the liberal tradition last noted in connection with the *rouges* of mid-century. The most influential politician in Quebec in the decade and a half before the First

World War was Henri Bourassa, editor of *Le Devoir*. He had been a Liberal and very close to Laurier. But in 1899 he began to move away from his former leader, and he resigned from parliament. What he was protesting was the dispatch of a contingent of Canadian troops to aid Britain in her war against the Boer farmers in South Africa. That, argued Bourassa, was a British quarrel, not one that involved the empire. But lying behind such objections was the feeling that Quebec, above all, was not to be dragged into what was an anglo-saxon undertaking. Quebec separatism, which as will be seen had been growing ever since Confederation, was becoming inward-looking; French Canada was retreating into its shell. Ten years later the province had the opportunity to drive the fact home again, and it was Bourassa who led the crusade against the Liberal government of Laurier. In 1909–10 Laurier had undertaken to make Canadian contributions to the imperial naval effort. Bourassa fought to such effect that he helped lose Laurier and the Liberals the 1911 election. But what is important at this point is not so much Quebec distinctiveness but that it was articulated by one who was in many ways a liberal. Once more liberal cosmopolitanism had been defeated by the superior imperative of *la survivance*. That today Quebec votes Liberal is due to 'accident', as will be shown. The underlying mood has been in many ways profoundly illiberal.

If Quebec was retreating and ceasing to remain a member of the North Atlantic triangle, the rest of Canada was deeply involved with its on-going evolution. The competing attractions of the two major models, Britain and the United States, continued to be powerful. In terms of open declarations, however, those of Britain would seem to have had the edge. The Canada of the Confederation period had been formed largely from people who had immigrated during the 1830s through the 1850s, and they were overwhelmingly British; even the large Irish element made for increased loyalty, for it was mainly northern Irish Protestants with their Orange Lodges who came to Canada, the southern Catholics tending to take their anti-British sentiments with them to the United States. And loyalty to Britain in the last quarter of the nineteenth century was intensified by the interest in empire that was abroad at that time. Since Disraeli's symbolic articulation of imperial sentiment in 1876 the jingo spirit had been increasing, shown in a series of colonial skirmishes that culminated in the Boer War of 1899–1902. Despite Bourassa, some seven thousand Canadians took part in that war. And in a less bellicose way, imperial solidarity was shown by the Colonial Conferences (after 1902 known as the Imperial Conferences) that were held from 1887 onwards. Canadian belief in the imperial connection was dramatized when Empire Day, an annual holiday, was inaugurated in 1898.

To add strength to this pro-British feeling was the persistence of anti-Americanism. In central Canada especially a tradition of anti-Americanism had developed over the years. The early memories of aggressive intentions on the part of the United States were kept alive during this period. At the end of the Civil War a factor in encouraging Confederation had been the Fenian raids, attacks on British North America by Irish-American Civil-War veterans who wanted to revenge Irish wrongs by harming Britain through her colonies. Then in the very year of Confederation Alaska had been bought from Russia, largely at the instigation of William Seward, a believer in Manifest Destiny, and this purchase seemed to suggest American interest in taking possession of the Hudson's Bay Co.'s territories north of the forty-ninth parallel. And indeed, at the time of the formation of Manitoba in 1870 and the organization of the North West Territories in 1875, there was a good deal of American intrigue over these areas. American designs on Canada, it was felt, persisted into the twentieth century. In 1903 the Alaska boundary dispute between the United States and Canada was settled, a ruling that granted America valuable land and access to Skagway at Canada's expense; what especially rankled was President Roosevelt's underhand tactics, a win-at-any-cost approach, and a new round of American utterances that Canada was destined to be absorbed into the republic. It was this anti-American resentment that the Conservative Party was able to mobilize in the 1911 general election, which helped defeat the Liberals. Laurier had taken up the liberal tradition of free trade and sought to renegotiate reciprocity with the United States, which had last existed between 1854 and 1866. But his opponents could make much of the danger that such a policy posed for the imperial connection, and it was repudiated.

But if obvious loyalties were to Britain, the pull of American ways was extremely powerful. Sometimes there could be dramatic, open declarations that underlined the logic of continentalism. Thus Goldwin Smith, an ex-Oxford don who settled in Toronto after a spell at Cornell, a staunch Manchester liberal and Canada's outstanding ideologue of the period, abandoned his original belief in Canadian autonomy and declared for Canada's absorption into the United States. Sometimes there were signs of more general dissatisfaction with the British connection. For example, anti-Americanism over the Alaskan boundary dispute was accompanied by a feeling that Britain had abandoned Canada. The three American representatives had been balanced by two

Canadians and one Briton, and it was the latter's almost unanimous agreement with the Americans that had settled the issue against Canada. But such formal examples of anti-British feeling and of pro-American attitudes were rare. More common was a steady drift away from British presuppositions towards the American.

In one very important area Canadians were in fact to show themselves more American than the Americans. Liberal nationalism in Canada could never be so purely individualistic and anti-statist as *laissez-faire* theory demanded or even as Britain practised it; nor as it existed in the United States. By the time of Confederation the United States was already so advanced economically as to pose a standing threat to the Dominion; indeed that was a reason for encouraging the union of the individual colonies in 1867. It was clear to John A. Macdonald that only a policy of forced growth could provide Canada with the prerequisite for continued independence. The initial steps were taken during his first period of leadership, 1867–73. The Canadian Pacific Railway was chartered, and the promised task of linking British Columbia to eastern Canada was assumed. Such an undertaking was a frightening one; the United States had accomplished its first transcontinental in 1869 at a time when California had two million inhabitants and the entire Union almost 40 million people, but in 1872, when the CPR was chartered, British Columbia had some 28,000 white inhabitants and the Dominion considerably less than 4 million. The work was supposed to take ten years. But in 1873 the drive of Macdonald was replaced by the caution of the Liberal Alexander Mackenzie, for the fact that the Conservative Party had accepted vast sums from the backers of the CP charter became public knowledge and forced Macdonald's resignation. The government contracting of Mackenzie's régime, 1873–8, was once again turned over to private enterprise when Macdonald returned to power, and the line was finished in 1885. From start to finish the state had provided the push, sinking huge amounts of land and money into the venture.

On this basis two further elements were to be built. The prairie regions were to be peopled by great floods of immigrants; the newly established CPR would bring the settlers in and also take out their agricultural products, mainly wheat. At the same time the railway would bring these newcomers the industrial products of central and eastern Canada. And so that these infant industries could be built up, sheltered from British and American competition, a tariff wall would be raised to provide the needed protection. This crucial element in the 'National Policy' had been foreshadowed in Macdonald's first premiership, but only became explicit during the 1878 election. In 1879 it went into operation, with Conservatives rejoicing that either the wall worked and so encouraged Canadian ventures, or else goods still entered, in which case the revenue would help pay for the cost of the CPR. In this interlocking way the Canadian economy would be built up in defiance of geography, which seemed to dictate a north-south flow of trade and the eventual triumph of American control.

Reaction to the National Policy provided a further clue to the way in which American styles were taking over. It has been maintained that whereas British political parties have always retained a core at least of ideology, American practice has been otherwise, 'interest' politics not 'issue' politics. What is striking is that the Canadian Liberal Party, the heir of the Grit and Rouge traditions, direct descendant of Brownite Reform, accepted the Macdonald policy. The Liberal leader in succession to Mackenzie, Edward Blake, began moving away from free trade ahead of his party. His successor, Sir Wilfrid Laurier, led the Liberals to an electoral triumph in 1896 after the tariff had been accepted by the party. Liberals became so wedded to transcontinentals that during the Laurier years *two* additional lines were added to the CPR (this was overexpansion, and public ownership as the Canadian National Railway became necessary in 1923); as has been aptly remarked of this period

Whatever party may be in power, what do you find? The government is building a railway, buying a railway, selling a railway, or blocking a railway.

Nor was this need for additional outlets from the west surprising, for the greatest success in the Macdonaldite policy of prairie settlement had been shown by Laurier's Minister of the Interior, Clifford Sifton, the man responsible for the tremendous wave of immigration just prior to the war.

But was anything else to be expected? North American societies experienced a common problem, that of overcoming raw nature and constructing the rudiments of civilization. The need to conquer the sheer physical obstructions can easily be overlooked, especially by the observer of the 1970s. It was a problem that encouraged the centrist, pragmatic approach and that branded party conflict on an ideological basis as a luxury not to be afforded. From the earlier days this had been recognized. Long before Confederation, essential agreement had been the norm; putting aside the unrepresentative Mackenzie and Papineau traditions, there had been no great gulf between the Baldwins and the Family Compact, or between Howe and the Nova Scotia establishment. The first governor of reunited Canada, Poulett Thomson, the first Lord Sydenham, had actively pushed what today would be called a 'technocratic' concept of government; this middle-class bureaucrat, close to Utilitarian circles, who had been personally assisted by Bentham when seeking a seat at Westminster, set out to be the centre about which all able politicians, regardless of party, could gather. Even later, when Elgin took the governorship out of active politics, the centre party was seen as desirable. During the Union period the dominant grouping was none other than the Liberal-Conservative, the very name of which speaks volumes. Nationhood then was but making evident what had always been implicit in Canadian politics.

Another area where original British style was being abandoned was the constitutional. As was pointed out in the last chapter, the Fathers of Confederation would have preferred as unitary a legislature as possible, and even when it became clear that a federation would be necessary they took care to build up the powers of the central authority and to give it the ability to intervene in provincial affairs in the national interest; in all this, remember, they were consciously influenced by what they saw as too great an attachment to states' rights in America.

Against this thrust towards centralized unity, however, were arrayed powerful forces. Each province had its own long history and had developed a distinctive identity; Quebec's might be the most salient, but Ontario was also very different from, say, New Brunswick. And then there were the terms on which the provinces were to be treated when once in Confederation. Even within the year of Confederation disagreement on this score had taken place. In Nova Scotia both federal and provincial elections returned anti-Confederation majorities. The assembly was emboldened to put out the following resolution, redolent of American sentiment:

> That there being no Statute of the Provincial Legislature confirming or ratifying the British North America Act, and it never having been consented to nor authorized by the people . . . the preamble of the Act, reciting that this Province has expressed a desire to be Confederated with Canada and New Brunswick, is untrue, and when Your Majesty was led to believe that this Province had expressed such a desire, a fraud and imposition were practised on Your Majesty.

The threat of secession was averted by the grant of better terms, and by having the anti-Confederate leader, Howe, taken into the federal cabinet. In the eighties it was Manitoba that championed provincial rights against Ottawa; that province sought to challenge the CPR monopoly by chartering railways provincially, only to have the federal authority disallow the legislation. But the leading exponent of provincial rights was the Liberal leader of Ontario from 1872–96, Oliver Mowat. As the leader of the richest province he had the means and the incentive to insist upon the largest possible measure of autonomy.

Three factors conspired together to weaken the ability of Ottawa to withstand this rising tide of provincial rights. In 1873, when the dual mandate was abolished and politicians had to choose between being elected to Ottawa and to their provincial assemblies, there was the question of patronage. Provincial leaders were led to claim increased provincial powers in order to extend their ability to reward followers and injure opponents. Then in the eighties and nineties there were a series of crucial judicial decisions that interpreted the British North America Act in favour of the provinces. By the Supreme Court Act, 1875, the Judicial Committee of the Privy Council in Westminster remained the supreme court of appeal. Thus it was possible for British judges, not familiar with the intentions of the Fathers of Confederation or with the needs of the Canadian nation, to decide on matters of Canadian concern. In fact the trend of these decisions was against the extension, against even the maintenance, of a strong federal role. And finally there was the effect of the depression, which was general throughout the crucial period 1873–96. Given buoyant times and surplus resources it might have been possible to avoid many of the conflicts or, where they were unavoidable, to outbid the provincial champions. Unfortunately such influence was not available.

To back up such provincial autonomy there was worked out a theory of Confederation known as the 'compact' theory. Against those who would argue that the BNA Act was an imperial imposition that made of Canada an all but unitary state in which the provinces existed merely for convenience's sake—does not the Act state that 'Canada shall be *divided* into Four Provinces, named Ontario, Quebec, Nova Scotia, and New Brunswick'?—arose those who stressed the frequent references by the Fathers of Confederation, including Macdonald, the leading centrist, to the fact that Confederation was a 'treaty' or 'agreement' between the provinces, a 'bargain' to which Westminster merely lent its sanction. The compact theorists attempted to underline their contentions when in 1887 the Quebec government invited provincial régimes and the federal authority to send representatives to an interprovincial conference in Quebec City, where they took the title of the *Second*

Quebec Conference; the first had been that meeting in 1864 that had laid the groundwork for Confederation itself. Macdonald's government naturally refused to attend, and so these compact claims were not officially recognized. But that today meetings of provincial and federal authorities regularly take place gives a good deal of support to the compact theory.

Finally the issue of pluralism, which had been a vital part of the Confederation settlement, was one that was re-opened in this period. It is a difficult topic, since it was complicated by its involvement with the similar but distinct question of provincial rights. But because so much Canadian energy was expended over pluralism, and because it has so affected Canadian life down to the present, a discussion cannot be shirked. In outline the story will show a progressive abandonment of pluralism and increasing approximation to the American pattern of a single standard and majoritarian conformity.

The abandonment of pluralism was soon initiated. It came as early as 1871 over the New Brunswick Schools issue. The BNA Act had rightly seen education as a key area for pluralism and had entrusted education to the provinces; this in itself was a commitment to pluralism since the provinces differed so much that a federal control would have tended to impose too much uniformity. At the same time, however, the federal authority emphasized its concern for pluralism by writing into the BNA Act the provision that if any separate or dissentient educational system in operation in a province was abolished, then the federal authority could step in and pass remedial legislation to correct the situation. When in 1871, therefore, Catholic schools in New Brunswick were done away with the federal government could have taken action. A motion to do so was brought in but was heavily defeated on a free vote. Of particular interest was the reaction of George-Etienne Cartier, the leader of the Quebec *bleus* and spokesman for French Canada. He was opposed to any federal action against New Brunswick, for such action might constitute a precedent for future action even against the separate schools of Quebec. In other words French and Catholic rights were seen as centring in Quebec, and other French and Catholic claims would if necessary be sacrificed to preserve those of Quebec; at the same time there was also a suspicion that the drive to uniformity might one day be turned against Quebec.

The next significant demonstration that pluralism was on the wane did not come until 1890. To understand what happened in that year, however, it is necessary to digress and sketch in the background of the establishment of Manitoba in 1870.

Soon after Confederation the new Dominion began negotiations to purchase the Hudson's Bay Co. territories. In true imperial fashion no consultations took place with the people most directly involved, the inhabitants of the Red River colony scattered about present-day Winnipeg. The bulk of these people were Métis, halfbreeds of Indian and (mainly) French background, who took their lead from the French-Catholic missionaries sent from Quebec. The Métis resented the high-handed Canadian attitude, especially when it seemed that their lands were in danger of being confiscated, and late in 1869 they rose in protest and under their leader, Louis Riel, established a Provisional Government to protect their rights.

Riel's Provisional Government is remembered for two things. Early in 1870 opposition to that illegal régime broke out and Riel felt it necessary to make an example of a troublemaker. One Thomas Scott was courtmartialled and executed. What made this particularly infamous was the fact that Scott was from Ontario and was an Orangeman. Antagonism between Ontario and Quebec, between Protestant and Catholic, was inflamed. Soon after this episode emissaries from the Riel government went to Ottawa and there negotiated the constitution of the new province. It was a constitution that established a Quebec-on-the-Red-River—the French language was given official status alongside English, and the school system established both Catholic and Protestant schools, while the diminutive province was given an upper chamber, a favourite device for entrenching minority rights.

In the mid-eighties the slumbering resentments caused by these developments burst forth again. In 1885 federal mishandling of the Métis question, this time in the North West Territories, led to the return of Riel from American exile and a Métis rising that was quelled only after Canadian troops, sent to the west by the recently constructed CPR, had been risked in large numbers. This time Macdonald would do nothing for Riel, and he was executed as a traitor. Ontario was delighted but Quebec was enraged. Then three years later Quebec in turn enraged Protestant Canada. In 1888 the Quebec government finally settled the Jesuit Estates. Rights to these had passed to the crown on the suppression of the Order in the eighteenth century, and now they were to be settled. What infuriated Protestants was that the Pope was to be asked to apportion the Estates, and they vainly campaigned for federal disallowance of the provincial legislation on the ground that a foreign power should not be allowed to meddle in Canadian affairs.

In this atmosphere of poisoned relations the very able politician, D'Alton McCarthy, launched an attack upon the Manitoba Catholic

Schools. He had much to work upon. French migration to Manitoba had failed to match that of English, particularly that from Ontario. From being a majority in 1871 French speakers had plummeted to less than 8 per cent by 1891. They were, in the context of Manitoba, just another minority group to be placed alongside the Mennonite and Icelandic communities, say. A series of changes took place to jeopardize the French-Canadian position; the upper chamber was abolished; redistributions tipped the balance of constituencies increasingly away from the French; an attempt to abolish French as an official language in 1879 was defeated only by the lieutenant-governor's action. There was in the province a good measure of anti-French and anti-Catholic prejudice. In 1889 McCarthy made a speech at Portage la Prairie, Manitoba, in which he demanded an end to separate schools in Manitoba. The call precipitated political and popular desire for a change and in 1890 separate schools in Manitoba were abolished. For the next six years the faltering Conservative government in Ottawa attempted to dodge its responsibility to pass a remedial act, but eventually on the eve of the 1896 election decided to act. It became a main issue in the election.

Laurier came out against a federal Remedial Bill. And of the support which he received, that from Quebec was crucial; it was that province's forty-nine Liberals out of sixty-five seats that enabled him to win the election. This revolution in Quebec politics, the abandonment of the alliance with the Conservatives, had been prepared in the years after Riel's execution. The execution had such an impact on *nationaliste* feeling as to cause a realignment of politics in the province, and it paved the way for the emergence of a Liberal allegiance. And the switch to Laurier emphasizes what was noted in connection with the New Brunswick Schools issue; when it came right down to it, Quebeckers were more concerned to vote for Quebec's interests than for abstract Catholic rights; they preferred to vote in 1896 for the success of their compatriot, Laurier, than for the rights of their co-religionists, even if this meant defying their bishops. With this support from Quebec Laurier became Prime Minister and negotiated a settlement of the Manitoba Schools question that, if it preserved something of Catholic education, was in fact a setback for pluralism.

That the mood of the country was basically in agreement with this abandonment of the earlier stand was made clear in 1905. In that year the provinces of Alberta and Saskatchewan were set up. The original Autonomy Bills drawn up by the Laurier government attempted to give the French language extensive rights and to establish Catholic separate schools, but the protests against these provisions were such that the government had to amend them seriously. The interest finally affronted by the settlement of 1905 was the *nationaliste* one of Bourassa, and it encouraged his formulation of the 'racial compact' theory, the idea that Confederation was a compact between two founding races that should remain co-equal throughout the Dominion.

But if pluralism was in retreat, pushing Canada further away from the original British model, it did not mean that Canadian liberalism would become a mere variant of the American pattern. The separatism of Quebec had too long a history, had too many points of support, notably in the BNA Act, had too many leaders like Bourassa prepared and able to champion the French-Canadian identity, for it to be in danger of disappearing. Rather, in the face of anglo-saxon Protestantism (in Canada the WASP mentality is simply the ASP mentality) Quebeckers dug in their heels. Indeed they raised the level of their demands. It was Bourassa who elaborated the compact theory of Canadian nationhood into the racial compact theory, arguing that ever since the Conquest there had been an undertaking to keep the two founding races co-equal and co-extensive throughout the widening nation. So successful has this argument been that in 1963 the federal government appointed a Royal Commission on Bilingualism and Biculturalism and followed up in 1969 with the Official Languages Act, which extended French-language rights across the Dominion. The fruit of this new attitude to the French fact may be seen in St Boniface, across the river from Winnipeg; whereas in France cars are halted by signs saying STOP, in St Boniface they are halted by signs saying STOP/ARRET.

This last small example draws attention to something specifically Canadian. In the example there is a desperate leaning over backwards, and this points to the fact that, while in Britain there have been few problems because that country has taken pluralism in its stride, and while the same has been broadly true of the United States because there formal subscriptions to one set of values has been the norm, in Canada there has been suspicion and resentfulness. Feeling between the two sections of the country has often been embittered, and concessions to the French fact have been deeply resented in certain areas, notably the prairies.

An awareness of this growing split between English and French Canada on the eve of the First World War modifies the optimistic outlook that Canadian liberalism exhibited in those years. Paradoxically, Canadian liberalism was more in tune with British liberalism, perhaps in having revealed fundamental flaws in the system, than with the American, where no such realization was evident. But whether the

American system was thereby better fitted for the future than was the Anglo-Canadian is by no means so clear, for in this period liberalism was not the only creed for society.

❋ ❋ ❋

> ... though we may insist upon the rights of the individual, the social value of the corporation ... like the Trade Union, cannot be ignored .... I would strongly maintain that the general conception of the State as over-parent is quite ... truly liberal ....

These unliberal sounding sentiments came from the book already referred to by Hobhouse. They re-emphasize the principled liberal's anguish, at the opening of the twentieth century, when the old liberal certainties no longer seemed to suit the times. And Hobhouse's despairing attempt at a defence reveals in spite of himself how reform was moving on to a new plane. The politicians mentioned above, the Lauriers, the Wilsons, the Lloyd Georges, no matter how their actions might deviate from liberalism, always claimed to be acting within the established tradition and the prevailing orthodoxy. But now there were those to suggest that liberalism itself was outmoded, and that what was needed was some solution that would go *beyond* the existing framework. Hobhouse himself recognized this, acknowledging that 'individualism, when it grapples with the facts, is driven no small distance along Socialist lines'. He was, in fact, echoing the comment of Sir William Harcourt, Liberal Chancellor of the Exchequer in Gladstone's last cabinet, that 'We are all Socialists nowadays'.

The socialist philosophy is a broad one, and a myriad different systems claim the title. But the judgement may be ventured that the clue to the essential difference between the liberal and the socialist lies in the value each assigns to tension. A liberal instinctively sees life as a tension-filled arrangement, the economic corollary of which is competition and the social corollary upward mobility. The socialist looks to a day when tension will have been dissipated, when co-operation will have replaced competition and egalitarianism replaced stratification. At the same time the socialist repudiates the atomistic individualism that underpins the tension-filled world of the liberal, and it was for this reason that Hobhouse had to qualify his praise for Bentham, since 'the life of society is rightly held to be organic'.

The longing for a tension-free society may be found throughout history; Plato's *Republic* was one such, and more recently Münster was, too. But the full flowering of the socialist doctrine had to await the modern world, the world of the French Revolution and the Industrial Revolution. It was not simply that the process of fragmentation had to go so far that a countervailing *social* structuring became necessary to hold things together and to return to man a sense of being in charge of affairs. It was also necessary to build the mass power that could force developments on to a new plane. The changes in western society at the beginning of the nineteenth century mobilized the masses, made them literate, and politicized them. It was a slow process, and in Britain, the most modern of the states, this evolution was in its embryonic stages during the Chartist period; isolated socialists wrote and taught, and even tried experiments like Owen's New Harmony and Lanark ventures, but no real socialism as yet existed. But by the end of the century the conditions were ripe. The intellectual tradition was by then a full one; the urbanized masses were now schooled; working-class organizations had developed a life of their own, trade unions in particular having flourished since the dawn of mid-Victorian prosperity and having been given protection by both Gladstone and Disraeli. A critical date was 1889, when the bitter London Dock strike was fought; until this strike it had been assumed that trade unionism would be practicable only among the artisans, the skilled élite of the working class and the very people enfranchised in 1867, and that the great mass of the lower classes were unorganizable and unimprovable. The strike of 1889 showed that this was not correct, that casual labour could be disciplined into union activity. This New Unionism meant that the numbers involved were greatly increased and a vast army became available to socialism. During the 1880s the British socialist movement suddenly blossomed forth.

In Britain as in other countries a bewildering variety of sects spanned the socialist spectrum. At one extreme were the British followers of Karl Marx, the Social Democratic Federation, a tiny band of purists. Their appeal was hamstrung by the dictatorship of their leader, Henry Hyndman, a rich gentleman who in haranguing the crowds never failed to wear the frock coat and top hat of the stockbroker. (Though the prize for aristocratic condescension to the socialist cause must go to the Countess of Warwick, mistress of Edward VII, who attended socialist conferences in her private train.) At the other extreme was either the Guild of Saint Matthew, an even smaller organization of ritually inclined high Anglicans who eschewed Marxian ideas to concentrate upon the beauty of brotherhood, or the various anarchist groupings, both violent and non-violent, united only in their passionate hatred of *all* coercion and of all but the most minimal structure. But the most representative of the many socialist groupings in Britain were the Fabian Society and the Independent Labour Party.

The former, founded in 1884, took its name from the Roman general Fabius, who wore down the enemy commander by a patient program of delay and limited engagements. From the first the Society repudiated revolutionary solutions and put its faith in the power of argument, backed by a compelling mass of statistics; the pamphlets that it issued on specific abuses were a powerful means of influencing public opinion. Naturally such a Society attracted the middle class, and never had a large membership. But among its members were George Bernard Shaw, H. G. Wells, and the quintessence of Fabianism, the husband and wife team of Sydney Webb and Beatrice Potter; of these two plodders, whose vision of a future society was 'a discretely regulated freedom', it was said that they did not have children, only blue books (a reference to the many factual but dry reports that they compiled). Never a force in its own right, Fabianism took pride in 'permeating' other organizations and moving them imperceptibly in a mildly socialist direction. They were, in fact, the intellectual heirs of the Benthamite tradition, stressing bureaucratic expertise, what was still a form of middle-class paternalism, but playing down the *laissez-faire* side of Utilitarianism in favour of the collectivist implications.

Very different was the Independent Labour Party. This organization was founded in 1893 in Bradford, a typical Yorkshire wool town. It set out to be a mass party and its leadership indicated its working-class character. Its early leader was James Keir Hardie, a Scots miner, and a little later its two most prominent figures were James Ramsay Mac-Donald, the illegitimate son of a Scots miner, and Phillip Snowden, whose father was a Yorkshire weaver. And while the party did contain some with a grasp of the economic argument for socialism, the main driving force of the movement was not so much intellectual as moral-emotional. The overlap between sectarian religion and the ILP was marked, and many a local leader was also a lay preacher. The antagonism between socialism and religion that marked the Continent was missing in Britain, where the more dogmatic Enlightenment tradition had never been strong, and that had missed the French Revolution.

It was the ILP that took the initiative, along with the Trades Union Congress (the organization of the various trade unions, which had first met in 1868), in calling a meeting in 1900 to form the Labour Representation Committee; the Fabians also attended. The aim was to secure the return of representatives of the working class to parliament, for those who had appeared in the past had been too few to be effective and their trusting dependence upon the Liberal Party was clearly not showing dividends. And although socialism was very much a factor in the new party (for that is what it in fact was, though the name Labour Party was not taken until 1906) there was the same ILP-Fabian willingness to play down dogmatics and work pragmatically for the required end. The initial success of the Labour Representation Committee was meagre, however, only two seats being won in the 1900 general election. But in the following year the House of Lords, the highest court in the land, found for the Taff Vale Railway, which had sued a union for losses suffered when the union members went on strike against the railway. This assault upon the strike weapon led to a dramatic rise in the fortunes of the new party, and in the 1906 election twenty-nine members were returned.

By the outbreak of the war socialism in Britain had shown itself respectable and had been accepted. It was not simply that the Labour Party was successfully launched, that the socialist parties proliferated, and that the case was argued throughout the land and on every level. Rather it was the absence of unthinking, prejudiced dismissal on any significant scale that was so striking. For instance, when the Taff Vale decision seemed to undo the strike weapon, the Liberal Government passed the Trades Disputes Act in 1906 to rectify the situation. When the Osborne judgement of 1909 denied that trades unions could spend funds on supporting members of parliament, thus threatening the life of the infant Labour Party, an Act of 1911 provided an annual salary for all M.P.s, and legislation of 1913 once again permitted unions to spend for political purposes. Above all Britain was largely free from violent attempts to muzzle socialist agitation. The British movement does remember 'Bloody Sunday' of 1887, when socialist attempts to hold a protest meeting in Trafalgar Square in London were beaten back by the police and troops. But what did it amount to? Several injuries, and but two deaths. Bad enough, but insignificant when set against Peterloo or the contemporaneous confrontations in other countries. From time to time there were instances of repression, notably during the hysterical years just before the war chronicled by Dangerfield, and modern research is qualifying some of the self-congratulatory accounts of a perfectly calm climate of worker-employer relationships. But even so, labour relations and socialism in Britain were characterized by moderation on both sides.

This could not be said of America. Indeed so outlandish was socialism in America, so much outside the mainstream of political life, that Werner Sombart, an outstanding German historian and sociologist at the turn of the century, entitled his book on the subject *Why is There No Socialism in the United States?* There were, it is true, socialists and socialist parties to be found far back in the nineteenth century. And a significant breakthrough, comparable to that in Britain in the 1880s, took place in the 1890s. Then it was that the astonishingly successful socialist weekly *Appeal to Reason*, edited by J. A. Wayland, was established, soon selling over a quarter of a million copies and on its way to a circulation of over half a million by 1912. The first significant marxist party in the United States, the Socialist Labour Party, founded in 1877 but not then marxist, took its permanent form in 1890 with its new leader and interpreter of Marx, Daniel DeLeon, and began to make a bigger mark. And at the end of the decade in 1900 various socialist groups including a dissident faction of the Socialist Labour Party met to form the Socialist Party of America. For the next dozen years this party, under its charismatic if woolly thinking leader, Eugene Debs, was to represent the burgeoning hopes of American socialism. By 1912, the peak year for socialism in the United States, the membership of the Socialist Party was over 125,000, and when Debs ran for president in that year against two avowed Progressives and the incumbent, he picked up over 900,000 votes. By this date socialists had been elected to a fair number of offices at the municipal and state level, and had even elected one congressman, Victor Berger of the Socialist Party of America.

Yet a cursory evaluation of these gains reveals how small they were. Even Debs' vote, respectable as it was under the circumstances, was less than 6 per cent. And a comparison with Britain shows clearly the 'failure' of American socialism; one congressman against twenty-nine Labour M.P.s was a stark contrast, and moreover it must be borne in mind that the British movement was destined to go on to much greater things within a short while whereas for the American movement 1912 was a high point from which decline had already begun. And even more revealing than the bare statistics is the tone of socialism in America and the way in which that philosophy was received by the main body of the nation.

In America there had been a long and continuing tradition of violence surrounding socialism, and even the wider labour movement. Soon after the Civil War there appeared the 'Molly Maguires', a secret organization of coal miners who used terrorist tactics to maintain themselves against employers and black-leg labour; in return the authorities moved with exemplary force against them, smashing them by executing ten of their leaders on flimsy evidence. The following years were dotted with such incidents as the Haymarket riots of 1886, when, it was

alleged, an anarchist hurled bombs into a Chicago crowd that was protesting the police killing of strikers; the Homestead strike of 1892 when
strike-breaking Pinkerton guards (ironically this private law-and-order
enforcing agency had been founded by a Chartist obliged to flee to
America in 1842) clashed with the workers, leading to twelve deaths,
and when the national guard was used to protect further strike breakers;
the Pullman strike of 1894, which began as a protest against wage re-
ductions by the Pullman Car Company but which spread to paralyze
the nation's railways, led to rioting in Chicago in which twelve lives
were lost, and to the imprisonment of the railwaymen's leader, Debs,
who used his enforced leisure to read and be converted by socialist
literature; all these and many others were symptomatic of labour strife
in America. That it was deeply and officially engrained was seen in the
way in which the Sherman Anti-Trust legislation could be turned
against unions. This interpretation was upheld in 1908 by the Supreme
Court in the *Danbury Hatters Case*, which allowed a firm hit by union
boycott to sue the union and recover punitive damages. And although
President Wilson passed the Clayton Act in 1914 to exempt unions from
the Sherman Act, later events were to show that this new protection
was not so effective as it seemed.

The truth was that the climate of Social Darwinism was still sufficiently powerful to warp labour-management relations. Thus the
authorities were ready to use troops and injunctions to aid employers
in smashing labour protests. Thus the mine-owner's representative,
George F. Baer, at the height of the bitter Anthracite strike of 1902,
could speak of the owners as 'the Christian men to whom God in his
infinite wisdom has given the control of the property interests of this
country'. And thus an extreme form of socialism arose to fight this
attitude. In 1905 was formed the Industrial Workers of the World (the
IWW or Wobblies as they were known). Under the leadership of Big
Bill Haywood, the IWW used dynamite and murder as a means of getting across its message. Never a large organization, and not destined for
a long life, the IWW was yet a very American phenomenon and testimony to the inability of socialism to obtain a fair hearing in the United
States.

Matching this physical violence was the readiness of American socialists to take up intransigent, 'impossibilist' positions. On occasion this
could lead to farcical results, as in 1899 when two factions of the SLP
came to blows, not only had the police to step in to restore peace but,
supreme irony, the two sides took their disagreement—property, no
less—before the bourgeois courts. And if this example was extreme, it

was not isolated. Socialist groups were constantly splitting, forever taking up dogmatic stances. There was little of that tolerant give-and-take, little of that pragmatic working with other groups that characterized British socialism. Indeed, when in 1908–9 the British example was urged as a means of countering a decline in the movement's appeal, American socialism repudiated the suggestion; even the relatively broad SPA, not nearly so purist as the SLP, even the emotional and unintellectual Debs, agreed with this decision. Nor was there anything surprising in this; the roots of American socialism lay in the many communitarian colonies (for instance New Harmony, Oneida, the Mormons even; and Wayland himself founded a commune at Ruskin, named for the contemporary British art critic and opponent of materialism) that had dotted its history. Each of these was a repudiation of the greater society, a very particularist response. Unlike the British variety, American socialism never lost its bias towards narrow orthodoxy.

The vacuum left by socialism's failure was filled by the American Federation of Labor, founded in 1886. Unions had long existed in America, and after the Civil War the leading organization was that of the Knights of Labor. It had begun in 1869 as a secret organization, a fit comment upon the atmosphere still surrounding unions, and it became open only in 1881. It was not until 1885, following a successful strike against a railway, that the membership began to increase significantly, shooting up to over 700,000. The aim of the Knights under their Grand Master Workman Terence V. Powderley (the Masonic ritual was never wholly given up) was to organize One Big Union, the mobilization of the entire work force if possible; all were eligible for membership except doctors, businessmen, sellers of intoxicating drink, and lawyers. And their chosen weapon was not the strike but the even more mass-based boycott, the consumer's rather than the producer's weapon. But by the 1890s the Knights were well into decline. Powderley's leadership was defective, and the whole organization had been tarred with the anarchist brush in the Haymarket Riots and was never able to live down that false identification. And most significantly they could not compete with the newcomer, the AFL.

The leader of the AFL, Samuel Gompers, was determined to try a very different tactic. This was no One Big Union but, as the name indicated, a coming together of independent unions, each with needs and aspirations peculiar to itself. The aim was not to use a massive mobilization of forces in a big set-piece confrontation, but rather to engage in a series of limited actions for specific ends, e.g., better wages and conditions, shorter hours, etc., and to do so the strike weapon was used with care. The AFL studiously refrained from setting itself or its members apart from the mainstream of American life. Thus Gompers became vice-president of the National Civic Federation, a 'do-gooder' organization at the turn of the century to promote reasonableness in place of narrow partisanship, whose president was Mark Hanna, the boss of the Republican machine. And when it came to politics Gompers refused to have anything to do with the socialists, a very different tactic from that of the Trades Union Congress in Britain. His preferred way was to use the AFL as a pressure group, rewarding friends and punishing enemies, not confronting the system but demanding that it accommodate his members too. It suited the American worker.

And here lies the clue to a main reason for the failure of socialism to 'take' in the United States. In a rich, 'open' country, washed by wave after wave of immigrants most of whom saw material success and upward mobility as a means of self and group pride, the attractions of a head-on confrontation with the system were minimal. It has been pointed out by David Bell in his excellent contribution to Egbert's and Persons' *Socialism and American Life* that socialist literature was curiously filled with advertisements for home-improvement courses in the Dale Carnegie manner and for get-rich-quick investments. And Sombart answered his own question by saying 'On the reefs of roast beef and apple pie, socialistic utopias of every sort are sent to their doom!'

In many ways the problems facing socialism in Canada were even more daunting than in America. That continuing lag characteristic of Canadian industrialization inevitably had an inhibiting effect on the growth of socialism. The urban concentrations so necessary for effective socialism were only just forming on an appreciable scale. Canada was still dominated by its staples. The geographical isolation that many of these staple industries imposed on the work forces was a powerful obstacle to the effective emergence of socialism. At the same time industries like fishing, lumbering, and mining were marked by a boom-bust style, and if this predisposed the workers to radical critiques it also inhibited the expression of those critiques by denying the workers the settled conditions and steady incomes without which organization is all but impossible.

A further structural weakness of Canadian socialism was the way in which the country was broken up into regions that had little in common with each other. The Maritimes, long conscious of their basic identity, were finding confirmation for that fellowship in shared depression as their once mighty staple and carrying trades declined; central Canada, taking advantage of the St Lawrence, railways and the National Policy, was booming, though already Ontario was drawing further ahead of Quebec; the prairies were prosperous, but on a staple, wheat; and British Columbia's mineral and timber wealth and growing Pacific trade were setting it apart. To compound difficulties posed by regional diversity was the simple fact of size and distance; the Canadian population was still a sparse one and communication remained relatively poor.

Important though these structural weaknesses undoubtedly were, others were equally significant. In Quebec, long reluctant to espouse liberalism, there was continuing prejudice against socialism. The Church was very suspicious of industrialism but was also suspicious of radical movements, and since socialism in Europe, the example best known to the Church, was so frequently atheistical or at least anti-clerical, this reaction was perhaps understandable. Coupled with this antagonism was a *nationaliste* aversion from anything imported into Quebec from anglo-saxon (and Protestant) North America. Thus in 1886 the Quebec clergy came out against the Knights of Labor, which had made significant headway in Canada. And even when the labour organization in question was the Trades and Labour Congress of Canada, founded in 1886, there was antagonism in Quebec. When in 1902 the TLC split, Quebec unions took advantage of the fact to develop their own organization, the Canadian Labour Federation. That separateness that Bourassa was even then stressing in the political-cultural sphere was being paralleled in the industrial-cultural, and the Quebec labour movement was well launched on a distinctive development that would stress Catholic principle of social solidarity in place of the class basis of other socialisms.

It was the philosophy of Quebec, then, rather than its structural peculiarities, that inhibited socialism there. And in a very different way, philosophy in the rest of Canada also had the same effect. By and large Canada enjoyed boom conditions from the end of the great depression in 1896 right down to the outbreak of the war. Of course the United States did too, but in Canada the contrast with the uncertain economy of Confederation day was startling. The imagination of the country was captured by the expansion triggered off and kept going by the opening up of the prairies. Between 1870, when Manitoba was founded, and 1914 millions entered Canada and many of them came to the west; Winnipeg, the gateway to this booming region, confidently expected to become a second Chicago. And as grain poured out to world markets, so did manufactured goods pour in from central Canada, thanks to the National Policy. There seemed to be no reason why the expansion should slow for many years, and, as Prime Minister Laurier observed, the twentieth century would belong to Canada. In such an optimistic setting doubt was but a passing mood, and if there were a check then the tendency was to look for the slight technical flaw that was causing the system to malfunction; thus anti-monopoly sentiment was strong, and hardly surprisingly the Single Tax movement of Henry George was powerful and persistent in Canada.

This attitude on the part of English Canada was recognizably American. There were also other examples of Americanism. Capital from the United States was beginning to move into the country, and whereas British capital, which until the twentieth century had supplied the bulk of Canada's needs, was accompanied by Canadian management, the Americans tended to run their Canadian investments as part and parcel of their own business—in short the American 'branch plant' system was becoming the norm. And as management was increasingly American, so too was the workforce; during this period significant proportions of the two populations drifted back and forth across the border. Given these facts, and given the totality of shared background and experiences, it was no surprise when American styles in the world of labour became apparent.

One characteristic that was shared by America and Canada was the attitude towards class consciousness. In Canada, as in the United States, there was a great reluctance to visualize society in terms of competing classes. The comment of Macdonald in 1872 when responding to the workmen who thanked him for securing the Trade Union Act is very revealing. 'I might be said to have a special interest in this subject,' he observed,

> Because I am a working man myself. I know that I work more than nine hours every day, and then I think that I am a practical mechanic. If you look at the Confederation Act, in the framing of which I had some hand, you will admit that I am a pretty good joiner; and as for cabinet making, I have . . . much experience . . . .

This was politicking of course; but even so, could any British prime minister have spoken in that way? But an American could; Lincoln, the splitter of rails, did.

Macdonald's speech was an appeal to social solidarity. The same was true of successful Canadian trade unionism. The form that did best was that of Gompers, and indeed so powerful did the AFL become in Canada that the Trades and Labour Congress of Canada was reduced in effect to being an appendage of the American body. And given the prominence of the AFL, the opportunities for socialism were restricted. The Canadian movement was precluded from using the mass-union membership as a base on which to build, as the British Labour Party had done on the TUC. Some members of the TLC did make the attempt and at the 1908 convention of the TLC the British leader Keir Hardie made an impassioned plea for the British tactic. His efforts were in vain, however, for the majority of the union movement would have nothing to do with organized socialism.

As a corollary of this mainstream reaction against socialism, what manifestations did appear tended to be small, unstable, and extremist. The American-derived Socialist Labor Party was the first such group in Canada, in 1895; it fared no better than the original. This limited extremism was especially true of British Columbia about the turn of the century. The mining and logging camps that characterized much of the province and that set the tone for the remainder were ideal breeding grounds for intransigent movements. In these areas the appeal of the violent American Western Federation of Miners was strong as was, somewhat later, that of the IWW. In the first decade of the twentieth century British Columbia spawned socialist sects, including the Revolutionary Socialist Party of Canada, which announced that 'it has no compromises to make'. And accompanying this impossibilism was a tendency to industrial violence. At the miners' strike at Rossland in 1901 the militia was used to maintain order, and in effect to break the strike. But if British Columbia was the centre of extremism, this did not mean that other parts of Canada did not experience the same kind of thing. Tiny dogmatic socialist groups were to be found in other provinces, and bitter industrial clashes took place in, say, Winnipeg in 1906 during a streetcar strike, and at a sawmill strike at Buckingham, Quebec in the same year fatalities occurred.

Yet the socialist experience in Canada was not simply a copy of the American. If Canada was 'colonial' it was not the vassal of America only; there was the link with Britain too. Many of the immigrants to Canada had come from Britain, and of these a significant number had been artisans. In other words they represented a proletariat that had been through several generations of industrialization, that knew and accepted that world, and that had learnt how to protect its interests by the use of suitable tactics. As a result they could inject working-class expertise into Canadian life, expertise that was often socialist and usually moderate but efficient. Because these leaders tended to be the élite of the labour force they found their way mainly to Ontario, the most sophisticated economy and the one best suited to their skills. But the big cities such as Winnipeg received their quota. And even in British Columbia, the most Americanized economy and workforce, there was a British leaven at work; a major organizer of the Socialist Party of British Columbia, formed in 1902, was Ernest Burns, an ex-colleague of Hyndman—though it ought to be added that Burns had been a Populist in Washington state, a reminder of how rich was the North Atlantic, especially Canadian, heritage. This British socialist source was important in a second way. Not only did it provide moderation and experience, it brought validity. In the United States socialism had also been imported, but there it was an especially continental European phenomenon and consequently viewed with suspicion as alien and un-American. The fact that at the beginning of the twentieth century Canada was still very British, together with the fact that there was never the same degree of nativism there anyway, meant that socialism was viewed with much less suspicion than in the United States.

Secondly, Canadian socialism was not simply a copy of the American, because it was a success. This is not to compare Canadian results at the polls or in the legislature with those of British socialism. But bearing in mind the structural and philosophical disadvantages against which Canadian socialism had to struggle, its successes were not negligible; set alongside the United States it was a creditable record. Berger had been the only congressman elected by the socialists. But Ottawa saw A. W. Puttee returned for Winnipeg in a by-election in 1900 and again in the general election of the same year, and Alphonse Verville was returned in Montreal in 1906. Admittedly their record as socialists was not impressive, the former being defeated in 1904 and the latter going over to the Liberals almost at once. But they *had* represented socialist successes. Above all there was in Canada a readiness to accept socialism as a valid outlook, even if it were thought to be a wrong one. Thus whereas in the United States the period just before the war represented the high point, in Canada it represented merely the beginning of slow but steady growth.

6
The
Post-modern
World

The half century or so since the First World War has not only provided
the opportunity for the working-out of the patterns traced above, but
has also faced the North Atlantic community with challenges of a totally
new order. Three shocks in particular have affected the development of
these three societies, that of war, that of the new science, and that of
depression. Of the three the most salient has been the first—war.

The First World War had a shattering impact upon men's consciousness. The scale and intensity of the fighting dwarfed anything known
hitherto. And this grim gigantism was all the more shocking because of
the contrast it made with the popular attitudes of August 1914. When
Britain declared war on Germany in that month it, like all the combatant
nations, looked forward to a victory by Christmas. Europe was bored
with peace, and Britain had not had a European engagement since the
Crimea, 1854–6, and nothing of real importance since Waterloo. The
tiny British Expeditionary Force that landed in France, 100,000 men,
left in a light-hearted mood and to the delighted patriotism of the
crowds. In the same first flush of enthusiasm Canada recruited 30,000
men, fitted them out and confidently despatched them to England.
Within the year such attitudes had evaporated. Victory had not come.
The two enemies had settled down to trench warfare stretching from
Switzerland to the Channel, in which casualties were enormous. Soon
Britain was calling for the then unheard of number of 500,000 volun-

teers; by October 1915 Canada had authorized no less than 250,000 soldiers. Even such huge increases proved inadequate as the war dragged on. When the Armistice came on 11 November 1918 Britain had six million in the armed forces and Canada 630,000. Those killed were 750,000 and 65,000 respectively, figures that defied comprehension.

And by this time the United States had over a million troops in France and many more in training. As the war had progressed Germany had turned increasingly to submarine warfare. The Allied command of the seas won by their surface ships imposed an effective blockade on Germany, denying it vital war supplies brought in neutral shipping. A submarine offensive was seen as a means of forcing Britain to relax its blockade, and in addition it would curtail the flow to Britain of essential food supplies, Britain being reduced at one point to only a six-week supply. But because of their vulnerability, submarines were obliged to use extreme methods, and sudden sinkings could be made to appear barbarous. Moreover neutral shipping was often confused with British. The United States in particular was incensed by the sinking of her ships and her nationals, a sentiment that British propaganda played upon with good effect. A particularly good example of this came over the sinking of the *Lusitania*, a British liner sunk in 1915 with the loss of 128 American lives; that along with civilian passengers the *Lusitania* was carrying contraband war material was kept from the public for a long time. Given this and similar incidents, President Wilson was able to bring the country round to a declaration of war in April 1917. Its troops were spared the worst of the trench warfare, but even so 117,000 were killed before the war was ended.

The numbers involved and the numbers killed and wounded were appalling. But even those who were physically unharmed suffered cruelly. The conditions were indescribable, the mud at Passchendaele in 1917 so glutinous that men and machines could be swallowed up in it; the weight of *matériel* was awesome, the rain of bullets and shells, kept up for days on end, enough to cause complete mental breakdown —'shell shock' was the term used. The wonder is that instances of desertion, of organized mutiny, were not more frequent. The futility of war had never before been made so evident, and so it was no surprise, though it yet shocked the older consciousness, when in 1933 the Oxford University Debating Society overwhelmingly resolved not to die for King and Country. Pacifism, or at least a determination to avoid war at almost any cost, was an enduring legacy of the First World War.

Appeasement, however, was unable to prevent the Second World War. Though it lasted two years longer, battle casualties were much lower than in the First War, for this was a war of machinery and move-ment. At the same time, though, the shock to society was a profound one. The evidence of man's inhumanity to man was more brutally re-vealed in this war, and its final stages were climaxed by the revelation of the destructive power of nuclear weapons, a trauma that has haunted mankind ever since. And in the years after 1945 there have been enough conflicts to keep the possibility of holocaust constantly before the imagination; Britain and the United States, world powers, have some-times been involved as belligerents, while Canada, a middle power, has been prominent on United Nations peacekeeping missions.

War, the fact of war, has precipitated change in the North Atlantic community as in the entire western world. That votes for women were granted not as the result of abstract argument, but in recognition of the fact that women had contributed to the war effort and that they had shown that they were capable of doing a man's job has already been noted. And there were, too, the altered patterns of international rela-tions caused by war. Britain lost ground in both world wars; the cost itself was great and there was also the bitter fact that markets lost in wartime could not be recovered in peace. On the other hand North America increased its wealth and power, and Canada in particular vaulted into world rankings when during the Second World War it acted as the industrial reservoir for Britain. And accompanying the changes in wealth and power were constitutional changes, too.

A case in point was Ireland. War had always been an occasion for Ireland to embarrass Britain, and in 1914 Ireland was further antago-nized by the withholding of promised Home Rule. When the Irish Nationalist party supported the war effort, more extremist groups came to the fore, notably Sinn Fein ('Ourselves Alone') and the Irish Repub-lican Brotherhood, an offshoot of Fenian activity. With backing from Germany and from Irish-Americans, these forces mounted the Easter Rebellion in 1916. Although it was put down in a week, the execution of the ringleaders furnished martyrs to the nationalist cause, which continued to grow and to press for freedom. In the 1918 elections Sinn Fein won 73 of the 102 Irish seats and, refusing to attend Westminster, proclaimed themselves the Parliament of Ireland at a meeting in Dublin. Britain's answer was to recruit a force of ex-army thugs and loose them in Ireland, and these 'Black and Tans', so called from their makeshift uniforms, vied with the Irish Republican Army in ruling through terror. By 1921 a compromise settlement was arrived at. The greater part of Ireland acquired dominion status (i.e., that enjoyed by Canada) as the Irish Free State, while Northern Ireland remained part of the United

Kingdom. In 1949 the Free State left the Commonwealth and became the Republic of Ireland.

The changing status of Ireland was only the most dramatic instance of a wider change that was transforming the British empire into the Commonwealth. In this transformation Canada played a leading role. The impetus to a reordering of the empire had been provided by the ready response made by the Dominions to the war effort, and in 1917 it was agreed in the Imperial War Conference that a new system would have to be worked out as soon as peace was restored. The chance for asserting Canadian sovereignty was provided by the Versailles Peace Conference, where Canada was recognized in its own right apart from Britain. These beginnings were followed up in 1920 with the appointment of a Canadian High Commissioner in Washington, and by the signing in 1923 of a treaty governing the American-Canadian Halibut Fisheries without any formal British participation. This changed reality was recognized formally in the Statute of Westminster, 1931, which applied to the entire Commonwealth. Canada was still bound in some ways; the constitution could be altered only by Westminster, and appeals to the Judicial Committee of the Privy Council were still possible. But foreign policy was now Canada's alone, and only Ottawa could legislate for the country. The new autonomy was underlined on the outbreak of the Second World War; whereas Canada had been a belligerent in the First War automatically on Britain's declaration of war, in 1939 Canada itself declared war and waited an extra week to do so. And after that war the drive to independence was continued. Within two years of the ending of hostilities Canada instituted its own citizenship. Within two more years appeals to the Privy Council had been abolished. By 1952 Canada had her first Canadian Governor General, Vincent Massey.

Such changes were undoubtedly important. But they were the result of the fact of war, and probably the wars did nothing more than speed up a process that was inevitable. Much more significant was war as an experience, for in that sense it affected much more than merely technical relationships. The assumptions of the nineteenth century were destroyed in 1914 and liberalism itself became a casualty. It was a traumatic loss because the rhetoric of the war was the epitome of the liberal creed. The patriotic outpourings against the enemy had stressed the need to subdue German militarism and the autocracy. What this last term drew attention to was the contrast between the North Atlantic triangle's adherence to parliamentary democracy and Germany's attachment to a dominant executive—the Kaiser—and minimal representation of the people; a further contrast was between the voluntary-ism of the North Atlantic societies and the imposed discipline in Germany—to put the contrast in stark terms, and in terms that encompass the propaganda of the war against Hitler too, the North Atlantic belief in the primacy of man over the state was being challenged by its antithesis, that the state was more important than the individual. But the irony is that in upholding liberalism the North Atlantic societies were obliged to retreat from that very liberalism.

A dramatic instance of this retreat came over conscription. It had been a cardinal point of liberalism that man should not be constrained to anything; if a course of action was right then rational men would see that it was right and choose to do it. To force a man to fight was therefore immoral. Britain had maintained this attitude through the first two years of the First War. But the insatiable demands of the trenches convinced the Liberal and Conservative coalition government that conscription would have to be introduced. This was done in 1916, but that it offended against deeply held convictions was made evident when Sir John Simon resigned from the Cabinet in protest. In Canada the same reluctant introduction of conscription took place. The question was complicated in Canada by two pockets of opposition to any Canadian participation in the war. On the prairies were many recent immigrants, a great number of whom had arrived from countries that had no interest in Britain's quarrel and some of which were at war with Britain; in addition the farmers were enjoying boom conditions and did not wish to see the harvest suffer from a want of hands. More serious, though, was the opposition from Quebec. The anti-French sentiment last noted over the Autonomy Bills was further shown during the war years when in 1915 Manitoba abolished teaching in French, and when in the following year, under the so-called Regulation 17, the same was done in Ontario. Bourassa and the *nationaliste* press were able to make much of the similarity with German autocracy, and wondered aloud why Quebeckers should fight for an anglo-saxon power that did not hesitate to crush its minorities. Recognizing French-Canadian isolationism, the Canadian government put off bringing in conscription, and when in 1917 it felt obliged to, it provoked anti-conscription riots in Quebec. So powerful were Quebec's feelings that in the Second War, which could more easily be portrayed as a crusade against an evil threat, the Canadian government hesitated long over the question, taking refuge behind Prime Minister Mackenzie King's pronouncement 'Conscription if necessary, but not necessarily conscription'; when conscription was brought in resentment in Quebec was fierce, and only the fact that soon after its introduction in 1944 Germany was seen to be beaten kept the province quiet. Only in the United States was conscription not a major issue. In the Civil War both sides had been obliged to draft troops, and by half-hearted measures (in the north a substitute could be hired on payment of $300) had caused bad feeling. Thus in 1917 the United States implemented a selective draft using a lottery system and in this way the vast numbers needed could be mobilized with ease from the beginning.

Conscription to fight was an indication that liberalism was under attack. But it did not stop there. Wealth was also being put to the service of the state by conscription. The taxation system in each country was overhauled. This was most noticeable in Canada, perhaps. Britain had had an income tax as far back as 1798; America had authorized a federal income tax by the Sixteenth Amendment, ratified in 1913. It was only in 1917 that Canada introduced such a direct tax. But all countries were having to find new ways of increasing their taxing powers. The rates of income tax were drastically pushed up. New taxes were added; corporate taxation was introduced; there was an Excess Profits Duty in Britain, a Business Profits Tax in Canada, and an Excess Profits Tax in the United States, designed to return to the state something of the abnormal profits realizable in wartime.

Additional taxation in wartime had good precedent; the British introduction of income tax in 1798 to finance the war against France was an early instance. But what was unprecedented, however, was the way in which the state was intervening directly in the economy. Early in the war material for sandbags became so much in demand in Britain that the government stepped in and confiscated it, paying but one-third of the expected profiteers' price. But as time went on it became clear that attempts to control the price of essential goods merely moved back the area of profiteering, and in the end the British government was obliged to contract for the entire Indian jute crop, say. Bit by bit state control of the economy was pushed further and further, and by the end of the war the Ministry of Food was buying by far the greater part of the country's supplies. The state's quick action to remedy shortages of shells was a particularly good example of what could be done, and in 1915 the choice of Lloyd George to head the Ministry of Munitions gave him the opportunity to show his powers of war leadership. In Canada the same trend was observed; shell production was early coordinated via the Imperial Munitions Board; a War Purchasing Commission was established in 1915; the Wheat Exporting Company of 1916 was formed to handle the national crop when Britain and other countries established single buying agencies—it later became the Canadian Wheat Board; and the first steps were taken in the reorganization that led to the emergence of the Canadian National Railway system. Even the United States, late into the war, moved quickly to set up national administrations to deal with food, fuel, railroads, and other key areas; perhaps the greatest service was tendered by the War Industries Board, which by encouragement and command rationalized the production of many industries.

Two things may be noted here. The collectivism that liberalism had shunned, especially in the actual production of wealth, had been put to work. The need for planning, to see the whole process as one, had been underlined. And secondly, within that co-ordinated approach there was a new insistence upon bureaucracy and rationality. A technocratic concept of the economy was emerging, a kind of generalized Taylorism. Not that it triumphed at once. Britain had gone to war in 1914 parroting the silly cry 'Business as usual', and if it and other countries had been forced to change their ways they yet tried to get back as soon as possible to the old methods, to what Wilson's successor, Warren Harding, called 'normalcy'. The United States government quickly relinquished its control over the railroads, say. Britain did likewise with most of the concerns that had, in effect, been nationalized. In Canada the drift to provincial rights, stemmed by the need for a strong federal authority to fight a total war, was once again under way. But the impressive achievements of a technocratic structure were a matter of record, and they could not be ignored forever.

The First War fostered the collectivist and technocratic mentality in a second sense, on the more purely social level. Mass war had killed, but it had killed selectively. The officer class, which was to say the rising generation of the natural ruling class, had been decimated. It has been argued that in Britain, the member of the triangle most affected by this factor, a dearth of leadership allowed the country to drift at the very time when firm guidance was needed. And perhaps equally significantly, the concept of a natural ruling class was being undermined by the war. It became apparent that the conduct of the war was poor. In particular it was seen that the old virtues of bravery, coolness under fire, loyalty to one's code, which had been suitable for earlier and colonial battles, were not enough in modern war. The war was increasingly a technocratic matter; the tanks and planes that made a marginal appearance in the First War had become the dominant arms in the Second, and the men to use them were a very different kind of soldier from the stereotype. Indeed, as the 'poor bloody infantry' declined in importance and *matériel* took over, war itself became a reflection of the bureaucratic-rational business that industry had already become. The upward mobility that war always encouraged was especially marked in these world wars of the twentieth century. And finally this social collectivism was sealed by the trench experiences. The privations of war, extended in a desperate continuous effort, brought the various sections of society together in ways that were new. An extreme illustration of this breakdown in mutual ignorance was provided by that last exemplar of the Whig patrician type, Lord Curzon, once Viceroy of India and almost Prime Minister of Britain in 1923; on observing a large number of British working-class soldiers bathing he is reported to have remarked with wonder on how white their skins were—just what he expected is not clear, but evidently he thought of them as almost a different race from his own. The First War was matched in this respect by the Second, for the bombing raids of that war made all ranks realize their common danger; the evacuation of children from the towns to foster homes in the country was an especially potent means of inculcating social solidarity.

In short, modern war was a great levelling agency. Naturally Britain, the country closest to the firing line and the one most marked by stratification, was the one most affected by it. But the others were not immune. The blacks in the United States were encouraged to press for a new round of concessions as a result of their Second-World-War experiences (particularly since it was a war fought against racism); that segregation in the American armed forces ended in 1948 was a signal advance.

The second major factor affecting the development of consciousness in this period were the breakthroughs in science and technology. Since the closing years of the nineteenth century science had been taking giant steps, so vast that the familiar features of the Enlightenment world-picture were being left behind. But these changes, which were to make Einstein and relativity familiar words to the man in the street, were because of their very magnitude and daring understood by few. In time their implications would filter down through more and more layers of society, their message would be internalized, and a new way of thinking would prevail. But that takes time, and the process is still too young for an adequate account of its social impact to be given. But the technology of the twentieth century was altogether different. There the time-lag was much reduced and the impact may be charted with some facility.

In many cases the new technology was simply 'more of the same'.

Thus even before the war the principles of mass production had been known and had been extended in the form of Taylorism. But now a new expansion began, a movement whose messiah was Henry Ford. The standardized methods adopted at his factories at Dearborn were the subject of many jokes—Chaplin's *Modern Times* has been alluded to already, and we may add Ford's offer that anyone could have his Model T in the colour of his choice, provided that that choice was black—but the results were impressive. The price of cars was slashed drastically, and motoring, which had been a sport for the well-to-do in Britain and France, the pioneer countries of motoring, became a way of life for all kinds of Americans. Much the same was true of the telephone, a pre-war invention but now in the inter-war years greatly extended; once again North America took to this expansion with much more zest than Britain.

But some of the most interesting developments were quite new. Radio was a prime example. The principle had long been understood, the German Hertz having worked it out by 1887. Practical application had been made by the Italian Marconi, who by 1907 had made contact across the Atlantic. Indeed on the eve of the war the British government awarded a contract to the Marconi company to unite the empire via a chain of radio stations. But radio as a form of popular entertainment and information was not yet a fact. That had to wait until the inter-war period. It was an overnight success. It is interesting to note the basic difference between British and North American response to the novelty. In America private enterprise soon realized the possibilities. Within a few years of the opening of the first radio station in 1920, hundreds of competitors had entered the field. Eventually a Federal Communications Commission was established in the United States with minimal powers in 1927–34. In Canada the Canadian Broadcasting Corporation was set up in 1932–6 with rather more authority. But in Britain broadcasting was a state monopoly from the first. The British Broadcasting Corporation, established 1922–7, had regional variations, but essentially there was one central direction to the entire concern. Advertising was not permitted, and the necessary funds came from general revenue and from a license fee that had to be paid on each radio set owned. (This principle was later applied to television, but with the subsequent amendment that an Independent Television Authority was established alongside the BBC; the former uses advertising and is commercial, the latter is still free of advertising; all sets must carry a license annually renewed.) And whereas the major emphasis in North America was on entertainment, which meant seeking the lowest common denominator of taste, in Britain it was on improvement. Until very recently the BBC radio had what was called The Third Programme, a channel that catered to intellectuals only and that put out material of a *recherché* kind. The first controller of the BBC, Lord Reith, was ideally chosen to see this aim of improvement carried out. A dour Scots Presbyterian, he was so exacting that he had his news announcers dress in evening dress—and this for radio, not television!

This is not the place to go into a detailed account of the manner in which radio and television have altered people's ways of looking at the world; anyone interested in that fascinating subject may be referred to the works of Marshall McLuhan. But the very evident point may be made that radio was the most obvious manifestation of the general levelling trend of technology. Radio, for all Reith's paternalism, was essentially a levelling phenomenon. It reached into the houses of all strata and brought the same basic message and style. In Britain a 'BBC Voice' is referred to. The distinction between urban and rural, already breaking down, was even more swiftly eroded, for the radio was over-whelmingly the voice of urbanism. This was especially true perhaps in the commercial setting of North America where the latest city fashions would be communicated swiftly to the most out-of-the-way hamlet. At the same time regional distinctions tended to be broken down, and it is significant that Canada, which came to maturity with the radio, has not developed well-marked regional accents such as one finds in Britain or even in the United States, both of which pre-date the radio.

Levelling was also fostered by the mass-production techniques that have been mentioned. Mass-produced, standardized clothes made it less easy to tell a member of one class from another merely by outward appearance. Car travel was a boon in knitting scattered communities together and in increasing mobility in general. And in its own way the internal combustion engine, too, decreased regionalism and strength-ened the central pull. This paradox is beautifully illustrated in the case of Winnipeg. That city boomed as the gateway to the west, and main-tained its position as capital of the region. But it could do so only so long as it was a gateway, and this depended on its position astride the railway when that means of communication was virtually the only one. With the displacement of the steam engine by the internal combustion engine it is now possible to by-pass Winnipeg. The spread of tele-phones, radio, television, and other means of communication at a dis-tance have also served to undermine the regional capital and centralize power in even bigger centres. Finally, of course, the coming of cheap air travel has completed the decline of cities like Winnipeg. In these ways, then, the old truth was again vindicated that levelling means collectivization.

Technological change reinforced the effects of war, therefore. In this there was nothing surprising, for their compatibility has been touched upon. Their affinity, in fact, may be underlined by noting how in the modern period war has been accompanied by educational reform—and it may be indicated best in connection with Britain for there inertia has been strongest and so the impact of war has been most needed to bring about change. The big landmarks in educational development have been 1870 (a response to the emergence of technically minded Prussia at the head of an expansive Germany), 1902 (the shock of the Boer War, which was in fact a defeat for Britain), 1918 and 1944 (responses to the two world wars). But even the United States was affected; the G.I. Bill of Rights encouraged servicemen to pursue their education and helped spark a dramatic expansion of university work in the fifties and sixties, while the shock caused by the Russian sputnik led to a presidential inquiry and a tremendous increase in educational spending; this last example may have been cold war, but it was still war. And in all these instances the gain was to technology; if it was not formally favoured, at least the expansion of literacy and numeracy was beneficial to a work force increasingly technical.

The third major determinant was the depression. The ending of war in 1918 was followed by a short-lived boom. Wants had been bottled up during hostilities, and now that peace had returned many seized the chance to satisfy their long-thwarted wishes. But by 1921 this boom was over and the three societies experienced hard times. Slowly the economies picked up again, and this was especially true of North America. Even so the buoyant mood belied underlying structural weaknesses, and that the basis of prosperity was precarious was revealed late in 1929 when the New York Wall Street crash occurred.

The crash itself was essentially similar to the South Sea Bubble of 1719–20. For some time before the fall of 1929 a mood of rash confidence had gripped the American investor. *The New York Times* index of share prices, which had stood at 106 in mid-1924, was up to 181 a year later, to 245 by Christmas 1927, to 331 by Christmas 1928, and to 452 by September 1929. As in 1720 there was no reason why this should not go on. But sufficient investors decided that prices had gone high enough and began to sell and take their profits. Within days the rush was on to sell before the bottom fell out, and this only hastened the fall in prices. The collapse revealed the essential unhealthiness of the economy.

This crash also intensified the problems of the industrialized world, and Canada and Britain were badly hit too. The bare statistics reveal something of the enormity, though it is important to grasp what Blair Neatby stressed in his *Politics of Chaos*, that 'A depression is really a state of mind, a loss of faith in stability and security'. In America the per capita GNP, which had stood at $857 in 1929, had dropped to $590 by 1933. The unemployment rate by that year was over 25 per cent and this statistic says nothing of those forced to take jobs for which they were not suited and that did not pay adequately. Canada was similarly affected, but with the added disaster that her dependence upon staple products made her particularly vulnerable. Wheat, which had been enjoying a golden period in the late twenties, was terribly hit, the price per bushel falling from over $2 to 32¢ by 1932; and to compound the disaster was the arrival of drought, grasshoppers, and disease. Since so much of the prairies were dependent upon wheat, that region was particularly badly affected. The farmers, who had assumed large mortgages at high interest rates in the boom period, were in a much worse position than the Populist farmers of the nineties. The symbol of their comedown was the Bennett-buggy, a motor car with the engine removed and shafts added for the horse and called derisively after Canada's Conservative Prime Minister, 1930–5, R. B. Bennett. Though perhaps the biggest impact was upon Newfoundland, not yet a part of Canada but a separate Dominion. There the fish and newsprint staples were so badly affected that the island went bankrupt, lost its Dominion status in 1934, and, reverting to a colonial relationship, ceased to enjoy responsible government. In Britain it was the older areas of heavy industry and old-established concerns like the textile industry, now faced with cheap Asian competition, that were the hardest hit. National unemployment rose to an average of about 25 per cent, but infinitely worse were such pockets of unemployment as the ship-building town of Jarrow-on-Tyne, described in the book by Ellen Wilkinson as *The Town that was Murdered*, for there over 80 per cent were almost permanently out of work. Although the worst of the depression was over by the middle of the thirties it remained true that no real improvement had taken place and that only the Second World War could effectively break these three societies out of prolonged slump.

Depressions were nothing new in the capitalist world; they had been frequent, even cyclical, that of 1837 being but one of many. But this of 1929 was infinitely worse than 1837, worse even than that of 1873, which until now had always been the great depression. In part it was the magnitude of 1929, in part the way in which it spread its effects over a wider area, all economies being interdependent, in part its unrelieved persistence. But most of all it was worse because it came at a time when men expected better things; the war's suffering had been borne partly because it was expected to give rise to a better world—a 'world safe for democracy and a land fit for heroes' was the rhetoric of the day; the time had gone by when the trade cycle was seen as something God-given to be borne in resignation, and the faint beginnings of welfare legislation, mentioned in the last chapter, were being taken for granted and as but the first stages in a widening program. And it was worse because a new class of people were the sufferers by it; previously a depression would throw out of work the flotsam and jetsam of society or the more precarious businessmen who accepted the harsh logic of boom and slump anyway; but now those out of work were frequently white-collar, educated individuals, people who would be articulate about conditions and organize to do something about them. In a different way, then, the depression too was a levelling force. And it was a collectivizing one, also. Both in the short run, in terms of immediate aid, and in the long run, in terms of avoiding similar depressions in the future, the depression provided a powerful push in the direction of bureaucratically controlled, centrally planned economies.

※ ※ ※

The nature of the three main impacts, of war, of science and technology, and of the depression, has been dealt with so far on a general level. It is time now to look at the ways in which the three societies handled these problems of the twentieth-century world. This may be done by considering their responses under the headings of crusading movements, political flexibility, and economic novelty.

The first term draws attention to that mood of idealism that gripped the countries at war and of expiation they experienced when it was over. From what has been said so far of these three societies, it may be guessed that the United States would best exhibit this mood. A look at two crusades will bear this out.

Prohibition had been a major plank in the reform movements of the North Atlantic communities all through the nineteenth century. It had been intimately connected with the sectarian religious tradition, and in America the first victory for the Prohibitionists, the Maine Law of 1851, had fittingly come in a Puritan New England state. In time other states went dry, and it was mainly rural America, the bastion of WASP values, that showed this trend; William Jennings Bryan was a leading advocate of Prohibition. And just as the crusade against slavery had thrown up its antinomians such as John Brown, so too did the crusade against drink; Carry Nation from Kansas was one such, who would take an axe to saloons and physically destroy them. The movement against intoxicants fed into the Progressive wave. The WASP basis of Prohibition, the tendency to see drink as a foreign evil and one particularly connected with the Catholic immigrant, found a sympathetic echo amid the ranks of the Progressives who, as has been noted, were more than a little tinged with nativism. (This American identification of Catholicism and alcohol was alive as late as 1928, for in the election of that year the Democratic candidate, Al Smith, was assailed both as a 'wet' and as a Catholic.) This long tradition of crusading, together with the impetus of the Progressive movement, climaxed during the war. The eighteenth amendment, banning the sale of intoxicating beverages, was passed by Congress late in 1917 and it became law at the beginning of 1920. For thirteen years the experiment was persisted with. But the forces of corruption were too much for those of law and order; underworld gangs moved into the business, and so large were the profits to be made that widespread violence occurred in the attempts to control the 'market'. Rather than an improvement in the morals of the nation, there occurred a decline. But that the experiment had been tried at all was very American.

Something of the same determination to legislate the conditions for morality was to be seen in Canada. The same long tradition, the same motivation (ASP in this case) were to be seen, facts borne out in New Brunswick's following the example of neighbouring Maine in 1852 and 1856. But a clearer example came in 1898 when a national referendum was held on the subject of Prohibition; all the provinces voted to go 'dry' (by small margins it is true) except Quebec, which overwhelmingly rejected the proposal. As it was, the small majority for Prohibition and the low turn-out of voters enabled Laurier to avoid taking action, and the already existing patterns of local option were all that could be managed at this stage of the campaign. But in 1915 Saskatchewan went 'dry', to be followed by every other province but Quebec. Finally in 1917, following the American decision, Prohibition became national. But it lasted only until 1919 and from this high point the 'drys' were in retreat. One by one the provinces abandoned Prohibition until by 1930 only Prince Edward Island was left. And as the liquor trade was once again permitted, the provincial governments sought to control it by establishing monopolistic liquor authorities. Incidentally it may be noted that the Canadian experiment did not produce the same antinomianism as did the United States; not only was there no Carry Nation, but there was not nearly so much flouting of the law while Prohibition was in effect—indeed there are those who argue that the experiment in Canada did cause an improvement in the morality of society and that the experiment should have persisted.

In Britain the Nonconformist Conscience had seen its campaign against drink recognized by the inclusion of the 'local veto' plank in the Liberal Newcastle program of 1891. In fact, though, the Liberals showed little determination to come to grips with the trade. The war did have some moralistic effect upon the question; King George V declared that he would abstain from alcohol for the duration of the war. But what little impact the war had was from a practical standpoint only. In the interests of war production government controls over the liquor trade had been tightened up, of course, and in certain cities where drinking problems were particularly bad the state had nationalized the breweries and the pubs; Carlisle was the best example, for its beer remained a state monopoly down to the seventies, long enough to be tested by *Which?*, the British consumer magazine, which rated it number one in Britain, an odd triumph for nationalization. But this was all, and after the war commitment to Prohibition evaporated.

The second crusade the United States embarked upon was an even more ambitious undertaking. President Wilson was determined to take seriously the slogan that the Great War was the war to end all wars. Even while the hostilities were raging, even while the original belligerents were still thinking of a peace in terms of old-fashioned territorial acquisition, Wilson was pledging America to the search for principled ways by which the fighting could be ended. Early in 1918 Wilson formulated a Fourteen Point program that should guide any peace conference. It was a monument to idealistic liberalism, even down to including a demand for the removal of tariff barriers between nations, and it stressed the idea of national self-determination that led to the re-creation of Poland and the setting up of Czechoslovakia; the Irish were particularly happy with this point about self-determination.

The clearest expression of idealism, however, was the last point of the program, which called for the setting up of a supra-national organization that would see to it that war became a thing of the past by adjudicating quarrels between member states. This plan eventually led to the establishment of the League of Nations. This too was a very American crusade, and reaction to it in the North American triangle is revealing.

Britain responded as did most of the European powers. It was difficult to come out against such 'motherhood' sentiments, and Britain did join the League and remain a member until it faded away with the coming of the Second World War. But there was little genuine commitment to the spirit of the Wilsonian approach and Britain was always more taken with the urge to hang the Kaiser or to squeeze Germany till the pips squeaked. Canada was committed to membership of the League, for this was another way in which her growing autonomy could be recognized. But there was never any deep enthusiasm for the idea. Canada felt remote from the world's trouble spots and was reluctant to give up her American isolationism.

And here was a most potent factor that brought down Wilson's own schemes in his own country. The deep commitment of the United States to a new moral order was challenged from within the country and Congress refused to accept the idea of the United States' membership in the League. It must be admitted that Wilson's handling of the issue was not blameless, and that the stroke that paralyzed him undermined his leadership at the crucial moment. Yet it must also be acknowledged that the country was revealing its tendency towards a very different tradition from that of moral leadership. American isolationism, which could be traced back to the pre-Revolutionary sectarian conviction that American morality was to be shown not in participation but in self-righteous withdrawal, was the stronger force; significantly it was especially strong in the mid-west and among the surviving pockets of Populism-Progressivism.

It remains true, however, that crusading in America was represented in great part by a commitment to the League. In Canada and Britain, however, there were alternatives. In Canada the mood was a diffused one that was first seen in the Union movement. In May 1917 the Prime Minister, Sir Robert Borden, asked Laurier and the Liberals to enter a coalition government. Laurier himself refused but many prominent Liberals did join. In the election late in 1917 the Union government was easily returned. It is true that this result was helped by rigging the election: the women relatives of servicemen, who would be expected to vote for an aggressive war policy and conscription, were given the vote and duly voted Unionist; at the same time citizens who had come from enemy countries since 1902, that is brought in by Liberal immigration policies in the main and disposed to vote Liberal, were disenfranchised; the members of the armed forces were asked to vote not for a certain candidate but simply for or against the government. But even so the Union government was seen by many as a force to represent the purer aspirations of the country, and much was expected of it. In the event, little did come of it, and the mood was dissipated among competing political ideologies even as the Union government itself split up by 1919. It is worth stressing, however, that the mood of idealism was channelled into practical politics and not into any chimera like the League of Nations.

The same point may be made about Britain. There expiation took the very concrete form of concentration upon an overhaul of the country's amenities. The Education Act of 1918 has been mentioned already. Then in 1920 the Unemployment Insurance Act was greatly extended. It was housing, however, that showed the new social concern to greatest advantage. Whereas the intervention of the state in housing remained tentative and minimal in both Canada and the United States, Britain's commitment to public housing and slum clearance was on an impressive scale. This is not to say that the evils of urban overcrowding were removed overnight, but a serious attempt was made and the state had indicated its determination to safeguard the environment.

The crusading mood was short-lived, surprisingly so. This is not to say that the reform, indeed revolutionary spirit was wholly dead, but to suggest that it quickly became part and parcel of movements that were political. The nature of politics, in particular the degree of flexibility with which situations were handled, must now be examined.

Political developments in the North Atlantic community have been fought out since the First World War against a continental European background; whereas in the nineteenth century the countries of the triangle were the pacesetters, now in the twentieth they have become the followers. In Russia war weariness and criticism of the Tsarist régime led to the overthrow of the autocracy in the spring of 1917. A liberal constitution took its place and the general reaction in the west was akin to that which had greeted the first stages of the French Revolution. But like the French model, it proved impossible to maintain such a moderate alternative. The Russian war effort was still going badly, food supplies were short, and in the unaccustomed freedom of debate there was too much discussion and bickering and not enough united action. As the French Revolution threw up its Terror so did the Russian produce its second rising of 1917; in November the Bolshevik wing of the Russian Marxists under the leadership of Lenin seized power and within a relatively short period had established a totalitarian régime even more repressive than the Tsarist. At the same time the Bolsheviks, who took the name Communists, announced that the Russian Revolution was but the first episode in what was to be a world-wide revolution. The Comintern was established in Moscow in 1919 to co-ordinate and foster such risings, and central Europe in particular was hit by communist risings.

Reaction to the Russian Revolution was profound. Many were favourably impressed, but equally there were those who were appalled both by the methods used and by the aims professed by the Communists. A right-wing force developed to fight this drift to the left. The most notable early example was Italian Fascism in the twenties, but it was soon overshadowed by that of the National Socialists who captured power in Germany in 1933. The western world split between these appeals of left and right, and opinion increasingly polarized. And it is important to grasp that such a division was as much psychological as anything else; even without knowing anything about communism or fascism people would instinctively know they were for the one and opposed to the other. Thus when in 1936 the Spanish Civil War broke out the world took sides; Americans fighting against Franco and for the Republic in the Abraham Lincoln battalion, Canadians in the Mackenzie Papineau battalion, and British in the Saklatvala battalion (after an Indian Parsee elected to Westminster as a Communist in 1924; the absence of an 'above party' myth figure in British history may be pondered) may have been few, but many more were deeply interested in the outcome. Their reactions coloured their attitudes to the domestic politics of the North Atlantic communities.

In one respect there was unanimity within the triangle. Democracy, even egalitarian democracy, was taken for granted. With the granting of votes for women it might be thought that in North America there was little scope left for demonstrating belief in a thoroughgoing democracy. But in fact the spread of radio and television did provide an opportunity. President Franklin D. Roosevelt, elected in 1932, was particularly adept at using radio talks, 'fire-side chats', to get close to the citizen and make him feel a part of the governing process. And as the use of TV coverage during the Watergate crisis has shown, the American determination to ensure participation whenever possible has not weakened. This conception of politics as popular drama has never been so fully developed in Canada, though Bennett, a conscious follower of Roosevelt, did go a good way in this direction. In Britain the practice of government is still kept apart from the wider life of society.

But in other ways Britain was exhibiting a move towards wider participation. The widening of the franchise has been noted, and it may be rounded out with mention of the 1945 Act, which removed the last vestiges of plural voting—additional votes in respect of business premises and the university seats were abolished. Even more meaningful was the decline of the oligarchic element. It has been mentioned how Lord Curzon was almost prime minister in 1923. The reason why he was passed over was that he was a peer, and it was felt that to have the prime minister not in the Commons and able to reply directly to the representatives of the people was no longer possible. The final *coup de grâce* to the oligarchy came as late as 1957 when Lord Salisbury resigned from the Macmillan cabinet because he disagreed with the Conservative policy. Salisbury was the grandson of the Conservative Prime Minister of 1885–6, 1886–92, and 1895–1902, and he came of a long line of English statesmen stemming from William Cecil, adviser to Queen Elizabeth I; it was in recognition of this tradition as much as of his own abilities that the fifth marquis was included in the Macmillan cabinet. In an earlier period the defection of such a notable would have been disastrous for the party and the government, and Salisbury was no doubt intending this effect. But in fact his going was hardly noticed. And confirmation of the trend was given in 1965 when the Conservative leader, Sir Alec Douglas Home, 14th Earl of Home, resigned. It had been Tory practice to avoid the election of a leader—it smacked too much of democracy, and the party preferred to discover a leader by sounding out the chief members and seeing who evolved as the natural ruler. But in 1965 for the first time a formal election was held, all Conservative M.P.s being allowed to vote. Their choice was similarly revolutionary; Edward Heath was of lower-middle-class parentage, if not from artisan stock. It was a sharp contrast from his patrician predecessor. At the same time the residual deference in British life and the reluctance to make clean breaks with past practice should not be overlooked. As late as the fifties half the Eden cabinet had been to the same school, Eton, and the House of Lords still plays a role in the Constitution. That role has been reduced and now the Lords can hold up legislation for one year only; but the upper house has not been abolished, and the fact that life peers have existed since 1958 (peerages not transmittable to heirs), that since 1963 a peer has been able to relinquish his title and sit in the Commons (the contemporary Labour minister Antony Wedgwood Benn won this right by refusing to take his Lord's seat as Lord Stansgate), and that since 1965 no more hereditary peerages have been created point to the fact that Britain is still committed to the expedient of changing an institution not by an outright attack on it but by allowing time to do its work.

If there was broad unanimity on the rhetoric of democracy there was by no means the same unanimity on the actual scope to be allowed to that democracy. In a polarizing world it was inevitable that tension become acute and that there be disagreement over the extent to which society should adapt to meet the new challenges. Would there be repression or a flexible compromise?

The First War itself, a total war, had provided an impetus towards repression. Some control was inevitable, but excessive hostility was directed to anyone or any group that could be suspected of being less than one hundred per cent behind the war. For being critical of the war Bertrand Russell was deprived of his position at Cambridge University; D. H. Lawrence, who was already known for his 'advanced' and 'shocking' views and whose wife was German, was persecuted; the leaders of the Clydeside workers who protested against the war profiteering were arrested and 'deported' to other parts of Britain. In Canada the government was armed with the War Measures Act, which went much further than Britain's Defence of the Realm Act. Under the War Measures Act, whose draftsman had taken the line that 'no one could foresee what it would need to contain to be effective and that the only effective Act would be one of a "blanket" character', the government had enormous reserve powers—as was shown when it was resurrected during the Quebec FLQ crisis in 1970. In addition, the publishing of material in a foreign language was controlled, it being feared that Bolshevik propaganda would be attractive in this guise. And radical organizations like the Canadian cells of the IWW were banned.

But it was in America that the most thoroughgoing assault upon dissidents was mounted. The official campaign for conformity was carried on under the Espionage Act and the Sedition Act of 1917 and 1918 respectively. Particularly hard hit were the already declining socialist groups. The IWW was harried out of existence, and the Socialist Party of America reduced to a shadow of its former self; its leader, Debs, was sentenced to ten years in jail for his opposition to the war, and its Congressman, Berger, was denied his seat in the House, and there were many other instances of persecution.

Such activities were deplorable, but given the fact that governments were facing the demands of total war for the first time some excuse can perhaps be made. The real test came with the restoration of peace. How would the various governments react, and in particular what would their attitude be towards the radicals, notably the Socialists and the Communists?

In Britain there were ugly episodes. In 1919 serious riots broke out in Glasgow when the Red Flag was raised. In 1921 there was a bitter miners' strike. Five years later the miners struck again, this time to be joined by almost all other workers. This General Strike of 1926 paralyzed the country for several days; volunteers, protected by police and troops, attempted to keep essential services going, and Winston Churchill, then Chancellor of the Exchequer, made tough speeches on the need to smash the workers. The TUC called off the strike before too many physical confrontations could develop. When later during the depression the government applied a 'means test' to those seeking welfare, a prying assessment of a person's total assets, and relief was given in proportion to those assets, there was street fighting in Liverpool. Above all, as a sign of a repressive attitude there was the Trade Disputes Act of 1927, a measure prompted by the General Strike. This Act took away the right granted in 1913 (to right the Osborne judgement) for unions to collect dues from members and apply them to political purposes unless the member 'opted out' of the arrangement; under the Act of 1927 the member wishing to pay the political levy was required to 'opt in', and this was clearly intended as a device to weaken union political power. By and large, however, it may be said that society was calm and reasonably prepared to engage in dialogue. No anthology of the General Strike is complete without its photograph of the strikers playing soccer against a police team.

And all the while there was the growing appeal and credibility of the Labour Party. In 1918 the party was reorganized. Previously a federation of groups, it now permitted individuals to join directly; membership rose in this period and there was an especial increase in intellectuals. At a time when the Liberals were splitting between the followers of Asquith and of Lloyd George, the Labour Party was well placed to pick up recruits and to become one of the poles of a reorganized political system. At the same time the Labour Party took advantage of the reorganization to proclaim openly what had been taken for granted, that it stood for socialism.

This reinvigorated socialist party was improving its standing at the polls. At the 1918 election it returned 59 members; in 1922 it increased this figure to no less than 142; and in 1923 to 191. When early in 1924 the Conservatives were defeated, Labour was asked to form a government. Ramsay MacDonald did so, and it lasted almost a year. Labour had a second chance to show its style in the inter-war period, for in the election of 1929 it was the biggest party. But the economic crash prevented any possible innovation. Indeed so critical did the situation become in 1931 that a National Government was formed, with MacDonald as prime minister. The Labour Party repudiated MacDonald and went into opposition. In effect the National Government was a Conservative government, and after the election of 1931 Labour was reduced to a rump of 46 members. Finally the real breakthrough came at the close of the Second World War. The 1945 election gave Labour a majority of 204 over the Conservatives alone and of 146 over all other parties combined. Even before this triumph, however, it was clear that socialism was accepted as valid in Britain. There had been, it is true, the Red Scare of 1924; a letter purporting to be from Zinoviev, the head of the Comintern, which advocated making British diplomacy serve revolutionary ends, was seized upon by some in an attempt to discredit the left. But even that manifestation of the Red Scare was minor. Much more revealing was the fact that when the first Labour ministers went to kiss hands upon appointment they elected to wear court, i.e., aristocratic, dress. It was a far cry from the cloth cap that Keir Hardie had aggressively worn to Westminster back in 1892.

The acceptance of socialism was accompanied by an acceptance of communism. Not that the party ever commanded the votes of many in Britain. From its foundation in 1921 it has enjoyed few parliamentary successes, Saklatvala being one of a handful. But it was accepted in the sense that there were no serious attempts to have the party outlawed. At the same time it may be noted that Britain had been quick to recognize the U.S.S.R.; Lloyd George did so *de facto* in 1921 and MacDonald *de jure* in 1924. Repressive attitudes towards novel developments were not widespread in Britain.

It was far otherwise in the United States. The coming of peace saw little let-up in repression, and the twenties may have been the most repressive decade in American history. There was, for instance, a generalized nativism abroad in the land. This was the time when the traditional open-door immigration policy was replaced by a quota system. This was the time when the Ku Klux Klan was rampantly active. Minorities were under increasing pressure, and of none was this more true than the blacks.

In some ways the negro might have been expected to improve his position. Just before the First War a race riot in Springfield, Ohio (not that such riots were rare, but this one produced positive reaction) had encouraged white and black to come together in the hope that race relations could be improved; in 1910 was formed the National Association for the Advancement of Colored People (NAACP), the leading figure being the negro, W. E. B. DuBois. Soon afterwards the war situation ought to have improved the negro position. In fact segregation and discrimination in the armed forces was so bad that German propaganda could make much of negro degradation. At the same time the war economy had the effect of stepping up the migration of negroes from the south to the urban north and industrial jobs. This was in the long run to lead to increased black militancy and gains; in the short run however it produced a new racial confrontation where both sides had to learn the etiquette of race relations from the start.

During the inter-war years the negro was able to do little to improve his position in a climate where improvement might have been expected. No civil-rights legislation was secured, and in one crucial decision the negro seemed to have lost even more ground: in 1935 it was decided that it was legal for a Democratic organization to keep negroes from voting in primaries. So disillusioned was the mood that the most impressive black crusade of the period was that of Marcus Garvey, a Jamaican negro. His plan was to repatriate negroes to their original homeland, Africa, and if it collapsed due to bad management it yet showed the dawning sense of repudiation that was increasingly marking the black community. Since the Second World War this repudiation has been taken further with the Black Muslims and the Black Panthers.

Hard hit indeed was the labour movement and its tentative political manifestations. Industrial disputes still tended to become violent confrontations. This was especially true after the reorganization of the union movement in the thirties. Certain workers argued that in the newer industries, say auto manufacture, it made more sense to organize industrially than by craft; to organize in the former manner would mean a monolithic institution able to withstand the closed ring of employers, whereas to organize in the latter would mean fragmentation of effort and enable the employers to play craft off against craft. The AFL, however, was not in agreement and in 1935 a split occurred; by 1938 the industrial unions were structured as the Congress of Industrial Organizations. The bosses were determined to resist this new antagonist, and fierce struggles took place. In 1937 a steel strike in Chicago touched off rioting in which police killed ten workers.

Amid this bitterness there was no significant declaration for a labour or socialist party. At the end of the war the American Red Scare had been a savage and widespread outburst. Radical organizations came under intense pressure and were discredited in the eyes of the vast majority. In the election of 1928, admittedly a boom year, Norman Thomas, the socialist candidate, could poll only .72 per cent, and even in 1932, three years into the depression, he managed but 2.21 per cent, well below Debs's showing in 1912. So committed to the existing party system were the unions, in fact, that they became the biggest contributors to the Democratic Party.

In such a climate the Communist Party had no hope. The United

States did not recognize the U.S.S.R. until 1933. The Communist Party might attract some intellectuals but it was far beyond the mainstream of American political life. So far beyond, indeed, that it could become a convenient scapegoat in troubled times, a focus for those inclined to a conspiracy view of history. Legislation that effectively outlawed the Communist Party was passed in 1940, 1950, and 1954, and Senator McCarthy was to make his reputation as the exposer of communist infiltration. Only in the last few years has there been a softening of this attitude, yet even mild accommodation has sent many scurrying to the John Birch Society, to the Minutemen, and to other extremist anti-Communist groupings. The contrast with Britain was striking, and perhaps nowhere better summed up than when Saklatvala arrived for an American tour; this Indian Parsee, chosen by his London constituents to represent their interests and so a member of the British legislature, was denied entry to the United States because of his political beliefs.

Canada also represents a contrast to the United States. This is not to deny that the level of intolerance was high at times, significantly higher, for instance, than Britain's. Nativism was a powerful force, and in the twenties the Ku Klux Klan flourished, in Saskatchewan especially. When during the depression a march set off for Ottawa it was brutally stopped in Regina. When in 1937 the nascent CIO began to organize in Ontario the provincial authorities determined to break it up; and significantly, the CIO was tagged with the communist label as a means of discrediting it. From the first feeling against the Communist Party had been marked in Canada, and the original party had had to be a secret, underground organization when it was set up in 1921; twice since then, in 1931 and in 1940, it has been persecuted by the authorities.

And as an example of rigidity there was always Quebec. Such rigidity could be seen in labour organization and attitudes. That separate structure foreshadowed in 1902 was openly developed in 1921 when the Confédération des Travailleurs Catholiques du Canada was formed, in which membership was open only to Catholics and where direction was in the hands of the Church. It was separate from, and indeed hostile to, the Canadian Trades and Labour Congress. Out of this inward-looking, defensively minded society there evolved a specifically Quebec movement to embody its nationalism. The underlying mood of the province had always been conservative, and the vote had been Conservative until the execution of Riel, the emergence of Laurier, and the Conservative pressure for conscription. And if therefore the name Conservative now had to be avoided, it did not mean that the fundamental leaning had to be given up. In the mid-thirties the remnant of the provincial Conservatives and dissident Liberals, drawing upon the basic conservatism of the province, formed the *Union Nationale* and swept to victory in 1936. Under its leader Maurice Duplessis it showed itself to be well within the long tradition of political absolutism. The 'Padlock Law' of 1937 was a law, nakedly used against dissident opinion, to close down those places of assembly thought to be subversive of the *status quo*, that is those to the left. The urge to reform, which had motivated the dissident Liberals in particular, was quickly put to one side and driven underground, to emerge only much later. What remained was an intense *nationalisme*, the political counterpart to the intellectual manifestations that received their most dramatic form in the writings of Abbé Groulx.

Only in the fifties did Quebec begin to change. The educational system was overhauled. Students in grades 9 to 12 more than doubled, and university enrolment increased by fifty per cent. There was also a shift in emphasis away from the classical curriculum towards more modern subjects, and sociology in particular experienced a sudden popularity. The result was to prepare a new class of people who would find it difficult to fit into the traditional intellectual niches of the learned professions, and who would further find that their modern skills brought them into sharp competition with the group that until then had a near monopoly of such training, the anglophones. Direction for this urge was provided by a new-style intelligentsia that stressed the end of clerical domination and the spread of more modern bureaucratic and technical outlooks and that centred about the periodical *Cité Libre*; prominent in this grouping was Pierre Trudeau.

While this breakthrough was being accomplished in the intelligentsia, developments were taking place in the labour world that had a similarly shattering effect on the old fixities. The Duplessis régime had favoured management over unions to a frightening extent, and the Padlock Law was merely the most extreme example of a determination to crush anything even remotely subversive. But in 1949 there took place a major strike at Asbestos. It was major not simply because of its bitterness, nor because of the tremendous support, amounting to $300,000 in monetary terms, shown by unionists and people generally. It was major because it represented a change of attitude, first on the part of the strikers who were challenging the system as such, secondly on the part of the CTCC, the Catholic union founded in 1921 to keep the workers in line but that now saw its role as an adversary one, and thirdly on the part of sections of the Roman Catholic hierarchy; for instance Archbishop Charbonneau of Montreal charged that 'The working class is the victim of a conspiracy which wishes to crush it', and went on to claim that 'when there is a conspiracy to crush the working class, it is the duty of the Church to intervene'.

The Union Nationale collapsed in 1960 and Jean Lesage and the Liberals took over. What is known as the 'Quiet Revolution' was inaugurated. The structural changes referred to above in schools, offices, and industry were accompanied by a sudden flowering of the arts, and the demand for recognition of Quebec nationalism was again raised. But this time it was overwhelmingly from the left and not from the right, from progressive forces and not from the reactionary, that the cry was heard. Thus when the Queen visited Quebec in 1964 she was received coolly, if not with hostility. The more extreme nationalists, the separatist Parti Québécois under the ex-Liberal René Lévesque, look to an independent Quebec in which there will be a large measure of socialism; and in the recent election, 1974, there were overtures between the NDP and the Parti Québécois. And even further to the left of the Parti Québécois are small groups of the *Front de Libération du Québec*, communist terrorist cells whose campaign of violence culminated in 1970 in the kidnapping of British diplomat James Cross and the assassination of Liberal politician Pierre Laporte; significantly those involved chose exile in Cuba.

The case of Quebec was a special one where rigidity once challenged meant a violent flip-flop in attitudes. In the rest of Canada there was a more flexible development, though in the years immediately after the First World War it must be confessed that this did not seem likely.

In 1918 there was unrest throughout western Canada, with tension running especially high in Winnipeg. Early in the summer of 1919 the metal and building trades struck over the question of wages and union recognition. The Winnipeg Trades and Labour Council voted to call a general strike and on 15 May an almost total stoppage of work took place. For some six weeks the city was paralyzed; perhaps equally significant was the outbreak of sympathy movements in other Canadian centres. In the end the strike was broken; police and citizen specials charged the crowds, one fatality occurred, the leaders were arrested, accused of seditious libel, and sent to prison. The authorities in their fear added provisions to the Criminal Code that made mere attendance at a meeting of an unlawful association a crime.

It looked as though the Canadian Red Scare was to be as total as that in the United States. But the Canadian government's repression was not wholly successful. Within a short while the leaders were victoriously back in city politics, one even becoming mayor. And still more striking, one leader, J. S. Woodsworth, originally a Methodist Social Gospeller but increasingly a socialist without doctrinal Christianity, was elected to Ottawa in 1921 for one of the Winnipeg seats; once in the Commons he became the 'leader' of a two-man 'Labour Party'. In other words, whereas the early 1920s were the end of the road for American socialism, they were the beginning for Canadian.

It was however a faint beginning, and at the time a second and very different protest movement loomed larger. The farmers began to organize their own movement and to enter politics both provincially and federally. Not surprisingly it was essentially a prairie movement. The Maritimes, though swept by anti-federal feeling, yet chose to channel their discontent via the existing major parties, a conservatism that still remains true today. Ontario, on the point of transition from an agricultural economy into an industrial, did, it is true, produce a successful farmers' party. In 1919 the United Farmers of Ontario formed the government of that province. Their success however was short-lived, and a better example of farmer politics was to be found further west. Alberta in fact provided the best illustration, and the United Farmers of Alberta, successful in 1921, held on to a provincial power uninterruptedly until 1935. A national counterpart to these provincial organizations was formed in 1919. In the summer of that year T. A. Crerar, a representative of Manitoba's farmers and Minister of Agriculture in the Unionist government, resigned in protest against the continued high-tariff policy. At once he became the nucleus of a farmer grouping, the National Progressive Party. In the election of 1921 this new organization did amazingly well; with 65 seats, 28 of them from the prairies, they were the second biggest party at Ottawa, the Conservatives having been reduced to a mere 50 seats.

The Progressive Party could draw upon a tradition of farmer discontent going back in a formal way to the turn of the century and informally right back into the nineteenth century. Yet the new party lacked a coherent philosophy. The broad outline of its beliefs might be discernible, its criticisms especially might be plain. But too much was left undecided and there was a good deal of disagreement between the members of the movement. In particular two wings may be identified, a 'Manitoban' wing and an 'Albertan' (not all members of these subgroups came from Manitoba or Alberta, only the most prominent). The former was represented by Crerar who was little more than a nineteenth-century liberal and believer in strict laissez-faire. The latter was represented by Henry Wise Wood, who was prepared to go much further and could perhaps be claimed as a socialist of sorts. And it is this second wing that is of interest. In the early days it infused the Progressives with its thinking, and as by 1926 the Progressives began to break up, the 'Manitobans' drifting into a Liberal position, it was the Albertans who held together to continue a radical critique. By this time, indeed, they were known as the 'Ginger group', and under that name they were to exist down into the thirties when they were in a position to play a crucial role in a realignment of politics. The nature of their radical critique therefore deserves to be examined.

The most distinctive contribution of Wood was his theory of group government. It is a basic assumption of the parliamentary system that a member of parliament represents all the people in the constituency that returned him; he must, therefore, seek to defend the interests of miners, shopkeepers, farmers, all manner of occupational groups. Wood rejected this as impossible. Far better, he argued, if farmers, say, had their representatives, miners theirs, and so on, such that parliament would cease to be a forum of individuals each claiming to represent the nation and would become one where group bargained with group. It marked in fact a return to a medieval notion of representation, that of interests. A further objection to the parliamentary system was its practice of formed opposition; it is now accepted that the second biggest party shall consider itself as a potential governing party waiting the call, and that until that call comes its duty is to criticize and oppose the government whenever possible. Wood's hatred of such a system was at once pre-modern and post-modern. The eighteenth century and earlier had feared formed oppositions because they suggested an unbearable split in the body politic that ought to be united. The post-modern technocrat, assuming that efficiency will dictate a course of action regardless of party distractions, looks to the same unanimity for very different reasons. Both outlooks were delighted with Wood's impatience with partyism. When in 1921 the Progressives' 65 seats entitled them to become the opposition they refused to consider themselves in that light.

The American element in the Canadian Progressive party is plain, and not surprising when it is remembered that Alberta had been settled by many with American experience and that Wood himself was an American of Populist background. The reluctance to function as an opposition is the best indicator of this background, but the group representation was also paralleled in the United States where lobbies, formal registered interest groups, are recognized to play a major role in legislation. There was too a common stress upon the mechanics of direct government, initiative, referendum, and recall. And given this background it was only to be expected that the Progressives should dissipate, for Ottawa after all was patterned on the parliamentary model.

But the Progressive mentality for all its contradictions was yet fertile ground. The depression seemed to prove the bankruptcy of the traditional parties and there was a willingness to consider alternatives. The first sign of this occurred in 1932 when the Ginger Group and urban labour groups came together to plan joint action. The key meeting, at which Woodsworth was elected president, was in Calgary, heart of Progressive country. But that there would be a vital infusion of British ideas was ensured by the fact that a crucial element in the merger was the League for Social Reconstruction, a gathering of Labour people in the main, many of them intellectuals, and consciously modelled on the Fabian party. The new organization, which soon took the title Co-operative Commonwealth Federation, held its first convention in Regina in 1933 where a Manifesto was put out outlining its commitment. It was socialist.

Federally, success for the new party was slow in coming, but provincially, and especially in Saskatchewan, it did much better. Eventually it made a key breakthrough in 1944 when it captured power in Saskatchewan under its leader, T. C. Douglas; it is an interesting example of the British strain that Douglas, like Woodsworth, was a minister of religion, a Baptist in fact. This election victory was a first for socialism in North America. The attractiveness of the CCF was such that organized labour, which in the American pattern had held aloof from formal participation, reconsidered its stand. The old Trades and Labour Congress of Canada united with the Canadian Congress of Labour (the industrial organization, the equivalent of the CIO) in 1956 and five years later this Canadian Labour Congress and the CCF took the lead in establishing the New Democratic Party, the Canadian counterpart to the British Labour Party. By 1972 the NDP had 31 seats in parliament and controlled British Columbia, Saskatchewan, and Manitoba. That year seems to have been a temporary high point, but enough has been shown to indicate that in major ways Canada is sticking to the British rather than to the American pattern.

It remains now to look at the extent of economic innovation that these communities brought to bear upon the problems facing them, notably depression and its possible recurrence. The first clue to a new way of managing the economy came during the First World War. Men had long been familiar with the old paradox of poverty amidst plenty; now it reappeared in a new guise. At a time when economies were being geared for destruction, not construction, when governments were spending far above their incomes, the productive capacity of society was increased enormously and the average worker enjoyed a standard of living never previously known. Neither condition seemed to make sense, neither could be explained adequately on the basis of existing orthodox economic theory. But new theories were appearing that explained both paradoxes by stressing the danger of underconsumption. Poverty in the midst of plenty had been possible because sufficient purchasing power had not been in the right hands. The purchasing power was there all right, in the form of say prairie grain, but it was not in a form that could be translated into effective demand; thus people stopped buying, soon people stopped producing, and eventually the whole economy spiralled downwards. But if blocks to purchasing could be removed, then demand would be brisk, production would increase, and boom conditions would be at hand. And this is just what the war had demonstrated; a nation in need of essentials would not let a temporary lack of purchasing power stand in the way—credit would be granted and the project undertaken. It showed that the way out of a stymied productive process, in effect out of depression, was not by cutting wages but by the reverse; handouts to consumers would translate potential demand into actual demand. 'Priming the pump' was to be the key to the new economics.

This insight appeared in many forms, but two need to be noted in this account. There was the academically respectable version developed by the Cambridge economist, John Maynard Keynes, and the earlier but less sophisticated version by the British engineer, Major C. H. Douglas. This second scheme, Social Credit, may be given in outline form.

The essence of the Social Credit theory was that the existing capitalist economic system, otherwise the best ever devised for producing wealth, was failing because a single flaw prevented it from distributing that wealth efficiently. The famous principle of the A and B payments explained the flaw; A payments were those to individuals (wages, salaries, etc.) and B payments those to organizations (mortgages, fixed costs, etc.). Now the price of goods produced was A + B, but the money to buy them, purchasing power, was only A. Thus an amount equal to B was lacking, goods could not be bought, and the economic machine was obstructed and faltered; the end result was slump and depression, and Douglas did predict the 1929 crash. (It will be objected that B payments ultimately became A payments, which means there is no gap in purchasing power. Douglas replied that the rate at which B payments became A payments was not fast enough.) The solution, then, was for society to distribute purchasing power equal to B, a national dividend, which would be given to every citizen irrespective of contribution.

Social Credit languished in Britain from 1917 onwards, the date of its first publication. It had a very different impact in western Canada, however. At the very time when the Progressive Party was splitting up, Douglas's message was taken up by an Alberta high-school teacher, William Aberhart. Aberhart did not fully understand the Social Credit case. But he was impressed by the attention it drew to the paradox of poverty amidst plenty and the belief that a simple technical change in bookkeeping could restore the capitalist system to full efficiency. And once converted he was in a good position to lead a Social Credit campaign. For several years prior to his conversion Aberhart had been leading a fundamentalist, back-to-the-Bible crusade over the radio. This message was widely diffused over Alberta, the Bible-belt of Canada, and he had a tremendous following. Slowly at first, and with great skill, he began injecting Social Credit ideas into his religious broadcasts. It was here that a great transformation of Douglas's ideas took place. As originally formulated Social Credit proclaimed the end of the work ethic. Given modern technology and the bookkeeping adjustment the theory called for, industrial productivity could be expanded hugely. Few would have to work, and the hours of labour could be shortened greatly; work in fact would become something done for enjoyment. As was to be expected, such a philosophy had little appeal for the Nonconformist sects either in Britain or in Canada, and Aberhart could never grasp the idea of payment for no work, but it did appeal greatly to Catholics and High Anglicans—the Archbishop of Canterbury, William Temple, was a Social Crediter. In Canada Social Credit made less initial impact in Quebec than in Alberta, but it seems plain that it will last longer there than in the west and that it is more genuine in the Catholic setting than in the Fundamentalist.

But the Aberhart version, although eventually repudiated by Douglas, was at first glance the real thing, and by 1935, the year of the provincial election, its theory was the topic of general discussion. Candidates were put forward, though Aberhart did not run, and in the election the United Farmers of Alberta were destroyed. Of 63 seats, 56 were won by Social Credit. A seat was found for Aberhart and he became premier. Whether Social Credit theory would have been able to do anything about the depression was never determined, for the federal government disallowed the Alberta bills that would have implemented the doctrine by tampering with the money supply and currency; it was held that provinces did not have such powers under the BNA Act.

That Social Credit was an 'American' solution is clear. There was that concentration upon a single flaw in the system, a technical adjustment, that has been noted in United States history. There was the connection with fundamentalist religion. The Populist suspicion of eastern interests was present, and there were echoes of Donnelly's bankers' plot to enslave the world. Conspiracy, in fact, was a leading theme in the movement, and there was enough anti-semitism to make the movement an ugly one at times. But if this is so, Social Credit should have been a force in the United States too. There was a Social Credit movement there, but it was insignificant. However there were schemes that had a good deal in common with that of Douglas and Aberhart. Fr Coughlin, the radio priest of the Catholic church, approached closely to that theory. Better known was the Townsend plan, named for its originator. Under this plan individuals, beginning with the elderly and retired, would be granted a certain sum of money each month on condition that they spend it at once. In this way an extra demand would be generated akin to that of the Social Credit 'national dividend', as purchasing power was increased through the injection of additional B payments. In fact one may say that Social Credit ideas permeated America in a diffused way. That a formal movement under that name was not more successful was due to this very fact, and also to the fact that the authorities themselves were acting within the scope of this approach. For without being too clear about it the American government was in effect embarking upon a Keynesian experiment.

It was not so much that Keynes had more disciples in the United States than in Britain, though that may well have been true. Nor was it that the new president elected in 1932, Franklin D. Roosevelt, entirely understood and championed the new economics. Rather it was that the enormity of the disaster coupled with Roosevelt's opportunist determination to try almost any remedy permitted America to discover the effectiveness of Keynesianism. For it must be remembered that the crash in America was much more serious than in Britain, since in America it had come suddenly and after a boom period. Worse, it had psychological dimensions lacking in Britain, for was not America the land whose business was business? The depression in the United States was so threatening that it produced apathy and incomprehension, and in his Inaugural Roosevelt had to point out that contrary to appearances 'the only thing we have to fear is fear itself'. That the country was ready for strong action without debate was shown when emergency banking legislation, prepared inside three days, went through the House in thirty-eight minutes and through the Senate in three hours.

One of the first things Roosevelt pushed through was a federal relief program of $500m, a truly vast sum in those days. Without fully understanding the theory, the administration had hit upon deficit spending. That they did not grasp the principle was seen a few years later in 1937 when Roosevelt attempted to get back to a balanced budget. It proved impossible, and demonstrated how crucial had become state spending to direct and fuel the economy. From the first, then, the new American broom had made a clean sweep of the liberal penchant for retrenchment and had launched out on a completely new course.

The impression of vigorousness of the Roosevelt program was deliberately encouraged by the appellation given to it, the 'New Deal'. The President and his advisers were not content with pumping federal funds into the economy; they were eager to move the entire economy away from the *laissez-faire* presuppositions of the Progressive-Populist era. This does not mean that they were socialists, determined to abandon the individualist, profit-motivated economy that had been America's from the start. But the essentially negative aspect of *laissez-faire*, the fear of the state and its role in the economy and society, was being given up and was replaced by a more positive conception. A leading example of this revolution was the Tennessee Valley Authority, established in 1933. Before this date dams had been built on the Tennessee River to control flooding and to generate electricity, but moves to extend this program and to make the benefits public rather than private had been thwarted. But under the New Deal the scheme was proceeded with as a federal one cutting across several states and operated as a public utility. Another example would be the National Recovery Administration, also established in 1933. Under its wing codes of practice for individual industries were worked out with the intention of harmonizing the aspirations of producers, consumers, and government. It was not a success because in practice the codes benefitted big business too much at the expense of the smaller, and finally because in 1935 the Supreme Court found the NRA unconstitutional on the ground that its codes amounted to legislation, something that only Congress was competent to do (in other words the idea of delegated legislation, which was being resorted to increasingly in Britain, was rebuffed). But the failure is beside the point; the state had indicated its determination to mould the economy, and to do so in the interests of efficiency rather than in terms of the Spencer-Alger tradition.

Much the same may be said of subsequent New Deal programs; the Civilian Conservation Corps was a scheme whereby young men were set to work under war department auspices on projects such as road building and the like; the Public Works Administration used funds to set private firms to worthwhile projects; by 1935 the administration felt emboldened to set up the Works Progress Administration, which spent huge sums on projects not covered by the two agencies previously mentioned. Yet it must be admitted that although these and other similar schemes did much good, the depression was licked only by the inauguration of a war economy in 1941. But for all its shortcomings the New Deal had marked a break with the older American tradition; to put it in terms of the pre-First World War dichotomy, the New Nationalism had won out over the New Freedom. When in 1935 the New Deal instituted a Wealth Tax Act to increase the rates at which the very rich paid, and in the same year the Social Security Act set up old-age pensions and unemployment insurance, it became clear that America had experienced a revolution. Americans, however, refused to acknowledge the fact.

Keynesianism was taken up in Canada too. If there was not the same dramatic manifestation of it, there was an even more wholehearted commitment to it. The role of the state had always been recognized in Canada, and here was but another way in which it could be demonstrated. The Conservative prime minister, R. B. Bennett, began to move to meet the crisis as soon as he was elected to office in 1930. At once $20m was allocated for relief. What has to be stressed here is not so much that this sum represented a large amount for that day as that for the first time federal funds were being committed to an area that had been a provincial concern. As time went on the pace increased. Labour camps, akin to the American Civilian Conservation Corps, were set up. Marketing boards were established, notably the Wheat Board in 1934. The Bank of Canada was instituted, a central bank to co-ordinate the fiscal policies of the existing banks. The climax came in 1935, election year. Bennett went on radio to proclaim 'The old order is gone. It will not return . . . . I am for reform. And, in my mind, reform means Government intervention. It means Government control and regulation. It means the end of laissez-faire . . . . I nail the flag of progress to the mast-head. I summon the power of the state to its support.' It was not enough. Bennett gave way to Mackenzie King and the Liberals. But Keynesianism was persisted with. The budget of 1938 was a breakthrough, for deficit financing was agreed to.

The impact of Keynesianism in Canada was significant for a second reason. It provided the central power with a new tool with which to shape Confederation. As federal intervention continued during the thirties it became clear that the whole question of federal-provincial relations would have to be re-examined. In 1937 Prime Minister King appointed the Rowell-Sirois Commission, which reported in 1940 and recommended adjustments that would give the Ottawa government increased powers. The Commission's road was not an easy one, for some provinces were so jealous of their rights that they co-operated badly or not at all—Duplessis of Quebec was the worst of them. Perhaps hardly surprisingly the government was not able to implement all the Rowell-Sirois recommendations; perhaps the surprise is that so much was achieved. The introduction of a federal Unemployment Insurance Fund in 1940, of Family Allowances in 1944, of an expanded Old Age Security scheme in 1952, were occasions for the recovery of initiative by the central authority after the long drift towards provincial autonomy, as well as being practical examples of Keynesian-type thinking.

Ironically Britain was the country most reluctant to apply Keynesianism. Lloyd George and his tiny band of Liberals were prepared to consider it. But other remedies for depression were narrowly orthodox. As the crisis in Britain deepened the Labour Government set up a committee under Sir George May to report on the situation. The May Committee predicted in the summer of 1931 that national revenue would be short of the required amount, and recommended in good nineteenth-century liberal fashion a program of retrenchment. In particular, cuts in unemployment benefits were suggested. When MacDonald and his Chancellor of the Exchequer, Snowden, showed themselves prepared to go along with these suggestions the cabinet split and the government fell. But the National Government, the all-party coalition that succeeded, implemented the policy. Government salaries were slashed as were unemployment benefits; especially disturbing was the institution of the 'means test'. Great store was put by the return of Britain to protection and the institution of Commonwealth preference. There was some special concern for those areas particularly badly hit such as the South Wales coalfields, but the aims of the Special Areas Act, 1934, were not fulfilled. It was not until the war had broken out that Keynesianism was given a trial. And when it was, it was in a form different again from that applied in the United States.

In Britain Keynesianism was grafted onto a more far-reaching commitment to social planning. During the war William Beveridge, a Liberal and a veteran student of social questions, who had been the organizer of the Labour Exchanges when they had first been set up in 1909, was appointed to examine the whole field of social welfare. His reports recommended that the state extend its responsibility to ensuring full employment and to providing protection to all members of society from cradle to grave. The Churchill government agreed to the first but did not commit itself on the second recommendation. But the victory of the Labour party in 1945 meant that the way was clear for the implementation of the second recommendation via the welfare state. In particular the policy of nationalization pursued by the Labour government enabled Keynesian control to be exercised with ease. The socialist implications that had underlain both Keynes and Douglas (though attention had never been drawn to them) had emerged most openly in Britain.

7
Retrospect: Towards a Theory of New Societies

The foregoing account has shown something of the way in which the three societies have differed in their origins and unfoldings. But scattered hints and asides apart, no explanation for this divergence has been given and it is the task of this concluding chapter to offer an outline of three major theories that have been advanced to account for the differences. In doing so, one society must be taken as the starting point and the others explained as deviations from that given norm. Theoretically, any one of the three could be chosen as the datum, though in practice Britain must be the one selected. Her society pre-dated those of the United States and Canada, being already mature by the time of separation of the United States in the eighteenth century. And in fact commentators recognize this fact and inevitably begin to explain American ways in terms of adaption, or repudiation, or acceptance even of British and European norms; and it is the same for Canadian patterns. This chapter then makes no apology for the fact that British developments are taken for granted, and that only the unique qualities of the American and Canadian experiences are analyzed.

❖   ❖   ❖

The first full-scale theory to account for the specific qualities of American development appeared in 1893 when the young historian Frederick

Jackson Turner presented a paper to the American Historical Association. What had sparked Turner's contribution, and what gave it its impact, was the finding of the 1890 census that there were no more unsettled areas available to homesteaders in the American west. Ever since the first colonists had precariously established themselves on the Atlantic coast in the early seventeenth century there had been land for settlement to the west of them. At first the westward movement of population had been slow, the Appalachian barrier being breached only on the eve of the War of Independence. But since then, thanks to an open-door immigration policy and a high rate of natural increase, the pace of occupancy had been stepped up, so much so that the land had been filled up by the closing decade of the nineteenth century. Now that this possibility of moving westward had come to an end, and in so doing had underlined its importance, Turner undertook to explain to his fellow citizens 'The Significance of the Frontier in American History' (the title of his paper of 1893), the way in which this constant factor in the American experience had affected development.

At the outset it is necessary to understand what Turner meant by frontier. It was not a boundary between two areas in the way that the forty-ninth parallel is a boundary between the United States and Canada. Rather it was itself an area, a broad band of territory intermediate between the settled area in the east and the full wilderness in the west; thus the frontier would contain a fair number of people—explorers, traders, military men, missionaries, and settlers—but the density of population would be comparatively low. The frontier, then, was in advance of the more civilized east, and always in process of being filled up and made over in the east's image. And when that happened, the frontier itself was pushed a little further to the west. Thus it is perhaps helpful to stress that the frontier was not so much a place as an experience, a constantly shifting area in which the formative sensation was that of being free of fully developed civilization. As it was, the census of 1890 did not say that all free land had been exhausted, and for a long time the work of homesteading went on, filling up the continent with settlers. But this did not affect the validity of what Turner was saying as early as 1893. Just as isolated capitalists could not give a tone to society, so too could isolated pockets of free land not support a distinctive way of life as had the frontier.

The most obviously distinctive characteristic of the frontier experience was its physical hardness. Western European man found himself in a strange environment devoid of any supportive institutions. From Sir Humphrey Gilbert's failure to plant a settlement in Newfoundland in 1583, or Sir Walter Raleigh's at Roanoke in North Carolina in 1587, the history of settlement on the frontier had been strewn with instances of disaster. And under such harsh and demanding conditions the settler soon learnt the necessity of subjecting his entire inherited customs and beliefs to a searching review. When it was a question literally of life or death it was not enough to take a line of action simply because that was the done thing back in Europe. Thus, for instance, it would not do to allow an individual to take charge simply because he was the son of the last leader, a member of the natural ruling class; that might be admirable in a settled community where continuity was prized, but on the frontier it would be necessary to ask if the would-be leader had the required qualities, was in fact the best man for the job.

But the rejection of the traditional went much further than this one instance, the rejection of oligarchy. Much else suffered in the harsh conditions of the frontier. Thus specialization itself was out of place. Small communities had not the demand or the manpower for esoteric professions, and at times this would be true even of the manual trades. Thus on the frontier the jack-of-all-trades was the desired type, the person who could turn his hand to almost anything. Abraham Lincoln, a frontiersman *par excellence*, comes to mind in this connection, a lawyer and politician who yet was proud of his skill in splitting rails for the family farm. Andrew Jackson was another in this tradition. And it is possible to bring the Jacksonian practice of the spoils system within the Turner thesis, for the belief that, since anyone can do any job, a turnover of civil servants may be expected to follow any political change is part of the anti-specialist outlook. A more important casualty on the frontier, however, was culture as such. Culture was a luxury that many communities simply could not afford, and it may be that that strain of anti-intellectualism that runs through American history had its strength in the continuing frontier experience. As has been mentioned American education, which has represented a tremendous commitment both of intellectual and material resources, has always stressed practical knowledge and directed expertise more than has European education, where the aim was the total moulding of the pupil.

The initial effect of the frontier, then, was to tear away much of the intellectual baggage that the settlers had brought with them from civilization, whether from Europe or, as time passed, from the eastern seaboard. But the frontier also had a positive role to play by fostering new values and then feeding them into the mainstream of American life. Hints of this have already been given; the emergence of the jack-of-all-trades, the spread of the common school—an institution free of sectarian control and direction that aimed to give a useful education to all children and not just to the élite. In short what the frontier valued were those things that worked, that enabled man to survive and prosper. Thus adaptability was praised, but even more so was inventiveness, technical inventiveness above all, and that tradition has been well-marked from the days of Whitney through Henry Ford down to the space triumphs. This strain, which has earlier been characterized as a preference for 'how' questions over 'why' questions, even produced its own brand of philosophy. At the end of the nineteenth century the American philosophers Charles Pierce and William James developed Pragmatism, a philosophy whose teaching may be summed up and only slightly caricatured in the slogan 'If it works, accept it'. Interestingly enough a major application of these ideas was made by the American John Dewey to education; it is to him more than to any other single individual that is due the so-called 'progressive education' where learning is fostered through group problem-solving experiences, projects and the like that reproduce on a miniature scale the life experiences of the adult.

But if the frontier experience encouraged Americans to apply the test 'does it work?', 'is it useful?', it remains to ask for whom should it work? for whom should it be useful? The answer, of course, was: for the individual, and one of the major elements of frontier life was the emphasis given to the notion of the autonomous being. It may be seen in many different contexts. A good example would be the lawlessness of American life, a generalized attitude whose religious equivalent is antinomianism. It was the essence of the frontier that it was the area ahead of settled society, and this meant first and foremost ahead of law and order. On the frontier each man had to take the law into his own hands, a tradition that is kept alive in each cowboy epic. And when anarchy became too much to bear and some antidote became necessary, it was vigilante justice that was supplied, that is, a rough-and-ready popular justice devoid of abstractions and legalities; the punishments often fitted the rough extremism of the frontier, and lynch hangings were frequent.

This was the less pleasant side of frontier individualism. In a more elevated guise the same values could be seen in the kind of democratic theory worked out under American conditions. Those manifestations referred to throughout this account—Jeffersonism, Jacksonism, Populism—may be seen as the natural product of an agrarian frontier where the mass of people were alike in being upwardly mobile, property-owning individuals who instinctively reacted against the slightest sign of privilege and hierarchy. That these suspicious, resentment-filled movements should also have insisted upon elective institutions (school boards, judges, and so on) underlines the point already made that frontier conditions will breed a distrust of the specialist. At the same time it may be noted that it was the more westerly states, those that had had the largest exposure to the frontier mentality, that were first in introducing 'progressive' legislation. Thus in the early nineteenth century, on the eve of Jacksonian democracy, it was the newer states that led the way in removing the last traces of property qualification for voting. It was western states in the latter portion of the nineteenth century that pioneered many of the social-security measures only later accepted by the east and federally, and it was in the western states that votes for women were earliest granted; after all, on the frontier a woman's worth was made abundantly evident as she took a full part in the work of winning a living from the land.

The frontier encouraged direct democracy, then, and an essential part of this was an emphasis upon localism. Unlike the British-Canadian practice, Americans have always insisted upon a representative's coming from the people he claims to represent; thus a senator from, say New York, must reside in that state. Then, too, there has long been a tradition of leaving the locality to settle its own affairs as far as possible without any interference from the outside. Schools, for instance, were always very local affairs, with control vested in a board locally elected. But the best example of frontier localism comes in religion. It has already been pointed out how in America, and especially at the time of the Great Awakening and in the western areas, the sectarian denominations were enjoying the greatest success. In part it was the nature of their message, but much of it was also due to their structure. Congregationalists, Methodists, and above all Baptists were ideally suited to frontier conditions and prospered accordingly. Even the Anglicans submitted to the frontier spirit. In Virginia, a state where the Anglican Church was strong, the normal practice of giving the parish priest security of tenure was modified so that the church wardens appointed an incumbent for a year at a time. In practice this frequently amounted to tenure, but the principle was crucially different, for the autonomy of the priest and bishop was replaced by that of the parish. (At the same time it must be pointed out that the frontier thesis somewhat contradictorily insisted upon the sense of nationalism that a frontier experience engendered; since the typical frontiersman was always on the move he could develop no lasting loyalty to his state, but only to something like America that represented an expansive idea; and since the new frontier needed help the inhabitants were encouraged to look to the centre for the required blessing—federal aid to the transcontinentals would be a good example, though undoubtedly the best would be the Louisiana purchase by that frontier democrat, Jefferson, to provide continuing opportunities for his beloved farmers; at the same time the varied population on the frontier, where each individual proved himself in equal competition with his neighbours, was the ideal setting for the melting pot that eventually produced Americans. But the sense of contradiction here need not be pushed too far; it is quite possible to hold to an American ideal and yet insist upon the necessity for very local articulation of that ideal—the Goldwater-Nixon philosophy in fact.)

Above it was asked to whom the pragmatic test 'does it work?' was applied. The answer was for the individual, and these instances just given provide some idea of the dimensions of individualism in America. But the answer is not complete, for another question remains. Just what is the test of whether it works? What, in fact, is that 'it'? Here one needs to be reminded of a point in connection with the frontier thesis made most forcefully by a disciple of Turner, writing quite recently. In his valuable book *The Great Frontier*, W. P. Webb defines the frontier as the area of unappropriated surpluses; on the frontier are vast amounts of land, gold and silver, other mineral deposits, timber, grassland, and other resources that belong to no one (the Indians being in no position to withstand the Europeans), which can be seized without too great an outlay of effort, and which within a short while can be made to yield splendid profits. With these dazzling prospects in view the initial work of merely surviving is quickly transmuted into something very different, a determination to realize the tremendous possibilities that exist. In the absence of inherited restraints and alternative cultural ends, themselves stripped away by the frontier experience, work becomes not only a means but an end. Good is what conduces to wealth and the free mobilization of wealth. Hence the Yankee bustle, the concentration upon quick service, the time-is-money syndrome. Hence the impatience with primogeniture and entail, legal devices that stand in the way of an individual's developing his own full potential through the use of freely realized assets. As Webb has pointed out, the indigenous American folk heroes have been characters like Paul Bunyan and John Henry, giants able to work in herculean manner to tame the frontier and make it yield up its wealth. The American realizes his individualism less in being than in doing, and preferably in doing something tangible that will transform raw nature. It is in this sense that the American people are the people of the boom, not in the superficial sense of the

Wall Street surge of the late twenties but in the deeper sense of a four-hundred-year commitment to subduing challenge after challenge, each greater than the last.

One final point made by the frontier thesis may be noted here. The frontier acts as a safety valve. Whenever discontent builds up in the settled areas there will be a movement away from the sources of frustration to the new start possible in the west. In this way the pressure of reform within the main body of society is always kept within reasonable bounds and outright, fundamental rebellion is unlikely. At the same time it has been argued that the drain of manpower from the east meant a perpetual shortage of workers. Consequently those who remained were in a position to demand good wages, which further lessened the likelihood of revolution. (It has also been held to be a factor in the rapid mechanization of America; producers unwilling to pay high wages were prepared to sink large amounts of capital in labour-saving machinery.) In particular the lack of long-contained discontent, together with the possibility of land on which a settler could become his own master and start moving upward in the socio-economic scale, was held to be a major factor in inhibiting the rise of an independent labour movement and above all of socialism. As indicated previously, the American worker thought less of overthrowing the bosses than of eventually joining them, and the continued existence of the frontier made this a valid belief over many years—and even after the 1890s, of course.

Naturally the Turner thesis came in for its share of criticism. It was pointed out that his terminology was vague and that certain of his observations were contradictory. Others went to the facts to claim that they disproved Turner; thus the safety-valve aspect was declared rejected when it was established that long before 1890 the urban areas were being peopled not solely from overcrowded Europe but also from the frontier. Then, too, it was urged that any aggressive, progressive attitudes discernible in the west might be due not so much to the frontier setting as to the fact that the population in these parts was a self-selected one, made up of younger, more ambitious types than those in the settled east; in other words migration rather than frontier might be the key. This is not the place to go into the revision in detail, and it may also be noted that the latest trend seems to be revising the revisers so as to re-establish the essence of what Turner was saying. The frontier thesis still provides valuable insight into American development, and may profitably be reflected upon.

And so presented, the frontier thesis is an environmentally determinist one; a transitional area between civilization and wilderness exists and has certain consequences for the total society. At the same time it is a thesis that stresses the independence of America from Europe. To take one major example; on the Turner theory, American democracy must be seen as something indigenous, not as the taking over of European ideas; as it is often put, American democracy was 'forest born'. Those who incline to the frontier hypothesis must play down the European heritage of American civilization, and at the same time must tend to see American civilization in its widest sense, i.e., not simply as the United States but possibly as the entire Northern and Southern American hemisphere, and certainly as the whole of North America: the United States and Canada. Thus the question inevitably arose, can Canadian history be explained in terms of the Turner hypothesis?

The attempt has been made on several occasions. Those eager to fit Canadian developments into the frontier thesis would point to the following facts. It was the intention of the authorities to impose absolutism in New France, an undertaking in which they were in the main successful. But there were certain departures from the blueprint. Thus the lightness of the feudal obligations is striking when set against those in the mother country. The tithe, in particular, is a case in point. It was not until 1663 that a tithe was made compulsory, and even then it was fixed at the low level of one twenty-sixth of the wheat crop as against (usually) one thirteenth of the total farm produce in France. This lightness was to be explained, it was held, by the fact that the frontier's existence made it possible for settlers, if pushed too far, to leave the main area of the colony and escape burdens altogether. Then it was noted that for a while at least the militia captains were elected officials, that is democratically selected, and that even the later appointments were a disguised form of popular choice. This fact pointed to the democratic spirit and the need to elect the best that marked frontier conditions.

Upper Canada was held to provide even better evidence of the frontier spirit. In its early formative years the province had been settled by the 'Late Loyalists', that is, by the natural westward push of settlement that even then was founding such states as Ohio. Thus in time Upper Canada produced its American-style democrats—Gourlay with his probing inquiries and 'conventions', and better still Mackenzie with his Jacksonian tinge. That it was the western, i.e. frontier, portion of Upper Canada that was prominent in the 1837 rising was taken as very powerful confirmation of the frontier thesis. And then when the democratic impulse revived in the 1850s and 1860s that same frontier spirit was detected at work; conventions abounded again and the Clear Grits were committed to universal suffrage, elected governors, elected upper houses, elected public functionaries, and the secularization of the clergy reserves for public education along American lines.

And finally the Progressives of the inter-war years were pointed to as major examples of the frontier spirit. The roots of this movement had been laid down in Alberta on the eve of the war, at a time when that province represented the last significant frontier still open and when it was attracting a large proportion of settlers from America. The views of Wood and the repudiation of party government have been outlined above; they may be seen as manifestations of a frontier mentality.

But no sooner had the applications been made than the unsatisfactory nature of the case became evident. New France really yielded little confirmation of the theory. To set against the lightness of the tithe obligations and the existence of a quasi-elective official were the more important facts that individualism in the Turnerian sense did not develop in that society, that democracy was always a weak growth (witness the failure of the *Rouges* to develop into a viable political party), and that extensive genuine radicalness was, until the very recent period, missing from the province. Indeed the French-Canadian experience of colonization is a very significant one. By 1870 Quebec was over-populated and many French Canadians were moving to the north-eastern United States. This drift away from the traditional occupation on the land was viewed by many influential people with regret, and colonization societies were formed to keep the *habitants* on the land. Now just at that time Manitoba was opened to settlement. But very few French Canadians could be tempted there. What agricultural settlement there was went to the unpromising areas of northern Quebec; in other words the French-Canadian population lacked that pioneering spirit that, say, took the Mormons to Utah. Considerations like these have led A. I. Silver, writing in the *Canadian Historical Review* of 1969, to question the frontier thesis by asking whether Turner did not have the cart before the horse; in other words, did a certain mentality form the frontier rather than the reverse?

Against this rejoinder it may be urged that French Canada never had a frontier in the sense that the United States did. Turner, who did not bother with comparative studies, instinctively took as the norm a frontier where the settler was cut off from more settled society and more civilized pressures and where the preferred unit of settlement was the individual family farm. It may be said that both these were lacking in New France—Quebec. There the power of absolutism was great from the start and there never was a significant time and area free from such control; the few exceptions were the *coureurs de bois* and they were by

definition not settlers but traders incapable of communicating any positive values to a society (except, perhaps, that because the employer, the
fur trade, needed Indian co-operation the French had a better record of
Indian relations than the Anglo-Americans whose farming settlement
was so dominant that possession of the land became all-important and
Indians were driven off or exterminated; but such a point is peripheral
to the main argument). And French-Canadian farms were never such
individualistic enterprises, the basis of speculators' fortunes, as in the
United States; the static farm, often subdivided among children, and
the static parish, were the characteristics of Quebec. Thus, it is argued,
the frontier as Turner assumed it had no chance to work its impact
along the lower St Lawrence.

Unfortunately for this counterargument, the example of Upper Canada is no better. Again the instances of frontier impact may be sub-
merged in contrary examples. United States history has been full of
frontier risings—the Regulators, Shays, and Kansas-Nebraska have
been mentioned, and there have been many, many more both before
and after these just mentioned. The same has not been true of Upper
Canada. The one real rising, Mackenzie's, had to wait until 1837, and
it took a world trading depression to trigger it off. Even then the
impressive thing about 1837 is the lack of support that Mackenzie could
drum up; the province was soon restored to peace and quiet with little
bloodshed, and Mackenzie could eventually be allowed to return and to
take part in political life. Basically the same may be said of the Grits;
how quickly were their universal-suffrage ideas and elective proclivities
forgotten in an acceptance of more British notions championed by
George Brown and his *Globe* newspaper.

And briefly to round out this questioning of the applicability of
frontier theory to Canada, the passing impact of Progressivism may be
noted. The Progressive independence did not long maintain itself in its
non-party guise but quickly transformed itself into the more British
experiment of the socialist party.

And here the root failure of the frontier thesis for Canada is touched
upon. Although Canada does share some North American traits with
the United States, there is still an awkward amount of 'Britishness' (or
possibly it would be better to say 'Old Worldness') about the country.
In particular there is the fact that while the United States has failed to
produce a socialist tradition, Canada, like Britain, has. Recognition of
these facts has encouraged historians to develop alternative theories to
account for Canada's distinctive evolution.

The origins of an alternative account, more sophisticated than the early theories that simply accepted that as a colony Canada would be essentially British, are to be found in the economic histories of H. A. Innis, many of which were studies of individual staple trades. Innis stressed the point that these trades required the financial help and marketing skills of the already developed mother country, and in particular that the dominance of the St Lawrence as a continuation, so to speak, of the Atlantic helped to structure trade and society about that river. So prominent did this great highway loom in his writing, and in that of the similarly orientated D. G. Creighton, that a school of interpretation known as the Laurentian was recognized. And just a little later the impact of the Second World War encouraged other scholars to stress the trans-Atlantic links; J. B. Brebner's *North Atlantic Triangle*, first published in 1945, was originally intended to be a study in Canadian-American relations but was widened as the author felt more and more obliged to take note of British impact. More recently still, these strains have developed into the theory known as metropolitanism, a theory in Canada connected above all with J. M. S. Careless.

This theory seizes upon the fact that certain centres grow to unusual prominence. The economic historian who first used the term in this way, N. S. B. Gras, noted four stages in the growth of the super-centre; first the market in the surrounding area is organized to hinge on the centre; then the centre develops an industrial base; transportation is next improved so that industrial goods may be better distributed over the metropolitan hinterland and agricultural products and other goods may also flow easily in the reverse direction; and finally the metropolis develops major financial institutions and know-how, so that it may continue to finance and direct the economic activity of the area tributary to itself. But Careless's emphasis is upon the socio-cultural control that may parallel such economic dominance. Thus the entire St Lawrence trading system down to 1849, when it was undermined by the establishment of free trade and the repeal of the Navigation Acts, was a means of ensuring the dominance of London and London values over the area, since the headquarters and finance of the trades were based there. At the same time, however, metropolitanism can operate at a subordinate level; thus within Canada itself Montreal acted as a metropolis, establishing its cultural imperialism over the hinterland. And at different periods and at different levels other Canadian centres have acted as metropolises; Toronto early became the focal point and 'organizer' of Ontario, especially the southern portion; Winnipeg performed the same function for the prairies, but as hinted earlier modern communication means that Winnipeg is losing that status as the emphasis moves as far afield as Toronto or Montreal. Meanwhile Vancouver, thanks to a growing Pacific orientation on Canada's part, has risen to metropolitan rank, and as the far north opens up Edmonton may do the same.

Careless would say that in terms of historical development the interaction between the metropolis and the hinterland is complementary. The hinterland is the area where grievances develop; thus in the 1830s the western Upper Canadian farmers felt discriminated against and exploited; in the fifties and sixties there was much the same feeling as the possibilities of further settlement became less and less; by the first decades of the twentieth century the prairies were convinced that eastern interests were ruining western potential. But it is in the metropolis that the solutions are worked out, that the grievances are formed into a political movement. Mackenzie was a newspaperman in Toronto and it was from there that his *Colonial Advocate* was put together and sent out to the smaller towns and rural areas, giving form to the inchoate protests of the backwoods. By the time of the Clear Grits it was George Brown and *The Globe*, again Toronto-based, that performed this service. And in the case of the western Progressives there was the Winnipeg-based *Grain Growers Guide* to offset the mainline liberalism disseminated through the *Winnipeg Free Press* of John Defoe.

It will be seen that metropolitanism does not wholly contradict the frontier thesis, for it too allows that frontier conditions may destroy the old loyalties and certainties. But whereas Turner held that the frontier could supply its own positive antidote to its negative work, Careless stresses the fact that more civilized forces were at work in the task of building up. And what makes metropolitanism more attractive to historians of Canada than to those of the United States is the realization that geography and history have helped in Canada's case to magnify the impact of the capital city. Canada has always been thinly populated, and with the exception of the *coureurs de bois* who were unable to make a lasting impact, the people always found it necessary to huddle together; the *habitants* of Lower Canada found this particularly natural since their religion and its parish structure held them to centripetal forces; in Upper Canada the Canadian Shield prevented the early spread of settlement and acted as a dam to keep the settlement relatively more compact and metropolis-bound than was the case in the American middle west. And when that dam broke in 1870 the settlement of the prairies coincided with the development of the railway and the telegraph-telephone, methods of communication that enabled the 'frontiersman' of Canada to be kept in touch with the more settled values.

The United States equivalent had taken place crucially earlier, and so it had been possible to escape the eastern influence more completely and for longer. This point is always neatly summed up by contrasting the two traditions of law and order, especially as applied to the Indian question. In the United States it was vigilante justice at first, and the Indian was usually provoked to war; in Canada the opening of the prairies was accompanied by the formation of the North West Mounted Police (today the Royal Canadian Mounted Police) and a determination to provide law and order *in advance of* settlement, and Indian wars were avoided.

If the frontier thesis stresses environment and isolation, metropolitanism stresses heritage and connections with older ways, mainly British. However its weakness lies in its failure to distinguish between the sources of these older ways. Thus how is Mackenzie's radicalism to be evaluated in metropolitan terms? It may be that he got his ideas from more developed centres and then passed them on to his readers; but were they picked up from British proto-Chartist notions brought to Upper Canada, or were they rather from the United States? The same may be said of Clear Grit ideas and of Progressivism. And even if it is possible to decide in any particular case the source of the ideas—for example George Brown was himself much more influenced by British mid-Victorian liberalism than by American equivalents—the metropolitan theory does not account for the whole tone of Canadian development, it cannot predict the amount of British as opposed to American influence in Canada. Metropolitanism describes a method of communicating influence; it says little about the content of that influence.

Much more useful in this connection, then, is a second theory that values heritage over environment. This is the theory worked out by the American scholar, Louis Hartz. But before going on to describe the theory the warning must be given that Hartz writes a dense, elliptical style, and that it is not always easy to follow him. And it must also be pointed out that his entire argument is built upon what is known as a dialectical framework. This awkward-sounding term draws attention to the need for tension in any account of change; in abstract terms it holds that any statement or condition (the thesis) throws up its opposite (the antithesis), and that the interaction of the two produces a resolution (the synthesis) that contains the elements of the original thesis and antithesis in a satisfactory and no longer contradictory blend; but no sooner has this state of affairs been arrived at than the synthesis itself becomes another thesis, and the whole process must be repeated. To translate this abstract formulation into terms that have been used in this account, the medieval social ordering (thesis) will interact with its denial, the demand for an end to status (antithesis), to produce Lockean liberalism (synthesis). In turn this Lockean order (new thesis) will interact with a continuing demand for an end to even modified status (the new antithesis), and a higher synthesis will result, a Chartist-style outlook. The process will continue, giving rise to socialism and even communism (or perhaps the New Left). Some readers will recognize that such dialectical evolution has underlain many philosophies, notably those of Hegel and Karl Marx; this is not to say that Hartz is a Hegelian or a Marxist, merely that he adopts this kind of framework to account for the evolution from one outlook to another.

Armed with this understanding, Hartz proceeds to consider what he calls 'fragment cultures'. Certain colonial societies differ from their parents because they do not contain a representative cross-section of the classes and outlooks that were present in the original. Thus New France was not the mirror-image of old France, but rather of how the absolutist kings would have liked old France to be. By maintaining careful controls over immigration, by keeping out any hint of Enlightenment thinking, New France was settled by those who overwhelmingly adhered to the standards of feudalism, of the pre-modern outlook. In the case of the future United States the fragment operated in the reverse way but essentially with similar implications. There the settlers, especially the Puritans, were those who did not fit in to the attempt of the Stuarts to impose absolutism on England; they were, so to speak, the modern spirits who could not abide the already out-of-date notions of seventeenth-century England. Thus New England, like New France, was unrepresentatively composed of likeminded people; as Hartz says, 'All fragment cultures are by definition distinctively homogeneous.'

Granted this fact, it means that these colonial societies are denied the possibility of evolution. Since, according to Hartz, societal evolution takes place by the interaction of two distinct social outlooks, New France and New England are fated to remain frozen at their point of fragmenting. In France a normal, continuing evolution was possible because the medieval philosophy could interact with the contrary one of the Enlightenment. In England much the same could, and did, happen. But New France lacked the Enlightenment critique that could spark any development, and so Quebec society remained essentially unchanged, static, clerical, medieval even, down until the 1960s when the pressure of outside forces became too strong to resist. Thus in the 1830s the unrest could produce a Papineau who held many seigneurial, élitist views, but not a Jacksonian figure. The *Rouge* tradition was always very weak in Quebec. New England lacked the pre-modern critique and so Lockean ideas never received their check; the United States never developed a true conservative party—and so could never develop a true liberal party, and so, in fact, could never develop a genuine party system at all—and was prevented from ever evolving a socialist tradition. For on the Hartzian model, socialism is the result of the collision between the medieval notion of a society where there is group, even state, responsibility for individuals (witness the guilds and the Just Price) and the liberal notion of progress and the recognition of individual worth. America has the second, and as the popularity of Herbert Spencer showed has it in plenty, but never having had the first can not develop socialism.

The Hartz thesis has further applications to North American history. A homogeneous, frozen fragment that never experiences an internally validated critique of its values is tempted to erect those values into unquestionable absolutes. Indeed Hartz would go further, and claim that in its urge to find completeness the one-sided fragment must make these values into the equivalent of its nationalism. Thus Quebec has been driven to make subscription to Catholicism, the French language, and the sanctity of the land the test of French Canadianism, a test that was applied with an intolerance under, say Duplessis, which would not be found in the France of that day. Thus New England was driven to its own brand of intolerance, the Salem witch trials say, a tradition whose continuance has been outlined in the account above; today 'Americanness' is still something that is recognized, and citizens of the United States are constantly being reminded of the need to be true to the 'American way'. Those who would suggest alternative values *must* be seen as misfits, tools of a foreign system, and so the conspiracy mentality is forced into existence.

A particularly important application of the Hartz thesis is to the problem of relations of immigrants with the indigenous peoples and with the blacks who were brought in to replace those natives exterminated by the white man because they would not work adequately for him. A feudal fragment has little difficulty in coming to terms with, say, the Indians. Notions of status are so inbred that it is easy to add one more level and slot the Indians in at the bottom (or if it is a question of an Indian chief, to decide at which point in the pyramid he should be entered). In this way it is possible to accept the Indian as a human being and a full member of society (in theory at any rate), a viewpoint that, incidentally, is buttressed by the universality of the Catholic religion. But a Lockean fragment faces a terrible problem. On the one hand there is the democratic imperative, as enshrined in the Declaration of Independence. On the other is the fact of negro slavery, as seen in the Constitution's counting of the negro as three-fifths of a person. The way out of such a dilemma was to deny the humanity of the negro, for in this way democratic aspirations could be maintained for the rest of the population. The way out of such an impasse could only be by a violent revolution, and the Civil War might have been predicted on a Hartzian analysis; the feudal method would allow the possibility of a gradual rise in the status of non-whites, however, and this may be a factor, then, in the better relations that existed between the Indians and the inhabitants of New France.

Both New France and the United States pose little difficulty for the Hartzian analysis. But what of English Canada, in particular of Upper Canada/Ontario, which has so dominated the Canadian tradition? It may be argued that this province was settled in a way very different from the U.S.A. The United Empire Loyalists were the Tory residue that the liberal Americans refused to tolerate within their new polity. And just as this Tory element was lacking in the United States, so it was dominant in the formative years of Upper Canada. This Toryism did not have to be a thoroughgoing and powerful one; indeed Horowitz, the most successful applicator of the Hartzian analysis to Canada, agrees with Hartz that it was merely a 'touch', but it was enough to distinguish the province from its neighbouring states. And it was enough for there to be tension between the older and the newer outlooks, the proof of which is the fact that, however attenuated, socialism *has* developed a tradition in Canada. Another indicator of this fact that Upper Canada, and Canada for that matter, is not a fragment culture in the way that the United States was, would be the lack of intolerance claimed by many Canadians as distinguishing their society from that of the United States; the difference between the melting pot and the mosaic may be re-emphasized in this connection.

Further Reading

National surveys for the period from c.1760 include: W. L. Arnstein, *Britain Yesterday and Today: 1830 to the Present*; J. H. Plumb, *England in the Eighteenth Century*; D. Thomson, *England in the Nineteenth Century*; and also his *England in the Twentieth Century*; W. B. Willcox, *The Age of Aristocracy, 1688 to 1830*; J. M. S. Careless, *Canada: A Story of Challenge*; D. G. Creighton, *Dominion of the North*; W. L. Morton, *The Kingdom of Canada*; S. E. Morison and H. S. Commager, *The Growth of the American Republic* (two volumes); R. B. Nye and J. E. Morpurgo, *A History of the United States* (two volumes). If more detailed surveys are required there are: for Britain the Oxford Series; for Canada the Centenary Series; and for the United States the New American Nation Series; the volumes for 1760 are J. S. Watson, *The Reign of George III*; H. Neatby, *Quebec, The Revolutionary Age 1760–1791*; and L. H. Gipson, *The Coming of the Revolution*; the names and titles of subsequent volumes in the series will be found inside the end papers of these books. For Ireland there is E. Curtis, *A History of Ireland*. And since Quebec has always been so very much apart, M. Wade's *The French Canadians, 1760–1945* may be added. More political-constitutional frameworks may be found in: D. L. Keir, *The Constitutional History of Modern Britain*; J. D. Lees, *The Political System of the United States*; and H. M. Clokie, *Canadian Government and Politics*; while J. A. Corry and J. E. Hodgetts compare the three systems in *Democratic Government and Politics*. Finally special mention may be made of J. A. Blyth, *The Canadian Social Inheritance* (which brings in British and

American patterns and assembles some useful information); of R. Kelley, *The Transatlantic Persuasion: The Liberal-Democratic Mind in the Age of Gladstone* (which is keen to stress the similarities to be found in the three countries); and of W. L. Morton, *The Canadian Identity* (since Morton is always aware of Canada's position between Britain and the United States).

CHAPTER ONE

In addition to the works mentioned in the text: P. Miller, *The New England Mind* (two volumes); H. R. Niebuhr, *The Social Sources of Denominationalism*; B. Semmel, *The Methodist Revolution*; W. Stark, *Sociology of Religion* (especially volume 5, which deals with types of religious cultures). Erich Fromm's *Escape from Freedom* is a provocative work by a psychoanalyst-cum-sociologist. Fascinating but even more demanding is G. R. Taylor's *The Angel Makers*, a study of eighteenth-century social psychology. For Enlightenment ideas: E. Cassirer, *The Philosophy of the Enlightenment*; and A. R. Hall's *Scientific Revolution 1500–1800* is useful but dry. The various political systems may be examined in R. A. Smith, *Eighteenth Century English Politics*; C. Rossiter, *Seedtime of the Republic: the Origins of the American Tradition of Political Liberty*; B. Behrens, *The Ancien Régime*; Y. Zoltvany provides a useful account in his *The French in North America*. The Eccles's viewpoint mentioned in the text may be found in his *Canada under Louis XIV*. The Acton thesis is in his *Essays on Freedom and Power*.

CHAPTER TWO

L. B. Namier's concentration upon the structure of politics, the links that bound the members of the political classes together, revolutionized the history of the mid-eighteenth century when he wrote in the 1930s; see his *England in the Age of the American Revolution* and *The Structure of Politics at the Accession of George III*. More recently G. Rudé has taken the enquiry further by looking into the composition of the crowds that rioted for change; see his *Wilkes and Liberty*. Also on the impetus to reform, I. Christie, *Wilkes, Wyvil, and Reform*. For the reaction and the French Revolution's impact the older P. A. Brown, *The French Revolution in English History* is still useful. R. B. McDowell,

Irish Public Opinion 1750–1800, covers a crucial period. American developments may be followed in J. T. Main's statistically based *Social Structure of Revolutionary America;* B. Bailyn's *The Ideological Origins of the American Revolution;* J. P. Green's 'The Social Origins of the American Revolution', *Political Science Quarterly,* 1973; G. S. Wood, *The Creation of the American Republic, 1776–1787;* D. Boorstin, *The Lost World of Thomas Jefferson;* J. C. Miller's *Crisis of Freedom* deals with the Alien and Sedition Acts. For British North America, in addition to the H. Neatby volume mentioned above, there are G. M. Craig's *Upper Canada, 1784–1841* and W. S. MacNutt's *The Atlantic Provinces, 1712–1857.* W. Nelson, *The American Tory* should be supplemented by D. Bell's article on the United Empire Loyalists in *Journal of Canadian Studies,* 1970. The diplomatic aspects of the triangle in these years may be followed in A. L. Burt, *The United States, Great Britain, and British North America* and in V. T. Harlow, *The Founding of the Second British Empire, 1763–1793.*

CHAPTER THREE

A background survey of British economic history is E. J. Hobsbawm, *Industry and Empire: An Economic History of Britain since 1750.* For the Agricultural Revolution there is the recent survey by J. D. Chambers and G. E. Mingay, *The Agricultural Revolution, 1750–1880.* Outlines of the Industrial Revolution may be found in T. Ashton, *The Industrial Revolution, 1760–1830,* and in P. Deane, *The First Industrial Revolution;* a particularly important development is traced by N. McKendrick 'Josiah Wedgwood and Factory Discipline' in *Historical Journal,* 1964. The disastrous example of a country that did not industrialize or diversify, Ireland, may be read in C. Woodham-Smith's *The Great Hunger.* An account of the economic philosophy of the new industrialism may be found in W. D. Grampp's *The Manchester School of Economics.* H. Perkin, *The Origins of Modern English Society* provides an overview of the total change and yet also manages new insights. American patterns may be traced in G. R. Taylor's *The Transportation Revolution,* which is wider than the title suggests and deals with the period 1815–60. For the same period more or less there is D. N. North's *Economic Growth of the United States, 1790–1860.* The later flowering is treated in T. C. Cochran and W. Miller, *The Age of Enterprise: A Social History of Industrial America.* J. Dorfman's *The Economic Mind of American Civilization* is encyclopedic. R. Hofstadter's *Social Darwinism in American Thought* deals with a specifically American phenomenon. Canada's economic history is outlined by W. T. Easterbrook and H. G. J. Aitken, *Canadian Economic History*. A brilliant study of the St Lawrence centrality is D. G. Creighton's *The Empire of the St Lawrence*, which covers the period between 1760 and 1850. Finally there are the various publications of H. A. Innis, most of which deal with the individual staple trades.

Banking is covered by B. Hammond, *Banks and Politics in America* (which includes material on Canadian patterns). For educational developments there are B. Bailyn, *Education in the forming of American Society* (the colonial period only, but very provocative), and R. F. Butts and A. Cremin, *A History of Education in American Culture*; J. W. Adamson, *English Education 1789–1902*; A. M. Kazamias, *Politics, Society, and Secondary Education in England*; and S. J. Curtis, *History of Education in Great Britain*; F. H. Johnson, *A Brief History of Canadian Education*; while C. B. Sissons' *Church and State in Canadian Education* draws attention to a very Canadian preoccupation.

CHAPTER FOUR

A basic introduction to liberalism is still G. de Ruggiero, *The History of European Liberalism*. Its British variant may be examined in J. Plamenatz, *The English Utilitarians*, and in S. E. Finer, *The Life and Times of Sir Edwin Chadwick*; also J. L. Hammond and M. R. D. Foot, *Gladstone and Liberalism*. G. M. Young's *Victorian England, Portrait of an Age*, and G. K. Clark's *The Making of Victorian England* and his *An Expanding Society: Britain 1830–1900* should be consulted. The links with the earlier developments will be found in A. Briggs, *The Age of Improvement, 1783–1867*. For the Anti-Corn Law League, N. McCord's book of that title should be consulted. M. Hovell's *The Chartist Movement* and J. L. and B. Hammond's *The Age of the Chartists* need to be supplemented by A. Briggs (ed.), *Chartist Studies*. E. P. Thompson's *The Making of the English Working Class* is vital. The struggles of Ireland may be followed in P. O'Hegarty, *The History of Ireland under the Union, 1801–1921*. The American variant is treated in L. Benson, *The Concept of Jacksonian Democracy: New York as a Test Case*, and in A. M. Schlesinger, Jr., *The Age of Jackson*. The nature of the south may be explored in E. D. Genovese, *The World the Slave Owners Made*; E. M. Elkins, *Slavery*; and K. M. Stampp, *The Peculiar Institution*; but with the very recent publication of the statistical and revisionist *Time on the Cross* by R. W. Fogel and S. L. Engerman, the whole question is up in the air. The crusade against slavery is the subject of L. Filler's book of that title. Also see A. Kraditor's *Means and Ends in American Abolitionism: Garrison and his critics*. K. M. Stampp has dealt with immediate post-Civil War developments in *The Era of Reconstruction*, while a more extended treatment of the new south is C. Vann Woodward's *Origins of the New South*. Links between British and American reform in this period are traced by F. Thistlethwaite in his *Anglo-American Connection in the early nineteenth century*. The Canadian variant of liberal reform is to be followed in A. Dunham, *Political Unrest in Upper Canada*; W. Kilbourn's *The Firebrand: William Lyon Mackenzie and the Rebellion in Upper Canada*; and in F. London's *Western Ontario and the American Frontier*. Lower Canadian developments are in H. T. Manning *The Revolt of French Canada, 1800–1835*, while Maritime patterns may be seen in the life of Joseph Howe by J. A. Roy. Traditional interpretations of the coming of responsible government, centring about Lord Durham, have been shaken by the recent *The Durham Report and British Policy* by G. Martin. Post-1840s developments are examined by J. Monet, *The Last Cannon Shot: A Study of French-Canadian Nationalism 1837–1850*, and in English Canada by J. M. S. Careless in his study of *Brown of the Globe*. The wider nature of Canadian liberalism is explored in F. H. Underhill's *In Search of Canadian Liberalism* and by W. L. Morton in *The Critical Years*, where the achievement of Confederation and its nature are described.

CHAPTER FIVE

The formal triumph of liberalism in Britain is examined in C. Cross, *The Liberals in Power, 1905–14*. But the shifting reality may be understood through J. F. Glaser 'English Nonconformity and the Decline of Liberalism', *American Historical Review*, 1958, and H. Hynes, *The Edwardian Turn of Mind*. H. Pelling has two very useful studies, *The Origins of the Labour Party, 1850–1900* and *The History of British Trade Unionism*. R. E. Dowse's *Left in the Centre* is an account of the ILP. *The Story of Fabian Socialism* is a readable introduction by M. Cole, herself a Fabian and the wife of G. D. H. Cole whose many works on labour and socialism may be consulted. N. Mansbergh's *The Irish Question, 1840–1921* continues the story of Britain's greatest colonial failure, which climaxed in this period about the Great War. Reform in America has been studied in depth. J. D. Hicks, *The Populist Revolt* is the standard account; a more recent study by one who would defend the Populists from their detractors is N. Pollack, *The Populist Response to Industrial America.* Accounts that span Populism and Progressivism are R. Hofstadter's *The Age of Reform* and E. F. Goldman's *Rendezvous with Destiny.* G. Kolko in *The Triumph of Conservatism* argues that little was accomplished. The seamy side of this reform tradition may be traced in R. Hofstadter, *The Paranoid Style in American Politics*; J. Higham, *Stranger in the Land: Patterns of Nativism, 1860–1925*; and in V. C. Ferkiss, 'Populist Influence on American Fascism' in *Western Political Quarterly,* 1957. Accounts of the American labour and socialist movements include D. Brophy, *The American Labour Movement*; P. Foner, *History of Labor in the United States*; C. Green, *The Rise of Urban America*; P. A. Taft, *The A.F. of L. in the Time of Gompers*; D. A. Shannon, *The Socialist Party of America*; P. F. Brissenden, *The I.W.W.* Much of Canadian work on labour and socialism is still in theses. There may be mentioned H. A. Logan, *The History of Trade-Union Organization in Canada, 1827–1959*; there is the turgid *Radical Politics and Canadian Labour 1880–1930* by M. Robin; a much more attractive start would be K. McNaught's *A Prophet in Politics*, the biography of J. S. Woodsworth. The energies that Canadians put into bicultural and provincial separateness may be gauged through J. Levitt's *Henri Bourassa and the golden calf: the social programme of the Na-tionalists of Quebec (1900–1914)*; R. Cook's *Provincial Autonomy, Minority Rights, and the Compact Theory, 1867–1921*; and H. B. Neatby, *Laurier and a Liberal Quebec.* For a special case of tension see E. M. Armstrong, *The Crisis of Quebec 1914–18.*

CHAPTER SIX

A convenient survey of British developments in the recent period is A. Marwick's *Britain in the Century of Total War, 1900–1967*; other works by the same author will repay study. A pleasant description of the inter-war period is *The Long Week-End* by R. Graves and A. Hodge. The growth of the Labour Party is described in H. Pelling, *A Short History of the Labour Party.* For an account of the crash, limited in its definition, there is R. Skidelsky's *Politicians and the Slump: The Labour Government of 1929–31.* M. Bruce, *The Coming of the Welfare State,* deals with a concept that is more accepted in Britain than in the rest of the triangle. The political ferment in Canada is particularly well covered. The Winnipeg Strike has attracted a plethora of works; the latest is

D. J. Bercuson's *Confrontation in Winnipeg*. W. L. Morton has written the definitive *The Progressive Party in Canada*. The CCF in Saskatchewan has been studied by S. Lipset in *Agrarian Socialism*, and the wider socialism in W. Young, *The Anatomy of a Party: The National C.C.F.* Among the many works examining Social Credit there is C. B. Macpherson's *Democracy in Alberta*; if nothing else the student should read its last chapter 'The Quasi-Party System', a concept that may apply to Canadian politics in its entirety. For developments in Quebec see H. Quinn, *Union Nationale* and S. H. and H. Milner, *The Decolonization of Quebec*. For the Prohibition crusade there is J. Gray's *Booze*; other works by Gray may be consulted for a vivid evocation of western Canadian life between the wars. The literature on Prohibition in the United States is much more copious and includes A. Sinclair, *Era of Excess*, and H. Asbury, *The Great Illusion*. The entire inter-war period in America is the subject of D. A. Shannon's *Between the Wars*. The repressive climate just after the First War has been examined by R. K. Murray in *Red Scare*. The New Deal may be evaluated via W. E. Leuchtenburg's *Franklin D. Roosevelt and the New Deal*; D. W. Brogan, *The Era of Franklin D. Roosevelt*; while those wanting more detailed treatment may consult A. M. Schlesinger Jr.'s study.

CHAPTER SEVEN

Perhaps the best way to examine the richness of the Turner controversy is to look through R. Hofstadter and S. Lipset (eds.), *Turner and the Sociology of the Frontier*. There are also useful insights in W. J. Eccles, *The Canadian Frontier, 1534–1760*, while the Turner approach suffuses S. D. Clark's *Movements of Political Protest in Canada*. (Incidentally the other works of Clark will greatly repay study.) Metropolitanism in the economic sense is discussed in N. S. B. Gras, *Introduction to Economic History*, and J. M. S. Careless' application appeared in his 'Frontierism, Metropolitanism, and Canadian History', *Canadian Historical Review*, 1954. L. Hartz's ideas on fragment cultures may be seen in his *The Liberal Tradition in America*, and in the series of essay he edited as *The Founding of New Societies*, which contains K. McRae's application of the theory to Canada; G. Horowitz's application, 'Conservatism, Liberalism, and Socialism in Canada: An Interpretation' is in *Canadian Journal of Economics and Political Science*, 1966.

INDEX

Date Due

Carl Bethe Fredo. 8/82			
MAR 13 1984			
MAR 28			
OCT 14 1988			
APR 10 1991			
NOV 26 1991			
FORM 109			

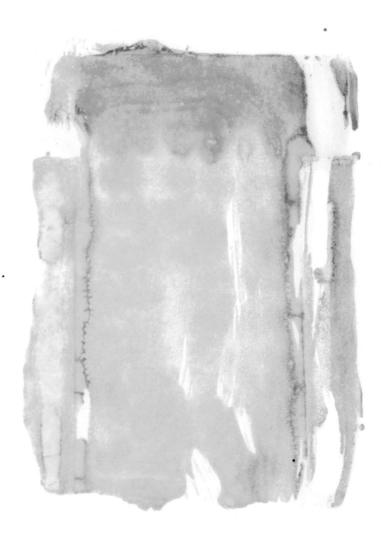

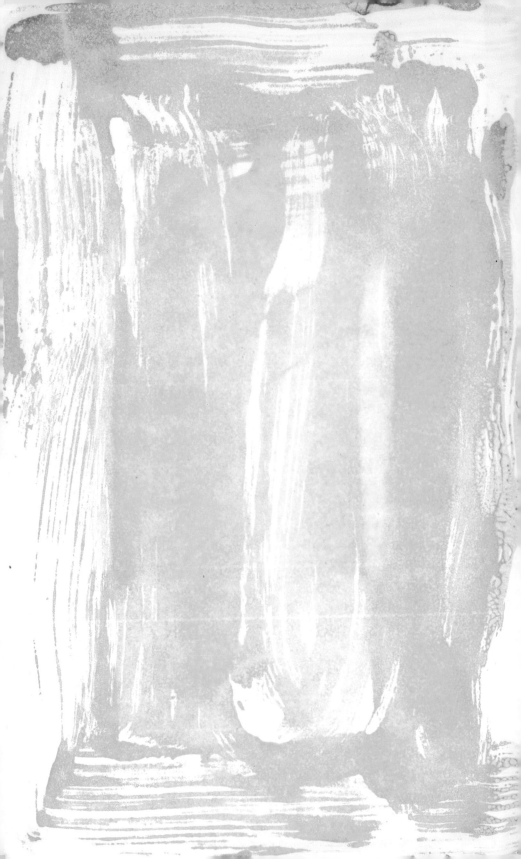